PENGUIN BOOKS

The Condé Nast Traveler

Book of Unforgettable Journeys

THE *CONDÉ NAST TRAVELER*

Book of Unforgettable Journeys

GREAT WRITERS ON GREAT PLACES

EDITED AND WITH AN INTRODUCTION BY
KLARA GLOWCZEWSKA

PENGUIN BOOKS

PENGUIN BOOKS

Published by the Penguin Group
Penguin Group (USA) Inc., 375 Hudson Street,
New York, New York 10014, U.S.A.
Penguin Group (Canada), 90 Eglinton Avenue East, Suite 700, Toronto,
Ontario, Canada M4P 2Y3 (a division of Penguin Group Canada Inc.)
Penguin Books Ltd, 80 Strand, London WC2R 0RL, England
Penguin Ireland, 25 St Stephen's Green, Dublin 2,
Ireland (a division of Penguin Books Ltd)
Penguin Group (Australia), 250 Camberwell Road, Camberwell,
Victoria 3124, Australia (a division of Pearson Australia Group Pty Ltd)
Penguin Books India Pvt Ltd, 11 Community Centre,
Panchsheel Park, New Delhi – 110 017, India
Penguin Group (NZ), 67 Apollo Drive, Rosedale, North Shore 0745,
Auckland, New Zealand (a division of Pearson New Zealand Ltd)
Penguin Books (South Africa) (Pty) Ltd, 24 Sturdee Avenue,
Rosebank, Johannesburg 2196, South Africa

Penguin Books Ltd, Registered Offices:
80 Strand, London WC2R 0RL, England

First published in Penguin Books 2007

5 7 9 10 8 6

Copyright © Condé Nast Publications, 2007
All rights reserved

The essays in this book first appeared in issues of *Condé Nast Traveler*.

LIBRARY OF CONGRESS CATALOGING-IN-PUBLICATION DATA
The Condé Nast traveler book of unforgettable journeys : great writers on great
places / edited and with an introduction by Klara Glowczewska.
p. cm.
ISBN 978-0-14-311261-7
1. Travel—Literary collections. I. Glowczewska, Klara.
PN6071.T7C66 2007
808.8'032—dc22   2007026230

Printed in the United States of America
Set in Adobe Garamond • Designed by Elke Sigal

CONTENTS

INTRODUCTION   *ix*

CZECH REPUBLIC

Rock Around the Clock,   BY FRANCINE PROSE   *I*

    Plus: *Finding Kafka*   *9*

ENGLAND

Haunted by Beau and Beauties,   BY EDNA O'BRIEN   *12*

    Plus: *Literary Bath*   *20*

ETHIOPIA

Heaven's Gate,   BY PICO IYER   *23*

    Plus: *Seeing Ethiopia*   *47*

FLORIDA

Primal Dreams,   BY RUSSELL BANKS   *50*

    Plus: *The Animals of the Everglades*   *64*

FRANCE

A Country Made for Living,   BY PATRICIA STORACE   *67*

    Plus: *Ultimate Provence*   *84*

GEORGIA

Sip It Slow,   BY NIK COHN   *88*

    Plus: *Savannah Secrets*   *102*

GREECE

The Secret Lives of Athens,   BY PATRICIA STORACE   *108*

    Plus: *Athens Essentials*   *130*

HAWAII

The Haunted Land, BY JAN MORRIS 133

Plus: *The Big Island's Sacred Sites* 143

THE HIMALAYAS

Lost Horizons, BY SUKETU MEHTA 146

Plus: *A Map of the Mountains* 164

ICELAND

The Loneliest Place on Earth, BY PICO IYER 166

Plus: *Iceland's Hot Springs* 182

IRAN

Gods, Kings, Mystics, and Mullahs, BY JAMES TRUMAN 185

Plus: *Reading Iran* 209

ITALY

The Glory That Was Not Rome, BY ROBERT HUGHES 212

Plus: *Etruscan Essentials* 240

ITALY (CAPRI)

Bella Capri, BY SHIRLEY HAZZARD 243

Plus: *Island Highlights* 250

ITALY (THE VATICAN)

Treasures of the Popes, BY JOHN JULIUS NORWICH 253

Plus: *Walking the Vatican* 267

JAPAN

Eight Ways of Looking at a Garden
(or, the Art of Setting Stones), BY NICOLE KRAUSS 276

Plus: *A Garden Guide* 286

JORDAN

Jinn City, BY EDMUND WHITE   289

  Plus: *Visiting Petra*   297

THE PHILIPPINES

Beauty and the Beast, BY SIMON WINCHESTER   299

  Plus: *Volcanoes Explained*   311

ROMANIA

The Red Danube, BY GREGOR VON REZZORI   315

  Plus: *Of Castles and Counts*   330

SPAIN (BARCELONA)

Portrait of the City as Genius, BY ROBERT HUGHES   334

  Plus: *Barcelona's New Masterpieces*   353

SPAIN (SANTIAGO)

Pilgrim's Pride, BY WILLIAM DALRYMPLE   360

  Plus: *A Pilgrimage How-To*   382

TANZANIA

Where the Wild Things Are, BY PHILIP GOUREVITCH   384

  Plus: *A Safari Packing List*   402

ABOUT THE AUTHORS   405

ABOUT *CONDÉ NAST TRAVELER*   413

ACKNOWLEDGMENTS   415

INTRODUCTION

"This is Heaven," a guide in Lalibela, Ethiopia, tells Pico Iyer, one of the contributors in *The Condé Nast Traveler Book of Unforgettable Journeys,* as he shows him around a complex of churches carved entirely, unimaginably, belowground. Lest the traveler miss the point, he repeats it again: "As soon as you step here, you have set foot in Heaven."

It's not another tourist scam. The man is being literal: The marvels built nine hundred years ago out of red rock in the heart of Ethiopia were meant to represent the geography of salvation, Paradise included. But heaven—the perfect place, the transporting experience—is also one of travel's most potent metaphors, its Holy Grail, its ultimate allure. We all want to go there, or at least get close to it, if only for an unforgettable moment—be that while consuming a positively divine meal in Provence, or contemplating the transcendent beauty of a Japanese garden, or simply awaking at dawn in a flimsy safari tent in the African bush, wild things jabbering all around, to find oneself, miraculously, uneaten ("triumphantly whole," as Philip Gourevitch puts it in his account of a journey through Tanzania).

Since its founding in 1987, *Condé Nast Traveler* has been dedicated to the proposition that while hell can be a trip gone bad, all a traveler needs to find his or her bit of heaven is the right travel information—inspired, accurate, unbiased. It is our mission to provide that knowledge, on our own scrupulous terms: Writers on assignment for the magazine accept no free or discounted travel—not from the airlines, not from hotels and resorts, not from tour operators—a simple yet liberating prohibition that allows them to report freely and fully on what they see, feel, learn, and experience (the good and the bad). They are what every traveler wishes for—consummately knowledgeable guides with no ulterior motive, no hidden agenda or allegiance.

For *The Condé Nast Traveler Book of Unforgettable Journeys,* we have selected twenty-one reports from the magazine's last two decades by eighteen eminent contributors—art critics, novelists, poets, political reporters, and more. These are deeply felt, beautifully told tales of time spent in some of the world's most desirable and fascinating places. (One might debate which of those two adjectives best describes the ominously unpredictable Mount Mayon volcano in the Philippines, object of Simon Winchester's obsession. See "Beauty and the Beast.")

With more and more of us traveling, much of our daily discourse on travel is, of necessity, about its nettlesome mechanics—booking strategies, reservation policies, fare negotiations, crowd avoidance, security procedures. Each month, the magazine supplies the best, the latest, and the most reliable advice possible on these matters and many more like them. But the stories in this volume speak to travel's other dimension—its magnificence, its enduring power to transport us, delight us, educate us, and enlighten us.

There is no more mesmerizing guide to Italy's Tyrrhenian coast than art critic Robert Hughes as he expounds on the mysterious footprints left there by the pre-Roman civilization of the Etruscans, and recalls his own early enchantment: "It would become sacred ground for me. . . . delicate gold ornaments buried in the earth, incomprehensible inscriptions, the echo—no more—of vanished flutes and sistrums caught by imagination's ear in the offshore Tyrrhenian wind whispering above the breastlike tombs of Cerveteri and through the blond grass of Tarquinia's long sun-struck ridges." Who wouldn't want to follow him there? Or Edmund White to Jordan's Petra, "where every outcropping of stone looks carved and every carving looks natural, [and] every turn of the path inspires an urge to pray to some strictly local spirit." Or Francine Prose to Prague, "with its profound, unstable beauty always at the point of crumbling, its penchant for amazing me as I turn a corner to discover a shockingly handsome square, or palace, or statue, or garden." Or Russell Banks to the Florida Everglades, where, he argues, it is possible to travel back in time to a heaven of another sort—"to view and imagine anew the planet earth without billions of human beings on it."

There are epiphanies everywhere and of every scale. Traveling through Iran, James Truman tries to train his Western eyes to appreciate the non-representational, non-figurative mosaics in the mosques he visits. And it comes to him: "Far from being hieroglyphic riddles, the wild colors and patterns emerged as explosions of life, molecular and biological, caught in a single moment of perception. One surrenders to it without sentimentality or storyline." Other revelations are more, well, secular. Why, you might wonder, are there so many jewelry stores in Athens? Patricia Storace divines the answer: Because "it would be incorrect for an Athenian man to buy his wife and his mistress jewelry at the same address." Now you know.

Walk with Edna O'Brien through the streets of Bath ("an enduring miracle it is—crescent after crescent of pale buff houses . . ."), or succumb to Savannah with Nik Cohn as he drifts "from one touch of magic to the next: the great stand of live oaks along Oglethorpe Avenue, or the chorus line of sweeping cast-iron stair railings on Gordon Row . . . a breath of eucalyptus within a fountained garden; or just the saturated warmth, and the creeping southern light." Tour the treasures of the Vatican with John Julius Norwich and see in St. Peter's Basilica "an explosion of glory so tremendous that you can almost hear the trumpets." View Capri through the eyes of longtime and frequent visitor Shirley Hazzard, who knows well the storied Italian isle's sun-filled, people-watching days but also its "nights of supernatural silence, interspersed as they are with grand nocturnal storms in which every declivity and grotto reverberates and the face of the mountain flares with lightning all night long."

Jan Morris is enthralled in Hawaii. Suketu Mehta ascends the Himalayas. Gregor von Rezzori is swept away on the Danube. Nicole Krauss is enchanted in Japan. William Dalrymple embarks on a pilgrim's progress through Spain. And more. Every story in the collection is complemented by a section of additional practical information. And each makes one thing eminently clear: that there is nothing mundane about travel. Done well, it is one of life's most consequential acts. And doing it well, as our writers demonstrate, is an art we can all aspire to. There is indeed plenty of heaven to be found on this earth. Happy trails.

—*Klara Glowczewska,*
editor in chief, Condé Nast Traveler
New York City, 2007

THE *CONDÉ NAST TRAVELER*

Book of Unforgettable Journeys

Rock Around the Clock

by

FRANCINE PROSE

Officially, I have come to Prague to teach, but my secret mission is to commune with ghosts, to contact the restless spirits of Kafka and Mozart. Here, in this atmosphere so conducive to deep philosophical brooding, even popular T-shirts seem to know some profound and complex truth about the different (and opposite) natures of those two heroes and saints of art. One shows lonely, tormented Kafka in silhouette, his tragic shadow looming on the cobblestoned streets he couldn't bear to leave and yet desperately longed to escape. MOZART LOVES PRAGUE! announces another shirt, on which the prodigiously energetic composer kicks up his heels and pirouettes through the welcoming town where "my Praguers" adored his work and salved the damage inflicted on his ego by chilly, unappreciative Salzburg and Vienna.

But as I drift through the around-the-clock party that Prague has lately become, Kafka's sad, solitary ghost seems distant, unavailable. As I glance up at a harem of fleshy Rococo nudes writhing on the newly restored butter-colored facade of a former palace, as I cross the lovely Charles Bridge, bordered by graceful eighteenth-century statues and mobbed with tourists, sword-swallowers, tiny dogs jumping through hoops, a musician playing "Feelings" on an eerie glass harmonica, tourists watching other tourists nervously posing for snapshots with a boa constrictor, the entire city seems possessed by the puckish, joyous spirit of Mozart.

Estonian ska-band and Finnish head-banger music pours from the CD shop. Dixieland swing, a ragtime pianist, Peruvian flutes and drums, vie for attention (and Czech koruny) on Karlova Street. A dozen concerts take place each night, often in venues where Mozart played the harpsichord or organ. At the exquisite Chapel of Mirrors in the Clementinum, where Mozart appeared, the talented violinist appears to feel—just as Mozart must have—that he was born for better things than the gig he is playing.

The staging of *Così fan Tutte* at the glittering Estates Theater—restored even beyond the grandeur it must have had when *Don Giovanni* premiered here in 1787—suggests something Mark Morris might dream up in a regressive moment. The heroines have pink and orange Marge Simpson hair; the women's costumes are pornographic; at some point a banner descends with that heraldic coat of arms the Rolling Stones' stuck-out tongue.

At Bertramka, the pale yellow villa where Mozart stayed with his passionate admirer and number one fan, Mme. Dusek, we sip champagne in the garden while an intense soprano trills arias from *Don Giovanni*. Moving me to tears, the chords of Mozart's final *Requiem* fill St. Nicholas Church, the same magnificent Baroque cathedral "my Praguers" thronged for a memorial service days after Mozart had been unceremoniously dumped in a common grave in Vienna.

But it's more than the music putting Prague in this giddy Mozartean mode. It's the renovation and restoration, the CD shops, the theaters, the boa constrictor, the buzz—all of which followed the

1989 Velvet Revolution, and more of it every day. Depending on whom you ask, Prague is Paris in the twenties, New York in the eighties, a celebration, the New Frontier, an ongoing three-ring circus.

"It's a zoo," growls Marta Zelezná, the director of the Kafka Society, an organization devoted to translating Kafka's complete works (finally) into Czech and fostering the multicultural harmony that, the Society seems to think, his work signifies. Her office faces Old Town Square, and she complains that she can't work, can't think, listening to the same lousy banjo play the same eight songs over and over. "In the past there were never these crowds, these horses and carriages, this noise, these . . ."

Why do I imagine that she is about to say Americans? And what exactly is this past for which she is so nostalgic? A shiver of Kafkaesque paranoia blows in, along with the roar of the crowd, on the breeze from Old Town Square.

In New York, a friend tells me one of those jokes that involve various nationalities riding in an airplane which for some reason must be lightened by each nationality throwing something out the window. The punch line (you can imagine the rest) features the Czech pitching the American out the window and saying, "We have enough of these back home in Prague." In Prague, when I tell the joke to a Czech student, he laughs, waits a beat, and says, "We used to tell that joke about the Russians."

So someone must think it's time for the next Defenestration of Prague, in which case a whole generation may go flying out the window. I hear wildly varying estimates: eight thousand . . . fifteen thousand . . . forty thousand young Americans now live in Prague. In any event, the community is large enough to support two weekly English-language newspapers, a popular bookstore/café, dozens of bars, restaurants, and clubs geared to satisfying homesick cravings for nachos, Cajun shrimp, tabbouleh, Guinness stout, and open-mike poetry readings.

One hears grumbling about the "American invasion," and often, after some sullen minor daily transaction in a café or shop (this is not a culture that trades on easy charm), I suspect that more than a few Czechs are still following the "Ten Commandments" broadcast by Prague Radio during the Russian invasion: "You don't know. You don't care. You don't tell. You don't have. You don't know how. You don't give. You can't do. You don't sell. You don't show. You do nothing." With its profound, unstable beauty always at the point of crumbling, its penchant for amazing me as I turn a corner to discover a shockingly handsome square, or palace, or statue, or garden, Prague keeps looking like Venice while it is acting like Eastern Europe.

Mozart had a fondness for low-life bars, of which there are still plenty, especially around the train stations and amid the fast-food joints and bargain-sale racks that (again, like the Russians in 1968) have invaded Wenceslas Square. Kafka preferred the smoky cafés where artists and intellectuals gathered, and these days it's hard to walk more than a block without passing a bar full of expatriate poets guzzling great inexpensive Czech beer or costly nostalgia-inducing Guinness. All over the city, painfully hip and painfully thin Americans and Czechs mingle in cafés furnished in scruffy Eastern European versions of fabulous fifties decor.

Early in my stay here, I give a reading at The Globe, the funky, congenial bookstore/café where one can buy the *International Herald Tribune* or a secondhand copy of a Raymond Chandler novel and sit around for hours eating oatmeal cookies and sipping absinthe. The crowd is hip, attractive, appreciative, and indistinguishable from the audience at similar cafés in New York's East Village. The only difference is that during my reading at The Globe I'm getting progressively looped on Becherovka, a surprisingly potent Czech herbal liqueur. I don't think I remember doing that the last time I read in New York.

———

Kafka would have loved The Globe, especially if he got a big crowd. For although we tend to imagine Kafka in solitude, writing all night long, enduring penitential bouts of angst and paranoia, the truth is he was a writer, with a writer's ego and no problem accepting admiration and acclaim. "Frankly, dearest, I simply adore reading aloud; bellowing into the audience's expectant and attentive ear warms the cockles of the poor heart," he wrote, describing a public reading of his story "The Judgment."

And for all his complaining about Prague ("This little mother has claws," he wrote. "We should set her on fire from both sides. . . . Then perhaps we should be free of her"), the writer also "adored" his native city. Kafka, wrote his friend Gustav Janouch, "was familiar not only with its palaces and churches but also with the most obscure alleys of the Old Town. He knew the medieval names of the houses even though their ancient signs no longer hung over their entrances. . . . He conducted me by crooked alleyways into narrow, funnel-shaped interior courtyards in Old Prague, which he called 'spittoons of light.'"

His birthplace, on the corner of Maiselova and Kaprova, is marked now by what must be the world's most unflattering commemorative plaque: a gaunt bronze portrait with radar-dish ears and psycho goggle-eyes. Most of the dots on the Kafka map (available at the Kafka Centre) marking the places where he lived are contained in one claustrophobic cluster surrounding Old Town Square—which, with its pastel Baroque facades, its Gothic steeples and sgraffito friezes, is (despite the crowds) grander, brighter, and more glorious than photos can convey.

Map in hand, I trace the peregrination of the Kafka family along that pale Art Nouveau confection Parizská Trída, around Old Town Square, and past the corner of Celetná, where Mrs. Berta Fanta, whose salon Kafka frequented, played host to Albert Einstein, Rudolf Steiner, and Mme. Blavatsky. I trace Kafka's footsteps into Josefov, through the cobblestoned lanes and well-preserved (or restored) synagogues of that former ghetto, during which, if I time my visit right—say, early on a drizzly, atmospheric weekday evening—footfalls seem to reverberate from another century, another era.

Eventually, the Kafka trail leads me to the Old Jewish Cemetery—with its hummocklike mounds rising high above street level because lack of space obliged the Jews to bury their dead in layers. Kafka came to meditate in this bristling forest of tombstones inscribed with Hebrew letters and symbols, jammed together, tipped at crazy angles, covered with furry green moss and pebbles left by the living as tokens of remembrance. Filtered sunlight stripes the headstones of poets and grande dames, the graves of mystics and cabalists. The most famous and frequently visited grave is that of Rabbi Loew, the sixteenth-century wonder-worker and proto-Frankenstein who created the golem from mud—and brought him to life. This legend of transformation passed down through the generations to Kafka, who in turn imagined that violent, overnight—and most modern—metamorphosis of man into cockroach. A brilliant yellow caterpillar crawls across the Rabbi's headstone—by far the brightest, most vital, and vibrant creature in the graveyard.

Kafka's grave is in the New Jewish Cemetery, in proletarian Zizkov—a sooty district to which a recent influx of young American residents has brought a faint whiff of gentrification. En route to the cemetery, I stop briefly at what may be the most Kafkaesque site in Prague: the giant Zizkov TV tower, visible all over the city, rising above the housetops like a silvery alien invader or a huge, grotesque relic from some hellish World's Fair. What lends a touch of the monstrous to the tower's basic ugliness is the fact that it was built on top of yet another Jewish cemetery: Coffins that had to be dug up and reburied are jumbled together in a narrow strip by the side of the tower.

Predictably, the tour groups don't make it here, nor do they shuffle through the New Jewish Cemetery, herded by guides with raised umbrellas. The cemetery is nearly deserted except for the elderly caretaker who gives my husband a yarmulke and declares my sons' baseball caps sufficient covering for their heads to show respect for the dead. An arrow points the way to the grave of Dr. Kafka; it takes me a moment to recall that he was a doctor of law. The arrow's hardly necessary—we could have found the grave without it. It's one of the few that seem cared for, that aren't overgrown with ivy.

Like Rabbi Loew's plot, Kafka's is covered with pebbles left for him by the living—in this case by impassioned readers, loyal fans, and literary neurotics who have made the tormented writer into a kind of modern saint. A middle-aged woman places a single red rose near the plain stone obelisk beneath which Kafka lies with his mother and father—the smothering parents whom he struggled against and tried to escape all his life.

We stay until everyone has left, and then we stay some more. I am teary-eyed and so distracted that we've walked nearly all the way to the cemetery gate when I remember I've forgotten to leave a pebble on Kafka's grave. I run back.

I carefully choose my pebble, solemnly kneel . . . and only then do I notice: There's a racket going on, a raucous chorus of construction noise from beyond the wall—jackhammers, power shovels, the shouts and whistles of workers, descendants of Mozart's Praguers, the symphony of a city rebuilding itself, celebrating its survival.

So once more, Kafka's spirit seems to have neatly slipped away. But there are moments—every evening, in fact—when I begin to suspect that his ghost has neither gone underground nor vanished. Perhaps his shadow has just relocated, picked up and moved to the suburbs.

In Dejvice, the somewhat out-of-the-way neighborhood where we've been lent an apartment, the technical college is on summer break, the wide streets are deserted, and our footsteps echo spookily as we pass the drawn curtains of the residences of Middle Eastern ambassadors. It's a neighborhood of state Socialist monoliths and rambling villas, popular with diplomats, expatriate families, and, in the past, Communist officials. The Hotel International (built in the Stalinist-Gothic skyscraper style at its most phallic extreme) looms above our tram stop, looking more like Kafka's castle than does the one at Hradcany. (Actually, it seems made for KGB agents to pitch dissidents out its high windows.)

On our streets are sensors (like the security systems in certain American homes) meant to turn on the street lamps when a moving body comes near. But something has gone wrong here, a reversal so strange that when I at last figure it out, my head simply swims with delight. And I can almost feel Kafka's presence beside us, alive with ironic, paranoid glee, accompanying us up the long hill, the empty road bordered with bright streetlights that sense our approach—and, one by one, blink out.

1995

FINDING KAFKA

Celebrating the godfather of existentialism

 "This small circle contains my whole life," Franz Kafka once declared to his Hebrew teacher, Friedrich Thieberger, as he looked out his window onto Prague's majestic Old Town Square. It was, perhaps, a wistful observation—the German-speaking Jewish author must have pondered many times the relatively tiny space in which most of his dreams and nightmares had played out. In one glance, he could see his high school at the Baroque Kinsky Palace; his former university; and a few of the many residences in which he had lived. In 1924, he succumbed to tuberculosis at the age of forty.

Kafka wrote his eerie masterpieces—1925's *The Trial* and 1915's *The Metamorphosis* among them—at the height of central Europe's brief, bright intermingling of Czech, Jewish, and German cultures. The multiethnic tradition of coexistence was so thoroughly destroyed by World War II and communism, however, that before the Velvet Revolution of 1989, his works were little read by Czechs. Today, a new scholarly interest in Kafka—as well as the writer's obvious star power—has led to a revival in Kafka's hometown. Nearly all of the important landmarks associated with the author are clearly marked and can be found within walking distance in the Old Town (Staré Město), the Jewish Quarter (Josefov), and the Lesser Quarter (Malá Strana).

Kafka's birthplace is just around the corner from Old Town Square, where Maiselova and Kaprova streets meet at the recently renamed Franz Kafka Square. In 1897, his original home was destroyed—except for its portal, which now fronts the one-room Kafka Exposition (420-222-321-675). The center is full of Kafka kitsch as well as some useful brochures. Back on Old Town Square is Dům U Minuty, a seventeenth-century *sgraffito*-covered building where Kafka's family lived from 1889 to 1896. The family also lived during two different periods at Old Town Square's Oppelt House (Staremětské 5 náměstí, third floor), where Kafka wrote "A Hunger Artist" (1922).

The insurance firms where Kafka toiled "for bread," as he put it, were Assicurazioni Generali at Wenceslas Square No. 19, today home to an H&M shop, and the Workers' Accident Insurance Company for the Kingdom of Bohemia, now the Hotel Mercure (7 Na Porici), which named its Brasserie Parisienne Felice for Kafka's two-time fiancée, Felice Bauer.

In the Golden Lane (22 Zlatá ulička) behind Prague Castle, Kafka sought out the peace and quiet of his sister Ottla's tiny apartment in 1916 to write most of the short stories included in *A Country Doctor* (1919). The cheerful blue house where Kafka is said to have meditated on scenes in 1926's *The Castle* is frequently overflowing with die-hard fans. The Golden Lane is only accessible to those who purchase a ticket to Prague Castle (hrad.cz/en/prazsky_hrad/obecne_informace.shtml). In 1917 Kafka moved to the Schönborn Palace (15 Trziste), where the United States Embassy is now located.

The Franz Kafka Society was established shortly after the end of communism in an attempt to bolster the writer's standing in his homeland. The society, which is in the heart of the Jewish Quarter (15 Maiselova; 420-224-227-452; franzkafka-soc.cz), offers guided walking tours of the places where Kafka lived, worked, studied, and reveled. The society's gem is Kafka's own one-thousand-book collection, which includes, among other titles, amateur Danish athlete J. P. Muller's 1904 *My System,* a guide to a fifteen-minute daily workout that Kafka took very seriously. In 2003 the society erected what it claims is the world's only Franz Kafka Monument (Dušní Street next to the Spanish Synagogue), a 12.3-foot-high bronze statue of a small man sitting on the shoulders of a giant suited body with no head. The sculpture was created by Czech artist Jaroslav Róna based on an image in Kafka's *Description of a Struggle.*

The Franz Kafka Museum opened in 2005 with "The City of K: Franz Kafka and Prague," a fascinating exhibition about how the Golden City provided both the inspiration and, occasionally, the topography for Kafka's writings. Particularly engrossing is a section that speculates about why Kafka did not marry any of his three great loves. The exhibition also explores Kafka's late-blooming interest in kabbalah, and his friendship with the author and journalist Max Brod. The world owes its Kafka knowledge to Brod, as he defied the writer's dying wish to burn his works and then dedicated his life to popularizing them (2b Cihelná; 420-257-535-507; kafkamuseum.cz).

Kafka's grave at the New Jewish Cemetery in Prague 3 (Izraelska 1) is marked by a modest vertical stone in the shape of a hexagon. To get to the cemetery, take the A line metro to the Želivského stop. Exit on the right and once above ground the cemetery entrance is a few feet to the right. Once inside, turn right. The grave is about halfway down toward the end. The grave is number 21-14-21.

Haunted by Beau and Beauties

by

EDNA O'BRIEN

 In the summer, from the window of the train, cow parsley, convolvulus, and loosestrife smother the steep bank that runs down to the railway line, and in the fields the herds of black-and-white cows stand very still, like dappled effigies. Often the conductors change midway, and the voice that announces hot and cold dishes from the buffet is West Country, thicker and somehow truer. I am on my way from London to Bath. I can never say *Bath* and not think of a whole galaxy of people— Jane Austen, Richard "Beau" Nash, Sarah Siddons, Richard Brinsley Sheridan, and a succession of voluptuous Bath Beauties who vied with one another not only in anatomy but in legend.

It is such a noble city, on such a patrician scale, that it gives any visitor a sense of grandeur such as one might derive from being in some perfectly designed amphitheater. The architects responsible for it were John Wood the Elder and, even more so, John Wood the Younger, and an enduring miracle it is—crescent after crescent of pale buff houses of local oolite stone dappled with black patches like frescoes and graced with long Georgian windows, Ionic columns, continuous cornices, each crescent rising as if it were from the meniscus of the previous one, and from the very top of the city a view of the seven hills of Bath and the narrow streets falling down, necklacelike, to the center of the town, where the hub is, as well as the Abbey, with its dark windows of lead as fine as filigree. Here, in summer, the crowds eat pork pies and ice creams and Sally Lunn, take photographs of one another, or wait to join one of the several city tours—the walking tour or the Stonehenge tour or the ghost tour. Bath has a population of over eighty thousand, and annually it's reckoned that more than a million outsiders grace, or disgrace, its precincts.

WATER IS THE BEST OF ALL THINGS, a sign in Greek proclaims on the north wall of the entrance to what is called the Pump Room, opened in 1706 by the Corporation of Bath to provide shelter for the bathers, along with music and entertainment. A story has it that around 500 B.C. a certain Prince Bladud was banished from his father's estate because of his leprosy, which it was feared would contaminate the court. Traveling to a village near Bath, he offered his services to a man who kept pigs and in turn infected the animals. To alleviate their pain, the pigs rolled in the muddy springs, and before long Bladud noticed that they were cured. He tried the springs himself and, finding that he was cured as well, had the springs cleaned, erected baths, and built a town around them. Later the Romans came and built their baths and a temple to the goddess Minerva, and centuries later the Saxons came.

Beau Nash went to Bath in 1702, an impecunious but swashbuckling young man who saw its potential as a watering town, especially now that Queen Anne had visited that same year, with fashionable men and ladies of quality following soon afterward. Nash was by profession a gamester, and he was lucky at it as well as able to charm the dignitaries of the town. He called himself the Master of Ceremonies and set about making it a city of splendors. Assembly Rooms were built where couples could meet to dance, an orchestra was brought from London, pavements were laid down, and the inhabitants were forced to hang out "lanthorns." Nash forbade the men to carry swords or wear boots. And with good reason: Bath was a rowdy town.

Nash also imposed strictures on ladies' dress. Anyone who appeared in the Assembly Rooms having the impertinence to wear an apron had it torn off, even the duchess of Queensberry, who wore an apron of point lace as a dare. "None but abigails appear in white aprons!" Nash shouted. Not everyone admired the required extravagant apparel. Mrs. Elizabeth Montagu, who lived for a time in Bath, said that a certain Lady Parker and her daughters looked like "state beds," so bedecked were they with ribbons and baubles. Though liking the waters of Bath, she had reservations about the houses, complaining that although they were large on the outside, the insides were nests of boxes where she might have stifled were it not for the winds that came through the holes in the masonry. Tired of hearing "What's trumps?" Mrs. Montagu decided to begin intellectual evenings during which people would discuss ideas instead of playing Old Maid, and in this she preempted Virginia Woolf and her sister, Vanessa Bell, by almost two centuries. In her Bath drawing room the expression *bluestocking* originated when one of the men, so poor he could not afford silk hose, wore blue wool stockings.

The rakes came to Bath; so did the invalids, along with the doctors and the quacks who gave the invalids goose dung or crab's tails. The beauties came to catch the eye of the eligible; and the nonbeauties, those too old for marriage or the young ones "who had not yet come to Perfection," were seated in the back rows of the Assembly Rooms or the Pump Room. Thomas Gainsborough came to paint the beauties and charged five guineas a head. The satirists came too, and many of the drawings and engravings show gouty creatures disgusted at having to take the waters. Charles Dickens happened across the name of one Moses Pickwick in Bath and used it in what is the funniest novel in the English language. Dickens sent his beleaguered gallants to Bath, where, as usual, their lascivious intentions turned to absurdity.

One cannot think of any other place in England so haunted, except, perhaps, Stonehenge. But we do not know what the Druids were up to, as they had no Beau Nash to mastermind their pleasures and their pastimes.

Right in the center of the Royal Crescent, occupying two houses in the curve of thirty identical ones, is the Royal Crescent Hotel. The sight of the doorman in top hat, French blue tails with gold braid aiguillettes, and white gloves—ready lest royalty should call—summons up the dashing world of Thackeray and the reverential world of *Upstairs, Downstairs.* One arrives in a bit of a tizzy, soon to be soothed by the chintzes and the needlepoint and the watercolors, all redolent of the illustrations in *The Country Diary of an Edwardian Lady.* There is, too, the Spanish barman Luis, who has devised some potent cocktails, has parried with the great, and knows who came with "womens" and who did not.

You order tea, because from your window you see those young girls—those Pollys, those Janes, those Emilys—in pairs, hawking trays across the garden, and you weaken, and you think, "This is English country life and to hell with it." Worse is to follow at dinner, because not only is it exquisite, it is lavish, and you are brought tidbits in between to tempt the palate—little *amuse-bouches,* as Michael Croft, the inestimable chef, calls them.

The visitors' book abounds with names: Actors who played the Theatre Royal testified to being overjoyed; James Coburn, resorting to French, wrote *"C'est magnifique";* Van Johnson simply drew a Picassoesque logo in cerise. The most tantalizing entry is perhaps that of King Hussein of Jordan, who stayed one June and claimed to be entering upon his eleventh year of honeymooning with his American wife, Noor. Donna and Lisa from Illinois confessed to "divine decadence."

Divine it is, with comfort and gentility at every turn: in the front hall a painting of Queen's Square in the coaching days; another, after Sir Joshua Reynolds, of Lady Waldegrave and her children, the mother a delicate creature—half invalid, half mother—wilting in her pale cream gown and powdered wig. Elsewhere, wilder creatures with décolletage and brazen expressions.

A short walk away, in the Museum of Costume, a guide who called girls "gals" described those bygone times and asked us to imagine "the silks moving in a minuet under the chandeliers." We were also told how the ladies' hair was treated with pork fat, trimmed into curls, and powdered with white or gray corn flour, since a lady did not expect to see her hairdresser more than once a fortnight. The museum's collection includes court dresses, wooden batons for curling ringlets, combs, gowns with stomachers, and gloves, "for favours, gifts, and coronations."

At the Roman Baths, the guide I happened to eavesdrop on had a more contemporary slant. She remarked on "the grotty color of the water," which indeed was like pea soup. Notices above the steaming and untreated water enjoined us not to drink it, not to slip, and not to dip our big toe or our fingers in it. All around were statues of Roman emperors and governors of Britain, which caused one visitor to feel that the place was "an all-male setup." Another woman, upon seeing a drain that went out to a river, grasped her husband's arm and said, "It's absolutely laden with history, Hank." A few steps away is the temple to the goddess Minerva, who was not only showered with coins and gemstones as favors and thanksgiving but was also beseeched to dispense curses. The curses were inscribed on small metallic sheets, some of which have been translated for our benefit, allowing us to savor the bile and rage of the wronged, for whom blood was the only recompense.

The more than twenty Bath antiques shops and markets are a collector's joy, a journey into an Aladdin's cave, full of temptations. On an inclement Saturday afternoon in the Bartlett Street market, I felt as if I had indeed stepped into the past, surrounded as I was with booths crammed with Bohemian glass, Georgian glass, carpets, silver, and furniture from every century and almost every country.

In one of the lace stalls, a woman who repairs, washes, and starches christening robes, stoles, pillow slips, nightdress cases, and bonnets spoke of each piece of lace as if it were a little person. There was hand lace, machine lace, chemically treated lace, and your Irish crochet, which she rather sportingly said could be classed "almost" as lace. Her prize possession was a tea gown with a sixteen-inch waist, which she was told had belonged to an Englishwoman who had been governess to the czar of Russia, but of course she could not prove it. In her heart, she hoped that a museum would buy the gown, where it might be kept undamaged forever.

As a concession to literature, I was installed in the Royal Crescent Hotel's Jane Austen Suite. It was everything one might have imagined—a tester bed with cream silk hangings, paintings, and engravings (including a copy of the one of Jane by her sister Cassandra). A secluded bower opened onto a sun-room with, of all things, a Jacuzzi under a wide white umbrella. The murals all around the sun-room depicted fruits and mementos, a shawl and pumps, which I presumed were to resemble those worn by Jane or by one of her characters. Austen lived five years in Bath, but after she left claimed she was glad to have escaped the place. Her caustic wit whetted, she wrote to Cassandra, complaining that the stone of Bath was a bit too white, a bit too glaring, that the Bath buns disordered her stomach, and that if she went to the gardens for a concert, at least the gardens were large enough for her to get beyond the reach of the music.

It is said that while Jane lived in Bath she underwent two traumatic experiences: A young man whom she might have married died, and another who proposed to her was accepted and then rejected because, although she liked him, she did not love him. Her heroine Anne Elliot, in *Persuasion*, upon seeing Captain Wentworth, who unbeknownst to her had come to Bath to seek her hand, is given a whole crop of conflicting emotions—"agitation, pain, pleasure, a something between delight and misery." Austen does give her lovers a happy ending, sending them climbing up the hill to Camden Place, "exquisitely happy . . . in their reunion."

As I walked up, or rather climbed up, to Lansdown Crescent, which overlooks the town, I felt that I might easily have been in the heart of Somerset. Black sheep moved deftly as they grazed on the common, picking their way between the thistle and the dandelion, the city itself a basin, an avalanche of purplish-pink roofs girdled by the hills.

Although Jane enshrined Bath in her fiction, it belongs more truly to Thackeray. The vicissitudes of the town's characters resemble those in *Vanity Fair*. The widow of John Wood the Younger was in penury and had to appeal to the Corporation of Bath for a stipend; Beau Nash, no longer lucky at the gaming tables, moved to a smaller house where he was looked after by his mistress, Juliana Papjoy, but was ridiculed as being a toothless old fop who lived with a whore; Marie Thérèse, Princesse de Lamballe, lady-in-waiting to Marie Antoinette, broke off her long sojourn in Bath to return to France and the guillotine; and, most prodigal of them all, Richard Brinsley Sheridan, who, having fought duels to win the beautiful Elizabeth Linley, lost her to an early death. When he died in 1816, his body had to be smuggled in a blanket to avoid the bailiffs. Worse still, the monarchy and the nobs eventually moved on to Brighton. And the waters fell into disuse.

One thing remains—it is the Georgian architecture of the two John Woods, defying the schlock and barbarity of modern times, austere and yet friendly, the voluptuousness of Imperial Rome made chaste. Impregnated with beauty and history, the ghosts of those who flourished there are surely lying in wait to cut a second swath through history.

1989

LITERARY BATH

In these books, Bath is a character itself

Francis Frith's Around Bath (2000)
By Francis Frith
(The Frith Book Company)
An extraordinarily evocative collection of archive photographs of Bath, from the mid-Victorian era through the twentieth century. Eclectic, imaginative, and unexpected, these images reflect the dramatic changes the city has undergone in the past 150 years or so.

Funeral Music (2005)
By Morag Joss
(Bantam Dell)
A zippy, postmodern detective story starring Sara Selkirk, a world-class cellist who, while on vacation in Bath, stumbles upon a juicy murder case. The killing takes place in the Roman Baths, forcing Sara to follow a trail strewn with dark secrets and damaged lives—only to discover that the killing may not be quite finished yet.

The Image of the Georgian Bath, 1700–2000 (2000)
By Peter Borsay
(Oxford University Press)
Bath reached its architectural apogee in the eighteenth century and in this book, Borsay, a history professor at the University of Wales Lampeter, focuses primarily on the period from 1700 to 1830. In this serious historical study, he explores how the city was depicted in contemporary maps, diaries, guidebooks, and letters. The illustrations are spectacular.

The Killing of Cinderella (A Bath Detective Mystery) (1998)

By Christopher Lee

(Orion)

The third in the successful Bath Detective Mysteries series, starring the intrepid Inspector Leonard. Set in contemporary Bath, *The Killing of Cinderella* revolves around a curvacious, top-heavy ex-Bond girl by the name of Lynda Elstrom who arrives in Bath to audition for the Christmas pantomime show. She fails to turn up for the photo call, but does show up, center stage, the next morning, hanging from the Fairy Godmother's wire. Irritating and dumb she may have been, but who would have wanted to kill her?

Northanger Abbey (1818)

By Jane Austen

(Penguin)

The silliness, vulgarity, and excess of Bath society form the background for Catherine Morland's adventures in this very early work of Jane Austen's (published posthumously). In no other book does Austen have so much fun setting up her heroine as the clear antidote to all the folly and insincerity of the kind of people who flocked to Bath in the early years of the nineteenth century. Read it for laughs and for Catherine's triumph over the fops and simpering snobs she encounters in the town.

The Pickwick Papers (1837)

By Charles Dickens

(Penguin)

Written when he was only twenty-four, *The Pickwick Papers* was Charles Dickens's first book and catapulted him into literary superstardom. Mr. Pickwick's adventures in Bath, where he lodges in a house in the Royal Crescent and "takes the waters" in the Great Pump Room, provide some of the book's funniest sections.

Dickens pokes fun at the whole experience, as poor Mr. Pickwick drinks endless pints of water, declaring himself "much improved," even though his friends "had not been previously aware that there was anything the matter with him."

The Waters of Sul (1997)
By Moyra Caldecott
(Bladud Books)

Set in A.D. 72 in Aquae Sulis (the Roman Bath), this is a surprisingly convincing story of a Celtic rebellion against Roman rule, led by a fiery heroine, Megan. The action swirls around this conflict between the native Celts and their Roman oppressors, and also concerns a nearby settlement on Glastonia Island that has embraced the hot new religious cult of . . . Christianity.

Heaven's Ga

by

PICO IYER

"This is the new Jerusalem," said our guide, a former deacon. "These churches were built with the help of angels. Once upon a time, an angel came to King Lalibela and asked him to build a city in the heart of Ethiopia, in rock. This is Heaven," he went on, pointing to the divide along which we were standing. "As soon as you step here, you have set foot in Heaven."

We walked in the silence above the plain, across the Jordan, through Bethlehem and Nazareth, through all the places reconstituted here by the king so that the faithful would not have to journey to Jerusalem, and, sitting outside one of the eleven seven-hundred-year-old churches carved entirely out of red rock—the only such marvels in the world—we let the centuries fall away, on this, St. Mary's Day.

The next morning, at dawn, I went out to see the hillside beside the churches scattered with figures—hooded, robed figures all in white, with priests above, under rainbowed umbrellas, half-obscured by the mists of their frankincense, reciting prayers and sermons from the tops of rock faces. Farther inside the complex, by a maze of tunnels, the chapels were alive with the gaunt estral faces of pilgrims called Bethlehem and Solomon and Abraham, who had walked two weeks—or two millennia—across the emptiness to be here; with withered nuns staring out from the darkness of their cells, small lightless spaces in round two-story huts, white crosses on the iron doors; with priests, burning-eyed and bearded, moving back and forth in purple robes to the ancient, hypnotic sound of drum and sistrum, golden crosses in their hands.

Motes of sunlight danced in the air, and boys flashed smiles, and gradually the silence descended, seeping out of the round huts, drifting through the network of underground passageways, floating into and out of the chapels. Something in the air—the children playing in the light of ragged corridors, the aged pilgrims clambering toward the doors, the priests in raiment—made me think of Tibet. For I had never before seen such fervor and devotion except in the Himalayas. Sometimes, in the dark, I could see nothing but priests and their crosses; sometimes only the outline of figures, archetypal almost, biblical, bowing toward the altar.

I had heard for years that Lalibela was one of the secret, undiscovered wonders of the world, and now I was being told that it was Paradise. But in truth, it seemed to me, it was something more than that: a living, singing replica of Paradise in our midst. And not just a collection of old buildings and stones for archaeologists, but a breathing, pounding, chanting place with a sense of worship so powerful that it made me shake.

Lalibela, like all the truly sacred places in the world, is distinguished, in fact, by all the things you cannot see: most of all, the silence, the sense of spun calm as luminous and clear as glass polished by forty generations and more of worship. You sit in the cool darkness of a church, light streaming through the cross-shaped windows, the sound of murmured prayers all around you, and you leave the world you know. And enter one you had forgotten you inhabited.

I hadn't come to Ethiopia to be spiritually awakened. Quite the opposite, in fact. I'd set off (for reasons that should remain obscure) with a box of plain Cheerios, some chocolate-covered espresso beans, and an English investment banker with a mosquito net. The I.B. (as I shall call him, for reasons of diplomacy) was a disciple of Evelyn Waugh's, anxious to set back any Anglo-Ethiopian relations that might have healed since the great man's visit. The Ethiopian National Tourist Operation was, I had found, in the Ethiopian Airlines office in New York City, but when I went there, they had no knowledge of it (or, indeed, of tourists), and fobbed me off instead with a months-old copy of the *Ethiopian Herald*. A large headline said, AMATEUR BOXING LACKS KOCK-OUT APPEAL.

On the Ethiopian Airlines flight into Addis Ababa, one toilet was soon flooded to the point of being unusable, and the other needed to be reassembled by the time the feature movie—*Dennis the Menace*—began. Every five minutes, like clockwork, the armrest of the woman in front of me came down to concuss my knee. And, for some atavistic reason, wrenching country-western music accompanied us over the great plains of Africa, culminating in a stirring rendition of "America the Beautiful" as we touched down at Bole International Airport (which was dominated by a six-foot-high replica of a pack of Winstons and a sign: WELCOME TO ETHIOPIA. CENTRE OF RECREATION AND RELAXATION).

Within an hour of arrival in the country, I found myself (unknowingly) in a house of ill repute, where a plump, denim-jacketed houri called Franca was shaking her hips and calling "*Rico, Rico,*" while a bearded man walked in and out, bearing a copy of *Franny and Zooey*. Another woman sat at a brazier in her shorts, cooking up coffee in some traditional fashion, while Kenny Rogers sang "We don't need money" out of a super-woofer twin-drive radio. We were there because we had been picked up by an Eritrean named Haile ("Haile Unlikely," said the I.B.), who had promised that this was the only place where we could get a visa to his newly independent homeland.

A top dog in the Eritrean embassy came here to "re-create himself," said Haile, red-eyed with drink and bad intentions. "If we do some trouble, maybe you can give us some favorable attentions."

"I got you," sang Kenny Rogers, "you got me, we got love."

A few hours later, still reeling from the twenty-four-hour flight from Los Angeles, I found myself standing under a huge full moon outside the room of the Somali warlord Mohammed Farah Aidid. Aidid, the most wanted man in the world just a month before, was staying in the same hotel as we were, as it happened ("Oh, General Aidid—room 211, over near the swimming pool," the receptionist had said), and now, surrounded by khaki-covered men with guns, his private secretary was pulling up his pant leg to show us the shrapnel he had received from "U.S. helicopter gunships."

The very next day, though, we drove out of Addis, away from Franca and Aidid, away from Kenny Rogers and Haile Unfortunate, and within minutes we found ourselves in an utterly different world: a Stone Age world, almost, of antique figures and shawled old crones and donkeys who seemed to have walked in from the Book of Kings. Abyssinia has, of course, been veiled in mists and mysterious associations almost since the birth of Christ. It was a haunt of the Queen of Sheba and, by some accounts, the original site of the Garden of Eden. It is the oldest Christian country in the world, and the only one in Africa to have defeated a European power (the Italians, in 1896). I had only to look at the ancient Phoenician script on my visa, with its air of old parchment and sacred Coptic texts, to realize that I was traveling into antiquity.

Compounding this remoteness in space—Ethiopia is not really Africa, and yet not quite Arabia, either—is a remoteness in time, hardened by the watchfulness with which it has guarded its traditions. In medieval times in Europe, Abyssinia was known primarily as the domain of Prester John, a Christian priest-king ruling a world of unicorns and pygmies; and for centuries, hidden away in the mountains, with the oldest written culture on the continent and its own distinctive community of Muslims, Christians, and Jews, the country had kept up its own unlikely ways (whenever a crime was committed, the 1911 edition of the *Encyclopaedia Britannica* informed me, a small boy was drugged, and whatever person he dreamed of was fixed on as the criminal). Its sense of apartness from the world is only confirmed by the fact that Ethiopia still observes a pre-Julian calendar (so there are thirteen months in a year there, noon is at six in the morning, and New Year's is celebrated in September, four months before Christmas). "Encompassed on all sides by the enemies of their religion," as Edward Gibbon wrote, "the Aethiopians slept near a thousand years, forgetful of the world, by whom they were forgotten."

Even within my own memory, things were no less otherworldly. Just twenty years ago, Addis was still the center of a feudal medieval court, with pillow bearers and urine wipers and bodies suspended in front of St. George's Cathedral, ruled over by Haile Selassie (his heir apparent, Prince Zere Yacob, walking the same English high school corridors as the I.B. and myself). Then, in 1974, the King of Kings, Lord of Lords, and Conquering Lion of the Tribe of Judah was taken off his throne and driven away in a VW. There followed a more or less typical period of guerrilla warfare, Marxist misrule, and desperate food shortages, and when the country emerged again seventeen years later, in 1991, with a new "transitional government," it had a per capita GDP of under one hundred dollars a year and more than four million people dependent on international food aid. Now, under the thirty-nine-year-old Meles Zenawi, the 53 million Ethiopians (up from just 42 million only ten years ago) are experimenting with a kind of democracy by trial and error—no easy task for a land that had held, not long before I arrived, its first free elections in sixteen hundred years.

So as we journeyed out of Addis, along the so-called Historic Route, which takes one through many of the great historical sites of Ethiopia—Lalibela, Gonder, Bahar Dar, and Axum—we felt as if we were going into prehistory or into some dark and echoing otherworld. Rastafarians famously consider Ethiopia to be the home of the Messiah; others believe that the Ark of the Covenant and part of the True Cross of Christ are buried here. The high plateau is made for guerezas, geladas, guenons, and dog-faced baboons, I read, as well as the greater and lesser kudu, duiker, klipspringer, and dik-dik. The Ethiopian Orthodox Church is like nothing else in the world, observing a practice of singing and dancing, as in the time of King David, and a Monophysite creed. And even if (like me) one doesn't go to see the Surma women with clay plates in their lips, the tribes who reportedly still make fires with bows and sticks, or the "yellow people" of the south, one is going into a world charged with something spookily recessed.

As soon as we drove out of the capital, in fact, we were in a landscape of ancient spareness: shepherds on horseback, driving their flocks along roads white with dust; horses galloping across the openness; huge processions of petitioners, all in white, marching in long lines along the road to celebrate St. Gabriel's Day. The sky above the eucalyptus groves a burning blue, the ridges of the mountains forbidding before us, and everywhere a landscape untouched by anything we knew. Sometimes we stopped and joined little boys along the road at their games of foosball; sometimes we sipped sweet clove-and-cinnamon tea while introducing our hosts to the Neville Brothers.

And as we drove, I realized that I had never, ever, seen a place so bare: There were no road signs here—no roads almost—and no amenities or shops or frills. Nothing, in fact. And nothing to take one away from the ageless, changeless rhythm of men with crooks and staffs, and women with blue crosses painted on their chins, and patriarchs staring out from unlit doorways. In late afternoon, as we passed through villages lit up by the sharp last light, and six-year-old shepherds drove their animals home, and the sun declined behind the purple mountains, surrounded by silence and vast emptiness, I could think only of the lilting cadences of Gray's "Elegy Written in a Country Church Yard." For this really did seem a world pre-fallen; an intimation of some pastorale that sang inside us like a long-lost melody.

"What would it take for news to reach here?" asked the I.B., hungry for a copy of the latest *Financial Times*. It never could, I realized. An atomic bomb in Hiroshima; a coup in Moscow; the whole of China swinging on its hinges: None of it, surely, could ever touch this world or make sense even if it did get here. It belonged to a different age.

Driving in Ethiopia is not an easy experience—infrequent buses appearing on the wrong side of the road, children and donkeys swerving crazily in front of you, potholes sending you ricocheting from one side of the car to the other until you cannot move or talk or eat. And, in our case, conditions were not enhanced by a LandCruiser equipped with a tape deck that wouldn't work, seat belts that didn't engage, a front door that couldn't lock, and a driver who, when pressed, admitted that he'd been along this road only once before, twenty-eight years earlier, on a bus.

Still, there was redemption in the air itself, and in the unending vistas: camels, sometimes, running under a full moon; horses being ridden so fast in impromptu races that they raised up Mongol clouds of dust; village homes a blaze of apricot and sea blue and blinding green.

We drove past rolling hills and round straw huts, past monumental skies and conifers and hooded pietàs. "It's so cultivated," said the I.B., who had just come from Kenya, and though he was talking about the land, he could as easily have been talking about the sensibility. For there is nothing of the bush or the untended jungle here among these high mountain plateaus. And nothing without pride, and some degree of self-possession. The night of our first day on the road, helpful voices calling out directions in the dark, we stopped at a tiny rest house, and a man came out, cried *"Buona sera!"* and served up, with a Milanese flourish, steak Bismarck and Axumite red wine, a napkin decorously wrapped around the bottle (whose label announced, "The peculiarity of this wine makes it appreciated by everybody").

At daybreak, it was like seeing the face of the world before it was born, like shapes and figures from one's deepest subconscious. In the early light the mist still swaddled the mountains, and when I walked up the main street, little girls were skipping rope, women were sweeping the space before their huts, boys were carrying fuel home for their mothers. Cocks crowed. The mist began to lift. Horse-drawn carriages clattered over bumpy roads. It was not that there was so much poverty here; it was more that there was so little excess. No fat on the land, so to speak.

On a blazing blue day in Dese—the name means "my joy"—we stopped to get our roof fixed. Across from us, men bathed naked in a stream, their wives sitting on the grass under parasols. Above them, on a hill, villagers were selling sheep and goats and donkeys on this market day, while below, in the central market, boys sold empty bottles of Johnnie Walker and presided over cans of European Economic Community rapeseed oil. The I.B. lost himself in Richard Price, and I walked into a local video store, which carried seven copies of *Return to Eden* (and one of *Romeo and Juliet*), under a huge mural of Bob Marley.

"The Sudan is primitive," the I.B. pronounced. "This is basic. There's a difference." And there was some truth to what he was saying, in this land where eight people out of every ten live a half day's walk from the nearest road and ninety-five percent are still agricultural peasants. There was no sugar in the Ethiopian diet until recently, and there has always been a fierce wariness of the modern: Even when Haile Selassie brought the first airplane from Europe, in the twenties, many of his people took him to be a necromancer, importing instruments of Satan.

We drove on, through enchanted light, over mountain passes where men were carrying whole beds of leaves, and when we got to the town of Weldiya, we stopped to ask directions. If we went on, we were told, we would be attacked by bandits. "If they see us," the driver said, turning around, eyes wild, "they will take money, bags, everything. Even they will kill us. They do not care. They will kill us like the animals." Deciding not to put this prognosis to the test, we procured three rooms in a waterless shack and beguiled the last of the light with games of Ping-Pong along the main street, fifty or so boys cheering and laughing all around us and calling out "Bravo!" whenever one of my slams nicked the table.

The final five miles to Lalibela, over unpaved road, the car's wheels spinning in dry creek beds, the cans of fuel in the back all but suffocating us, took almost three hours. It was, we noted sorrowfully, December 31. "The end of the year in the end of the world!" cried the I.B., with a gaiety brought on by hysteria.

And then suddenly we were there, in silence and in mystery. Inside the rock churches the white figures were everywhere in the dim light, leaning against pillars, standing in front of windows, reading old leathery, hand-size Bibles or letting out unearthly, mumbled chants that reverberated around the ancient spaces. Sometimes I could see only their eyes in the dark, and hear only their song.

Lean, bearded priests with piercing eyes made strange movements with their crosses, and pilgrims slept in empty spaces, and somewhere in the rafters pigeons whirred. Incense rose up from the shrine, and deacons sang, and figure after figure came into the darkness, kissing the cool stone before they entered. "I weary of writing more about these buildings," the first foreign visitor to describe them, a Portuguese priest in the early sixteenth century, wrote, "because it seems to me I shall not be believed."

Often, in Lalibela, I took just to sitting on a hill and listening to the sounds of the village: the chatter of old men with crooks, gathered in the shade, a mother shouting to her child; the sound of other children playing in the distance. Birds with gorgeous iridescent turquoise wings—Abyssinian rollers, I later learned—lit up the branches. Often there was nothing but the calling of the birds and the wind, whistling in my ears.

Occasionally there were vultures in the trees and bells to summon priests to church. And everywhere a sense of piety and fervor, a world inscribed by nothing but devotion.

"It isn't Africa," a Swiss medieval historian said over dinner that night, on New Year's Eve. "It's more like a cross between medieval Europe and Arabia. In this village, for example, there are seven thousand people. And one thousand of them are priests. That too is medieval: In Europe, in the Middle Ages, one tenth of the population were priests."

The next day, the I.B. and I got on mules and rode through the dust-colored mountains, over a landscape as majestic and humbling as Monument Valley, the I.B. listening to Dead bootlegs on his Walkman as we passed donkeys and cedar trees and olive trees and juniper and peasants with long black beards, seated under trees sharing food. As so often happens in Ethiopia, it felt as if we were traveling through an illuminated Bible from the thirteenth century, except that all the figures moved.

When we arrived in Nakutola'ab, a tiny settlement two hours away where twenty-five anchorites live in rock caves, we came upon a group of pilgrims—mud-grimed grandfathers and sunken-cheeked women and young girls in pockmarked gowns—all of them clapping and singing their joy, ululating wildly and pounding on drums, in a circle, to vent their pent-up pleasure after arriving at the place that they'd been dreaming of all their lives.

I asked one of the men (through a translator) how old he was—a strapping man, tall and lean, his eyes alight with glee. He was seventy, he said, and he had walked twelve days and nights to mark Christmas (celebrated in Ethiopia on January 7) in this sacred site.

"And why do you come here?"

"Because this is heaven. We believe if we are here, we go to heaven."

"Then I'll see you in heaven," said the I.B., clapping him on the shoulder, and there were wild shouts of approval and laughs all around.

Lalibela was not just an extraordinary medieval mystery play in stone, I thought, not just a place where the emperor had come to pray when the first of Mussolini's Blackshirts arrived; not merely a marvel that had taken twenty-three years to construct, with the help of angels, and masons from Syria, from Greece—even from India. It was one of those rare sites where the spirit vibrated not only through the buildings but through all the spaces in between.

And then we took to the road again and drove for hour after hour, past deep canyons and bleak wasteland and lunar spaces, with nothing to remind us of where we were, or when. It felt more than ever as if we were driving through some ur-terrain, archaic, ancestral, through some lost part of ourselves, almost.

And everywhere, the sheer grandeur of the mountains and an immensity of sky. A landscape before whose gravity and purity one feels very small, and young. A bareness that takes you back to something very essential, and elemental, almost to life before it was lived. In the Ethiopian language of Gallinya, I had read, the word for sky is the same as the word for God.

I had seen empty spaces before I came to Ethiopia—in the Australian Outback, say, or in Patagonia. But what made these so much more rending and exalting was that there were people living amid this nothingness, walking across it, trying to eke out a living from it—nomads pale with grime, men wielding axes, women bearing staffs. And in the midst of the desolation, long lines of people, most of them rail-thin, bedraggled, barefoot; long lines of people walking, walking, walking, from nowhere to nowhere. The sadness of Ethiopia is that even in the areas that are relatively prosperous, all the lean figures look as if they are walking out of the photographs of famine that shocked the world a decade ago; next year, we were told, a million people would be without food, and there was nothing that could be done.

And the fervor and the desperation, the piety and the suffering, threw light on one another. Amidst this extreme deprivation, one could see how extreme devotion could arise; amidst this barrenness, the burning brightness of the religious rites and buildings made better sense. Prayers in the wilderness, I thought; water in the desert. It was easy, in Ethiopia, to understand how religions caught fire (easy, too, to see why people became monks in a world that was already naked, unaccommodated, and bare); and it was possible in Ethiopia to see how people who have nothing will give everything to faith.

Every now and then we stopped in cafés for the national staple of *injera,* or foam rubber bread, the I.B. crying out, "This could be *injerious* to your health. Did you take out multiple-*injera* insurance?" Sometimes as we left, we heard the haunting, biblical cry of children in the distance, *"Abba! Abba!"* Every now and then we saw figures in the distance, silhouetted against rocks or proceeding across the emptiness in search of shelter. The only signs of the world we knew were the occasional huts of relief agencies or four-wheel-drive jeeps with LOVE FROM BAND AID on their sides. Mostly, though, it was just emptiness stretching on and on toward the mountains.

After what seemed like days, or aeons, of travel, we arrived in Gonder and were reminded again of how sadness and fervor fuel each other here. There is a faintly threatening air to the old capital now, as its Amhara people chafe against the dictates of a non-Amhara government. Gonder was at its prime 350 years ago, and now, with people from the province of Tigray in power (Zenawi is Tigrayan) and the memories of civil war everywhere apparent, the city has a decidedly guarded feel. A Martyrs' Memorial stands in the heart of town, with messages scrawled in blood red across it, and nearby is a large painting of a skeleton, with a fierce old woman holding the former governor of the province by the hair and crying, "You killed my child! Wherever you go, I will find vengeance!" Men in hoods watch you from dark corners in cafés, sipping their orange-colored mead, and boys in denim jackets tell you the difference between Kalashnikovs and M-14s, and how their fathers were killed by Communists and their sisters, fleeing the fighting, raped in Sudanese refugee camps. Strung between the pretty Italian buildings at the center of town, a banner proclaims NOV. 20 IS THE BIRTH OF THE OPPRESSED PEOPLES!

"All this the Italians built in five years," a local boy told us, motioning around the two main streets of town and referring to the Italian occupation of 1936–1941. "Some people are saying, if they stay ten years, Gonder becomes like Paris."

In Gonder there was not a great deal to do. I bought some Yemenite sandwich biscuits and visited the Falasha village where the last few remnants of Ethiopia's Jewish community, yet to be airlifted to Israel, stand by the side of the road and sell stone figurines of Solomon and the Queen of Sheba making whoopee. I parted with thirty-five cents to attend a wedding in Revolution Square, and saw groups of men in their best Bon Jovi T-shirts gathered around a video camera. And, dutifully, I went to the ruins of the castle of Emperor Fasilades, the seventeenth-century ruler who built the capital here, with its Enigma Gate, Gate of the Flute Players, and Castle of Songs. For all the lyrical names, however, they are much like ruins anywhere: dead clumps of stone and broken towers and piles of forgotten rubble.

But as I sat one Sunday morning in the corner of a tower, looking over the pieces of rock, suddenly I heard wild chanting and the steady, insistent pounding of drums, and a trilling, thrilling ululation of women down below, and when I looked down, I saw them moving all as one, swaying back and forth, with the jacarandas behind them. And when I went down, I found myself in a whole avenue of churches, crowded with worshipers, the streets all but palpitant with prayer, and, along the ancient mud walls, long lines of mendicants.

On every side, around the center, people were gathered under trees, and children were scampering around broken gravestones, and petitioners with white crosses chalked upon their foreheads were giving alms. There were golden robes and rows of multicolored umbrellas, and bells tolling constantly, and, lined up outside the round churches, a terrible, haggard row of people in rags—the leprous, the lame, the palsied, and the blind. The notion of a savior had never made more sense to me; I half expected to see Jesus and the apostles walking down these muddy lanes.

The other site in Gonder that we inspected closely was the Ethiopian Airlines office (which pins POSITIVE ATTITUDE posters from Fairfield, New Jersey, on its walls). E.T., as the experts call it, has a sterling reputation but is not without its extraterrestrial elements. Its schedules seem to follow the solar calendar, it insists on security checks at every stage of check-in, and in many places the only terminals in sight are trees. "Ethiopia is a land where the great unknown yonder still exists in plenty," says the legend on every ticket.

Undeterred, we took our lives in our hands (and out of the hands of our driver, who had taken now to plaintive moans of "I am very suffering") and flew low over the high plateaus toward Bahar Dar. The town itself is a pleasant palm-fringed settlement along the banks of Lake Tana. Tissisat Falls is nearby, a rainbow punctually arcing across its rush of water every morning and marking the place where James Bruce, the Scottish explorer, excitedly hailed the waters of the Blue Nile. Boys cross the river on papyrus boats and hoist stalks of sugarcane taller than themselves. On the quiet lake there are tens of little islands, most of them given over to monasteries, some so strict that no female is allowed to set foot on them (not even a hen). The round, dried-mud churches at their center, three hundred years old, swarm with naive, brightly colored murals bursting with angels and stories from the Bible and even—a typical Ethiopian anachronism— Jesus surrounded by gun-toting men.

That strain, in fact, was beginning to hit me more and more forcibly. As soon as I went to change my money at a local bank, a security guard came up to frisk me and to ask me to deposit my camera next to the rifles laid neatly against the wall outside; an hour later, walking through quiet villages to see the falls, I was accompanied by a sharp-talking teenager and a barefoot peasant with a rifle (whether to ward off bandits or to perform banditry himself, I never knew). Pride is only a hairbreadth from machismo here, and when it does not take the form of guarding Jesus—or General Aidid—with guns, it involves overtaking around blind turns and driving the other man off the road.

The most obvious reason for this is that the country is only just emerging from decades of civil war. Ever since their region was annexed, in 1962, the Eritreans had been fighting against central authority in Addis, and then their guerrillas had joined the rebel fighters to overthrow the Communists. Meanwhile, more than a hundred other ethnic groups were pursuing their rivalries and interests in the north and south and east. The result is that everywhere you go in Ethiopia, you see the scars and remnants of thirty years of war: Airports are blasted, and the tarmac is littered with helicopters and junked Aeroflot planes. Rusted tanks line every road, and faded replicas of the hammer and sickle. Once, in Bahar Dar, coming upon a car crash (there are more crashes than cars in Ethiopia, it often seems), I ended up spending a long day in a local hospital, a place of terrible cries and whimpers, where boys with bandaged heads and sunken faces writhed under rough blankets. The doctors were courtly and efficient, but it was not a place where I would like to fall ill.

"Are there many car accidents here?" I asked a pretty young nurse.

"No," she said, nonchalant. "Usually it is bullet wounds. But that, too, not so often. Usually the people here shoot to kill, not wound. So we let them just go ahead with it." And, smiling, she went off to another victim.

We explored Bahar Dar in an old car decorated with pictures of Rambo and Jesus on the windshield, driven by Solomon, with Mikael at his side, both of them breaking into smiles of good-natured perplexity as the I.B. recited a poem about a duck-billed platypus entering the diplomatic service. We visited the U.N. Shoe Shine store and the Marine Bingo Club, and in the evening, we got the manager of the local cinema to screen *The Border* just for us, though the print was so washed-out and mutilated that the picture was over in a matter of minutes, and somehow the classic last scene of Freddy Fender singing Ry Cooder's "Across the Borderline" was lost. Nonetheless, it was a cheerful experience, sitting on long wooden benches, like pews, in what looked like a school assembly hall, the boys in the balcony eating egg sandwiches and sipping *shai,* and scarcely missing Freddy Fender.

For the few foreigners who visit it, Ethiopia is a very small country, and when I arrived, I had no hesitation in calling up Richard Pankhurst, perhaps the West's leading authority on the country and a resident of Addis, on and off, since 1951. He was rather ill, he said, the first time I called, and the next time I tried, he was out of town. But one day, as I walked toward a monastery on an island in Lake Tana, suddenly I heard his inimitable Oxbridge tones, and when I looked around, there he was, in a green suit, explaining the iconography of the church to a group of birders from America: the usual Ethiopian gallimaufry of St. George slaying the dragon, the "crucification" (as they always call it), the local Saint Abbo, Moses, and the Virgin.

The Ethiopian Orthodox Church is unusual, Professor Pankhurst explained, in that it still gives great honor to the Old Testament, believing not that the New supersedes the Old but, rather, that the Old prophesies the New. The Ethiopian Bible contains all the books of the so-called Apocrypha, and, in fact, the Book of Enoch comes down to us only in the ancient Ethiopian liturgical language of Ge'ez. Ethiopians also observe all the Old Testament rites of circumcision, fasting, and the like, to the point where many Ethiopians fast, one way or another, for roughly half the days of the year.

Ever since it was brought here in the fourth century by Syrian missionaries, Christianity has taken a distinctive form in Ethiopia, not quite Coptic and certainly not Western. Nestled in the isolation of the highlands, unsettled by the constant threat of Muslim invasions, it has gone its own individual way—to the point where it is now almost a talisman of the nation (thus Muslims participate in Christian rites).

It is wise to remember this when one flies out into the hot plains and scrubland of the east, for there one seems to have left the ancient land behind and entered Africa. Women in brilliantly colored robes, swirled like saris around their bodies, green and violet and pink, walk with a stately grace across the desolation of the desert. The air feels sultry, strutting, spiced with heat and menace.

Dire Dawa, my first stop in the east, had Stars of David on its doors and signs for the Ethiopia-Somalia Democratic Movement among stores that were nearly always called "Moderen." Not far from the old *chemin de fer* station (there is a strong French influence here in this hot, dusty, squat, rectangular town redolent of the Foreign Legion), I came upon a swirl of calèches and minivans and Peugeot taxis, and tall boys with insolent stares selling nuts and oranges. A man guffawed at my copy of *Le Rouge et le noir,* a boy with kohl-lined eyes ushered me into a van, women pulled up their saffron scarves, giving off a cloud of fragrances. A fight broke out nearby, and the combatants sprawled in the dust.

A couple of denim dudes collected our cash, and then we set off for Harar, passing proud dreadlocked girls and small, muddy African villages, tall cactus by the side of the road. Flirty teenagers jangled their bracelets and stared back defiantly at passersby. The girl next to me had a ring on every finger.

Harar, at its heart, is all North Africa, all whitewashed passageways and Moorish curves, the cry of "baksheesh" from the boys, and, in the house where Haile Selassie once lived, a man called Sheikh Mohammed, offering traditional healing ("The treatment is given by the help of God," his sign explains. "Although the Medicine is given without payment, the patient and all other peoples including organization help us if you can").

I put myself in the tender care of a bleary-eyed gent called Astaw Warhu, and he gave me a highly colorful tour of a Muslim enclave that was like a rich and heady concoction: of tribal girls with yellow-chalked faces, and others with rolling white eyes; of Oromo women with red dots around their eyes, and men with lips of foaming green. As soon as I turned down the traditional healing, he whisked me down a tiny alleyway and then up some dusty stairs, to a place with panes of dirty stained glass and a lightless room where two men were sprawled on cushions, phlegmatically chewing khat (the coca leaves of North Africa, of which Harar is the world's leading producer).

"You know Rimbaud?" asked Mr. Warhu, pointing to the two dazed men who were splayed out like opium addicts. "This is where he lived. Sometimes he sells arms to Menelik II. Sometimes he is a postman." I thought, gloomily, of the exiled author of *Une Saison en enfer.*

Then Mr. Warhu led me up some more stairs, to where there was some wallpaper covering the ceiling. "Rimbaud!" he declared. "All this he paints!"

We went down into the dust and confusion and red and yellow loudness of the market, surrounded by five gates and ninety-nine mosques, so they say, with *Les Jeunes Bonzes du temple de Shaolin* playing in the local cinema, and the children, without exception, crying out to me, *"Ferengi, ferengi!"* ("Foreigner, foreigner!") or, more often, "Cuba, Cuba, Cuba!"

"They think you are Cuban," said Mr. Warhu. "The Cubans are no good. They think every day, every night, about war. They are walking in town with guns, with pistols." This seemed an odd objection in a country where more people carry guns than handbags, but Mr. Warhu concluded, "Every people is come back to the gods."

Then, disconcertingly, he added, "You know Heinemann?"

Was he referring to the English publisher of V. S. Naipaul?

"Heinemann?"

"Yes. Heinie-man. Every night he feeds heinies. You can make photograph."

I decided to pass on the hyena man, while thinking that Harar has come a long way from its traditional status as a closed, walled city with its own chieftain, language, and coinage, a hidden metropolis that had never seen a European face until Sir Richard Burton stole into it in 1854. For centuries, ever since the Muslims had taken it over, it had flowered in secrecy behind its walls, closing its doors each night at dusk and keeping all Christians out.

Harar today seemed to me stench, flies, dust; flashing-eyed girls in golden scarves; the cry of the muezzin above green-domed mosques; women with nose rings and dangling bangles, walking so straight they were able to carry bundles of twigs on their heads. Along the main street was the Ogaden National Liberation Front and next door to it, the Commission for the Rehabilitation of Members of the Former Disabled War Veterans East Haraghe Office (the C.R.M.F.D.W.V.E.H.O.?). I checked into the best—actually, the only—hotel in town, which promised BOTH TRADITIONAL COMFORT AND MODERN HOSPITALITY. Did either of these include water, I asked the friendly receptionist? "No," she said. "There is no water in the town. For two months there has been no water."

Addis Ababa, through which almost every visitor must pass while coming and going, is a sleepy, eerie, rather bedraggled town—less tranquil than torpid, and less a town, indeed, than a collection of grand monuments set against shacks and vacant lots and open ditches: a sad, rather abandoned place of relief agencies, and faded, sun-bleached ads for the United Colors of Benetton, and small, hand-painted signs along the road to the airport directing you to embassies. It is, in fact, the most rural city I have ever seen, encircled by dun-colored hills and haunted by the recent discovery that the last emperor was buried in a secret vault beneath the central palace. "Goats and cows grazed on the lawns along the main street, Churchill Road," wrote Ryszard Kapuściński, "and cars had to stop when nomads drove their herds of frightened camels across the street." And that was during the golden age, when Haile Selassie ruled!

Indeed, what gives the city its forlorn, halfhearted air is that the half-finished relics of an imperial past are placed amid the tin-roofed shanties. Addis—like much of Ethiopia—has the air of an exiled prince, long accustomed to grandeur and full of pride but fallen now on very hard times. There are broad streets lined with jacaranda, and the emperor's palace dominates the center of town ("At night the visitor can hear the lions roar from the grounds of the nearby palace," my 1969 guidebook said of the hotel where I was staying). There are boulevards named after Queen Elizabeth and King George VI, and ceremonial gates. There is even a Hilton Hotel. But incense clouds the lobby there, and the only papers on offer are ten days old.

Much of the capital feels remaindered now, and dispossessed (even the envelopes in my hotel proclaimed, not very ringingly, THE TRANSITIONAL GOVERNMENT OF ETHIOPIA). Along the streets where Haile Selassie used to cruise in his green Rolls-Royce, the signs say HOPE ENTERPRISES FEEDING CENTER and LIFE SAVER CAFETERIA. Across from the National Museum, there are stalls with names like NEIL A. ARMSTRONG TYPING TRAINING SCHOOL (typing in Amharic, with more than two hundred characters in its alphabet, must be almost as difficult as walking on the moon) and hooded people clutching inflight magazines as if they were glossy treasures. And the city of palimpsests still has a spooky, nerve-wracked air, the air of a city with a bad case of the shakes, in the midst of a bad sleep troubled by dark dreams.

Yet on the day before Christmas—as flawless and blue as every other day I spent in Ethiopia—the streets were bright with cross-shaped wreaths of purple and gold, and as night began to fall, the bars put on their single tube of neon lighting and I could see bright candles in shacks and twinkling trees in cafés. Children let off fireworks in small parks, and women in gorgeous silks, with painted feet, trooped into my hotel.

And on a misty Christmas Eve, the streets were filled again with white-robed worshipers. The bells of the Selassie (Trinity) Cathedral tolled and tolled and tolled, and soon all corners of the glowing church were crowded with gaunt white figures in hoods, and deacons in white with red crosses on their backs, and priests in black robes with small white hats, and women with gold sandals underneath their white: a whole swirl of half-mythic figures, ragged, barefoot, but upright, filling all the pews in the church's ornate interior, the green and red and yellow flag of Ethiopia fluttering above them.

Upstairs, in a gallery, a group of robed deacons were standing in a circle, chanting slowly and solemnly, as if to some age-old rhythm. One, on the ground, banged a slow, slow drum, and all the men around him, clutching their T-shaped prayer sticks, slowly waving their sistrums, let out a slow, solemn, wailing chant that carried into the night and down into the nave below.

Outside, in the pitch-blackness, worshipers were making deep prostrations, extending their whole bodies along the ground and mumbling prayers, or standing in nooks and corners with their Psalters. Candles had been placed in the hands of every saint, in all the twelve alcoves along the church, above the stained glass;

believers circumambulated the darkened building bearing tapers, their figures making ghostly shadows on the walls.

Around them, in the dark, from the trees, I heard a banging drum. Cries and chants and ululations from somewhere among the gravestones. A haunting, unworldly, ancient chant that went through me to the core.

I followed the sound through the trees and the abject darkness and came upon a wondrous sight: a whole avenue of people, lit up by candles before them, outside the entrance to another church, old and small and round. Around it on every side, barefoot, bedraggled, hooded bodies, all in white, more bodies than I could count, hardly visible by the light of the candles they were holding, and gathering in small groups under straw roofs, or standing against headstones, or assembled in a circle under a tree, just praying, or listening in silence to a sermon, or singing hallelujahs in the night.

Everywhere I turned there were figures, some of them asleep. They had not eaten all day, and many of them had been fasting for two months—no meat, no eggs. Others stood on either side of distant tombs, a candle on each side of them. Others were lined up in what looked to be a manger, their sweet high voices rising up into the dark.

Within the church there were so many people that one could hardly move. Boys were playing ox-skin drums, and lines of men in multicolored raiment and gold and violet hats were singing from their holy books, the altars in front of them shaking with their piety. Outside, one of the groups struck up a hymn and started clapping, and others picked up the rhythm, and then there was a wild ululation that signaled, thrillingly, glad tidings to the world, and the arrival of something bright.

All across the candlelit city it was like that on Christmas Eve: white-robed people from another age, with laughing eyes and beads and crosses, chanting by the light of tapers. And sometimes, as I looked around me at the round church and the rough ground and the ragged, hopeful figures sitting or standing and singing through the night, I felt that this must have been how it was in Bethlehem two thousand years before. There was no sign of the modern world, no electricity or hype. Only ragged figures, with candles, singing their devotion.

"You really feel it," said the I.B., moved. "You really feel the joy that must have arisen when God was born." And he was right.

Before I went to Ethiopia, I had said, half-facetiously, that I was going there to "get around Christmas," leaving on December 25 to avoid the commercialism and loneliness and impossible expectations that constitute the holiday for us. I never knew, though, that Ethiopia really was the way to get to the heart of Christmas, and of almost everything else. I am no Christian, but Christianity made sense to me in Ethiopia—and many things as basic as hope and dignity, necessity and faith—and as I looked at the stars through the branches and the flicker of candles, I really could imagine three wise men coming to a manger, following the skies. Everything revved up and complicated fell away, and I was left in Ethiopia with the small, forgotten soul of the whole thing: thanksgiving amid hardship and songs of glorious praise.

1994

SEEING ETHIOPIA

How to navigate a timeless land

 It sounds like a daunting place to visit, but in reality, Ethiopia has never been more accessible. There are new terminals and a new runway at Addis Ababa's Bole International Airport, and the government has improved access roads to the four main towns—Lalibela, Bahir Dar, Gonder, and Axum—that make up the Historic Route.

Aside from the improved infrastructure—which the government hopes will encourage tourism—the country can claim other points of pride as well. In 2005, Ethiopia recovered from Rome the seventeen-hundred-year-old Obelisk of Axum, which had been stolen by Mussolini in 1937. After a decades-long campaign, the seventy-eight-foot-tall granite tower lies for now in the Axum stelae field; plans are under way to re-erect it. And in late 2006, in one of the most publicized paleontological finds in years, scientists announced the discovery of the remains of a 3.3-million-year-old baby in the Rift Valley.

Here, some of the best and most reliable ways to see the new (and old) Ethiopia.

The "Northern Historical Tour" is an eleven-day trip organized by **Custom Safaris.** The Bahir Dar stop includes a side trip to the Blue Nile Falls in addition to the famous monasteries on Lake Tana. The Gonder leg adds a day tour into the volcanic Simien Mountains (301-530-1982; customsafaris.com).

Throughout the fall and winter, **Abercrombie & Kent** offers half a dozen different departure dates for its twelve-day tour

"Ethiopia: An Ancient Dynasty," which covers the basic Historic Route stops as well (800-554-7016; abercrombiekent.com).

Two areas are expected to become more visitor friendly in the coming years: the Rift Valley, where Ethiopia's large animals roam, and the largely undiscovered South Omo region, which sits just across the Sudanese and Kenyan borders. Many of its tribal villages have never had outside visitors. A ten-day trip organized by the San Francisco–based **Geographic Expeditions** begins with an unusual visit to the Fistula Hospital in Addis before heading north to Axum and Lalibela. The Historic Route is followed by a U-turn south to the town of Jinka, Mursi villages in Mago National Park, and visits to the Konso people in coffee country (415-922-0448; geoex.com).

The Africa Adventure Company combines twenty-day trips to the north (including the Simien Mountains) with a full week exploring even more remote tribal villages of southern Ethiopia. Much of the travel is rugged, and includes a boat ride down the Omo River and lodging in mobile campsites. Depending on the timing, visitors will have opportunities to witness local ceremonies like the Hamar people's bull-jumping rite of passage for boys (954-491-8877; africa-adventure.com).

For those interested in shorter trips from the capital, many reputable tour operators in Addis can provide four-by-four transport—drivers included—for one hundred dollars and up per day. (Inquire at the Addis Ababa Hilton or Sheraton for details.) One of the best day jaunts is a drive to the walled city of **Harar,** Rimbaud's onetime haunt. Famous for its dense alleyways, the World Heritage Site near the Somali border is often compared to Zanzibar. **Lake Langano** is a convenient three-hour drive down the main southern highway from Addis, and is the country's only bilharzia-free—and thus swimmable—lake. The country's first eco-property, **Bishangari Lodge,** has bungalows and traditional mud huts on the banks of the lake. It's a great place, even for non-guests, to hike, ride horseback, and witness the elaborate traditional coffee ceremony in the outdoor restaurant (251-11-551-7533; bishangari.com). The truly intrepid can follow the tracks of Evelyn Waugh and take the century-old rickety train, which travels three days a week from Addis to Djibouti, five hundred desert miles away.

Primal Dreams

by

RUSSELL BANKS

When you come into Miami International Airport from Newark, as I recently did, and drive south and west for two hours on Florida's Turnpike, you have to travel through the end of the twentieth century in North America. Condos and malls and housing developments, like orange-capped mushrooms, spring up from horizon to horizon. Fast-food outlets, trailer parks, used-car lots with banners crackling in the breeze, and in Homestead the lingering wreckage of Hurricane Andrew—stripped live oak trees, decapitated palms, boarded-up buildings, temporary housing—give way to tomato and sugarcane fields, where migrant workers from Jamaica and Mexico toil under the subtropical sun. It's the inescapable present.

But then, suddenly, you drive through the entrance to Everglades National Park, and it's as if you've passed through a gate into another time altogether, a distant, lost time aeons before the arrival of the first Europeans, before even the rumored arrival of the Arawak in dugouts fleeing the Caribbean archipelago and the invading Caribs. Out on the Anhinga Trail, barely beyond earshot of the cars and RVs lumbering toward the lodge and marina in Flamingo at the southern end of the park, the only sounds you hear are the wind riffling through the saw grass, the plash of fish feeding on insects and on one another, and the great long-necked anhingas diving or emerging from the mahogany waters of a sluggish, seaward-moving slough. You hear a hundred frogs cheeping and croaking and the sweet wet whistle of a red-winged blackbird. A primeval six-foot-long alligator passes silently through the deep slough to the opposite side, coasts to a stop in the shallows, and lurks, a corrugated log with eyes. An anhinga rises from the water and flies, like a pterodactyl, to a cluster of nearby mangrove roots and cumbrously spreads and turns its enormous wings, glistening black kites silhouetted against the noontime sun.

A rough carpet of water lilies—clenched, fist-size buds about to bloom—floats on the surface of the slough, while just below, long-nosed gars luff in threes and fours and bass and bluegills collect in schools, abundant and wary of the next upper link in the food chain, but strangely secure, like carp in a Japanese pool, as if here they have no unnatural enemies. And they don't. A large softshell turtle hauls herself out of the water and patiently begins to lay her dozens of eggs in the gray limestone soil, depositing them like wet vanilla-colored seeds. Farther down the embankment lies the wreckage of an old nest broken open by birds, the leathery shells smashed and drying in the sun. A dark blue racer snake slides into the brush. Mosquitoes gather in slow, buzzing swirls. The sun is high, and it's hot, ninety degrees, with a slight breeze blowing from the east. It's mid-May, yes—but what century?

In our time, much of travel that is freely elected by the traveler is time-travel. We go to Paris, tour Venice, visit Athens and the Holy Land, mainly to glimpse the past and walk about the cobbled streets with a guidebook and a furled umbrella—emulating as best we can Henry James in Rome, Flaubert in Cairo. Or we fly to Tokyo, Beijing, Brasília, perhaps, for a safe, cautious peek into the future. Sometimes, for both the past and the future at once, we make our way to cities such as Lagos, Mexico City, Lima. It's time-travel, but it's strictly to the past and future of humanity that we've gone.

For some of us, that's not enough. We want to travel even farther in time, to view and imagine anew the planet earth without billions of human beings on it. For this we get up an expedition and float down the Amazon on a raft, or we go off to Africa and clone ourselves a Teddy Roosevelt safari, this time shooting the large animals with cameras instead of guns. Some of us traipse off to the Arctic or to uninhabited deserts or to mountaintops— journeying to the last remaining places where a traveler can be alone, more or less, and view the planet as it was before we started killing it.

But who can afford that? Who has the time? With only a week or two available and a modest amount of cash in hand, most of us are obliged to look for places closer to home. For me, when in search of this type of time-travel, one of the most satisfying places to go is the Florida Everglades. The reasons are many and complex. First off, and of no small importance, the Everglades is easy to get to, especially for a traveler living in the eastern United States. The park is a smooth seventy-mile drive from downtown Miami. And it is vast in size; you can get lost there. It is the second-largest national park in the Lower 48—2,200 square miles, an area approximately the size of Delaware. And despite its proximity to one of the most densely populated regions of America, it is, for its size, one of the least-visited parks in the system, especially from April to November, so you can be alone there, or nearly so.

But more to the point, every time I climb into my time machine (usually an air-conditioned rental car picked up at the Miami International Airport) and travel into the Everglades, I journey to a place that has a shivering personal resonance for me. I almost always go by myself. It's less distracting that way, and I don't want to be distracted, because, once there, my imagination is instantly touched at its center and all the world seems significant and personalized, as in a powerful dream. It's my dream-time, and I don't want anyone, even someone I love and trust, to wake me.

Most people, if they're lucky, have a place or two where this happens, but for me it occurs in the Everglades. Who knows why? Childhood visions of pre-Columbian Florida and the Caribbean, maybe, induced by hagiographic stories of Columbus, DeSoto, and that master of time-travelers, Ponce de León, in which I help-lessly identified with the wide-eyed European explorers. Followed years later by adolescent pilgrimages to the Keys in naive search of Ernest Hemingway's source of inspiration—as vain an enterprise as Ponce's, of course, but who knew that then? And then, over the years, repeated visits to the Glades, by accident or casual circumstance, building up a patina of personal associations, until now I always enter the park with an expectancy based on nostalgia for a lost self—nostalgia for the New England boy reading about the Arawak and Columbus, for the youth trying to become a novelist, for the reckless young man footloose in South Florida.

And it's an expectancy that is almost always met. I park my time machine and walk out onto the Anhinga or the Gumbo Limbo trail, step by step moving along on the catwalk of my own personal time line. I keep going back, and with increasing clarity, I see more of the place and more of my past selves. And more of the past of the planet as well.

Beyond any other national park, perhaps, the Everglades bears repeated visits, justifying a traveler's return trips, but maybe requiring them too. Without intending it, over the years I've ac-quired from these visits a gradual accumulation of information—about my layered self, I suppose, and, more important, about the place—which has helped me learn to look at the Everglades and see it for what it is instead of for what it isn't.

The first few times I didn't get it. There are no high mountains, no rushing cataracts, no grand panoramic vistas. There's no rain forest, no powerful continent-draining rivers, no rocky seashore. No, the Glades is quiet and low and slow, a shallow, almost invisible river of grass, an intricate, extremely fragile subtropical ecosystem that seems shy and difficult of access to the human eye, which is, of course, one of the reasons humans have come so close to destroying it—and may yet succeed.

To see the Everglades for what it is and not what it isn't, however, you have to develop a kind of bifocal vision, as if you were floating down the Mississippi on a raft with Huck Finn. You have to learn to switch your gaze constantly from the concrete to the abstract, from the nearby riverbank to the distant sky. You need an almost Thoreauvian eye for detail and the interrelatedness of nature's minutiae, for it is a 1.5-million-acre Walden Pond we're talking about here, the largest wetland in the United States. From November through May there are between fifty thousand and a hundred thousand wading birds in the Everglades. More than one hundred species of butterflies have been identified in the park. Fifty species of reptiles, including twenty-six species of snakes and sixteen of turtles. Eighteen species of amphibians. Three hundred forty-seven species of birds. Forty species of mammals. More than one thousand species of plants. There are fifty-two varieties of the small striped liguus snails that you see clinging to the trunks of the live oaks along the short Gumbo Limbo Trail, where, as you stroll, you can catch the skunklike smell of white stopper buds opening, used in ancient times by the Arawak and the first white settlers as a specific against dysentery.

The Gumbo Limbo Trail winds through great twisted old live oak trees with epiphytes and bromeliads clinging to the trunks and upper branches and dead-looking brown resurrection ferns at the roots that burst greenly into life after a rain. The trail is circular and begins and ends at the hundred-foot-tall royal palms of Paradise Key. The key is a hammock, a gentle, almost imperceptible rise in the blond, watery plain, more like a solidified limestone sea swell than an actual key or island. The majestic palms, which these days tower photogenically in front of Miami hotels and cluster around the old Bebe Rebozo compound on Key Biscayne and a thousand other estates, appeared first on the continent here in the Everglades, their seed carried by wind and water from the Caribbean thousands of years ago to catch and eventually prosper on this very hammock. A short way off the trail, I notice a small, still pool of water covered with bright green slime—duckweed—which, seen up close, turns into a glistening skin, as clean and beautiful and serene as snakeskin over the dark, turbulent, fecund water below. I lean down and look closer and imagine I can see into the thrashing molecular soup of life itself.

But the swarming details of the Everglades can overwhelm you. It's almost too much to absorb and organize. In this finely delineated and particularized landscape, to gain perspective you have to step away from time to time and abstract it. Thus, along with Thoreau's eye, you need to develop an almost Melvillean appreciation for the vast circular canopy of blue that stretches unbroken from horizon to horizon and the broad watery swale under your feet. It's as if you are at sea and are standing upon a shimmering grassy plain that floats like the Sargasso between the firmament above and the firmament below. The light is spectacular and shifts constantly, as clouds build and dissipate and build again. But the intensity of the light and its movement are dizzying. And to steady yourself, you shift your gaze almost involuntarily back to what's close at hand, clinging to it as if to the rail of a ship. In so abstract a landscape, to ground yourself you have to look again at the details.

And so it goes—back and forth, the long view and the short, the abstract and the concrete—for here you are situated in an infinitely complex world whose parts, and the tissue of connections between them, can be seen only if the viewer keeps shifting his focal point. By comparison, the city of man, from nearby Miami to distant Calcutta, seems stilled, frozen, caught in a snapshot in relatively recent time, and serving either as all foreground or all background, with no movement between them. The central figure, the subject, is always us; humanity is the figure and the ground; we are content as well as context. In the Everglades, the central figure is the ancient planet itself and its immense plenitude.

Sometimes, instead of visiting the southern end of the Everglades, I drive out from Miami along Route 41, the old Tamiami Trail, cross through the Miccosukee Indian Reservation, pass the airboat rentals (banned inside the park but ready to rent all around it) and the solitary fishermen sitting by the canals built by the Army Corps of Engineers, to reach the north side of the park and spend the day at Shark Valley. It's less a valley than a broad, shallow slough twelve miles wide, a one-to-three-foot-deep scimitar-shaped depression in the limestone bedrock that carries the overflow from Lake Okeechobee in a tectonically slow drift south and west at barely one hundred feet per day, sliding the fresh, nutrient-rich waters across the saw grass plain to the mangrove estuaries of the Gulf of Mexico. Out here, South Florida seems freshly emerged from the ocean, still dripping and draining back into the Gulf, as if the Ice Age had ended only yesterday. Its highest point is barely eight feet above sea level, but from it you can see for miles.

At the Shark Valley Visitors Center there's an open rubber-tired tram that carts tourists into the Glades a ways, with a Park Service guide on a loudspeaker who'll describe what you're seeing. But there's also a bike-rental shop and a fifteen-mile bike path to an observation tower and numerous trails where you can walk in silence. In a half hour, I'm under the hot May sun a few miles out on the bicycle path, pedaling a wobbly old one-speed bike I rented next to the visitors center. I'm finally far enough into the Glades that I can no longer hear the visitors or their cars and RVs or the guide on the tram, so I pull off the path and stop.

Purple pickerelweed is flowering everywhere, and bladderwort, like yellow stars, blooms against the dark water of the slough. Deerflies cruise by and then swerve hungrily back toward me, a new warm-blooded mammal, and hairless, too. All I can hear now is the sound of the links of the food chain clanking. Herons and egrets stand knee-deep in water, waiting motionless, like the fishermen I saw earlier on the Tamiami Trail alongside the canal, and now and then I hear the splash of a gar or a bass busting into the air for a low-flying dragonfly. For a long time, without making a ripple, a six-foot alligator on the far side of the slough stalks a spindly white egret, drawing closer and closer, undetected, until suddenly there is a great, furious roil and splash of water, then feathers floating, and silence as the gator slides away.

Later, out at the observation tower, I pause halfway up and look down, and in the copse below, a rust-colored fawn with pale spots across its belly lies curled and hidden by its mother. Intent only on protecting her offspring from the huge gator snoozing in the slough fifty feet away, she obviously has not considered aerial reconnaissance, especially by a human. Down below, the fawn is as still as a statue in the cool shade of the copse, and lovely, but I feel oddly invasive for watching and quickly resume climbing to the top of the tower. There I gaze out across the watery, veldlike plain of saw grass, where in the west I can make out a bank of cumulus clouds piling up over the Gulf near Everglades City, promising rain. For a moment I consider hurrying back to the car, but then decide no, let the rain come down. And within the hour it does, and as I walk my rented bike the eight miles back to the visitors center, I find myself feeling finally invisible, lost in time and space, afloat inside a dream of a lost and coherent world.

Crossing Shark Valley by foot in the warm torrential rain, it's almost inconceivable somehow that my points of departure—Newark, New Jersey, and Miami, Florida—are in the same time zone as the Everglades. Not just longitudinally, as on a map, but literally, as on a calendar or a wristwatch. Here and in Newark and Miami, today's headlines and stock quotes are the same, the historical facts still hold, and thus all three places bear, at least abstractly, the same relation to the onrushing millennium, to its ethnic cleansings, genocidal massacres, famines, global floods of refugees, children gunning each other down with automatic weapons, wanton destruction of the planet—everything that drives a modern man or woman nearly mad with grief and despair, so that finally all one wants is to get out of this time zone. "Anywhere, so long as it's out of this world," said Baudelaire. And here I am, out of that world. Astonishing!

Later in the day, after the rain has passed east toward Miami and the Atlantic, I drive out on Route 41 to Everglades City in the northwest corner of the Everglades, where there is another visitors center and a marina located at the entrance to the Ten Thousand Islands, a huge chain of mangrove islands that stretches about forty miles from Marco Island in the north to Pavillion Key. It was Ponce de León who guessed there were ten thousand islands, but the modern count, via satellite, is 14,022. The number keeps changing, because most of the "islands," even those several miles across, are built on clustered red mangroves and are constantly being broken apart and restructured by hurricanes.

It's close to five o'clock, though midafternoon bright at this time of year. The sky is washed clean of clouds, and the still surface of the cordovan-colored waters of Chokoloskee Bay is glazed with a taut silvery skin. In these calm tidal waters there is an abundance of snook, tarpon, redfish, blue crabs, and bottlenose dolphins, feeding, breeding, and being preyed upon by each other, by the thousands of cormorants, ospreys, cranes, pelicans, egrets, and ibis that flock year-round on the mangrove islets and rookeries, and by the sport and commercial fishermen from the tiny villages of Everglades City and Chokoloskee as well. They're not preyed upon in such numbers as to endanger them yet—except, of course, for the elusive, mysterious manatee, that fifty-million-year-old watery relative to the elephant, a seagoing cow with flippers. The manatees are protected, but their death rate may exceed their birth rate: These gentle two-thousand-pound animals are being decimated and cruelly wounded by the propellers of the fishing and pleasure boats that roar up and down the waterways here. Nine out of ten of the remaining eighteen hundred manatees bear ugly prop scars on their smooth backs. But there are about 700,000 registered powerboats in Florida, and, thanks to persistent lobbying in Tallahassee by the owners, there are no speed limits in these peaceful, secluded waters. The boats race along the thousands of interlaced channels and crisscross the myriad unnamed bays at thirty to fifty miles an hour, chopping through anything too slow or confused by the noise to get out of the way. Generally the manatees keep to the channels among the islands, feeding on sea grass in waters so darkened by the tannin from the roots and dead leaves of the red mangrove that the animal cannot see the bottom of the boat approaching; nor can it hear the roar of the motor until the boat is nearly on top of it, and thus cannot flee in time to elude death or maiming.

There's enough daylight left to tempt me to rent a canoe at the visitors center, and I push out into Chokoloskee Bay and paddle slowly along one of the scores of channels that cut into and around Sandfly Island in the general direction of the Turner River Canoe

Trail, the start of the Wilderness Waterway that winds for ninety-nine miles through the most extensive mangrove forest in America, all the way to Flamingo and Florida Bay in the south. All I want today, however, is a few hours of solitude on the water, a closer look than was available onshore at the cormorants and frigate birds and the tricolor Louisiana heron I glimpsed heading low over the bay toward Sandfly Island.

Halfway out, barely a quarter mile from shore, a pod of bottlenose dolphins, maybe four or five, swimming a short way off my bow, notice the canoe and slice through the water to investigate, their dorsal fins racing toward me like black knife blades. After circling the intruder several times, they move off again, apparently satisfied or bored, but the last in the pod—an adolescent, probably—makes a show-off's grinning leap. It practically stands on the water and plops over, splashing me and rocking the canoe, and then cruises back to join the others.

I move out into the bay another half mile and notice that atop many of the channel markers, ospreys have built their nests, turning the poles into tall, branchless trees. They are incredibly stable birds, mating for life (fifteen to twenty years), and they use the same nest year after year. Off to my right a ways, one of the smaller islands has been converted into a rookery by a huge flock of fork-tailed frigate birds. There seems to be a great flurry of activity, so I paddle over. Fifty or more parent frigate birds are huddling protectively over their fuzzy gray hatchlings, while another fifty make a great racket and fight off dozens of predatory, sharp-beaked cormorants screeching and hungrily diving for the offspring. I draw near in my canoe and watch the fight for a long while, an invisible witness to a savage siege and great acts of parental courage and sacrifice.

To see what's there, most national parks get you up high on a mountain or make you gape into a canyon or a gorge, playing with scale and fostering delusions of human grandeur without your even having to leave your car. "This car climbed Pikes Peak, Whiteface Mountain, Mount Washington," and so on. In the Everglades, though, you're kept on the same plane as the natural world. You can't see the Everglades at all, really, unless you get close up and keep it at eye level, which humbles you a bit. ("This car drove through the Everglades" is not much of a claim.) This sort of viewing is interactive, and your travel backward in time to the continent's beginnings is all the more convincing for it.

Maybe it's especially true for us Americans—we whose present is too much with us, whose future looks worse, and whose past is increasingly paved over or deliberately erased—that, for our emotional and intellectual well-being, for our moral health as well, time-travel has become more essential than ever. Maybe it's this need that explains the growing popularity and proliferation of historical theme parks, the desire to build a Disney World near a Civil War battlefield, for instance, or the whole Jurassic Park concept, which surely, as much as the animated dinosaurs, accounts for the extraordinary popularity of the movie. It's the idea of safe passage to the distant past that appeals. (One wonders, is that what's behind the success of *The Flinstones*?) This idea may also account for the rapidly increasing popularity of our national parks. The total number of visitors is up ten percent overall in the last decade, and it's much greater in some parks (seventy percent in Yosemite, for instance), bringing, especially in those located within easy striking distance of urban areas, traffic jams, environmental damage, graffiti, crime—all the woes of life in the here and now that we're trying to escape.

The Everglades, which in an odd way is more demanding of its visitors' imaginations than most other parks, has not yet suffered as they have. The greatest danger to the Glades comes from outside the park, from the agriculture industry and real estate developers who for generations have been blocking and draining off its freshwater sources in central and southeastern Florida for human use and polluting the rest with chemical fertilizers and run-off. In recent years, the National Park Service, the state of Florida, and the U.S. Army Corp of Engineers have begun cooperating to restore the old flow of water from Okeechobee as much as possible and to control with great rigor the amount of pollutants allowed to enter the system. In May of this year, Florida governor Lawton Chiles signed the Everglades Forever Act, a complicated, expensive compromise between the environmentalists and the agricultural interests, brokered with the assistance of Interior Secretary Bruce Babbitt. The bill requires the state to construct forty thousand acres of filtration marshes around Lake Okeechobee at a cost of $700 million, with the farmers paying a third of the costs and the rest coming from Florida taxpayers. No one is happy with the deal, which suggests that it's as good a deal as anyone is going to get right now. This act sets a temporary clean-water goal of fifty parts of phosphorus per billion parts of water while delaying a final goal for up to ten more years, which means that the pollution from chemical fertilizers, though diminished, will nonetheless continue. It's a start, but saving the Everglades is an ongoing, extremely costly fight, and for some species it may be too late. A Florida panther, for instance, whose numbers have dwindled to less than thirty, was recently found dead inside the park, and its body contained mercury at a level that would kill a human being.

The sky in the west has faded to pale rose. Ragged silver-blue strips of cloud along the horizon glow red at the edges, as if about to burst into flame. I turn my canoe back toward the marina and am paddling fairly energetically now, for I don't want to get caught out here after dark among ten thousand islands and ten million mosquitoes. You could easily get lost in this maze of channels and not be found for days and be extremely ill by then. I'm reluctant to leave this primeval world, however. Once again, the peaceful, impersonal beauty of the Everglades has soothed and nourished my mind and heart and has restored some of the broken connections to my layered selves and memories. It's time, however, to return to the city of man.

Then suddenly, a few yards ahead of my canoe, I see a swelling disturbance in the water. It smooths and rises, and the water parts and spills, as first one, then two large, sleek-backed, pale gray manatees surface and exhale gusts of mist into the air. They slowly roll and dive, but a second later they reappear, and this time there is a calf the size of a dolphin nestled safely between them. I can hear the three animals inhaling huge quantities of air, and then they dive again and are gone. The water seethes and settles and is still. A low-flying pelican cruises down the channel ahead of me and disappears in the dusk.

For a long time I sit there in my canoe, thrilled by the memory of the sight, feeling unexpectedly, undeservedly blessed. Jurassic Park, indeed. This is the real thing! For a few wondrous seconds, a creature from the Paleocene has let me enter its world and has come close enough almost to touch. It's as if the old planet earth itself contained a virtue, a profound generosity of spirit, that has allowed it to reach forward in time all the way to the end of the twentieth century in North America, and has brought me into its embrace.

1994

THE ANIMALS OF THE EVERGLADES

The wetlands' endangered fauna

 The Everglades is in rehab, and not a moment too soon: The area is being treated to an $8 billion, thirty-year government-sponsored restoration project, an expensive and controversial attempt to reverse the trends of waters drying and species dying that have been written on the wind here ever since land developers began fiddling with the region's natural water flow.

The project, known as the Comprehensive Everglades Restoration Plan (CERP), aims to recapture as much as 1.7 billion gallons of the freshwater currently being flushed out to sea every day and redirect it back to the ailing wetlands—all without flooding South Florida's farms and booming cities. Plans include eliminating some 240 miles of canals and levees to increase water flow through the River of Grass; constructing new filtering marshes to cleanse the runoff from seven hundred thousand acres of farms and sugarcane fields; and periodic releasing of water stored in the reservoirs and underground aquifers to mimic the area's historical wet-dry cycle. That's an ambitious plan in itself, but CERP must contend with other problems as well: The human population of South Florida is 6 million, and droughts seriously curtail water use. By 2050 the population is projected to surge to more than 12 million, which means that even if CERP goes as planned, increased water use and pollution could imperil the good health of the Everglades.

CERP's proponents are in for a long haul, but there's no doubting that the Everglades, which is home to scores of endangered and rare plants and animals, needs the help more than ever:

Canals, levees, roads, and even reservoirs have fragmented the Everglades's delicate ecosystem, restricting the movement of many species of fish, which has in turn reduced the range of birds who feed on them. In addition, invasive plant and animal species are quickly replacing natives, and phosphorus agricultural runoff has severely diminished water quality.

There are currently fifteen endangered species living within the Everglades's borders (a sixteenth, the Red-Cockaded Woodpecker, disappeared from the park in the 1940s). Here are some of the local inhabitants you might see while on safari in South Florida—one hopes they'll be around for many years to come.

The **Florida panther** once lived throughout most of the southeastern United States, but due to expanding urban development, it has been virtually eliminated. The six-foot, long-tailed, pale brown cat gives birth to two or three kittens every few years. Nomadic animals, they travel up to twenty miles in one journey, and eat mostly deer and wild hogs. In 1986, scientists began collaring panthers with electronic tracking equipment, leading them to believe that by 1990, there were fewer than fifty surviving in the wild. Habitat destruction is only part of the rough hand the panther's been dealt—genetic inbreeding, shootings, mercury poisoning, and car collisions also spell doom for this poster cat of the Everglades.

The **manatee,** or sea cow, is a gray-brown, thick-skinned mammal with paddlelike forelimbs. It weighs around one thousand pounds and grows from eight to fifteen feet long. Manatees inhabit slow-moving rivers, shallow estuaries, and saltwater bays, where they feed on aquatic vegetation. Essentially gentle animals, they have been used as agents for aquatic weed control, and are most threatened by collisions with boat propellers, vandals, poaching, and habitat destruction.

The **wood stork** is a long-legged wading bird up to forty-five inches long with a five-foot wingspan. A so-called "indicator species," its specific habitat requirements are closely related to the habitats of other species. It locates food with its bill by groping for small freshwater fish in shallow water, which is easiest during low-water periods. However, modern water control has led to excessive drying patterns, creating difficulties for the stork. While studying this species, scientists have discovered a ninety percent decline in all wading birds in the park since the 1930s.

The **American crocodile** is a lizard-shaped reptile that grows from a nine-inch-long hatchling to a fifteen-foot-long adult. Crocs are slimmer than their lookalike cousin, the alligator, and have a longer, more tapered snout. They feed primarily on fish, although as any South Floridian small-dog owner knows, they'll eat almost any animal that happens into their territory. Crocodiles in Florida inhabit the coastal mangrove swamps, brackish and saltwater bays, creeks, and coastal canals. Most crocodiles—along with their habitat from Biscayne Bay northward—have been lost due to human development along the coast and Keys. It is unlikely that many will remain outside Everglades National Park in another ten years.

To see the Everglades like a native, fall in with a Seminole guide at Billie Swamp Safari. Guides take visitors through twenty-two hundred acres of the Big Cypress Reservation, via swamp buggy, airboat, or a walk along a nature trail. Hardy types can rent a chickee to sleep in; these open-sided pavilions on stilts were the housing of choice for native peoples (semtribe.com/safari). Alternatively, Everglades National Park offers four contact stations throughout its 1.5 million acres, including one each in Homestead, Shark Valley, and Everglades City. The last location is the best jumping-off point to explore the Ten Thousand Islands, a maze of mangrove islands and waterways. Knowledgeable trackers can point you in the right direction (nps.gov/ever).

A Country Made for Living

by

PATRICIA STORACE

The ocher-red cliffs I see from the hotel dining-room window look like the smudges of a child's finger painting, especially when glimpsed through a shimmering double rainbow, an arc of color cutting across the sky. Here in Provence, a Roman colony for some five hundred years and still proud of this heritage, it seems appropriate to view a rainbow as a Roman architectural form, the triumphal arch.

I am at Le Phébus, a Michelin-starred restaurant in the tiny hamlet of Joucas. A pair of silver turtle doves preside over the table. Noiselessly, the server sets before me my first course, a hot cheese soup mysteriously consisting only of an egg enfolded in a tile-shaped pastry. This does not resemble soup. I compose my expression, waiting for enlightenment. She returns, bringing my companion's *petits gris de Provence,* those famous snails whose flesh is flavored by their diet of Provençale herbs. These delicate morsels, which the Provençal swear are superior to the more grossly plump snails of Burgundy, are so treasured they even play a role in the local Nativity scenes, in the figure of a snail seller on her way to the stable, bringing her offering to the Holy Family.

An elegant elderly couple, accompanied by a fine dog, are led to a table. They asked permission to bring the dog into the dining room, explaining that it cries piteously if left alone outside but will, they promise, sleep peacefully at their feet while they dine. Later, I hear them administer a gentle, quasiparental scolding to the youthful sommelier, who has recommended, they feel, a bottle on the basis of its costliness rather than its rightful place within the pattern of their dinner. This is not Paris, they rebuke him. With filial courtesy, he describes alternatives. The couple remind him that they expect a good dinner to be a matter not of consumption but of conversation, not of expense but of artistry.

Now the server reappears carrying a pitcher. She stands at a precisely calculated oblique angle to the bowl before me, then pours into it a flood of hot broth. The tuile softens like a Dalí watch, and the egg flows from it, thickening the broth into a rich, integrated whole, with different textures and intensities of flavor. Variations on the theme of cheese, and a wonderfully executed piece of gastronomic theater.

Provence is a place you taste as well as see, and Le Phébus's menu—which weaves into its text bits of Provençal, a language still studied but rarely heard—is itself an excursion through the region's history, topography, economy, and, in some ways, its society. Here is a version of a classic cod dish from chef Xavier Mathieu's great-grandmother Rose. The flavor of Provence is distilled in another dish of carrots cooked in lavender-blossom honey. Fantasias are founded on the region's olives, lamb, rabbit, red mullet, and chickpea-flour *panisses.* A fish course is accompanied by a witty, savory play on Provence's beloved nougat, in this instance one of ricotta, peanuts, herbs, and a confit of citron. A traditional leg of lamb, cooked for seven hours, is innovatively seasoned with cumin—a tribute, I think, to the new repertory brought to the region by North African immigrants. I am reminded of the great Provençal novelist Jean Giono's definition of the gastronomic experience: "There are things which by flavor or color make you taste joy when you have them on your tongue, and others which make you taste grief. Three parts of joy, one of mourning—that is the taste of life."

Four hours later, as I leave the restaurant, I think that what I have experienced tonight—from the array of tastes to the gibe at Paris—is nothing less than a portrait of Provence, a place where food represents culture, not gluttony, where the exercise of critical intelligence is itself a voluptuous pursuit, and no genuine delight is divorced from knowledge.

It was Virginia Woolf—like everyone in the Bloomsbury group, a devotee of Provence—who wrote that vacationing in the south of France is "undoubtedly what one will do in Heaven—motoring all day, and eating vast meals, and drinking red wine and liqueurs."

I myself, however, had long managed to resist the charms of Provence. Heaven for me is one place and one person, and both are my secret. A perfume of the self-consciously and ruthlessly expensive idyll seemed to waft from Provence, not unlike the Hamptons of Long Island. The place emitted a suggestion of a countryside transformed into a precious decor, all ceramic cicadas and "chichi pompons," as the wonderfully blunt gastronomic historian and radio chronicler Jean-Pierre Coffe once characterized a certain Provençal style—the kind represented by ridiculous tassels flapping from keys, curtains, and tablecloths; I remember a long formal dinner spent with a gargantuan tassel nestled in my lap.

Still, I was willing to explore Provence in spring, fall, or winter, when I might have a chance to glimpse her alone, without her maquillage, her throngs of admirers. I planned an ambitious and not always obviously logical route but one designed to emphasize

"Provence Profonde," the inland area between its great rivers, the Durance to the east and the Rhône to the west. I would linger for the most part in the many-villaged Vaucluse, one of the six *départements* that officially define the region, and would catch a glimpse of urban Provence in two of its important cities: Aix-en-Provence, its former capital, my first stop; and Avignon, France's Vatican, one of my last. In between, I would spend two weeks threading my way by car through the region's defining mountains: Cézanne's Mont Ste-Victoire, Peter Mayle's Luberon, and the peak sacred to the Tour de France, Mont Ventoux. I would taste the Provençal Alps and finish in the Dentelles de Montmirail, above the pebbly soil that makes the great wines of Châteauneuf-du-Pape. I would leave as much room as possible for impulsive detours, since famous towns can disappoint (like Isle-sur-la-Sorgue) and obscure ones charm (like Le Barroux). I decided on spring for my tour, when the almond blossoms, irises, and poppies enamel the fields—a compensation for the summer lavender I would miss.

The region is a place of celestial ambitions: The Christmas crèches that are its signature popular art invariably portray Provence as the birthplace of Jesus, with the three Magi wandering among lavender sellers and top-hatted mayors. Economically, it is surely a land of miracles, with sheepfolds and silkworm sheds reincarnated as multi-million-dollar holiday houses and recently repopulated villages now the hideaways of movie stars and investment bankers.

But this is nothing new. For centuries, it seems, nearly as many people have aspired to Provence as to heaven itself: Greeks, Romans, Moors, Ligurians, Jews, Spanish, Italians, Armenians. The current contenders are English and North Africans—as well as Japanese, judging by the busloads of food and wine pilgrims. And Americans too, of course, for if Boston is the capital of Puritan America, then Provence is the capital of hedonist America—

communicated to the United States by Richard Olney, Julia Child, M.F.K. Fisher, and Alice Waters, among others. Olney and Child both had houses in Provence; Waters expressed her love for Provence by naming her California restaurant Chez Panisse (after the Provençal character from Marcel Pagnol's "The Fanny Trilogy" films) and, even more profoundly, by translating for her own country a Provençal dream of cooking, of pleasure, as the foundation of life.

As always, Paradise has its snakes. Provence is filled with the evidence of both settled and unfinished quarrels: the feudal family struggles that continued even after the region was incorporated into the French kingdom in 1481; the wars of religion between Protestants and Catholics; the mortal battles between the French throne and the Knights Templar, the Christian military order whose wealth the French king coveted; the disputes between monarchists and republicans during the Revolution; the hydra-headed conflicts of the Second World War; and the ongoing spats between village and village, vineyard and vineyard, neighbor and neighbor, over water. But this history of darkness is somehow ignored by visitors; Provence has entered their collective unconscious as the sun-buttered, lavender-laved symbol of bliss, revealing the secret motive of travel itself: to get away from it all. The most perfect of holidays would be to escape from death. Heaven's our destination.

Aix-en-Provence was certainly Thomas Jefferson's idea of heaven. "The man who shoots himself in the climate of Aix must be a bloody-minded fellow indeed," he wrote during a visit in 1787. "I am now in the land of corn, wine, oil, and sunshine. What more can man ask of heaven?" This former capital of Provence, founded by the Romans around 120 B.C. for its springs, does honor to its essential resource, clothing its waters in the glory of the fountains studding the city. The Provençal novelist Pierre Magnan writes that in his native territory of Alpine Provence, water is so scarce that churchgoers bless themselves from the smallest holy water fonts in the world. I came to notice how many villages, with a poignant magic, evoke water in their names—Fontaine-de-Vaucluse, Pernes-sur-Fontaine, Greoux-les-Bains, Isle-sur-la-Sorgue, to name a few. When I first set foot in Aix, I saw the city's fountains as elegant urban decorations; by the end of the journey, they seemed instead outdoor chapels, places to worship water itself.

A bride and groom (during the May Day holiday weekend, Aix teems with men in morning suits and women in white lace) emerge from Ste-Marie-Madeleine, the church where Cézanne was baptized. They cross the Place des Prêcheurs, where the Marquis de Sade, a prominent Provençal noble, and his valet were executed in effigy in 1772, as a symbol of social death, after being convicted of violently mistreating a group of prostitutes he held captive in nearby Marseille. The bridal couple, though, are not concerned with these ghosts; they are on their way to be photographed near a fountain, making their city's waters a part of their sacrament.

Aix-en-Provence exists fluidly in many centuries. On an errand, I find myself in front of a shop that transports me to the Middle Ages—the storefront of a writer of letters and documents, who offers as one specialty translations into a pre-Islamic Yemenite language. A few doors down, a pharmacy with an encyclopedic collection of sunscreens—and an even more comprehensive selection of cellulite remedies—returns me to this century. Prominently displayed on one wall is a laminated poster with images of edible and toxic mushrooms. In France, mushroom gatherers may bring their baskets for consultations with pharmacists trained to distinguish between the delicious and the dangerous. On the street again, passing through a splendid square, I look up. Even overhead, on the eighteenth-century facade of the post office, are the waters—this time in the form of a god and goddess, personifying the Rhône and the Durance. The Rhône, massive and muscular, carries an oar, as is appropriate for a river critical to trade between northern and southern Europe. The luscious nymph Durance, as the giver of Provençal fertility, holds a cornucopia, and one of her legs dangles off the pediment, a witty allusion, possibly, to her propensity to overflow.

Late on May Day morning, impromptu stands spring up on the margins of the highway, selling pots and bouquets of *muguet* (lily of the valley), the traditional May Day gift. I am on my way to a *dégustation,* as quintessential a custom in Provence as tango dancing is in Argentina. The Commanderie de la Bargemone, a vineyard in the countryside neighboring Aix, is in its own way a dream of Provence. Built on the foundations of a garrison of Knights Templar, it became the property of a family of Provençal nobles, whose vineyards were eventually destroyed by the phylloxera virus. In the 1970s, the deteriorating buildings and vineyards were purchased by a wealthy industrialist who had been a hero of the French Resistance, and restored with the help of Claude Marriottini, who grew up on the property.

What I see is nothing less than a resurrection, a vision of French country life from a book of hours: A grand manor house emerges from the earth like a kind of geode. I wander the grounds, through an orchard with apricot, cherry, pear, and apple trees, past a yard with fat, beautifully kept chickens. Inside the cellars, I taste the Commanderie's wines; its white, its rosé, its robust, barrel-aged red, whose ambitions are revealed by its name: Cuvée Tournebride, named for a champion stallion that sired a number of horses at the Commanderie.

Back in the car, heading toward the Luberon Mountains, I turn on Beur (slang for "Arab") FM and listen to Arabic-language hip-hop while driving past vineyards blanketed with poppies. It is time to venture into the core of Provence; the region is above all a mosaic of villages, and travel here is less a matter of making climactic visits to monuments and landmarks than of meeting villages with almost humanly distinct characters, perched on cliffs, hidden behind strips of rock, expansive and confident on plains. They are all surprisingly different from one another, even when the distances between them are abbreviated. The guiding domestic impulse seems a distinctive feature of travel here—the magnet is not so much what you would like to see but where in Provence you would make your home, where you would like to live. There is an odd sense, at each destination, that you are not merely visiting but that you have settled here, however briefly. What Provence has to offer its visitors, above all, is a moment of its life.

The road to Cabrières d'Aigues, some forty miles to the north of Aix, is a pattern of sun-drenched fields, young olive plantations, peaceful valleys, and children wearing Provençal-patterned skirts. The prints are descendants of the *indiennes,* the imported cottons from India that were the inspiration for the now-famous Provençal cloth industry. This countryside gives a sheltered sensation, as of coves and inlets, as if the waters of the warm sea that covered it some ten million years ago had simply been peeled back to reveal it. The ground scattered with snail shells reminds me that escargots are simply shellfish that live on land; it is silly to be any more squeamish about a snail than about an oyster.

The exquisite illusion of peace along this route is in conflict with the remains of the plague wall to the north of the village, a wishful safeguard against the eighteenth-century epidemic that terrorized the countryside. It is also at odds with the brutal history outlined at Cabrières's Protestant church. For centuries, the Provençal mountains have been a refuge for resisters and dissidents of various kinds, and the sweet valleys have seen atrocities perpetuated on the pre-Protestant Vaudois sect, Catholics, royalists, republicans, Protestants, Jews, and anti-Fascists. Throughout Provence, you can see buildings ruined or damaged by human

folly, a force more unkind than time. In Cabrières's air are traces
of fear—the memories of crouching by the hill, praying against
detection. From the beleaguered Protestants of Cabrières, whose
eighteenth-century church, renovated in 1951, was a room above
an olive-oil mill, I drive to one of the seats of Catholic Provence,
the château of Ansouis, held for eight centuries by the same family, the Sabrans, who inhabit it still. The château floats above its
shimmering village like a perfectly cut and set jewel; hanging gardens jet from its walls like a gem's brilliant refractions.

Albert Camus used to enjoy watching the soccer games in Lourmarin, a village of apparently idyllic prosperity some seven miles
southeast of Cabrières. As I come up on it, I encounter what looks
like a roadside vegetable stand—it turns out to be a licensed dis-
tributor of foie gras. In Lourmarin, each house is more inventively
charming than the last, a peacock rainbow of painted shutters and
rose-draped doors.

The soccer games themselves are still played, luxuriously, on
emerald fields at the foot of a château that once belonged to the
powerful Agoult family, who held a network of fiefdoms throughout the region. Among the Agoult descendants were Marie de
Flavigny, the mistress of Franz Liszt, and her daughter, Cosima,
who married Richard Wagner. Provence still has a reputation as a
region in which power and influence are concentrated in families,
whether titled or peasant, a country where a well-placed cousin or
sibling is a substantial advantage. The Agoults incarnate that
characteristic on a grand scale.

The painstakingly restored château, now host to visiting artists and prestigious summer music festivals, is proof that Lourmarin's seemingly effortless beauty is hard-won. At the turn of the
century, it was a ruin of crumbling stones and floors upended by
tree roots, a place used as a midway camping point by Gypsies on
their annual pilgrimage to Stes-Maries-de-la-Mer to celebrate

their patron saint, Sarah, supposedly the maid to saints Mary Jacobe and Mary Salome. But Provence's encompassing loveliness is such that it mysteriously reverses the normal course of events; here, lost is found, and ruins fall not into destruction but into ever greater beauty.

It is in a very different kind of building that I spend the night, a fifteenth-century fortified farmhouse turned bed-and-breakfast, set among vineyards, newly leafed cherry orchards, and plashing fountains. There are parts of the world that attract visitors by offering them a sojourn in their private or media-made fantasies, writ large in the form of extravagant hotels. Provence, though, wants to offer the traveler an imagination of itself, a momentary dream of Provençal life: if anything, the traveler becomes the mirror in which the region can gaze at its image, and reflect. And so I find myself in this classic Provençal *mas,* a complex of buildings set around a central farmhouse and including some combination of stables, sheepfold, stone fountains, cypresses, and plane trees. Often one building was a silkworm nursery, until the late nineteenth century an important industry here, one colored by an eerie parody of maternity: The worms, sometimes incubated between the breasts of the women who reared them, would be assiduously fed with quantities of mulberry leaves, and then killed before they could leave their finished cocoons, nurtured to death.

The next morning, a long walk is in order, so I go to the nearby clifftop village of Goult, another Agoult family village, and climb uphill toward its windmill. A distinguished-looking middle-aged woman carrying a bouquet of wild irises and poppies—they grow in cascades on the hillsides, and anyone is allowed to pick a handful—urges me to take the path through the woods toward the village's restored olive terraces, to better understand the old agricultural ways.

The woods smell of rosemary, chamomile, thyme, and wild

mint; on the path, I pass a *borie,* a conical stone hut built for shepherds or tools. I stroll beside a wall perforated with niches for beehives. The steep terraces look like a separate village, a village belonging to the trees and crops. On the way back, I see an inviting path cutting deep into a cool glade, but a sign warns: Access to the truffle beds strictly forbidden. Truffle poaching is rife in Provence; one of the most successful savants of truffle culture, a Provençal dentist named Jean-Marie Rocchio, has written that the practice has become so sophisticated that poachers even make use of infrared technology to detect the beds.

I choose a restaurant called Clementine, in Ménerbes (a village that seems as narrow as a tunnel), partly for its panoramic mountain views and partly because of the controlled experiment I am conducting. My theory is that a restaurant which takes public responsibility for *"repas de noces"* will have in its kitchen a local cook of some distinction. The French take their wedding feasts very seriously; in wedding albums, I have seen nearly as many close-ups of principal dishes as portraits of the bride. A *blanquette de veau* with morels justifies the theory, as does the house white, produced with grapes from the proprietor's own vineyards.

My next stop, Cavaillon, a town that seems startlingly bustling after a series of country villages, is announced by an enormous sculpted muskmelon in the center of a traffic roundabout. Cavaillon is known for its melons: Alexandre Dumas famously accepted a yearly quantity of the fruit in exchange for supplying the town library with his collected works. I follow the signs to the local synagogue, made a museum in 1924. Housed in an eighteenth-century building that served a community of Jews who had originally come to Cavaillon in the fifteenth century under the protection of the Avignon popes, the synagogue shares the unusual joie-de-vivre and sensuality of Provençal ecclesiastical decoration, a confection of green and gold and floral motifs.

Circling back past a shop of jeweled Moroccan wedding

dresses, I stop in the plaza outside the town hall, getting a glimpse of Cavaillon's gastronomic livelihood. Here are posted the dates and rules for hunting such prey as partridge, hare, pheasant, and rabbit and fishing of sea and river lampreys and both red and green frogs. It suddenly seems not only unpleasant to leave before fall but downright foolish.

I don't sulk, though, for there is still opportunity ahead: a brief taste of the Provençal Alpines. Up here, among chalky cliffs and farmhouses that seem to float in velvety green valleys, there is a timeless silence, broken only by the equally timeless music of children's play. A road sign with a drawing of a sheep warns drivers—*Attention: Moutons,* and the fields above and below me are thick with ewes and baby lambs drifting like white blossoms on the green carpet. A landscape of natural hiding places, this was also Resistance country during World War II. The Provençal mistral winds, though, which at their worst are said to be able to strip the horns from a bull, posed new and unexpected dangers during the war, sometimes making landings on the camouflaged airstrips impossible, or blowing dropped matériel and provisions out of range. The beauty of this day makes that agony present: This is now, and was then, a country made for living, not for killing.

The radio announcer is advertising a weekend market featuring foods from local artisans in a parody of the breakneck American radio style: "Everything to satisfy the educated and passionate gourmand, which you certainly are." It is noon, he says, and he wishes an excellent appetite to all his listeners. The hostess of the fifteenth-century priory at the foot of Simiane-la-Rotonde, where I am staying, makes a quick telephone call on my behalf to the village of Banon to ask the restaurant on the square to keep its wood-burning oven hot enough for another customer. I make the short drive through silvery green fields of lavender and the brilliant green fields of wheat, whose legacy is not only apparent in

Provençale food but in its distinctive breadmaking furniture: the kneading table, the bread-keeper, the buffets with mechanisms for shifting flour, all sought after in the antiques markets of Isle-sur-la-Sorgue.

Banon is famous for its chestnut leaf–wrapped goat cheese, so my lunch is a wood-oven pizza topped with *chévre de pays,* eaten on the town square underneath the blossoming chestnut trees. Here the accents are unabashedly *chantant,* with the melodic vowels that distinguish Provençal speech. The Catholic youth group is holding a couscous dinner fund-raiser, proof of this dish's now-solid roots in France. I find a much more obviously native specialty in the shop of a gifted charcutier: Maurice Melchio, whose range of sausages—flavored variously with pine nuts, fennel, and savory—give new meaning to the phrase *être bien dans sa peau* ("to be comfortable in one's own skin"). More surprisingly, tiny Banon is home to another kind of feast—a feast of reason, as Monsieur Melchio describes it, in the form of Le Bleuet, one of France's great independent bookstores—and also to a May book festival that brings writers and readers to town to share picnics, wine, and literature (another Provençal melange of knowledge and delight).

May 8 is a holiday in Europe commemorating the end of World Ware II; there are processions in the villages and cities, and I hear elegiac music wherever I stop. Several large new wreaths decorate the foot of the war memorial in the square at Barbentane, a château and village on the edge of the Alps and just south of Avignon, a fifty-mile drive from Banon. The château, nicknamed the Petite Trianon of the Sun, was refurbished by a scion of the family who was Louis XV's ambassador to Florence, and survived the Revolution with even its superb furniture intact. It possesses a kind of architectural nostalgia for Italy, a domestic elegance, an air of having been created by inhabitants who took personal delight in conceiving it, evidenced by such details as the splendid three-hundred-year-old plane trees in the garden, imported from Turkey. The terrace overlooking the garden is punctuated by witty statues of eighteenth-century sirens, mermaids with chic laced bodices; one statue of a wild boar wears a smile of benign disillusionment, a creature that would have delighted Lewis Carroll; surely, he is the Cheshire boar. Inside, I covet a group of salon chairs, covered in needlepoint with imagery drawn from La Fontaine's fables; the wooden frames of the chairs are still painted black, a sign of mourning when the family learned that Marie Antoinette had been killed.

The village itself has a form not unlike a *croquembouche,* the French wedding cake of caramelized cream puffs; it rises from a rocky plateau as if positioned on a tray, climbing in tiers of stone houses, labyrinthine passages sugared with roses and honeysuckle, crowned at its summit by a stone tower. Aware that the still-sacred family lunch hours are upon me, I hurry back to the main square, catching sight through a window of a chef tenderly handing plates to his wife and little boy at a white-clothed table in his now-empty restaurant. From a bakery called Chez François et Céline, I manage to buy the last loaf, cracked but still warm, which I supplement with ham, sheep's cheese, and fava beans, young enough to eat raw. In Provence, the notion of buying local food does not just mean food produced nearby; it also means food of a particular character and flavor, the essence of a climate, a soil, a relationship evolved between the earth and the people who cultivate it. More and more these days, restaurant menus here are making the sources of their produce, cheeses, fish, and meat as identifiable as the producers of their wines.

The proprietress offers me some handsome strawberries imported from Spain, then the famous strawberries of the nearby market town of Carpentras. The imported strawberries are not bad, though a bit taut, as if they have had plastic surgery; the

Carpentras strawberries, however, are superb, as perfumed as flowers, and so melting that eating one is like a kiss on the lips. They are, though, so fragile that the lady insists on packing them herself, warning me to eat them today. I hurry for shelter to escape the passionate downpour whose approach has given me a glimpse of the cold and severity of a Provençal winter. A group of Muslim ladies are not so lucky; their heavy robes and veils are left soaked.

I have been saving the Rhône Valley, that needlepoint tapestry of vineyards, for last. Here, Séguret, overlooking a landscape out of a pastoral symphony, deserves its designation as one of France's most beautiful villages; its stone buildings set into a steep hill and walls shadowed with fruit trees are as sinuous and elegant as if an architect had designed the whole village as an ensemble. I fall in love with a group of *santons,* those painted clay crèche figures of villagers offering their lavender, cheeses, and game to the Christ child; after encountering them, it seems right to follow the Nativity toward the papacy, so I take the direction of Avignon.

In the walled heart of Avignon, echoes of which its native writer Henri Bosco later found in the walled cities of Morocco, a nun trailing some twenty sweetly singing children leads them toward a curving passageway, where all but their song disappears. It is a city of mysterious passages, curves, and apertures, designed for sudden encounters, perhaps one reason for its importance in the history of love. Petrarch famously met Laura here, and wrote over the years the cycle of sonnets that made even Casanova weep. John Stuart Mill is buried here, in the cemetery of St-Veran, the Père-Lachaise of the south. When his wife died unexpectedly during a stay at Avignon's Hôtel d'Europe, Mill purchased a house near St-Veran so he could visit her grave every day for the rest of his life.

After Séguret, I drive to Laurence Féraud's vineyard, Domaine du Pégaü, in Châteauneuf-du-Pape. In this land of profound wine-making, where a vintner's artful blending of the thirteen varieties of grape permitted to this appellation is a closely guarded secret, Féraud is queen, the producer of a cult wine, Château Pégaü, which earned a Robert Parker rating of one hundred points in 1998. From what looks like a field office, she emerges—small, dark, and indomitable, a dog at her heels. "Everything is going wrong today," she says good-humoredly, possessed by the problems of a shipment to Taiwan. For her, a year is not just a collection of events but a destiny to make into wine. When she thinks of 2003, she remembers that the grapes were ripe in August but their skins were still soft. This was the year of risk in her private zodiac: She daringly left them on the vine. The idiosyncratic soils of her vineyards, their clays, their pebbles, are as intimate to her as a child's personality is to its mother. In fact, her description of harvesting her grapes by hand is one of harassed but expert maternity: "I treat my vineyards like I treat my kitchen," she says. "I choose the vineyards to pick from by the smell and touch of the fruit. . . . My employees become my bosses. They see everything from high on their tractors. They shout, 'Laurence, pick here, pick quicker.'"

Laurence's ancestors are winemakers; in fact, one grandmother was a vigneron. She says that she hopes her children will want to do this work. "I teach them by teaching them to eat well," she says. "It is not proper not to give the children good products. It is in eating well that we develop the taste in wine." Perhaps I imagine it, but I think I taste that depth of relationship to the land in her wine, its concentrated impact the work of someone whose life's work is making life. A fleshy partridge is walking between the vines like a gleaner as I leave.

It is time for me to go. I drive up looping roads into the Dentelles de Montmirail, that natural Parthenon of limestone cliffs, on roads that give the sensation less of driving than of flight.

The mountains are crowned with great arches and battlements of limestone, like the châteaux of archangels. In the village of Beaumes-de-Venise, I look out over the tiaras of vineyards planted in intricate and complex formations on the slopes of these wild mountains. They are the image of the ancient aspiration to draw fruit from stone, to civilize. For me, as for so many others in centuries past and still to come, this is the landscape of the labor of humanism—not of heaven but of civilization itself, of *savoir-vivre.*

That evening, at the Auberge Saint Roch, I order a first course of foie gras and an aperitif of Beaumes-de-Venise, a wine which tastes of apricots, butter, and honey, and holds such a clear, sustained pattern of flavor in the mouth that it is like drinking dissolving lace. Perhaps it is the result of a day spent visiting the papal palace and tasting the papal wines, but it strikes me that the Provençal have performed a marvelous theological sleight of hand. Provence is not heaven after all, but earth. Unlike Adam and Eve, the Provençal have made a garden where knowledge is at the very heart of pleasure, and is essential to all that can be loved in life; they have eaten of the fruit of the tree of knowledge, and unlike their sacred ancestors, found it not bad at all.

2006

Ultimate Provence

The best tastes, sights, and smells from the land where pleasure was born

Best Olive Oil

Isle-sur-la-Sorgue is one of the most beautiful little towns in Provence. It is famous for its antiques stores, its open-air food market (Thursday and Sunday mornings), and for a shop called Les Délices du Luberon (1, Avenue du Partage des Eaux, 33-4-90-20-77-37; delices-du-luberon.fr.), which is really more of mini–olive museum that also happens to sell sensational tapenade as well as hundreds of different olive oils.

Best Roman Ruins

Between Orange, Arles, Nîmes, and the Pont du Gard, there's plenty to choose from, but the Roman town of Glanum near St. Rémy gives you the best idea of how the Romans in Provence actually lived. A triumphal arch marks the entrance to the site, and you can wander through the ruins of two temples, the Forum, and a grand private villa, its less attractive stone kitchen sink still intact at the back. Glanum has the added advantage of being only just over a mile from St. Rémy, with its chic shops, cafés, and restaurants.

Best Provençal Fabrics

The origin of this brightly colored traditional cotton fabric dates back to the seventeenth century, when the Compagnie des Indes began importing printed cottons from India. Les Olivades (Chemin des Indienneurs, 33-4-90-49-19-19; lesolivades.fr), which is based in Saint Etienne du Grès, in the Alpilles, is the only company left in Provence that still maintains traditional means of production. Its fabrics are sold by the yard and made into ready-to-wear items available in its shops throughout Provence.

BEST LAVENDER TRAILS

There are six different lavender trails in the region where you can explore all the deliciously scented aspects of this quintessential Provençal plant. The trails lead through some of the less-traveled villages and delve into everything from traditional folk medicine to garden design, perfume, the distillation process, and aromatherapy (for trail information, contact Routes de la Lavande, 33-4-75-26-65-90; routes-lavande.com).

BEST SANTONS DE PROVENCE

Christmas in Provence is celebrated with feasting and Mass on Christmas Eve, and also with re-creations of the Nativity scene, using small figurines called *santons*. These crèches became popular after the Revolution closed down the churches in 1793, and the region remained faithful to its religious traditions. The figurines are usually made of clay, but they can be wood, or even bread dough. Whatever the material, the scenes inevitably represent the Nativity as if it had taken place in a Provençal village, with garlic sellers, bakers, and butchers all represented. The best is Paul Fouque in Aix-en-Provence (65, Cours Gambetta, 33-4-42-26-33-38; santons-fouque.com).

BEST POTTERY

Less famous and, mercifully, much less crowded than Vallauris, where Picasso made his ceramics, the small town of Apt is home to one of the masters of the art, Antony Pitot. His glazed earthenware, known as *faïence*, draws on the traditions of the countryside, where the familiar ocher tones and greens of Provençal pottery are enhanced by a special marbling effect. Call ahead for an appointment at his atelier in Apt (RN100 Goult; 33-4-90-72-22-79).

BEST MOUNTAIN . . . AND VIEW

Known as the "Giant of Provence," Mont Ventoux is, at 6,273 feet, the tallest mountain in France between the Alps and the Pyrenees. Petrarch, clearly a man with brains and brawn, made the first recorded ascent in 1336, and you can either follow in his arduous footsteps or be a wimp and drive to the top. The mountain roads are still often included in the Tour de France (although the British cyclist Tommy Simpson suffered a fatal heart attack during the leg of the race on Mont Ventoux in 1967). The view from the top is, not surprisingly, quite *magnifique.*

BEST ROSÉ

Not all bottles marked "Rosé de Provence" were created equal. Don't be seduced by the rosy pink color, or the pretty label, or the laughable price you'll see on any wine list or the supermarket shelf. Instead, go straight to the tippy top—Domaines Ott. The Ott family has been producing wine since 1896, and although they make some perfectly respectable reds and whites, it is their rosés that they are famous for. Somebody had the brilliant idea of putting this rosy nectar into bottles based on the sexy shape of the Roman amphora. When it comes to tasting the wine of the gods of Provence, accept no substitutes (domaines-ott.com).

BEST (AND MOST TERRIFYING) DRIVE

There are plenty of good reasons to go to Cassis, a small fishing port just east of Marseille. The tourists may outnumber the fishermen these days, but the restaurants on the port still serve some of the best fish dishes in this part of France. But the real excitement here lies in a curvy, vertiginous road known as La Route de Crêtes, which runs along the cliffs of the Cap Canaille. It is 1,310 feet down to the sea from its highest point at La Grande Tete, but be warned: If the mistral is acting up and you are not driving a Hummer, you are in serious danger of being swept away, and not just by the spectacular view.

Sip It Slow

by

NIK COHN

I don't know her real name; we never really talked. She was simply an elderly woman with a cane whom I passed every day on my morning walks through the neighborhood. Because I saw her first on Abercorn Street, I thought of her as Miss Abercorn.

The formality of the title, with its whiff of Victorian starch, seemed to fit her. She was a fragile and birdlike figure, almost preternaturally thin, with the unblinking eye of a born headmistress. Crisply laundered in her white blouse and tailored skirt, she had the power to make me feel unwashed and obscurely guilty just by looking me over.

As days went by, I started changing my morning route, doubling back or sneaking through alleys, to escape that basilisk eye. Nothing seemed to work. Sooner or later, I'd hear the clacking of her cane at my back and would turn to find myself studied, measured, eternally found wanting.

What was it she saw? A man in free fall, I suppose. I'd come to Savannah in search of nothing more profound than a week off;

a little warmth and ease, a brief respite from northern austerities. And now I was sunk in quicksand. The warmth was becoming a meltdown, the ease a terminal torpor.

By the end of the week, I had no desire to move again. On my last morning, I found myself sitting in the Colonial Park Cemetery trying to read the paper. The day's major stories were a pie-baking contest in Ardsley Park and a widow in Skid-away who collected tea mugs, but somehow I could not seem to concentrate. Moisture from the live oak overhead dripped slowly on my head and shoulders, and the first faint waft from Wall's Bar-B-Que came drifting downwind, spiced with Confederate jasmine and magnolia. All I wanted was to let myself drown.

Before I had the chance, Miss Abercorn loomed up, came tapping, her gaze as unwavering as ever. And she spoke to me for the first time.

"It would not be prudent," she said.

There was a time when New Orleans used to have the same effect. A friend of mine called it *le mal doux,* the sweet sickness, and a potent addiction it was. Before I came to Savannah, I'd almost forgotten how good surrender can feel.

It is, in many ways, a secret city. Self-styled capital of the Georgia Coastal Empire, with a population of about 150,000, it stands in splendid isolation, penned in by forest and tidal flatlands. Approaching it from the north, though the South Carolina Low Country, you don't get even a hint of its existence until the road rises without warning out of the marshes and pine scrub and vaults you high across the Savannah River, and suddenly the whole town is spread out below.

At first glance, there doesn't seem to be much worth looking at. Apart from a scattering of church spires, two high-rises, and a plague of parking garages, the skyline is low and huddled. Then the road swoops and deposits you in a walled garden.

The scale is minuscule. The full extent of the downtown area, which the tourist board likes to call the Historic District, is only two and a half miles square. But its beauty is breathtaking. James Edward Oglethorpe, who in 1733 led the first British settlement of Georgia and laid out the original city, placed large public squares after every second block. Wherever you move, you are in sight of greenery and blossom, deep shade. Palms and live oaks overlord the squares; Spanish moss and wisteria fill the middle air. Below, the sidewalks spill over with oleander and Cherokee rose, bougainvillea and crape myrtle. And everywhere, as warm and consoling as new-baked bread, are the lush scents of subtropical damp.

The architecture, too, is dazzling: a fantasia of Southern styles and histories, clapboard, limestone, and brick. English Georgian mansions preening cheek by jowl with Greek Revival, American Gothic with high Victorian. Even the terrace houses are thoroughbreds, with high stoops and shuttered windows, perfect in proportion.

How was all of this preserved? One part luck and the rest good management. From the start, Savannah has been a pragmatic town. When William Tecumseh Sherman came marching through Georgia, burning and looting everything in sight, its civic leaders took one look at his marauding army and decided that the secessionist cause was not as sacred as they had thought; they surrendered without a shot. Sherman presented the captured city, with its guns and cotton, to President Lincoln as a Christmas gift, rested himself for a month, then marched on to Columbia. And Savannah lapsed into blissful obscurity, from which it has rarely stirred since.

It was not always such a backwater. In its early days, the town racked up an imposing list of achievements. Eli Whitney invented the cotton gin at Mulberry Grove plantation, and Juliette Gordon Low founded the Girl Scouts of America on Drayton Street; John Wesley was minister of Christ Church around 1736, and in 1819 the *Savannah* was the first steamship to cross the Atlantic. But the golden age died with the Civil War. The city's fortunes had been built on cotton, and the Cotton Belt started moving westward. By the 1920s, the trade was all but dead. Then a glut of hurricanes wiped out the rice fields, flooding them with salt. Many of the great mansions were abandoned, or demolished to make way for parking lots. Whatever money remained moved away to the suburbs and left the city center to rot. In 1946, when Lady Astor passed through on a visit, she called Savannah "a beautiful woman with a dirty face."

By the 1950s, one-third of downtown had been lost. Then, quite suddenly, a group of local ladies decided to call a halt. Organizing themselves into the Historic Savannah Foundation, they started rescuing and restoring the old houses. They drove out the prostitutes and junkies, replanted the ravaged squares with banks of blossoms, and brought more than a thousand buildings back to life. Piece by piece, the original nineteenth-century city was resurrected, until hardly a trace of its bad years remained.

Net result?

Urban paradise.

For the first couple of days, the blissful indolence of it all made me vaguely uneasy. Drifting through the streets at random, heat-dazed, I kept being stung by northern guilts. Surely I should be visiting some museum or taking a guided tour of a restored mansion? In some way striving?

It took an off-duty waitress named Valona, loafing through a drowsy afternoon at Big Al's Bar-B-Q, to set me straight. "Don't do a lot. And what you must do, do it slow," she advised. "The only way to grow old in this town, you have to learn how to honey-drip."

Seeking amplification, I visited Dick Richardson, one of the town's leading lawyers. "Everything in this town is feel. Your own point of angle," he told me. "If you want to work it out by logic, don't waste your time coming down. But if you have the gift of nose, this is the city of *savor.*"

We sat sipping martinis at dusk in a large white room full of echoes. Dick Richardson, a three-term representative in the Georgia legislature and a stalwart of the august Oglethorpe Club, was also a wild boy of seventy-one, with jug ears and raw cheekbones. "I worked a lot of years with the FBI up north—New Jersey, Washington, all over. But every time I changed assignments, I kept edging a little closer home. Until I reached Charleston, and then I quit. Just couldn't stand to be out of my own pond any longer."

What drew him back? "I guess I was sick of real life," he said. In Savannah there was no such thing. The Independent State of Chatham County, he called it. "We're a different breed of cat," he said, rolling his martini glass between massive palms. "We have our own rhythms, our own rules, our own cast of mind. Even our own language. It's like this old colored saying I've been hearing all my life. Someone mentioned it again at church this morning, and it just seemed to click in my mind: 'Nothing looks more like a bottle of liquor than a bottle of liquor in a paper sack.' Can you catch hold of that? Does it entertain your senses? If it does, you might as well stick around."

Sensual pleasure in words seemed to permeate the whole city. The day after I'd met Dick Richardson, the *Savannah Morning News* ran an interview with a lady named Doll Houstan. "They tell me I'm sixty-five. But I feel I'm twice sixteen," she said. "As long as you got your feet moving, you can go. Age don't get it. It's the way you carry yourself."

As for the Independent State of Chatham County, *oblivious* seemed more like it. There was no sense of rebellion, no Texas chest-banging; just the serene and unquestioning assumption that Savannah knew best. Outsiders might descend with plans to modernize the place, drag it out of its slumber and into the present tense. Gucci carpetbaggers, locals called them, and took not a blind bit of notice.

"We don't rattle easy. It's too much like work," Valona had told me, dreamily painting her toenails pink to match her beehive hairdo. When not waitressing, she tended bar at a disco and danced topless on the weekends. The combined proceeds were never quite enough to support her three dogs, mockingbird, gerbil, "two kids, and half a husband." Even so, she had no complaints. "I have my health and twenty-six bucks in cash, and I'm white in a town where the weather suits my clothes."

White, of course, was the critical word here. Away from the Historic District, life is less idyllic. Blacks make up fifty-five percent of the total population; their history in Savannah is notable. That does not mean they own many mansions on Lafayette Square.

To find out what they did own, I took a Negro Heritage Trail Tour ("Historic Savannah from the Black Perspective"). I was the only passenger, and the landscape that my guide, a hush-voiced man named Ben, drove me through was both dazzling and oppressive.

On the fringes of downtown, there were two squares and some streets of Victorian homes almost as spectacular as anything on the white side of town. Many of the houses had been restored; from a distance, they looked immaculate. But when I got out of the bus to look closer, broken glass scrunched underfoot.

Farther on, we passed through a section of tumbledown shacks, boarded windows. Groups of men stood outside the corner taverns, just staring. "It was worse," said Ben, his voice so soft I could barely hear. "Back when I was a kid, it wasn't a life at all."

"And now?"

"It's a life."

The lack of stridency seemed characteristic. Savannah was no place for rabble-rousers, and never had been. Even in the sixties, when other southern cities were blowing wide open, the civil rights movement here had moved softly, softly. There had been sit-ins at lunch counters, swim-ins at Tybee Beach, kneel-ins in churches, and an eighteen-month boycott of segregated stores on Broughton Street. "But barely no blood spilled," Ben said.

Much of the credit for that, he believed, belonged to W. W. Law, for twenty-six years the head of the local branch of the NAACP, who now lives in semiretirement on Victory Drive.

Mr. Law, when I called on him, had an old man's flesh, bitter chocolate, but a young man's avid eye. The floor of his front room was piled high with hardback histories; a rotating fan riffled stacks of yellowing newspaper cuttings. "Are you here with a serious premise? Or are you just raising a fuss?" he began. Once persuaded, however, that I had no insidious agenda, he started talking and did not stop.

In a sense, he said, he had been chosen. His grandmother had prayed at his birth that he would become a leader, and that was what he had always been. He had gone to college, expecting to become a schoolteacher. But after he graduated, with a reputation for activism, no black school would hire him. For many years he'd worked as a letter carrier. Then, in 1961, he was dismissed on trumped-up charges, accused of relieving himself on white folks' doorsteps. Rednecks dubbed him the Pissing Postman. When he fought his dismissal, they hounded him with death threats. A janitor who was minding his office at the NAACP was murdered in Mr. Law's chair. Still, he persevered. At last, on orders from Washington, he was reinstated. Which was nice and fine, as far as it went. But there were men in town who still called him the Pissing Postman, and would till the day he died.

Was he bitter? "That is not a word that tempts my mind," said Mr. Law. He had already helped found one black museum in town, the Beach Institute, and he was now working on another.

"A record of unsung heroes," he said. "The trash collectors, the street sweepers, the coal haulers." He smiled for the first time. "Yes," he said, "and the letter carriers too."

The keeping of records and mementos seemed a crucial part of Savannah's life, both black and white. The city was full of collectors and antiquarians, moss-gatherers of all description. That was how I came to find Willis Hakim Jones.

I had been visiting John Duncan's map and print shop on Monterey Square. The noblest square in the whole of the Historic District, it was also the site of the murder in John Berendt's *Midnight in the Garden of Good and Evil*. As a result, its stateliness was disrupted by a constant stream of tourists, best-seller in hand.

John Duncan's shop was the perfect refuge. I reached it through a garden gate, an alley overhung with blossoms, and walked into the Second Empire. Mr. Duncan himself, the courtliest of men, first showed me his wares, then led me upstairs through his house. Floor after rambling floor was filled with the fruits of a lifetime's scavenging—scores of regional paintings culled from flea markets, a set of 1830s Dutch marquetry cabinet doors, a 1920s wooden phone box from the Waldorf Astoria, and the four-poster bed of the scandalous Helen Drexel: "A witch. An absolute witch," John Duncan confided. "Her son said he could never sleep in her bed—its stories would wake him up screaming. My own dreams are delicious."

In a study full of leatherbound books and Mercedes Erixon watercolors, he pointed out three carved walking sticks, African-inspired. One showed a coiling vine that looked like a serpent, the second was clustered with geometric abstractions, the third seemed wrought of molten rock. They were the most desirable sticks I had ever seen.

Their maker worked shifts at the Union Camp Savannah paper mill and lived past Thunderbolt, past Skidaway, in the far suburb of Sandfly, near Pinpoint. When I phoned him, he said I could call him Willis Jones, Jr., or Hakim Azzam, or any combination thereof.

His home was in a subdivision. Downstairs, the house was neat, impersonal; upstairs was Aladdin's Cave.

Through a low door was a room filled, every inch, with black memorabilia: posters for Father Divine and Daddy Grace; tins of Sweet Georgia Brown pomade; a handbill advertising REAL ESTATE, NEGROES, STOCKS & BONDS ON COMMISSION; a World War I recruiting flyer—COLORED MAN IS NO SLACKER; photographs of the first black American magician, J. Hartford Armstrong, and his daughter Ellen, who used to advertise HALF-PRICE FOR ONE-EYED CUSTOMERS; and an action portrait of Peg Leg Bates, the monopedal tap dancer.

About two thousand items in all, Willis Hakim estimated, crammed into one tiny boxroom. At forty-one, a round-faced man with gentle manners, inordinately shy, he found his job in the paper mill a drudgery, this collection his one release.

It took every spare cent he earned. The extravagance drove his wife wild, but he couldn't help himself. Black culture and the black past was his life's obsession. His father had crafted twig furniture, a time-honored Georgian art. Every cane that he carved was sold the moment it was finished, the money spent on new treasures. "It isn't hardly sensible," he said. But his long fingers, as they stroked the skull of an old minstrel statuette, paid his mouth no mind.

Outside my hotel window was an outsize magnolia tree, one of its blossoms close enough to touch. When I arrived, it had been a baton, severely phallic, but by the end of the fifth day it had spread and opened, turned labial. Sun-dazzled, I wandered aimlessly through the streets, drifting from one touch of magic to the next: the great stand of live oaks along Oglethorpe Avenue, or the chorus line of sweeping cast-iron stair railings on Gordon Row, or the weathered brick facades on Jones Street; a splash of black-eyed Susans, spun gold against golden stone; a breath of eucalyptus within a fountained garden; or just the saturated warmth, and the creeping southern light.

At Bonaventure Cemetery, a few miles from downtown, a dense oak forest overlooked a broad, slow-rolling river. The poet Conrad Aiken is buried here. So is Johnny Mercer, the Tin Pan Alley songwriter whose hits included "Lazy Bones," "Jeepers Creepers," "That Old Black Magic," and "Blues in the Night." His stone, in the family plot, is simple; his epitaph, AND THE AN-GELS SING.

Conrad Aiken's grave is a more complex production. His father had shot his mother and then committed suicide when Aiken was still a child. Afterward, the poet had spent most of his life traveling, only to return to Savannah at the end and settle in the house adjacent to his childhood home, one wall away from the murder room. Now, in death, he is reunited with both mother and father. Their tombs sit close together in a small enclosure overhung with Spanish moss, and the poet himself is buried beneath a granite bench inscribed COSMOS MARINER, DESTINATION UNKNOWN.

John Berendt's book had led me here. When not awash in drag queens and murders and voodoo, it doubled as a first-rate guide, and it also brought me to Lafayette Square.

Few of the city's squares are quieter or more high-toned. Flannery O'Connor grew up in a limestone town house there, while the Girl Scouts derived from a pink Italianate villa, heavy on pomp and portico. But neither of these was the lure. What fetched me was the Hamilton-Turner Mansion.

It was a four-story château with a mansard roof, topped in

ironwork cresting like wedding lace. From outside, with its high windows and fine balconies, it looked imposing indeed. Even so, its real attraction was its owner, Nancy Hillis.

In *Midnight in the Garden of Good and Evil,* she appeared as the hero's girlfriend, Mandy—voluptuous, big-hearted, betrayed. The book's success having made her something of a local celebrity, she had rechristened her home *Mandy's House,* available for guided tours and dinner parties, as a weekend bed-and-breakfast.

With cotton candy hairdo and bounteous décolletage, Nancy Hillis was an authentic force of nature, somewhat on the lines of Dolly Parton, only more so. Within half an hour of our meeting, I'd heard enough of her history to fill five articles—her teenage career as a beauty queen and later modeling triumphs as a BBW (Big Beautiful Woman), her tangled finances and even more tangled private life, the recipe for corn bread muffins that her grandmother in Tennessee had taught her, the best friend who had tried to throttle her, the roller-coaster of her singing career, the state of her aching feet, and on and on. "Do you think I'd make a good nun?" she asked at one point. I did not. But it was a heroic image.

Somewhere in her monologue, Nancy spoke of sailors, great ships, far-off lands. And it came to me, with a small jolt, that Savannah itself was a port. The Historic District was so self-contained that I'd forgotten the river, just a few blocks away. But the moment I crossed Bay Street, I found myself in another town.

I entered it through a series of plunging, cobbled alleys. The Old Cotton Exchange and the massive brick warehouses of Victorian merchants loomed overhead like cliffs, and I burrowed deeper, level by level, via wooden walkways and wrought-iron ladders, until I seemed entombed. Then I groped my way around a blind corner, and the river was at my feet.

River Street itself was garish and tacky and brawling, all the things that a waterfront should be. Tourist traps peddled Confederate flags and plastic cotton bolls. Cavelike taverns blared the blues. Pickpockets lurked, cops cruised, and young ladies strutted the flesh. Meanwhile, out on the water, as if projected on a backdrop, a ceaseless parade floated past: steel-plated tankers from Riga and Caracas, Valparaiso and Tripoli; tubs and tramps; refurbished riverboats; speedboats and dredgers and coal-hauling barges; even the odd drunk on water skis.

In the bar where the jukebox kept playing and replaying "The South Is Gonna Rise Again," a man who looked like Grizzly Adams asked me whether I would like to have my nose driven into my brain. "Not particularly," I said and exited stage left, like Antigonus in *The Winter's Tale,* pursued by a bear.

Safely back across Bay Street, I settled my stomach in Franklin Square, hard by the New City Market. Until the fifties, this had been the heart of black Savannah. The First African Baptist, constituted in 1788, was the oldest black church in America, and the surrounding streets had been a hotbed of basket weavers and *conjure* women, street blues musicians, dispensers of folk medicines. Then the city had ripped the covered market down, to be replaced by yet another parking garage.

These days the streets were full of art galleries, boutiques, and chic bistros. But the rituals of Franklin Square were not much changed. Early each morning a group of black longshoremen forgathered beneath the live oaks, ostensibly in hopes of a day's work at the piers. Many carried bottles in paper sacks, oblivious to the Rev. Andrew Bryan, the First African Baptist's founder, glooming down on them from a plate glass window. Others preferred the pipe.

On Sunday mornings the paper sacks were carried more discreetly, but this only reinforced the truth of Dick Richardson's saying. Across the street, a stream of stately ladies in white dresses and white hats approached the church. The choir in their robes gathered on the porch; the sidewalk was lined with Cadillacs. "Seems like I ought to be departed," said one of the drinking men.

Stumbling a little, he made his way through the square, disappeared around a corner. A minute later, he was back again. "I thought you done said good-bye," one of his companions protested. "So I did," he said. "But every good-bye ain't gone."

My last evening in town, I got soaked to the skin. I had left my car at a car wash, where the attendant wore a T-shirt that read A CLEAN CAR IS THE SIGN OF A SICK MIND, and never noticed the thunderheads gathering.

This being the rainy season, tropical downpours marked the end of each working day. "Don't fret it. Only a Yankee or a born idiot ever gets caught," Dick Richardson had told me. So here I was, swimming upstream.

Blundering through the first door that opened, I found myself in a place called Bar Bar. The crowd in general seemed a typical Savannah mix—city aldermen and slackers, art students and business suits, flung together without prejudice. The bartender's name was Sarah Wood, and she was an Illustrated Woman.

Much of her was covered by a loose-fitting summer dress, but every part that showed was superbly tattooed. Each year she traveled in search of new artists, new works. Debbie Inksmith in Florida had done the skeleton on her spine, the cross on her breastbone; Will Schierer of Portland, Maine, the blackberries and bees on her right arm and the serpent on her left; Atomizer at 8-Balls of Columbus, Ohio, the spiderweb and spider, the fish, and the ladybug on her ankle. She also sported a scarlet heart saying ELVIS ("Who else would I love?" she asked).

She seemed, in many ways, to sum up Savannah's lure. Born in England, she had traveled all over the world, and then all over America, before she washed up here. That had been three years ago, and the sweet sickness still held her. "Where else is so easy? So free?" she asked. When she shrugged, the bees hovered and the serpent uncoiled. "People say that it's a town full of hopeless dys-functionals. But in Savannah you don't have to function. So what does hopeless mean?"

This was a question that needed some pondering. When my drink was finished, I splashed my way back to my hotel. Its balcony looked out over Columbia Square, and I sat smoking a farewell cigar.

For a long time, the only sounds were the splashing of the fountain and a piano in the next street playing Johnny Mercer songs—"Satin Doll," "Laura," "Dream." Then I heard the stuttering approach of a cane, and looked down to see Miss Abercorn.

At day's end, her white blouse and skirt were immaculate, unmarked by the heat and the storm alike, and her eye still looked me clean through. But its message seemed subtly changed. Instead of a schoolmarm's disapproval, there now seemed something challenging. A glint of wildness, almost of flirtation. As if she was daring me.

It was not a gaze I could meet. Pretending to fuss with my cigar, I ducked my head, and that was when Miss Abercorn laughed. "Not prudent at all," she said.

1995

Savannah Secrets

How to enjoy the city like a local

 When General James Oglethorpe laid out the streets of Savannah in 1733—following an easy, gridlike pattern and interspersing twenty-four lush, tree-filled squares every few blocks—he set the stage for one of the best walking cities in the United States. Today, visitors leave their cars parked at their hotels and explore the city's squares (all but three remain), parks, mansions, and monuments by foot.

After a starring role in John Berendt's 1994 best-seller, *Midnight in the Garden of Good and Evil,* Savannah was overrun with tourists. As of late, however, the artsy energy provided by students at the Savannah College of Art and Design (SCAD) seems to have given the city yet another life and a fresh gleam.

Best Way to See the City

Savannah's most intriguing bits of history are found in the city's nooks and crannies—in back alleys, private gardens, and tiny closets. And while riding in a trolley or motor coach may be a more comfortable option, you can snoop a whole lot more (or as much as the tour guide will let you get away with) on a walking tour. There are dozens of tour companies to choose from, including **Savannah Walks,** which offers daily guided tours of historic homes, private gardens, spots mentioned in *Midnight,* Civil War sites, and haunted squares (888-728-9255; savanahwalks.com).

Best Walk

Starting at City Hall, just in front of the river on Bay Street, turn onto Bull Street and walk through five of Savannah's most beautiful squares—Johnson, Wright, Chippewa, Madison, and Monterey—straight to idyllic Forsyth Park. It's a long walk (a few hours if you stop in each square), but the terrain is flat and there are plenty of cafés and benches along the way. Each square has its own place in history or intriguing bit of scandal: **Johnson Square** was the first of all twenty-four squares to be laid out, in 1773; **Wright Square** is the final resting place of Yamacraw Indian chief Tomochichi, who mediated between the English and Native Americans. **Chippewa Square,** which marks the center of the city, is best known as the site of *Forrest Gump*'s "bench scene" (although the bench now resides in the Savannah History Museum); on **Madison Square** is the Gothic Revival Green-Meldrim House, where General William T. Sherman stayed after presenting President Lincoln with the city of Savannah as a Christmas gift. Last, **Monterey Square,** considered by many to be the most beautiful square in Savannah, is the main locale of *Midnight.* Mercer House, the Italianate mansion where Jim Williams threw his lavish parties and Danny Hansford died (as did Williams, years later), sits on the southwest corner. Just two blocks away is thirty-acre **Forsyth Park,** always teeming with locals who gather around the large cast-iron water fountain—modeled after the fountain in Paris's Place de la Concorde—and enjoy the shaded walking paths, gardens, playgrounds, and ballfields (Green-Meldrim House, 14 West Macon St.; 912-233-3845. Mercer House, 429 Bull St.; 912-236-6352; mercerhouse.com).

Best Glimpse of Old Savannah

Most historic cities beg for the cavernous passages and cobblestone streets of the riverfront **Factors Walk,** where old cotton warehouses are now shops, restaurants, clubs, and, soon, residential lofts (between Bay Street and Riverfront Street).

BEST GLIMPSE OF NEW SAVANNAH

Three years ago, two SCAD graduates converted an old dairy and the area around it into the **Starland Design District.** Located just outside the Historic District, this is Savannah's new creative center, bustling with art galleries (and weekly art crawls), offices, theatres, cafés, and shops (from Drayton Street to Bull Street, between Forty-first and Fortieth streets).

BEST HISTORIC HOME

The **Owens-Thomas House,** designed by English architect William Jay when he was just twenty-four years old, is considered by many historians to be the best example of English Regency architecture in the United States. Although British in style, the honey-colored house was made from local materials—a concretelike mixture of lime, oyster shells, and sand, called "tabby," which is still found in some of Savannah's old streets. Ornamental columns, a brass-inlaid staircase with a bridge connecting the east and west wings, a Grecian veranda, and running water—with bathtubs—were all firsts for the area when the house was finished in 1819. Much of the former owners' eighteenth- and nineteenth-century English and American furniture is still on display, although the house is now owned and operated by the Telfair Museum of Art (124 Abercorn St.; 912-233-9743; telfair.org).

BEST RIVER STREET LANDMARK

Some say she waved in the name of Southern hospitality, others claim she was searching for a lost love; whatever the reason, Florence Martus faithfully welcomed, then waved good-bye to, every ship that came into or departed from the Port of Savannah from 1887 to 1931. Now **The Waving Girl** statue—the first memorial to a Georgia woman in a city park—stands in her honor, depicting Martus as a teenage girl waving a towel in the wind with her collie at her side. Martus was beloved by sailors from all over the world, and though she received thousands of love letters and hundreds of proposals, she remained single, living with her brother George, who was the lighthouse keeper (Morrell Park, East River St.).

BEST MUSEUM

With the addition of the modernist Jepson Center for the Arts in early 2006, the **Telfair Museum of Art** became more than just the South's oldest art museum—it's now a world-class facility befitting a town full of eager art students. The 64,000-square-foot Jepson Center allowed the museum, housed in a pair of nineteenth-century Regency mansions, to expand its permanent collection in both size and scale, so it now offers a gallery dedicated to Southern art, work by artists such as Gari Melchers and Romare Bearden, and traveling exhibitions, in addition to its vast decorative arts and Impressionist collections (121 Barnard St.; 912-790-8800; telfair.org).

BEST PEOPLE-WATCHING

It was the business and social center of early Savannah, and though locals frequent the area a little less often these days because of large tourist crowds, the promenadelike **Savannah City Market** is still a fun place to grab a slice of pizza, sit on a bench, and watch the world go by. Shops, art galleries, nightclubs, and restaurants fill the restored grain warehouses, and many tour groups pass through on their way to food maven Paula Deen's Lady & Sons restaurant (West St., Julian St. between Ellis and Franklin squares; savannahcitymarket.com).

BEST SOUVENIRS

Bypass the Confederate kitsch on River Street; instead bring home a memento from **ShopsSCAD,** a retail store/gallery that features the artwork of students, faculty, and alumni from the Savannah

College of Art and Design. Find one-of-a-kind paintings, jewelry, adorable handmade books, clothing, handbags—even beauty products—created by up-and-coming artists. Prices vary—from $135 for a vintage button cocktail ring to $4,000 for an original oil painting—but there's a pretty good chance these pieces will all be worth a lot more someday (340 Bull St.; 912-525-5180; shopscandonline.com).

BEST OF GOTHIC SAVANNAH

A visit to Savannah isn't complete without a visit to **Bonaventure Cemetery,** just a short drive east of the Historic District. Bonaventure became a hotbed for tourists after *Midnight* was published in 1994, but now that the popular "Bird Girl" statue, which appeared on the book's cover, has been moved to the Telfair Museum of Art, the cemetery has at last returned to its original quiet state. Massive 250-year-old live oaks protect the graves of Civil War heroes, veterans, Pulitzer Prize–winning author Conrad Aiken, and singer-songwriter Johnny Mercer, who penned the lyrics to songs such as "Moon River" and "Skylark" (330 Bonaventure Rd.; 912-651-6843).

MOST INSPIRATIONAL LANDMARK

The oldest African American church in the United States, Savannah's **First African Baptist Church** was founded in 1777 by George Leile, the slave of a Baptist church deacon. The church was built by its congregation, made up entirely of slaves, who worked on it after completing their daily labor. Finished in 1859, it became part of the Underground Railroad—the "tribal designs" on the wooden floors were actually meant to serve as ventilation for the people housed below. A small museum details the church's history, and Sunday services are always open to visitors (23 Montgomery St.; 912-233-2244; firstafricanbc.org).

BEST LEGACY OF A SAVANNAH NATIVE

Thousands of green-vested girls flock to the **Juliette Gordon Low Birthplace,** a stately 1821 English Regency–style mansion where Girl Scouts founder Juliette "Daisy" Gordon Low grew up. The Girl Scouts of the USA purchased and restored the house in 1953, furnishing it with many original family pieces and much of Low's artwork. Note: The home is especially popular on and around March 12, the official birthday of the Girl Scouts (10 East Oglethorpe Ave.; 912-233-4501; girlscouts.org).

BEST ANNUAL EVENT

Despite the popularity of Savannah's St. Patrick's Day festival (it draws the second-largest crowd in the United States, after New York), it's the yearly **Savannah Tour of Homes** that epitomizes this city's famed Southern hospitality. For more than seventy years, the owners of Savannah's most elegant and historic homes and gardens swing their doors open wide every spring for visitors to nose about (912-234-8054; savannahtourofhomes.org).

The Secret Lives of Athens

by

PATRICIA STORACE

"Abysmal Athens," the novelist Nikos Kazantzakis called it in 1937, after literary obligations forced him to spend more time than he wanted to in the city. And in certain moods, I agree with him.

"You are an Athenian and belong to a city which is the greatest and most famous in the world for its wisdom and strength," wrote Plato in the voice of Socrates in the fifth century B.C. And in certain moods, I agree with him.

Athens may be the most discussed city in Western history, and the voices idolizing and cursing it are as much a part of it as the cigarette-pack-shaped buildings that line it now, or the cascades of jasmine, hibiscus, bougainvillea, and gardenias pouring from the balconies of its banal apartment blocks, continuing the argument between beauty and destruction that is essentially Athenian. This city of marble and poured concrete still inspires passions, both of love and of hate.

Libanius of Antioch, the fourth-century philosopher, sounds almost tearful as he remembers his youthful ambition to study in

Athens: "I think that I would have followed Odysseus's example and spurned even marriage with a goddess for a glimpse of the smoke of Athens."

On the other hand, another fourth-century provincial Greek wrote venomously, "May the accursed ship-captain perish who brought me here; Athens has no longer anything sublime except the country's famous names." A contemporary piece of verse asks accusingly, "Athens, daughter of the gods, where is your beauty . . . you drank hemlock along with Socrates." Another contemporary voice contributed to the debate in the 1980s. The novelist Kostas Taktsis wrote in his valedictory essay, "My Grandmother Athena": "Many people say that, in the way it's degenerated, Athens is the foulest capital city in all the world. I don't know, and I don't care . . . for me it is special. She is the city in which my grandmother was born, lived, and finally died. It is necessary naturally to tell you that in many respects—exactly like Athens—she was a monster, and tortured me much of my childhood and adolescence, but what can I do; in my life, she was the only woman I ever loved."

This sequence of voices evokes a characteristic Athenian sensation, the feeling of being in an echo chamber, the disorientation of living in many worlds at once, in a place where everything that happens for the first time is also a repetition. Athens was, after all, a popular destination for Roman tourists well before the birth of Christ. In 79 B.C., Lucius Cicero remarked to a group of friends as they visited the sites of Athens, "There is no end to it in this city—wherever we walk, we set foot upon some history."

Athens is the city par excellence of the unconscious: It is part of the strange sleight of hand of this place that it is the modern buildings, reinforced against earthquakes, that seem impermanent, the ruins, both ancient and modern, that seem lasting. Here, where Europe ends and where Oedipus is supposed to be buried, there is a natural psychological crossroads. Athens has an uncanny power to draw to itself people who are themselves at crossroads, and to set choices before them. I had seen this effect myself in matters of personal archaeology, since I first visited, having grown up in the American South, which is so haunted by Greece. I left Greek Revival for the real thing. I lived in Athens last year, working on a book about Greece, and saw I was right about its habit of divination. Athens, where so much is underground, tells people their fortunes.

Athens has been a dream for as long as it has been a reality. One of the striking possessions of the Museum of the City of Athens is a set of fifteenth-, sixteenth-, and seventeenth-century engravings of imaginary views of Athens, fantasized as an Italian city and as a German one. It is also, of all cities in the world, the one most dominated by its own dream of itself. No other city I can think of is so uncompromisingly represented by one symbol. The vision of the Parthenon, part reconstruction, part ruin, rules Athens as no monument of Christianity has been able to do. How naive we have been to accept so unquestioningly the formula that this building represents reason and philosophy—it has held our imaginations because it is as inexhaustible and ambiguous as a dream. No experience of Athens is symmetrical, no impression of it uncomplicatedly romantic or easily consistent.

It is a village and a metropolis, a place where middle-aged women in slippers and garishly flowered robes shuffle unconcernedly onto neighborhood streets, coffee in hand, to send their children off to school, and a place where shipowners' pampered mistresses impulsively dispatch helicopters to islands to bring friends to the city for an afternoon of shopping. Here, even in shabby-genteel buildings, the lobby stairs and floors are marble, as are the kitchen sinks—marble is more common than wood in southern Greece, and Ajax cleaning powder promotes itself through its claims to whiten marble.

At the heart of Athens is the building that generations of architects have considered the most perfectly conceived in the Western world; but the city is also the source of unrivaled kitsch, a kitsch so inventive that it becomes a kind of doppelgänger artistry. Only in Athens would a child be presented with a candle for the Orthodox Easter Saturday service in the shape of a hulking figure dressed in wrestling trunks, his massive wax forearms flexed, his chest labeled with a banner that identifies him as MACHO KING RANDY SAVAGE. The combination bridal and christening stores in every neighborhood (unthinkable for one to be detached from the other) display dresses that look like ruffled plaster casts, every inch stuccoed with lace and spangles, while even the traditional tall wedding candles, some as high as five feet, wear drapery of organdy and ribbons, perhaps to mask modestly the inevitable suggestion that they are votive offerings dedicated to securing extraordinary feats by the groom. And yet next to these bazaars of kitsch masterpieces may well be a store offering some of the abundantly exquisite jewelry in Athens; the surprising number of these stores was explained to me as the result of a point of etiquette, since it would be incorrect for an Athenian man to buy his wife and his mistress jewelry at the same address.

Athens is a city whose coarseness can make New York seem genteel, with Athenian voices at fever pitch even in agreement, and the unrivaled Athenian pushing and shoving carried on with great intensity by deceptively frail-looking old ladies, the mothers and grandmothers who make Sophie Portnoy of *Portnoy's Complaint* seem a rank amateur. And there is the searchlight frankness of Athenian questions and the running commentaries that make the city seem populated by amateur investigative journalists. Perusing the magazines at a kiosk, you feel someone's expert fingers examining the details of your sweater. "Sexy," the stranger says. "How much did you pay for it?" An army barracks housing the soldiers who guard Parliament and the presidential palace is set in one corner of the National Garden, and a pedestrian walking down the busy thoroughfare of Vasilissis Sofias, or Queen Sofia Avenue, is often startled by the sudden resolution of trees and bushes into the shape of a soldier in camouflage, carrying a huge machine gun. "Ah, I like your earrings," I hear from between the iron railings one summer twilight on my way to a dinner party. This communiqué could only have come from the fierce-looking figure in combat boots on the other side of the fence, whose eyes never stopped scanning the street. The literal-minded might hear that whisper as a breach of discipline, but who could criticize the guard's power of observation, or feel less safe under the protection of a soldier with an appetite for life?

Brusque Athens is also, of course, a city whose elaborate network of courtesies is finer than silk, the Athenian streets a filament of wishes for good luck and health and long life, wishes more ardent and brave in their acknowledgment of the fragilities of the lives they would bless. And Greek courtesy has a fascination like no other. It is not a magnificent construction, a formal garden, like French courtesy, or a social contest following Marquess of Queensberry rules, like British courtesy; there is no stiff upper lip in Greek courtesy, but a volatile fusion of refinement and passion, a tough but breakable ceramic fired at high temperatures. A new baby makes a slow progress down the street in its mother's arms, halted by a series of neighbors and sometimes even passersby calling out, "May it live for you." After the credit card form is signed for the new radio or television set, the transaction doesn't end until the merchant wishes you *"Kaloriziko"*—"May it be well-rooted."

In the shops and restaurants of the Kolonaki quarter, still fashionable despite the current popularity of such suburbs as Kifissia and Glyfada, distinguished old ladies with fine gold jewelry, lace gloves, and hair arranged in what can only be called coiffures speak a Greek gilded with *katharevusa,* the "purist Greek," with its intricate declensions and vocabulary drawn from ancient Greek, a kind of linguistic museum. Among these ladies it is not accent that is the mark of social finesse but grammatical elegance and nuance. These women brought obligatory dowries to their future husbands, and their bookshelves are lined with the complete works of Jules Verne, Dumas, and Victor Hugo, which they purchase in translation to give to their grandchildren. Athenian toy shops feature the dolls they prefer for their granddaughters, dolls dressed in turn-of-the-century costume. The nineteenth century came late to Greece because of its liberation by degrees from Turkey. When you overhear these women buying their cakes, choosing their letter paper, here in this city of enclaves of time as well as space, you are overhearing the last nineteenth-century Europeans.

Athens is the only place I know where buying a present is also like getting a present; gifts are wrapped with a flourish, and nearly always a small extra gift is tucked into the ribbon—a pretty ceramic rose, a tiny piece of jewelry. Even the slices of chocolate cake in the windows of Athenian pastry shops—open on Sunday morning to sell to the cityful of guests and relatives on their way to a four-hour weekend lunch—come tied with delicate gold cord, or perhaps a fresh rosebud topping each slice. You can be trampled, shoved, and roundly cursed on an Athens rush hour trolley, but when you reach home, battered and hostile, a perfect stranger in your building may knock at your door holding a three-course meal on her best china, wish you *"Kali orexi,"* the Greek *bon appetit,* and disappear.

One of the glories, and annoyances, of Athens is that it is the most personal of cities, a gossip, a busybody, an intimate friend, a lover from whom you have no secrets. During my first month on the shop-lined street named for the sculptor Praxiteles' girlfriend, I struggled to get used to the Athenian view that each life is a drama to which all Athenians have been admitted free of charge. The doorbell rang constantly. A neighboring housewife felt free to drop by at 7:30 A.M., to offer me coffee, look at my posters, and inform me, "By the way, Macedonia is Greek. I hope you realize that," before she began her Monday laundry. I, who was used to working quietly at home, found myself awash in visitors, a flood of people selling books and furniture door-to-door, asking for donations, advertising, surveying.

"Good afternoon," someone says, thrusting a leaflet into my hand. "Do you know the perfect method for contraception?" Never certain, I hesitated, and the visitor seized her advantage. "Ha, I can see you don't. But here it is on page one hundred eleven of volume three of this excellent medical encyclopedia, simply take a sponge and a fresh lemon . . ."

After a week of buying papers at the local *periptera,* the news kiosk, I am known. "So," asks the proprietor, "how much money do you have to live on while you're here?"

The Athenian telephone system, like Greece, is given to fatalism. A number correctly dialed frequently yields an unexpected conversation; wrong numbers first apologize, then ask you out for coffee. A talk show host concludes a program by sitting down to a real lunch with his guests and toasting the audience from a carafe of white wine. Signs in store windows insist, encourage, scold, and even develop into full-scale personal letters, poster-size. An impeccably chic dress store informs passersby of its vacation dates with a message of barely containable exuberance: "We are not staying here for August! We are not going to the café across the street! We are going to the sea!"

The style of Athens is one of direct, theatrical communication, and most of its problems are introduced in the first act—the *nefos,* the pollution cloud that settles on the city on windless days, the dust that compounds it ("Direct from the Sahara," say Athenians proudly, always sensitive to ancestry), the lawless traffic, the

eccentric telephones, the electrical blackouts, the constant lightning strikes of taxi drivers, of farmers, of high school students, of
everything but Athenian chatter, which never pauses, the disappearing sidewalks that expose a pedestrian to oncoming traffic.
But if the irritations of Athens are immediately apparent, with the
daily litanies of *"Ti na kanoume, ti na kanoume"* ("What can we
do, what can we do"), this is also a city with an unmistakable
charm—the spicy, herbal smells of Attica, most concentrated in
the National Garden; the oranges and figs that drop straight onto
the city pavements from trees overhead; the way the entire city
becomes an extended living room after dark, with Athenians
strolling, shopping, eating at outdoor restaurants or by candlelight on their balconies overlooking the streets, balconies with an
Acropolis view the most prized of all. Night in Athens is not night
but another version of day. This city has always been ambitious
for immortality, and it is as alive in the dark as it is in its pour of
honey-colored light, driven to a divine sleeplessness relieved only
by the siesta from three to five in the afternoon, hours during
which a telephone call to a private house is a monumental gaffe.

The Parthenon is both a central motive for most visitors to Athens and a barrier beyond which they often will not pass to see the
living city that cups it. But the Parthenon itself is only partly visible, although of course hundreds of visitors climb the marble
steps every day to see a building that, though a human creation,
has acquired the stature of a natural phenomenon, like the Grand
Canyon or the Great Barrier Reef, rising above Athens like a man-
made moon. It is only partly visible, not because it is literally ob-
scured but because, like the rest of the city, it is not constructed
just of marble or limestone or cement but of materials here just as
substantial, of time and legend.

The history of the Parthenon, like the history of Athens itself, does not end when the conventional visitor's imagination of it does, with its construction under Pericles in the fifth century B.C. Its incarnations through time reflect with uncanny accuracy the panorama of Western politics and culture.

The visitor standing on the Acropolis often doesn't remember that Athena herself was evicted from the Parthenon when Theodosius II closed all the pagan temples in the Roman Empire with his edict of A.D. 435. The Parthenon, dedicated to the Virgin (*parthenos*) Athena, was later converted into a Christian basilica, the temple of a new virgin, the Panayia Atheniotissa, the All Holy Virgin of Athens. A medieval Greek Orthodox bishop distinguished the Virgin Mary from Athena by referring to Athens's previous patroness as the pseudo-Parthenos, the imposter Virgin. Masses were held where Athena had been dressed, at the culmination of the Panathenaic Festival, in the sacred gown woven for her by the girls of Athens.

During the schismatic struggle between the Roman and Constantinopolitan churches for domination, the Parthenon was reconsecrated after the Latin conquest as a Roman Catholic cathedral, known as Our Lady of Athens. Several hundred years later, in 1456, it underwent another identity change at the hands of the conquering Turks, who converted it into a mosque. An image rarely associated with the Acropolis is that of the black slaves living on its slopes during the Turkish period, brought over from Ethiopia by the Turks when the Acropolis functioned as a military garrison and the area around it was a largely Turkish village. Hans Christian Andersen recorded on his visit in 1841 that their descendants still lived in the neighborhood.

The Greek freedom fighters during their War of Independence (1821–29) against the Ottoman Empire fought hard battles against the Turks for the possession of the Acropolis; during the Ottoman occupation, Greeks were not allowed to enter it. On a moonlit evening in the fall of 1826, before a skirmish, the great memoirist of the Greek War of Independence, General Makriyannis, sang a song to his soldiers on the Acropolis, a song in which the sun narrates the pain of Greek men and women fighting to re-create their nation to an audience of the moon and the evening and morning stars.

Here, in 1854, another occupying army, made up jointly of French and English soldiers, was given a splendid banquet by the Greek government. The *Illustrated London News* reported the occasion, accompanying it with an engraving showing the feast amid the ruins, tables set with white cloths in the Parthenon, soldiers in full dress, with sabers strapped to their waists, drinking wine while the drums of columns lie at their feet.

Standing on the Acropolis, Sigmund Freud gained an unexpected insight into his relationship with his father, which became the core of the famous paper "A Disturbance of Memory on the Acropolis." A lame Cole Porter probably managed the ascent partly by mule, partly with the help of Greek sailors from his borrowed yacht, the *Eros*. And the fashionable decorator Elsie de Wolfe, when she saw the Parthenon in the thirties, said jubilantly, "It's beige—my color!"

The Acropolis even has its Romeo and Juliet, in Michael Mimikos and Mary Weber. In 1893 Mary Weber, a German governess at the palace of King George I of Greece, fell in love with a Greek army surgeon who practiced in a military hospital built, with the labyrinthine coincidence of Athenian history, on the old property of General Makriyannis. The lovers met every afternoon on the nearby Acropolis, but in February the doctor abruptly missed their daily rendezvous for three days running. Mary Weber sent Mimikos letters, which went unanswered, and even tried to signal his house by waving her scarf in its direction. She sent him another note, brief and desperate, which read, "Tomorrow at noon, I will go to the Acropolis, and if you don't come, I will kill myself."

The next day, she waited for Mimikos to respond or to meet her himself, and when she knew he would not come, she leapt from the Acropolis to her death. Visiting foreign tourists found her body and helped transport it to the nearby hospital where Mimikos was a staff member. He arrived later the same afternoon, to discover Mary's letters, none of which had been forwarded to him while he was in bed with a fever at home. Mimikos was guided to a medical officer's room where he found Mary laid out for burial, holding violets and dressed like a bride, as is still the Greek custom when unmarried people die. "I swear to you I will follow," he is supposed to have said, and during the night he shot himself. The couple were buried separately, but on the night of the funerals, a group of the doctor's friends entered the cemetery and reburied Mimikos in Mary's grave. Generations of Athenians, with their still-pronounced taste for tragic romance, have commemorated them with poems, novels, and even a movie. "Mimikos and Mary were pure as angels," one poem reads, "and like angels, they fell from heaven."

Morbidity has a kind of glamour for Athenians. Around New Year's time, the neighborhood stationery shops that are a fixture of every quarter of Athens are stacked with cheap matchbook-size page-a-day calendars filled with childish jokes, reminders of saint's days, recipes for *kataifi* (a death-dealing dessert of shredded wheat and honey), and doggerel verse promising varieties of eternal love beyond the grave, or asking for it.

The neighborhoods are studded with empty, once-grand neoclassical houses, with padlocked doors and overgrown gardens, their skull-like emptiness emphasized only by a stray cat or two skulking on the doorstep. Whenever I asked about the melancholy conditions of these houses, the explanations led back to the holy trinity of Greek motivation—family, money, government. There was an unresolved inherited struggle for the house on the corner; the family who owned the house on the hill no longer had the money to maintain a structure built on such a lavish scale. In some cases, I was told, when the government has forbidden the demolition of a fine neoclassical house, a family will try to force permission to erect a more profitable high-rise apartment building by letting the house deteriorate beyond repair. Many are said to be haunted, the sounds of sobbing or of parties from other eras issuing from them at night. There is the handsome house of the poet Sofia Laskaridou, in the neighborhood of Kalithea (120 Laskaridou Street), whose rejection of the poet Pericles Giannopoulos drove him to his dramatic suicide in 1900, when he rode naked on a white horse into the sea at the town of Skaramangas. Laskaridou is said to have rejected him out of pure caprice and to have mourned him for the rest of her life, a semirecluse until her death in 1963. In Kalithea, her ghost calls for him in her crumbling house.

This city is strangely haunted by its own present, as well as its past; behind the courtyards and surrounding the bland facades of the high-rises are the stories of modern Athens, a world rendered visible by events and personalities that visitors preoccupied by its classical past cannot see beneath its current camouflage.

Legends are alive here, but the immediate, the real, the daily, are ghostly. The visitors enjoying the shade and perfume of the National Garden are often unaware that it was a project representing in part the poignant ambition of nineteenth-century Athens to regain its stature as a European capital. Athens had been a Turkish village—the paradoxes of history are such that this ancient city became a new capital with none of the accoutrements necessary for a chief city of nineteenth-century Europe. The same visitors eating the grilled corn sold at the garden's entrance are even less likely to be conscious of the ghostly presence of the wounded and dead who lay on these grounds during the savage Greek civil war of 1946–49.

The non-Greek visitors climb the Acropolis, their heads full of images of Pericles but only rarely of the swastika-marked flag the Germans were so eager to raise on this site when they overran Athens in 1941. It is not only the darkness of much modern history that gives the present its disembodied quality here, but the fear of controversy, the habit of secrecy the Greeks learned under their various occupiers, and the bizarre, skewed Athenian sense of time. The past must have reached eternity in order to be dignified as the past; the more recent past simply isn't eternal enough. What will be remembered is what has acquired the status of legend, in the way that we remember Maria Callas costumed as Tosca, but we don't remember her at 61 Patission Street, a student wearing a Greek baptismal cross, learning about passion, betrayal, and courage—the things that would make her Tosca.

It is strange to realize how few familiar associations most visitors bring to modern Athens—visitors to Rome can request a song like "Arrivederci Roma," guests in Paris think of "La Vie en Rose," but who besides an Athenian knows "Athena, kai Pali Athena" ("Athens, Always Athens"), one of the cardinal songs of the Second World War period, part of the endless repertory of songs that are traded back and forth at dinner tables and tavernas? Athens is a city that has a second, separate existence in song, and its chameleon quality is traceable in these treasured fragments of air. In the decade between 1940 and 1950, the singer and composer Nikos Gounaris is singing in praise of "Beautiful Athens . . . with its modest girls, without painted lips," while only a short time later, in the seventies, the city stars in a song as a prostitute who will sell herself for a glass of wine.

The splice between past and present in Rome or Paris is less violent than in Athens—a city that has been made, unmade, and remade throughout the centuries. Even in Plutarch's day, Athens had the reputation of being a city manipulated into existence; he describes the strategy of the ancient kings of Athens for persuading the Athenians to develop a primarily agrarian economy, instead of one based wholly on shipping trade. "It was they who had spread the legend about Athena, how when she and Poseidon were contesting the possession of the country, she produced the sacred olive tree on the Acropolis" and became the city's patron instead of the sea god.

Plutarch's anecdote is early evidence, too, of the Athenian appetite for rumor, still the ignition key for intellectual and political life in Athens, a city in which the evening's bons mots are rehearsed in the morning, before being launched into the orbit that inevitably brings them back to the speaker in some new version. Through this means I learned one evening on the telephone the glad tidings of my own marriage to a mildly detestable man I hardly knew. A speculation in the morning had metamorphosed into a contract in the evening.

Here is the summary of the sixteenth-century martyr Filothei, whose bones you can visit in their elaborate reliquary in the Metropolis Cathedral, from which her relics are always carried in procession on February 19, the anniversary of her martyrdom, by one of her descendants, members of the influential Benizelos family: "They cannot stand firm, these Athenians. They are a low-class people, good-for-nothing and dishonorable; indeed irresolute, faithless, shameless, abominable, desperate; their mouths always open in mockery and complaint, speaking a barbarous language, eager to blame, loving strife, cavilling, pusillanimous, gossiping, arrogant, lawless, guileful, snooping, eternally on the lookout for the disasters of others."

Athenians adore well-crafted verbal abuse—the Sunday evening reentry into the city from the seaside towns and country houses resounds with cries of "Drive on, masturbator" and threats to a rich variety of mothers. On the grounds of verbal relentlessness alone, Filothei might have been canonized. At any rate, it is amusing to be reminded that the city's most popular church for weddings, booked months in advance, is named for her.

Because it seems to consist only of the sights most important to visitors—the ancient Agora, the Acropolis, Syntagma Square, Plaka, the marble Olympic Stadium, the temple of Olympian Zeus—Athens may look easily accessible at first glance. But it is in many ways a hidden city, its many vanished pasts alive in turns of phrase, in legends, in gestures, invisible to the uninitiated. As the British philhellene William Miller wrote in 1905, "There is little left to bridge over the chasm of centuries which separates the days of Perikles from those of Otho and his successor. . . . The traces of those intermediate ages must be sought in the manners and customs of the Athenians. . . ." This is a city which, after the fierce street-fighting between the Greeks and Turks in 1827, was left with only sixty houses standing. It became the capital of modern Greece only by default, after Aegina and Nauplion, because of the Bavarian royal family's romantic Hellenism. It was, according to the nineteenth-century analyst of Greek life Edmond About, an archaeological choice, not a political one. "Athens is surely not on the great road of commerce," he wrote, but "Athens is named Athens," and in Greece, legend is a strong legislator.

The Athens we see, with its unplanned sprawl, is in part the aftermath of the upheavals of the 1922 debacle of the Asia Minor campaign, during which the government of Kemal Atatürk came to power in Turkey and the three-thousand-year-old Greek presence in Asia Minor was decisively ended. The entire Greek population of Turkey, with the exception of the inhabitants of

Constantinople and western Thrace, poured back into Greece, doubling the population of Athens almost overnight. Athens's first high-rises were built to house the refugees, and one can still sense a refugee quality in the development of the city: the hastily built buildings, driven by considerations of need and profit alone, the insensitive use of land, a style of building extended by the later waves of emigrants from villages and islands, and by the custom of dowering Greek daughters with houses as a prerequisite for marriage, a custom that has not disappeared, although it is rarely referred to formally as dowry, since the practice is officially illegal. The chaotic growth of Athens is only beginning to be corrected through the efforts of such people as the late Antonis Tritsis, a visionary mayor of Athens, and by the current exemplary mayor of the Zoographou section of greater Athens, Mrs. Fotini Sakellaridou. Tritsis fought to save the Plaka district from degenerating into a street-sex and souvenirs district, and developed a scheme to ban traffic from the center of Athens, a city whose narrow streets are more natural for pedestrians than cars.

Athens is a city of neighborhoods, with the still-natural tendency of Greeks to form villagelike enclaves wherever they are, centered around a park or a hill, a view or an idea. Athens is essentially a city formed on the village pattern of clustering around a central *plateia,* or square. In and around the *plateia* are the neighborhood cafés, shops, and newsstands: The *plateia* is the backdrop for children's soccer games, newspaper-reading, pastry-eating, and people-watching. The central inner courtyard of an Athenian apartment building is a kind of feminine version of the *plateia*—if the men sitting at the cafés outdoors keep an eye on the community's public life, the women on the courtyard scrutinize its private life. In the elevator in my building, two women decoded my lingerie and the pattern of grapevines on the sheets hanging on the clothesline outside my apartment. The one with the poodle remarked, "There is a lot of black lace on her laundry line," and added, significantly, "and her lights go out very late. . . ."

Entire apartment buildings often house extended families, who wander in and out of each other's apartments, dandling each other's babies and stirring each other's pots of *stifado,* a beef stew with onions, wine, and cinnamon. A common and charming style of construction in all the city's quarters is a series of houses and gardens built on graduated levels of a hill, forming a kind of suspended cascade of residential gardens, momentarily separate worlds.

Among Athens's famous districts, there are Exarhia and Neapoli, the bohemian quarters, populated, as they were in the nineteenth century, by students, anarchists, the flocks of poets who still inhabit Athens, and the *philoloyika kafeneia* (literary cafés), where writers, critics, artists, and actors gather to sit over two-hour cups of coffee, 11 A.M. ouzos, and brilliant jokes. These were the neighborhoods of the turn-of-the-century *cantadori,* the bands of singers who would gather under the windows of their girls and serenade them, sometimes making the supreme gesture of cutting the strings of their guitars after the song, to give the music absolutely to the woman. The austere Greek fathers would call down the wrath of the police on the singers, afraid their daughters' reputations would be ruined.

There is, of course, Plaka, the oldest continuously inhabited village on the continent of Europe, settled since prehistoric times, with its unexpected grace of Cycladic Island houses in the Anafiotika quarter, built by settlers from the island of Anafi, a testament to the sheer unpredictability of Athens. There is Thissio, the area of the old Roman Agora, with its famous *House with the Caryatides,* painted by the definitive modern Greek painter Tsarouchis, in a canvas as familiar to Greeks as Edward Hopper's nocturnal coffee shop is to Americans. Thissio is the neighborhood for artists' ateliers, galleries, the distinguished frame shop Leonardo, said to practice its craft according to the aphorism of Tsarouchis (so celebrated for his aphorisms that in Greek they are simply called Tsarouchia) that "the frame is the pimp for the work of art."

The heroic center of anti-Nazi resistance, the leftist working-class neighborhood of Kaisariani, with its streets named nostalgically after their towns in Asia Minor by the refugees who settled it, is a popular Sunday refreshment, the urban equivalent of a country outing, as is the monastery of the same name on Mount Hymettus just beyond it, where Athenians picnic, play soccer, and gather the olives the signs strictly forbid them to pick. The slopes of Hymettus were the setting well into the 1920s and 1930s for a *nyfopazaro*, a "bride bazaar," in which eligible young women would be strolled up and down the green paths by their parents, getting together afterward to discuss whose eyes met whose with the most significance. The Kaisariani monastery was such a cherished Athenian expedition that it was nicknamed Seriani—"stroll"—and found a place in a couplet about the three monasteries on the edge of Athens that all Athenians can repeat:

> *In Seriani, strolling—and in Pendeli—honey*
> *and cold water that angels drink flows in Dafni.*

An Athenian year moves to a different rhythm than those of other European cities, and expresses itself with a different weather. At Christmas, possibly a better time to visit the city than the hot, crowded summer, the streets are full of vendors selling gilded fruit, and the fruit-shop and jewelry-shop windows are full of pomegranates, real and jeweled, symbols of good luck in the coming year. The fruit are thrown against the thresholds on New Year's Eve, and split open, symbolizing a fruitful year. You look through the glass windows to the bright fruit, the Christmas ornaments in the shape of pomegranates, the silver pomegranates in the jewelry window, half open to show their silver seeds, and realize—Persephone. In January come what are known as the "halcyon days," a mysterious cluster of days of warm, almost summery weather, slipped into the cold, damp Athens winter, days that in antiquity were supposed to have been granted for a princess to bear her child in gentle weather.

At carnival time, temporary shops appear on street corners, filled with masks and costumes, and the women's magazines are full of hints about the right makeup for Cleopatra, Carmen, or Madonna. The rubber faces of current politicians and figures from the gossip pages hang in the windows, too, as they did at the Carnival of 1875, reported by the *Illustrated London News,* when a "rollicking, popular humorist of the town, . . . reeling drunk . . . had put on the classic helmet of the princely Agamemnon, king of Mycenae, making a little fun of Dr. Schliemann's recent discoveries there."

At Easter, the racks of Easter candles in brilliant colors, wrapped with toys or charms of ships—the ship of Athena's festival, which later became a Christian symbol for the soul—appear on the sidewalks of neighborhoods like Pangrati, or along the streets of the handsome Mets quarter. And in summer the city moves out of doors. Tavernas are full at two in the morning with family parties, including young children, eating in gardens and savoring the cool night breezes. Some of the smaller streets are looped from house to house with grapevines that shield the street from the summer sun, and the *laiki agora,* the farmer's markets on the streets, are full of the magnificent Greek cherries, peaches, and melons, while competing vendors praise the perfumes and colors of their fruit with the chant *"Aromata kai chromata."*

The colors of the seasons are different from the ones we know; New Year's is full of dark blues, glass good-luck charms, antidotes against the evil eye, and silver-wrapped heads of garlic to hang over your front door. The champagne and dancing are imported here; Greek New Year begins with wishes, threats, propitiations.

Easter, unlike Easters farther west, is not pastel but ruby red, the red that is repeated in the eggs that appear in flower arrangements and braided into sweet Easter breads. The feasts of the Church calendar give the progress of the year a medieval quality, with the medieval world's blurring of the secular and the sacred; on June 30, there is an annual celebration of the icon of the Church of the Holy Apostles, the patron saints specially honored by the Association of Used Goods Vendors. Every season in Athens has its panoply of presiding supernatural beings, its angels and mermaids, its ritual foods, its reinterpretation of the coexisting ancient and modern worlds. There is a McDonald's on a choice corner of central Syntagma Square, but in Pangrati a local fast-food takeout offers *pastitsio* (a Greek baked-pasta dish needing hours of preparation), braised okra, peppers, and tomatoes stuffed with rice pilaf, along with demibottles of wine. Fast food here is understood as fast food for the customer but not for the chef.

Athens is a demanding city, one that can be known only through some relationship to it, of instruction, of finding out its family jokes and secrets, of growing up. There is a neighborhood jogging track, one of the few in Athens, that I run on with a friend, T.; on one side of the track the joggers are framed by the Acropolis, on the other by the chapel of St. George on Mount Lycabettus. We swing back and forth, from one to the other, held, like the city, between the pincers of classicism and Christianity. For me it is distracting to run in the presence of two such starkly contradictory metaphysics, but when I turn to look at T., I am reminded of how different it is to grow up in a place than it is to just live in it. For T., Athens is a place not only of symbols but of life, not just a memory but a fate. As I run, the shock of the Acropolis makes me blind to what T. might see: himself flying kites on Philopappus hill, being taken on the annual school trip to the Parthenon, meeting lovers. To me, these are places; to him, they are relationships.

The Greek poet Cavafy, acknowledged as one of the classic writers of the twentieth century, wrote a letter to a cousin describing his first visit to Athens in 1901: "I went to Athens—as to a Mecca—decided to like it and I kept my word . . . admiring with all the fervor—which is their due—the classical statues and columns; and I dwelt lovingly in the old churches in which I thought of the obscure generations that had there hoped and prayed for the third advent of our race; and was never shocked by the banality of the imitation French 'quartiers' for there too I saw . . . the interesting signs of an enduring people's new tendency. In all this, I assure you I was not activated by patriotism. I simply let myself be guided—as I like to do at times—by Sentiment and Illusion. They are not logical guides, I know. But . . . whoever despises them and exiles them from his life is either very strong or very rash."

I remembered his visit on an April morning walk, on Monday, the beginning of Megali Ebdomada, the Great Week of Easter, the central holiday of the Greek year. I passed stray roses growing in old cans of Mana olive oil, and the inevitable neighborhood religious-supplies store, its windows full of silver-plated icons and tin votive plaques stamped with houses, babies, and clasped hands over the raised script of the message I BEG YOU. The uglier buildings are covered with great swaths of the willing Athenian wisteria and lilac, like unattractive women with perfect jewelry. The grand buildings—like the house of the eccentric Duchesse de Plaisance, the French philhellene who was said to have kept her daughter's mummy preserved in her old room at home—all seem to be undergoing repairs at the same time. A giant delivery truck goes by; painted on its cab is a portrait of the Virgin Mary, whose face is framed with the word *Megalochari,* "great in grace." Between the railings of the National Garden, planted by Queen Amalia as the first queen of independent Greece before she and King Otho were sent back to Bavaria in 1862, a group of seven cats are intently giving themselves synchronized baths. Syntagma Square, once the site of the garden of the philosopher Theophrastus, is almost completely blocked off by subway construction; Athens vanishes even as it speaks to you, a city always in the process of disappearing and persisting. I choose another route for my errand, and as I wait for the traffic light to change, a bus speeds past, the destination lettered above its windshield reading METAMORPHOSIS.

1994

ATHENS ESSENTIALS

How to experience the seat of Western civilization

BEST ANTIQUITIES

It was Marcus Cicero's cousin Lucius Cicero who put it best—in 79 B.C., that is. Athens, he pronounced, was a huge, rambling museum; its ancient monuments as present in the city's subsequent reincarnations as they were when Socrates strolled its streets. "There is no end to it," he wrote. "Wherever we walk we set foot upon history."

Even today, antiquities seekers in downtown Athens are spoiled for choice. And uniquely—some would say miraculously—the antiquities have only gotten better, thanks to improved conservation and illumination. Begin your wanderings with a visit to the "sacred rock" of the Acropolis (30-210-321-4172), if only to prove to yourself, as Freud did, that it exists "just as we learnt at school." In addition to the temples, and the delightful, if small, museum perched beneath the fifth-century B.C. Parthenon, the site's entrance fee provides visitors with free access, over the course of a week, to most of the capital's other gems. These include the Theatre of Dionysos on the sanctuary's southern slope, the ancient cemetery of Kerameikós (arguably Athens's most evocative archaeological site), the Temple of Olympian Zeus, the marvelous ruins of the ancient Agora, and the Roman Agora.

BEST STROLL

For the 2004 Athens Olympic Games, the Greeks united their Golden Age wonders in a giant (and free) archaeological park. Widely seen as a masterpiece of innovative urban planning, the

2.5–mile walk takes you past Periclean and Roman antiquities, including the Hephaisteion, Greece's best-preserved classical temple, down to the buzzy, and distinctly more modern, districts of Gazi and Psirri. The best way to access the route is to stroll along Dionisiou Areopagitou. With its spectacular views onto the Acropolis and the second-century Odeion of Herodes Atticus, this cobbled boulevard is one of the most beautiful (and in real-estate terms) expensive avenues in Europe. Next, head for the pine-clad Philópappus hill for an unrivaled view of the Parthenon and a sprawling Athens down to the sea. The setting is particularly dramatic at sunset.

BEST MUSEUMS

Courtesy of its rich benefactors and even richer soils, Athens has a plethora of museums. Most are easily accessible from the city center. Stroll along Vassilissis Sofias, otherwise known as Museum Row, and stop in at either the Benaki Museum (30-210-367-1000; benaki.gr) or the Museum of Cycladic Art (30-210-722-8321; cycladic-m.gr), both of which have excellent exhibits and airy eateries. The Byzantine and Christian Museum (30-210-721-1027), which offers an unrivaled collection of period art and icons, and the War Museum (30-210-725-2974), whose showpieces include weapons dating from antiquity to modern times, are also farther up the street.

For one of the world's greatest collections of ancient treasures, visit the National Archaeological Museum (30-210-821-7717), housed in an impressive neoclassical building on Patission Street. The spectacular Museum of the Ancient Agora exhibits an array of eclectic relics that shed light on the everyday life of the ancients (30-210-321-0185). Lovers of modern art should head for the National Museum of Contemporary Art (30-210-924-2111; emst.gr); the National Art Gallery (30-210-723-5857), opposite the Hilton Hotel; and the new Benaki Museum Annex (30-210-345-3111) on Pireos Street, where the shows are often cutting-edge.

BEST SHOPPING DISTRICTS

As any shopper will soon discover, Athens is an amalgam of neighborhoods, all offering their own special fare.

For those hunting classy prêt-à-porter and haute couture, head for the fashionable Kolonaki district above central Syntagma Square. Here, Voukourestiou, Stadiou, and Ermou streets are crowded with big brand-name shops (often cheaper than in other parts of Europe). For museum-quality antiques and embroideries, visit Martinos (50 Pandrossou St.; 30-210-325-7414) in Monastiraki, near the bustling flea market, where real bargains are not uncommon. Finally, Mandra (75 Iraklidon and Pireos Sts.; 30-210-345-0003) offers a wealth of traditionally Greek gems to decorate gardens and homes (wooden chests, urns, and marble ornaments) and arranges shipments worldwide.

BEST DAY TRIP

Athens's proximity to the ocean and increasingly convenient modes of transport have made Greece's isles ever more accessible. Board a Hellenic Seaways hydrofoil (30-210-419-9000; hellenicseaways.gr) and scud over the seas to one of the nearby Saronic Gulf islands.

Quintessentially Greek Aegina is only thirty-five minutes away, and has fabulous walks, good tavernas, and the best pistachio orchards outside Iran. Car-free Hydra, which has one of the prettiest ports in Greece, is less than ninety minutes from Pireaus harbor and has a good selection of comfortable hotels. Or take a trip along the Athenian Riviera to see the spectacular temple of Poseidon at Sounion.

The Haunted Land

by

JAN MORRIS

 Down in the forest something stirs: me.

I am stirring a cup of tea, actually, and thinking about matters Hawaiian in one of the most absolutely Hawaiian of all possible places, the deep secluded valley of Waipio, on the island of Hawaii—which is not the island where Honolulu is, but the much larger, emptier, and more compelling place nicknamed the Big Island, some two hundred miles to the southeast.

The forest is sensually tropic, and hung with spiders' webs. The valley is accessible only by four-wheel drive, and its fifty or so inhabitants have no electricity or running water. I am sitting on a bench beside a taro patch in the twilight and imagining the rich pageant of Hawaiianness all about me.

The things that have happened in Waipio! Nenewe the Shark-Man lived in a pool. Pupualenalena the Dog-Spirit lived in a rock. The ghosts of the underworld periodically rise to the surface through a tunnel by the sea. In former times Waipio was a prodigy of well-tended abundance, but in 1946 a tidal wave swept away almost all its buildings and destroyed virtually all its gardens, leaving only a handful of houses, a few taro farms, and Mr. Tom Araki's simple lodging place, the Waipio Hotel, where I am staying.

Waipio has a black-sand beach, vertiginous waterfalls, and rushing, pebbly rivers. There are people in Waipio who still speak the Hawaiian language, and some folk whisper that the sacred bones of Kamehameha the Great, the king of all Hawaiian kings, lie somewhere in this retreat, hiding their mana under a rock with the Dog-Spirit, or in that tunnel among the shades.

So I stir my Earl Grey in the gathering dark, while the frogs begin to gurgle and Mr. Araki, who is very old and looks like a Manchu mandarin, lights the kerosene lamp on the veranda. There could be no better place than Waipio, in the dusk, at Tom Araki's place, for thinking thoughts Hawaiian.

The Big Island is the mother and father of the entire Hawaiian archipelago. It is bigger than all the other islands put together. Although less than a quarter of its 112,000 people are Hawaiian or part-Hawaiian (Caucasians and Japanese make up most of the rest), it is the fount of almost everything that we think of as Hawaiian.

Two thousand miles out in the Pacific from the U.S. mainland, some 260 miles around, the island is crowned by a 13,800-foot mountain, the Mauna Kea volcano, snowcapped for much of the year and surrounded by a landscape so majestically varied that it is like a little continent of its own. There are rolling downlands, dewy in the morning. There are rocky coasts, mountain gulleys dark with fern, and highways that sweep across high mountain wastes or through lowlands so lush that they are like splendid botanical gardens. Wild pigs and donkeys roam the hillsides, mongooses scurry across the roads; off the coast one often sees the exuberant spurts of water, the swish of giant black tails, that show the humpback whales are there.

But at the heart of the island's personality is something deeper and darker—for all these coasts, hills, and forests are under a spell, dominated by the volcanic substance of the place. The white summit of Mauna Kea, looking down upon so much beauty from its snowy, cloudy kingdom, truly is like a brooding throne. The erupting of volcanoes, the shaking of earthquakes, the bursting of fearful tidal waves, are social history on Hawaii. Grand resorts are built on the very edges of lava fields.

Pele the Fire Goddess used to live in the ever-active crater of Kilauea, in the southeast, and even the pussyfooting National Park Service, which has succeeded her as Kilauea's guardian, cannot dispel the mythical evocations of the volcano. No number of tour buses, no banality of guide, can make that great steaming crater feel merely geological or eliminate the atavistic dread that almost everyone must feel, contemplating its unappeasable force.

For some years a river of lava erupting from the flank of this old monster has been oozing down to the sea, demolishing houses in its slow progress, blocking roads, and finally entering the Pacific in portentous plumes of white steam. I walked one day over its hot, greasy-looking mass, like a desert of unmolded plastic, as close as I could get to the hiss and spout at the water's edge; and looking over my shoulder to the immense bare mass of the mountain behind me, its summit lost in mist, I thought I had never stood so symbolically near to the source of all energy.

But that evening I returned to the crater itself, and there I found an image of a different kind: In the blistered hole of Kilauea, riding the sulphurous fumes out of the earth's furnace, a white bird with a long tail was joyously flying.

No wonder the original inhabitants of this island were people of myth and magic, their imaginations haunted by the idea of secret power. Their chiefs wore robes made from the feathers of the o-o bird; their women were forbidden to eat bananas; they were strong believers in the advantages of incest. Blithely they rode the waves on surfboards, the chiefs' boards being statutorily longer than anyone else's, and merrily they slid down rocks on sleds. A system of awful social prohibitions called kapu governed all their affairs and kept their hereditary leaders on top; the authority of their many gods was emblemized in idols and in somber temples—heiaus—built of lava.

Such was what anthropologists call Pre-Contact Hawaii—Hawaii before the white man touched it. On the Big Island its artifacts, like its influences, are inescapable still. There is a place in one of the volcanic fields of the south where, in a bygone age, a party of Hawaiians found themselves trapped by hot lava, leaving only their footprints eerily implanted to tell the story of their passing. It seems to me that the whole island is rather like that—imprinted with the ineradicable traces of a very peculiar past.

There are heiaus grand and petty, sinister and benign, crumbled and restored. At Wahaula Heiau (Red Mouth Temple), within sight of the billowing steam-plumes of Kilauea, human sacrifice was first practiced on Hawaii. At Haleokapuni Heiau there is a stone against which, we are told, the high chief Alapi-kupalupalu-mano used to lean to watch the Shark-God propitiated in the bay below. At Puuhonua-O-Honaunau, offenders against kapu, if they could get there without letting their shadows fall upon the kingly palace next door, might be absolved of having eaten bananas or indulging in sexual intercourse before fishing.

Many and much-honored are the sites associated with Kamehameha the Great, still the presiding genius of this island 170 years after his death. Kamehameha, the "Lonely One," was the first of five Kamehamehas to rule the entire Hawaiian archipelago, and he is commemorated to this day in statues, street names, schools, and hotels, in the official Hawaiian anthem, and in Kamehameha Day, a public holiday throughout the fiftieth state.

Of all the sites in Hawaii Kamehameha's birthplace is the most moving. It stands near a great ruined heiau on the wind-swept, wide, and heart-lifting northwestern coast—grassy open country at the edge of the ocean. Today the royal house is hardly more than a wall of rubble, generally without a human being in sight, but it is as infused as any Celtic cromlech or Mayan pyramid with what mystics and Hawaiians like to call the earth-force.

Just as significant, though, if not so charismatic, is the re-constructed heiau called Ahuena, a cluster of thatched huts and wooden effigies immediately beside the swimming pool of the Hotel King Kamehameha in the touristy west-coast resort of Kai-lua. It was here that Kamehameha died. But more important still, here one evening in 1819 his successor, Kamehameha II, deliber-ately sat down to dinner at the same table as his womenfolk—thus, at a stroke, demolishing the whole oppressive structure of kapu. In no time at all the prohibitions were abandoned, the idols were destroyed, and anyone who audibly disagreed with the re-forms was eliminated.

Down a steep, winding road on the southwest coast lies the fish-ing village of Milolii. Here if anywhere one can feel to this day the pagan attractions of old Hawaii, before the Christians came. It is a gloriously bleached and ramshackle place, sans electricity or fresh water, it earns its living by catching mackerel, when in sea-son, from motorized outrigger canoes.

For much of the time, though, it seems to concentrate on en-joying life. Oh, the surfing, the swimming, the wading, the play-ing of harmonicas, the just plain lazing about that goes on at Milolii, which has nowhere for tourists to sleep unless they want to camp beneath the palms and eucalyptus trees! Children frolic in the sea just as they did before the Contact, while indulgent parents cook crabs, tinker with old cars, or drink beer on the stilted porches of their apparently all-but-derelict homes.

Once this was the general ethos of the island, especially after good King Kamehameha II, by abolishing the old gods, left his people in the fortunate position of having no religion at all. The gift for happiness proved very resilient. "When I was a child," a venerable Hawaiian-speaking lady told me, pointing toward a distant and inaccessible promontory, "we lived out there, and we didn't need nothing, no jewels, only food and flowers." Alas, the promontory has no people living on it now, only a solitary white obelisk ironically marking the spot where, on February 14, 1779, Captain James Cook from Yorkshire was bludgeoned to death by a resentful islander and the eventual fate of the Hawaiians was sealed.

There was a Mrs. Nancy Ruggles among the first batch of New Englanders who arrived forty-one years later, in 1820, to enlighten the savages. Her astonishingly ugly and forbidding face is pictured in all the history books and seems unfortunately to illustrate the effect of Christianity upon Hawaii. The first mission church stands incongruously amidst the raucous vulgarity of Kailua, and handsome though it is, and well provided with pamphlets pleading the missionary cause, it does seem a bit of a dampener. One cannot see Mrs. Ruggles parking her surfboard beside the porch. Inevitably the evangelists, in their Yankee way, were taken aback by the manners of the island—"benighted Owhyhee," as the *Missionary Herald* called it in 1821. Aghast at the seminudity and the emphasis on creature pleasures, they hastily clad their converts in more becoming clothes, gave them an alphabet so they could read the Bible, and encouraged them with mixed success to abandon the colorful traditions of the Hawaiian heritage.

"They came to do good," says a bitter Hawaiian apothegm, "and they did well." For capitalism soon profitably followed

Christianity and left its mark all over the island in cattle ranches and sugar plantations, nut orchards and coffee estates. Hawaii's chief port, Hilo, though it tries hard to be a resort, still possesses a slightly raffish, Conradian, traderlike flavor. Honokaa, in the northeast, is everyone's idea of a tropical sugar town—all false fronts and iron roofs, with somnolent dogs on sidewalks and gamecock supplies available at the agricultural store for the local Filipino cockfighters. Some of the missionary families indeed made their fortunes; yet they were not all money grabbers. They did good as well as harm, and there is much that is attractive in their legacies to the Big Island—the neat little churches here and there; the clapboard farm buildings; even the cotton muumuu, the long, bright granny dress, still so universally worn, with which the evangelists clothed the nakedness of their female charges.

I spent three nights at the hamlet of Waiohinu in the south. It is like a Connecticut village curiously mutated. The hills are green, the trees are fresh, the church is steepled and has weekly Singspiration meetings. But it is a Japanese family that has run the spotless little motel for the past half-century; Annie K. Wong Yuen is pastor of the church, and the congregation is an easy mix of Hawaiians, Japanese, Chinese, Caucasians, and multiethnic societal refugees. I went to one of those Singspiration sessions on a balmy starlit evening and, pagan as I am, thought it an enchanting blend of the pious and the carefree. The music would have satisfied Mrs. Ruggles, and the sentiments too, but they were presented with distinctly un-Puritan panache. Jokes were exchanged. Young men with Coke cans lounged beside the open door. Barefoot children ran about and squalling babies were communally comforted.

Some of the hymns were in Hawaiian, and when I left I could hear their slurry, scoopy cadences floating mellifluously on the night air all the way back to the motel (where Mrs. Shirakawa had kindly left in my room three mandarin oranges, freshly plucked from her garden).

I like to suppose that the Hawaiian kings and queens, though Christianized, Westernized, and eventually given the push by the Americans, retained to the end some of this hybrid charm. You can experience their later style in the modest summer palace they maintained at Kailua, suggestively situated opposite the missionary church. Hulihee Palace is a pleasant, airy house, open always to the sea breezes, plain but for a couple of Strawberry Hill–Gothic windows providing a vicarage effect; its mementos of the royal dynasty are touching.

As Victorian times went by, the seven kings, one ruling queen, and numerous princes and princesses became rather absurd, bemused as they were by the pretensions of European royalty. As you can see at the Hulihee Palace, they were seduced by crowns and orders, they maintained household guards, they made monarchical visits to other countries whose condescending mockery they failed to observe. Queen Kapiolani going to London for Victoria's Golden Jubilee looked like Charley's Aunt in her tight-corsetted, beribboned, and bemedaled finery, while King Kamehameha V, when dressed up in stiff white collar, waistcoat, and watch chain, looked remarkably like a Hawaiian bullfrog.

Yet there is something noble to their absurdity. Caught between cultures, trapped by history, they were groping toward dignity for themselves and for their people in the new world that had overwhelmed them. In 1820 not a soul in Hawaii could write; in 1887 Queen Kapiolani, dressed up to the Parisian nines, went off to London to visit her colleague the Queen-Empress of India—such was the speed and impact of the change to which these unfortunates had to adjust.

The last of the Hawaiian royals, Princess Kaiulani, whose wistful face looks out at us from her portrait in the palace, was not absurd at all, perhaps because her half-Hawaiian, half-Scots parentage allowed her to bridge cultures with more grace. She was heiress to the throne at the time when, in 1893, an American-engineered coup put an end to the monarchy. In vain this lovely and cultivated woman fought for the rights of her throne and, as she saw it, of her people. She died in 1899 at age twenty-four, some say of a broken heart.

So I sit in the Waipio dark and think. What, I wonder, have our own times brought to this strangely magnificent island? Nothing much to be proud of, I fear. Most of Hawaii is economically stagnant, while elsewhere the all-too-familiar corrosion of tourism gradually spreads in golf courses, resorts, and condominiums. Some damned company wants to build a commercial missile base in the south, some bloody developer has already tried to start a restaurant in Waipio. Junk food has betrayed the old Hawaiian staples of fresh fish, fruit, and vegetables, and year by year the ancient Hawaiian language is further lost to the people.

Yet in some ways Hawaiianness thrives in Americanness. The American manner of enjoyment, for instance, is not so different from the old Hawaiian hedonism—today's surf culture is just the Pre-Contact style, and so is skiing down snowy slopes 13,500 feet up Mauna Kea. The mountaintop observatories of modern Hawaii, remote and silvery in the sun, are like contemporary heiaus. American obesity, which can be so grotesque, is not out of place on this island, where a regal fatness has always been admired.

There has been something of a revival in the indigenous culture too. The Hawaiian language has been declared one of the two official languages of the state and finds some modern uses: *Kapu* generally means "Keep Out" these days; *Please no huhu* means "We don't want troublemakers"; and everyone who has ever heard a Hawaiian guitar knows about "Aloha." There are monarchists on Hawaii still, and nobody is allowed to forget the melancholy fate of the dynasty, or the ignominies suffered by the equivocal civilization that for better or for worse it represented.

Besides, the old gods have never quite died—one often sees flowers laid in tribute or supplication in the heiaus. The Park Service sanctimoniously proclaims the continuing holiness of the temples, if only to deter tourists from scrambling over their ruins, and at least one, Mookini Luakini, next door to Kamehameha's birthplace, still has its hereditary priestess—Leimomi Mookini Lum, formerly of the Honolulu police, who claims to be a direct descendant of the Priestly Order of Ku.

Certainly down here in Waipio, as night falls upon the valley, I feel the presence of old forces about me—if not the tramp and chanting of the processional ghosts, at least the emanations of im-memorial beliefs and inexpungible ideas. No doubt about it, Waipio is a place of powerful mana, and something of that same power, be it sacred or historical, geographic or merely mumbo jumbo, gives to the Big Island as a whole, even in the age of the rental jeep and the helicopter tour, a sense of hidden conse-quence.

"How come you can still see out there?" says Mr. Araki, shuf-fling over to attend to the edible water snails he breeds in tanks behind the house. "I don't need light to see," I say mysteriously, remembering the volcano and the whales, the ill-fated princess, the high, tufty grasslands, and the footprints of the dead men in the lava. Mr. Araki just grunts, though, and goes about his own sufficiently esoteric business.

1988

The Big Island's Sacred Sites

The places that remind you that Hawaii was once a land of gods and legends

Mauna Kea

 Today the home to W. M. Keck Observatory—which has the world's largest optical and infrared telescopes—and to intrepid skiers and snowboarders, this dormant volcano is also, according to legend, the residence of the fire goddess Pele's sister Poliahu, the goddess of snow. Pele and Poliahu never got along, and when Pele, who lived on the volcano of Mauna Loa, erupted, the lava would melt Polihau's snows. Then one day Polihau created a blizzard, forcing Pele back to Mauna Loa and forever covering Mauna Kea's summit in ice and frost.

Mauna Loa

This volcano, the world's largest and one of the most active—it last erupted in 1984 and is almost certain to do so again—is said to be the original home of Pele, the Hawaiian goddess of fire and the most feared (and respected) deity in ancient Hawaii. Pele was driven to Mauna Loa by her sister Na-maka-o-kahai, after Pele seduced her husband. Whenever Pele tried to dig a pit for a new home, her sister, the goddess of water and the sea, would flood her out. But on Mauna Loa—which rises 2.5 miles above sea level—Pele found safe, and dry, ground.

Kilauea

An active volcano that sits on Mauna Loa's southeast flank, Kilauea is said to be Pele's current home. Kilauea is still eruptive along its eastern ridge, where you can watch large, fiery platelets of hardened crust and molten flame spill into the sea and harden into satiny formations.

In ancient times, the volcano was a sign of Pele's fearsome displeasure. Today, travelers will find signs of the goddess everywhere, from the smooth, round bullets of cooled lava known as "Pele's tears" to "Pele's hair," thin filaments of volcanic glass. As tempting as it might be, though, removing them is strictly *kapu*—forbidden. Any local who has dared to do so has harrowing stories to share about Pele exacting her revenge, either through bad luck or through appearing, in the form of a young or old woman, in an unexpected haunting. Look, too, for the creeping vine with round leaves and a pale blue, cup-shaped flower—this plant, the *pa'u-o-hi'iaka*, is named for another of Pele's sisters, Hi'iaka, the godmother of hula; the flower is thought to resemble a traditional hula skirt.

Ka'u

This region, in the southern part of the Big Island, was known as the seat of kings and contains many sacred sites and ruins within its borders. Even today, its raw, windswept surfaces and often fierce surf give the area a lonely, haunted feel, as if it were not miles, but centuries, away from the glittering resorts of Kailua-Kona.

Among the best-known sites in Ka'u is Ka Lae; the southernmost point of the United States is also thought to be the first Hawaiians' landing point. Scattered along the shoreline are ghosts of Hawaii's seafaring past: canoe mooring holes, burial grounds, and the Kalalea *heiau* (temple), a stark yet somehow poetic gathering of lava rocks.

Another area within Ka'u, Koloa, is the home of the *'ili'ili hanau,* or birth-giving rocks, rough lava formations that seem to give birth to small pebbles as their pores are eroded by the surf. (In Hawaii, rocks are considered both sacred and alive—in 1893, a supporter of Queen Lili'uokalani, Hawaii's last monarch, wrote what has to be one of the loveliest protest songs ever, "Kaulana Na Pua" ["Famous Are the Flowers"]. The song's most famous lyrics declared that the royalists and queen's faithful would rather eat stones than accept anything from the United States, which annexed Hawaii that year.)

Pu'uhonua o Honaunau

One of the holiest sites in all of Hawaii, Pu'uhonua o Honaunau, also known as the City of Refuge, included both a *heiau* and royal grounds, which were a popular residence for Hawaiian chiefs.

Ancient Hawaiian society was ruled by a complex set of punishing laws that prescribed codes of behavior (everything from sartorial to gastronomic) for priests, laborers, commoners, and the *ali'i* (or royalty) alike. Breaking one of these rules resulted in death. If, however, the condemned could reach a *pu'uhonua,* or place of refuge, his sins would be forgiven and he would be granted clemency. Although it's now an idyllic National Historic Park, its waters busy with sea turtles, the reef that surrounds Pu'uhonua o Honaunau is treacherous and dense, making an attempt to reach its shores a particularly desperate and daring feat. Hale-o-Keawe, the structure protected by carved wooden gods, was once used as the royal mausoleum.

Lost Horizons

by

SUKETU MEHTA

The rhinoceros was looking at me meditatively. I wasn't in a zoo, and I wasn't watching the Discovery Channel. I was in Kaziranga National Park, famous for its rhinos, in the Indian state of Assam. All around me frolicked hog deer, hornbills, and wild buffalo. About forty feet away, it had raised its head from placidly eating in the tall grass, several birds perched on its massive body. It looked prehistoric; at forty million years, a rhino shows its age. The beasts, which weigh up to five tons, are covered in armor and their sight is terrible; they squint out at the world through beady little eyes. Then I saw him lift his horn, that piece of matted hair that commands up to $7,000—a staggering sum in a country where the per capita income is $465. Tipu, the guard accompanying me, told me that just last night two poachers had come into the park looking for this fabulous prize. The guards caught them on a boat in the river and shot one dead; the other fell off the boat and is presumed to have drowned. "We don't catch the poachers alive," he said. "We shoot them, from a distance or up close. If we hand them over alive, they'll just pay five thousand rupees [$110] to the police and walk out, and come back. We are all excited by the hunt when we're after the poachers."

I asked him if he felt any compunction in killing a human being. "No," he answered. "It's because of them that we don't know day from night, working out here in the jungle twenty-four hours. They are our enemies."

A senior forest officer who used to be in Kaziranga and now works in another Assamese forest confirmed what the forest guard had told me about the poachers. When he had first got to Kaziranga, the rhino kill was enormous—a total of five in just one particularly bad day. But then, by changing his patrolling schedule often, he started killing poachers—thirteen poachers eliminated in just one six-month period in "encounters." He laughed, and then reconsidered: "So-called encounters," he said. When he finds a poacher, he immediately starts shooting. "It's better to shoot and kill, it's better to be offensive than defensive," he explained. Besides knowing for a certainty that the poacher will be back, there is the risk of getting shot himself. When the account appears in the newspaper, he always has manipulated it so that the poacher seems to have fired first. With such tactics, Kaziranga's guards have been winning against the poachers, at least for the moment. There are now more than 1,250 rhinos wandering the park, up from 1,100 in 1988. In 1986, poachers killed forty-one rhinos; by 1997, that figure had declined to twenty-six. In 2000, the park achieved a record: As of August, only two rhinos had been killed by poachers. And the human count? Eighty poachers shot dead by the park staff in the last ten years.

But the rhinos face an even greater danger: unprecedented floods on the Brahmaputra River, caused largely by deforestation in the mountains where the river originates. In 1998, the river flooded its banks and drowned thirty-nine rhinos. Driven by the rising waters, others came out of the forests and onto the highway bordering the park, where they were run over by trucks or shot dead by poachers.

Kaziranga National Park is on the southern bank of the Brahmaputra River; the Himalayas technically begin on the northern bank. But the struggles between poachers and wardens in this 166-square-mile park, a World Heritage Site, are replicated throughout Himalayan parks. Few people in the Himalayan region seem to have much of a problem with killing poachers, because this is seen as part of a war. And all over the hill regions there are other battles being fought—against deforestation, against dams, against pollution, against the deterioration of cultural and architectural heritage.

For the past three decades, a crisis has been mounting in the Himalayas, the world's highest, longest, and youngest mountain range. Deforestation has triggered most of the degradation. During the past forty years, forty percent of the Himalayas' forests have been lost. Since the conquest of Everest in 1953, Nepal has cut down nearly half of its trees. In the Indian state of Himachal Pradesh, timber merchants and subsistence farmers have felled more than two-thirds of the hill forests. The consequence of the Himalayan tragedy is a dramatic increase in floods, leading to hundreds of thousands of deaths in the low-lying plains downstream, including Bangladesh. Then there are the dams: Along the fifteen-hundred-mile range, a seismic hotbed, twenty-two large dams have been built or are planned. Not only are whole valleys flooded and multitudes of people displaced during dam construction, but the very real possibility exists that the next earthquake could cause one of these to break calamitously.

For several weeks, I traveled the arc of the Himalayas, from Arunachal Pradesh in the east to Ladakh in the west, looking at the threats to the mountains and the interdependence of ecology and development. The issues are not simple. Environmental projects that work in one part of the hills may not work in another, because each country has radically different forms of government. Environment is intimately linked to local political issues, to local ideas about sharing and what a specific culture considers worthy of saving. Still, there are promising experiments: I went to Kaziranga to look at approaches, legal and otherwise, to wildlife preservation; to Arunachal Pradesh to see how a blanket ban on logging had worked; to Bhutan to see whether a mountain culture could be saved and at what cost; to Nepal to witness how a forest can be saved if you involve the people living in it; and to Ladakh to see how humans can live in modern times with the least possible toll on the environment. There were personal reasons for my taking this journey too; as a Hindu, my gods live there.

In countries such as India and Nepal, the law is not always safe from the lawmakers. In 1995, the Beas River, near the Indian Himalayan resort of Manali, in Himachal Pradesh, flooded a hotel built illegally on protected forestland on its shores. The river thereby incurred the wrath of a very powerful man—Kamal Nath, then India's minister for the environment, and part owner of the resort. Lesser mortals might have moved their property to keep out of the river's flood plain. Not the honorable minister. He moved the river. With bulldozers, earthmovers, and dynamite, a new channel was dredged, away from the hotel. A lawsuit by an environmentalist eventually drew the Indian Supreme Court's attention to this blatant destruction of the environment by the man who was responsible for protecting it. The court ordered the hotel removed from the river's edge, noting, "Rivers are not meant for ministers but for the poor people."

Eighty percent of Arunachal Pradesh, the Indian state just northeast of Assam and perhaps the country's most remote area, is covered by forests that supply fifteen percent of India's timber. I met the timber merchant whose interests in Arunachal Pradesh are some of the largest. We were in his car, pulling out of his palatial home in Calcutta, and I was asking him if it would be difficult for me to get a permit to travel to the state, which is restricted because it borders China. He dismissed my fears. "Laws are made," he said, "for those who abide by them."

That comment, I later realized, also applied to his attitude toward the forestry laws. Arunachal Pradesh has the greatest biodiversity of the entire subcontinent, boasting 550 species of orchid alone. But it has also suffered the most accelerated depredation of its forest—in just four years, from 1992 to 1996, 550 square miles, an area as large as all of Delhi, were lost to the axes and chain saws of the timber industry. In 1996, a vacationing Supreme Court judge saw the destruction, came back to Delhi, and made use of two unrelated forestry cases to impose a blanket ban on logging and sawmill operations in the entire northeast. A quarter of a million people lost their jobs.

The first day's drive took me from Tezpur in Assam to Bomdila in Arunachal Pradesh—from the northern bank of the Brahmaputra to the Himalayas proper. The road has been built by the army, which is much in evidence, and as it passed from tropical through temperate zones, I saw a stunning variety of trees. But there were also vast patches where the mountainsides were scabbed from clear-cutting. I constantly saw groups of workers removing boulders that had tumbled onto the roads after the trees, whose roots bind the topsoil, had been chopped. TREES ARREST LAND-SLIDES, a sign pointed out. At one point on my way back, I got out of my car and sank knee-deep in the mud. The road had been half washed away by heavy rains.

Tapek Riba is a very bored forest officer. His activities as district forest officer, Tawang, are limited to planting trees in the few acres of land that the villagers are willing to part with; he considers his posting an enforced vacation. We drove up into the mountains, half an hour up from Tawang, in the dense fog. At one point,

Riba stopped the car and we got out. At first I couldn't see clearly, but then I went closer and I drew in my breath. Acres of clearcut stumps stretched before me, the abandoned remains of an army camp. The original trees must have been destroyed fifteen years ago, and even now the stumps were being hacked for firewood; they showed red-brown where the bark had been stripped off. In the mist, a solitary bird chirped, accentuating the quiet. It was the silence of a graveyard.

As we drove along, Riba kept pointing out more and more such sites, where the army or the GREF (General Reserve Engineering Force), the equivalent of the U.S. Army Corps of Engineers, had cleared the trees for constructing their camps or for fuel for the machines building the mountain roads. At one spot, where we got out again, Riba showed me what the mountain had previously looked like. Walking down a little, he pointed out a majestic forest of fir and juniper, tall trees standing undisturbed. "Why have they been left alone?" I asked him. Riba pointed toward the road. It curved up and away from the forest; trees on the upward side of the road are always cut more easily, because you can just roll them down. "The main destruction of the forest follows the road," he explained. "It is . . . ," he savored the word, "natural." Where there is a road, poachers and timber fellers have motorized ease of access and exit. Roads kill forests.

The second great cause of the destruction of the forest near Tawang is population. According to the 1991 census, Tawang district had 28,000 people living in it. The current estimate is 40,000. The population has been swelled by outsiders, whom I saw everywhere, owning the shops and tea stalls: Nepalis, Bengalis, Marwaris. They work harder than the tribals. But they also get colder up in the hills, and so they need more firewood. It takes seven months to get a gas connection, after which a cylinder of cooking gas is delivered to your house every month. Firewood is cheaper and quicker to obtain. An average family, according to Riba, needs two truckloads, or nine cubic yards of wood annually, which currently costs around $240. The state government experimented with giving the tribals permits to harvest trees from the forests around their villages for their own use. In 1995, three thousand such permits were issued. Riba laughed, remembering the scheme: "People got permits in the names of dead people, for their pet dog, their pet cat. . . ." The permits were resold to timber merchants, and the permissible quota of trees was vastly exceeded—by about tenfold—and smuggled out by fast night trucks to the sawmills of Assam.

If the authorities subsidized cooking gas still further and made the cylinders readily available, the need for wood as a cooking fuel would be greatly lessened. But the jump in population has meant that the trees on the hillsides all around the hamlets have been stripped, and the villagers venture farther and farther inside the forest for wood. They are supposed to gather only previously fallen logs and not chop green trees, but they are not yet impressed with the necessity for conservation. The villagers see the forest department as their enemy. "Protection is very difficult," explained Riba. Deforestation causes landslides, which threaten their houses. "But we can't demonstrate a landslide. The effect is felt only by the next generation." The elders understand—they remember when Tawang was under deep forest cover. Now the streams are dry in the summer and flood in the rains. "The younger generation wants the forest but they don't want the forest department," Riba said.

That night, I experienced firsthand the passions of this younger generation. I was settling into my room at the tourist lodge in Tawang; I felt I had come to the last place on earth. I might have been the only tourist in town; tourism, both foreign and domestic, is minuscule in Arunachal Pradesh because of tight government controls. Behind me was the majestic seventeenth-century monastery of Tawang, the largest Buddhist monastery in

India, through which the Dalai Lama had been smuggled out of China. The impassable Himalayas stretched out all around me; the rudimentary facilities of the tourist lodge confirmed for me that this was off the beaten track, that I was in a far place.

Then I heard a thumping through the wall.

I went outside into the hallway and knocked on the room next to mine. A young man opened the door, and all of a sudden the thumping took on recognizable form: It was the bass part of "I'm a Barbie Girl." Inside was a wild scene: the room in near-complete darkness, many couples dancing, dressed, I could see when my eyes adjusted, in brand-new sportswear: Fila, Adidas, Nike. Bottles of booze lined tables along the walls. It could have been a club in suburban Detroit. The music was the same, the dress was the same, the poses the young people struck were the same. The young people of Tawang had rented out this room in the tourist lodge; it was the end-of-the-school-year bash, and it went on all night, the music filling the corridors of the lodge— Ricky Martin, the macarena song, that great international parade of hit songs that last exactly one summer but are impossible to avoid during that time. We are all Americans now.

These young revelers are not going to be satisfied with the se-date pleasures of yak herding in a pristine forest. An earlier generation gathered around a tree and propitiated it and asked its forgiveness before cutting it down, whereas this generation, its eyes turned firmly westward, has no use for such superstition. They want more: sneakers, stereos, motorcycles. But there is no industry in Arunachal Pradesh. There is only the forest. And there are outsiders who will give them quick money for their forests. The environment can be protected only if the whole cultural system of the people who live in it is protected.

Which is why, until recently, King Jigme Singye Wangchuk banned television in Bhutan, the country next to Arunachal Pradesh.

It was on the footpath to Cheri monastery, which begins at the Thimbu River, outside the Bhutanese capital. I crossed over on the most beautiful covered bridge I have ever seen. The blue water of the river rushed by below—in Bhutan, unlike the other Himalayan countries I visited, the rivers are blue even in the monsoons; elsewhere, they are muddy brown from the eroded soil washing down them. The sides of the bridge were festooned with prayer flags, and the vast protected forests of Jigme Dorji National Park, the biggest park in Bhutan, loomed before me on the mountain slopes. I climbed up through forests of maple, oak, blue pine, rhododendron, and poplar. They were untouched.

"We are in a very fortunate situation compared with our neighbors," observed Dr. Kinlay Dorjee, the representative for Bhutan at the World Wildlife Fund. The king decreed that sixty percent of the country should be under forest cover in perpetuity. Right now, seventy-two percent of Bhutan enjoys such forest cover. As a benchmark, the WWF is trying to persuade the governments of the world to designate ten percent of global forests as protected; the current world figure is six percent. In Bhutan, right now, government order protects twenty-six percent of its forests. "The forest act and rules are very strict and progressive. Anybody who wants to cut a tree from his own agricultural land, if it's over twelve years old, has to get a permit," Dorjee said. This edict was issued in 1979 by the king. I noted that the monarch had himself applied for such a permit, to cut a tree on land belonging to him. "Buddhist mythologies and beliefs contribute to conservation," Dorjee explained. "Most of the lakes and forests are considered the abode of deities. People believe that if you cut trees, the whole village will suffer from hailstorms or droughts."

Another way the king controls history is by limiting tourism only to those who can pay top dollar—$200 a day, to be exact. This has meant that other than Indians, who don't need visas, the number of foreign tourists—who must reserve through accredited travel agencies—has stayed below six thousand a year. Although the $200 includes everything, the travel infrastructure is severely limited. The capital, Thimbu, has only about 250 rooms for tourists, and those are often sold out a year in advance, particularly in summer and fall. The strict visa policy means two things: The environment is not burdened by the needs of five-star hotels, and the king gets to control the movement of poor people and their possibly subversive ideas into the country. As a result, most journalists allowed into the country write fawning profiles of the young, basketball-loving king and the antics of his four wives. Invariably, foreign journalists and aid workers, as well as the airline magazine, the newspaper, and every government functionary I met, approvingly quote one of the king's pronouncements: "Gross National Happiness is more important than Gross National Product." I heard this so many times during my stay in Bhutan that I found myself completing the phrase aloud whenever someone began to explain, "Gross National Happiness . . ."

There is no doubt that of all the places I visited, Bhutan has been the most successful at keeping its forests intact. But I was not completely at ease in the country. It is the only South Asian country I have been to where people were afraid to talk to outsiders about politics. The army and police were everywhere; before entering Thimbu, I had to register at a police checkpoint.

Expatriates and the various donor agencies love Bhutan. In the South Asian chaos, it is an exquisitely manageable country. But Gross National Happiness isn't for everyone. In the early '90s, according to the U.S. State Department, the Bhutanese government engaged in a systematic program of ethnic cleansing, "including arbitrary arrests, beatings, rape, robberies and other forms of intimidation by the police and army," forcing 87,000 ethnic Nepalis into refugee camps in Nepal, where they remain to this day. Many of them possess Bhutanese citizenship. The king argued that had the Nepalis been allowed to stay, they would sooner or later have swamped the Drukpas, the Buddhist Bhutanese, and eliminated the Himalayas' only remaining Buddhist state. Indeed, this is precisely what happened in neighboring Sikkim, which was swallowed up into India after a referendum in 1975, when its Nepali inhabitants outnumbered the native Buddhists. The king has further declared that anyone who cannot prove that he was in the country legally before 1958 has no right to stay there. "It's easy to have a good environment if you eliminate one-sixth of the population," noted Kunda Dixit of the Panos Institute in Kathmandu.

In June 1998, while I was there, the king abruptly dissolved his cabinet. Two weeks later, he announced a royal edict, or *kasho:* a cabinet to be elected by members of the National Assembly as well as a provision that its members could remove him with a motion of no-confidence approved by two-thirds majority. What caused the most unhappiness among the people? The prospect that they would be able to depose their king. For two days the 150-member parliament discussed the *kasho.* "Member after member pleaded with the king, gasps choking their voices, to take back the *kasho,* particularly the proposal for a vote of confidence in the monarch. Men and women in the visitors' galleries cried openly," the *Indian Express* reported. The king wanted to give his people democracy; the people pleaded with him not to.

Among the Drukpas, at least, this is one popular monarch. He has kept Bhutan, they say, from becoming another Nepal.

Kathmandu, the Nepali capital, is a textbook case of all the problems of modern cities in this part of the world. Most nights the power goes out for three hours, although always with advance warning from the authorities. Levels of air pollution here are some of the highest in the world; some time ago, the Nepali king's Mercedes failed an emissions test. All of Kathmandu labors under a severe water shortage; parts of the city don't get water for days on end. In nearby Patan, on the other hand, an underground network of acquifers built hundreds of years ago still provides drinking water to the poor: I saw water flowing out of several of these taps, called *dhunge dharas,* into sunken troughs. But the modern water supply system in the capital, built about a century ago, is already obsolete. The rich have pumps that dig far down into the earth, into the geological water table, water millions of years old that can never be replaced. Seeing the principles of town planning in Patan and then walking out into modern Kathmandu, my faith in the progressive view of human evolution was severely put to the test.

Still, not everything that threatens the Himalayan environment is in the control of the people who live there. In Thimbu, Kinlay Dorjee of the WWF had told me, one of the potentially greatest dangers to Bhutan and Nepal and many other Himalayan regions is GLOF.

"GLOF?" I asked, thinking of an aggressive, furry, creature, perhaps a newly discovered cousin of the yeti.

"Glacial lake outburst flooding," he explained. "We believe it's due to global warming. There's been a steady rise in the temperature over the last few years."

The upper regions of the Himalayas are sprinkled with lakes: water from retreating glaciers—some of which have moved a hundred yards in the last fifteen years—enclosed in moraine walls. As the temperature goes up, the glaciers melt at a faster rate than the lake drains. Too much pressure can cause the moraine wall to break, in which case the water comes gushing out—up to ten million cubic meters in four hours, as happened in 1985 with Dig Tsho Lake near Mount Everest. It swept away an entire hydroelectric project, along with scores of bridges and roads.

Tsho Rolpa, which holds more than 100 million cubic meters of water, is most seriously at risk of a GLOF. The surface area of the lake, which was .09 square miles in 1959, had increased by

1993 to .54 square miles. If Tsho Rolpa bursts, its GLOF will be greater than any other in recent decades. A burst at Tsho Rolpa, which sits northeast of Kathmandu, is the stuff of Nepalese nightmares. In June of this year, the government began a project aimed at removing seventeen percent of the lake's water.

Nepal has among the most successful models of social forestry in the world today, and people come from all over to study them, including the Nepal Australia Community Resource Management Project, the organization where Purna Chhetri works. In the 1950s, the government nationalized all the forests of Nepal. That policy didn't work; it assumed that the local population was hostile to the forests, and the people behaved accordingly, felling trees illegally and smuggling them out. The government, one of the poorest in the world, did not have the resources to police all its forests, so the new government policy, signed into law in 1993, made a radical turnabout: National forests would be gradually handed over to the communities around them. The tenure would remain with the government, but the management would be the responsibility of the local people, organized into forest user groups. These user groups have grown from a couple of hundred in 1992 to more than six thousand today, all over Nepal. Each group draws up a plan for managing its allotted forest and then harvests it accordingly. I went with Chhetri, a Nepalese forestry expert, to see one group's work.

Chhetri was pleased to get out of Kathmandu. "We go on field trips to clean out our lungs," he said, grinning. He took me to a forest nursery in the district of Kabhre Palanchok, which, the forest user group of the neighboring village had decided, would largely grow lokta, also called Japanese mitumata. Of the group's $1,800 budget, $1,500 had been invested in lokta. Why this concentration on one crop? Because money grows on trees—literally. The bark of the lokta is used to make the paper the Japanese yen is printed on; it fetches a hefty $2.50 a pound, and the group was expecting a return of up to $6,000 on its investment when the five-year crop is harvested next year. The money would fund literacy classes and other village activities. It's only a small forest—forty acres—that had been given to this user group, but the villagers were beginning to realize that the forest didn't have to have the bald patches I could still see in the district. It could be used for profit.

Steve Horn, the director of the Nepal Australia project, was emphatic about its participants making money, not just for subsistence needs, but also for a surplus: "We're trying to get them to view forest resources more as a crop than as a protected resource." The project has 52,000 acres: If the groups manage the forests well, they will be allowed to fell trees and sell timber to Kathmandu at market rates.

But Nepal is among the most corrupt countries on earth. How would the user group make sure any surplus was spread equitably? The money generated, Horn explained, goes to community groups, not individual households. It is a communal system that prevents people from taking more than their fair share. The surplus is used for reforestation and community development—electricity schemes, small roads, furniture and/or money for school buildings, drinking water schemes, and subsidizing salaries of health workers. The project has a special emphasis on women. "Women do ninety-five percent of all forest activities," so last year, explained Horn, the project ran four hundred literacy classes that educated some eight thousand women.

Kunda Dixit of the Panos Institute went to Sindhu Palchok and Kabhre in 1988. "It was barren. It was desert." The area was a leading producer of charcoal, for the smithies of Kathmandu, and the trees were felled for that purpose. Then he made another trip, in the spring of 1998. "I couldn't believe it. There were huge trees. Leopards are back, bears are back. There's one forest where a man toots a trumpet every time he sees a leopard and warns the villagers. There is no poaching, no barbed wire, no guards. The forests are coming back, near the villages. Community forestry is one of the success stories of the Nepali environment."

In transit between Nepal and Bombay, I stayed one night with a cousin who had recently moved to Delhi. At about ten o'clock, just as I was in the middle of Flaubert's *Sentimental Education,* the lights went out. They stayed out—for the next thirteen hours. A few weeks before, India had tested five nuclear bombs and demonstrated its technological prowess. Around the same time, Delhi was cutting off power to its residents for days at a time in 120-degree heat.

It is difficult for a person living in the United States or Europe to imagine what a thirteen-hour power outage is. But the subcontinent, the conflict between the need for power and the need not to dam the rivers of the hills is a very real issue. The activists fighting Himalayan hydroelectric power projects usually come from the cities; they operate out of offices with electricity. The rising middle classes of the hill areas resent being told that they should limit consumption, limit the amount of electricity they extract from the mountain waters. And their rivers are perhaps their greatest wealth: The Himalayan states are staking their future on exporting hydroelectricity to a power-hungry India. Here's a remarkable statistic—although ninety percent of Bhutanese rely solely on fuelwood for cooking and heating, the country exports ninety percent of its electricity to India, accounting for a full thirty percent of its export earnings. Huge new hydropower schemes are being envisioned; the same is true in Nepal. Some of the bitterest struggles in the region now are around the construction of large dams. It's all about big power.

To get to Gera, eleven thousand feet up in the Himalayas, I had to cross a footbridge over the Indus. But once there, I had traversed centuries. Electricity came to this hamlet in Ladakh, in the far north of India, only four years ago, and everyone remembered the difference it made. "Before the light came, people had to cook very quickly, and the children had to study with lanterns," explained Dolka, the schoolteacher. At her feet, on the porch of the one-room schoolhouse, sat eight children of varying ages, reciting multiplication tables.

In a simple stone shed, a stream that fed into the Indus below first flowed through a pipe, gushing onto a wheel. The wheel spun and turned a belt attached to a 3.5-kilowatt generator. Not that the boy who showed me the power plant thought in terms of watts or volts. "It runs twenty-five light bulbs," he explained. "And two or three tape recorders." When I asked him if he could use more electricity, he thought for a long time. "We would like to play our tape recorders in the day." The generator ran only from seven to ten in the evenings. During the day, a large disc of iron blocked the pipe, so that the stream flowed off in another direction, toward the village fields. When its work irrigating the fields was done, the stream lit the village houses and provided music for evening entertainment.

This was all being run by LEDEG (Ladakh Ecological Development Group), an environmental nongovernmental organization. I was taken to a house where three of the village women turn out traditional Ladakhi clothes that are sold through LEDEG in Leh. They had one of the tape recorders, decorated with a picture of Bruce Lee, on which they like to listen to Ladakhi tapes. It was the prettiest studio I'd seen: two big walls threw open the room to the mountains and the wheat field below, at that time in June studded with small yellow flowers.

The people of Gera, for the time being, had the electricity they needed.

The nearby hamlet of Ulley Topko has around fifty residents in seven houses. A man I met named Wangchuk runs a tourist camp there, and he showed me his house, which uses a traditionally Ladakhi method of heating: The stable for the animals is directly under the main living area, on the ground floor. The heat from the cattle radiates upward and warms the room above, making it quite toasty in the freezing Ladakhi winters. The disadvantage of this method of central heating is that your nose is very much aware of the cattle below, and insects from the animals and their droppings migrate upward along with the heat. Ladakh has nearly year-round sunshine, so Wangchuk also has a solar heater, which heats a few buckets of hot water. Then Wangchuk changed his mind. "Lukewarm. Lukewarm water," he said. That's the trouble with solar power. Unless the installations are huge, they are good for only very small jobs. And the cost of the equipment is out of reach for almost all private citizens, so it has to be heavily subsidized by the government.

Most of Ulley Topko's electricity needs were being met by a three-kilowatt generator, which Wangchuk runs from 6 P.M. to 1 A.M.; the tourists in the seventy-five-person camp were using the power for shaving and ironing. The power ran forty light bulbs. From 6 P.M. to 7:30 P.M., Wangchuk conducted a kind of electricity triage: He ran the camp's refrigerator, but not the lights; after 7:30 P.M., with the gathering dark, he shut off the fridge and put the lights on. The power went to the appliances where it was needed throughout the night; occasionally, a couple of tape recorders were put on. "This much electricity is sufficient," said Wangchuk. "We don't use more machines." The beauty and simplicity of the tourist camp was a convincing argument for this type of low-impact hoteling.

As soon as my plane landed in Bombay, the cell phones of the businessmen started ringing. Before they had even gotten off the plane, they had already begun urgently negotiating deals, making appointments. When I got into the city, it was a hot, steamy night. I drove through man-made canyons flanked by structures in which humans lived stacked above one another like colonies of insects. We are an urban species now; at the beginning of this century, for the first time in human history, more people are living in cities than in villages. We have voted with our feet. Through the highways of the city, expensive cars cruised, drinking the blood of the earth, emitting gases that cause glaciers to melt and flood the places I'd just been in. Most of the trees have long since been destroyed here, and yet this is where we all want to be, in cities like this, with one million people per square mile and the one million and first person just getting off the train from Assam. The young people of the mountains are willing to trade their rhinos, their rhododendrons, their traditional houses, their orchids, for life in vast shantytowns, without clean water, without clean air. This is what Kathmandu, too, will look like in fifty or twenty or ten years.

Early the next morning I sat in my study and looked out at the rippling Arabian Sea outside, and the white clouds on the horizon were ranged in formation, peaked, massed, in my fancy, just like mountains, abode of snow. Soon a monsoon wind picked up, the clouds darkened, gathered, and then the whole sky was just one solid sheet of black.

2000

A Map of the Mountains

The Himalayas play a critical role in the environmental future of southern Asia. Here are some of the problems facing both man and nature.

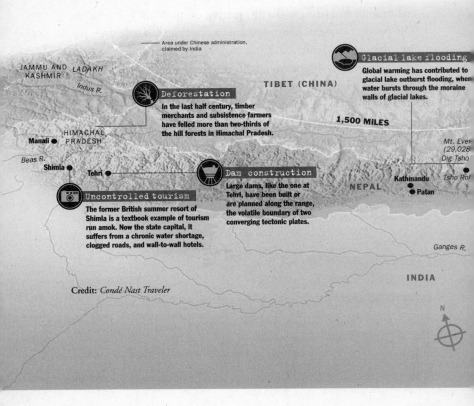

Area under Chinese administration, claimed by India

JAMMU AND KASHMIR
LADAKH
Indus R.
TIBET (CHINA)

Deforestation

In the last half century, timber merchants and subsistence farmers have felled more than two-thirds of the hill forests in Himachal Pradesh.

Glacial lake flooding

Global warming has contributed to glacial lake outburst flooding, when water bursts through the moraine walls of glacial lakes.

1,500 MILES

HIMACHAL PRADESH
Manali
Beas R.
Shimla
Tehri

Mt. Ever (29,028
Dig Tsho
Tsho Rol

Kathmandu
NEPAL
Patan

Dam construction

Large dams, like the one at Tehri, have been built or are planned along the range, the volatile boundary of two converging tectonic plates.

Uncontrolled tourism

The former British summer resort of Shimla is a textbook example of tourism run amok. Now the state capital, it suffers from a chronic water shortage, clogged roads, and wall-to-wall hotels.

Ganges R.

INDIA

Credit: *Condé Nast Traveler*

N

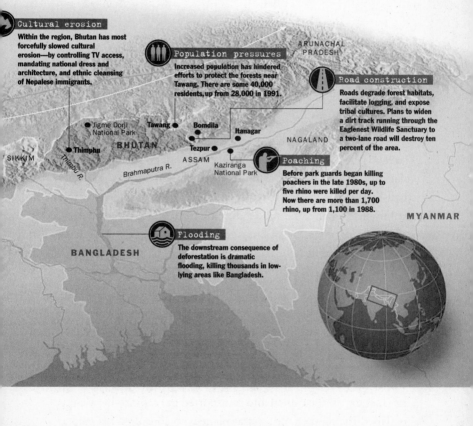

Cultural erosion

Within the region, Bhutan has most forcefully slowed cultural erosion—by controlling TV access, mandating national dress and architecture, and ethnic cleansing of Nepalese immigrants.

ARUNACHAL PRADESH

Population pressures

Increased population has hindered efforts to protect the forests near Tawang. There are some 40,000 residents, up from 28,000 in 1991.

Road construction

Roads degrade forest habitats, facilitate logging, and expose tribal cultures. Plans to widen a dirt track running through the Eaglenest Wildlife Sanctuary to a two-lane road will destroy ten percent of the area.

• Jigme Dorji National Park   Tawang •   Bomdila •   Itanagar •

NAGALAND

BHUTAN   Tezpur •

• Thimphu

SIKKIM   Thimpu R.   ASSAM

Brahmaputra R.   Kaziranga National Park

Poaching

Before park guards began killing poachers in the late 1980s, up to five rhino were killed per day. Now there are more than 1,700 rhino, up from 1,100 in 1988.

MYANMAR

BANGLADESH

Flooding

The downstream consequence of deforestation is dramatic flooding, killing thousands in low-lying areas like Bangladesh.

The Loneliest Place on Earth

by

PICO IYER

 Somehow I am always visiting Iceland—
whether in memory or imagination—and
always walking through its chilly, ghostly
streets, pale even after midnight in the summer, and hushed, no
dark to be seen for 2,400 hours or more. Somehow it is always
half-light in the Iceland of my memories, and I am walking across
empty fields alone, the sun landing on the sea at 1 A.M. and then,
after settling there for an hour or so, rising again as I walk back
through the pallid light and hitch a ride on an early milk truck
around the magical, cloud-covered coast. It seems I am always lost
in the ice blue poems of the Icelandic Romantics, and the images
from the light nights that I spent there keep returning: the man
with the chalk white face who accosted me in the café of a lonely
fishing village sometime after midnight and told me, through
piercing eyes, of his dreams of Jesus and a flock of angels robed in
white; the girl with the intense Egyptian gaze who picked me up
my first day in the capital and transported me off into her visions
of Tibet; the pilot of the six-seat plane who consulted his map as
we flew, just the two of us, low over ice fields and snowcapped

peaks, to the deserted fjords of the west. I am always standing on a hill in Iceland's golden quiet, my shadow stretching for forty feet or more, then walking through a sleeping world in the dove gray light of 2 A.M.

Perhaps because it is so otherworldly, Iceland leaves a curious impression on the mind. Days spent here are interludes from life, sojourns in some other, nether, twilight zone of the mind. Everyone knows a little about the epidemic oddness of the place: There was no beer when I first visited, and no TV on Thursday; there were almost no trees and no vegetables. Iceland is an ungodly wasteland of volcanoes and tundra and Geysir, the mother of all geysers, so lunar that NASA astronauts trained here; a place of fumaroles and solfataras, with more hot springs and mud pools and steam holes than any other wilderness on earth. One day I saw a crowd gathered on a Reykjavík street and went over to see what they were staring at: It was a dog (formerly illegal in the capital). Iceland is a duck-shaped island with eight million puffins and a thirteen-hand pony that can not only canter and gallop but *tölt*.

Even "civilization" here seems to offer no purchase for the mind: Nothing quite makes sense. Iceland proverbially boasts the largest number of poets, presses, and readers per capita in the world: Reykjavík, a town smaller than Rancho Cucamonga, California, has four daily newspapers. To match the rate of literary production of Iceland, the United States would have to publish six hundred new books *a day*. Iceland has the oldest living language in Europe—its people read the medieval sagas as if they were tomorrow's newspaper—and all new concepts, such as "radio" and "telephone," are given poetically chosen medieval equivalents. Roughly seventy-five percent of all first babies are illegitimate here, and because every son of Kristjan is called Kristjansson and every daughter Kristjansdóttir, mothers always have different surnames than their children. Every citizen of Iceland—even an erstwhile Wu Ziyang—must acquire a traditional Icelandic name, and the only exception ever made to this—for Vladimir Ashkenazy—prompted one disgruntled exile to ask if he could take on the new Icelandic name of Vladimir Ashkenazy. People are listed in the phone book by their first name, which does not make life easy when the Jons alone take up thirty columns of the country's directory (the hotels section of the Yellow Pages does not even fill a column).

Iceland is one of the largest islands in the world, yet so intimate that it has the same kind of tranquil dottiness as the northern village in the movie *Local Hero:* Every day promises to fetch up enigmatic mermaids, unlikely rock and roll bands, and the same faces that you saw yesterday and the day before. The first day I ever spent in Surprise City (as Reykjavík is called), I saw golden-haired princesses and sword-wielding knights enacting fairy-tale sagas on the main bridge in the capital. I came within two feet of the president (who seemed, unguarded in the street, just another elegant, blond single mother). And while staring at some life-size chess pieces in the center of town, I was interviewed by the biggest daily newspaper, *Morgunbladid,* so astonished were its reporters to see a foreign face. The Salvation Army hostel is only four doors away from the parliament building here, and the parliament building itself is a modest two-story house with a doorman less imposing than those in the nearby pubs. Prisoners are sometimes allowed to go home for the holidays, and on the main road out of town you can see the country's Nobel laureate in literature, Halldór Laxness, still writing at the age of eighty-nine.

Yet there is something deeper about the uncanniness of the place, something arising from its silences and space. You can feel it in the contained intensity of many people here, in the enormous calm with which they say *já,* and in the echoing way they say nothing at all. You can see it in their eyes, as shockingly beautiful, often, and as blue, as the sea suddenly glimpsed around mountain curves. You can sense it in the almost archetypal elementalism of the place, where honey-cheeked beauty queens rub cheeks with hatchet-faced yahoos (it is, as Jan Morris saw, the perfect setting for "Beauty and the Beast"): You can feel it in the settledness of the place, the weighty sense of *gravitas*. It is easy to believe, in this uninhabited space, that you are living once more amid the mead halls and monsters of *Beowulf,* within a tiny circle of light surrounded by an encroaching dark; it is easy to believe that the Irish hermits and the Viking warriors, who were the earliest settlers on the island, still possess it with their ascetic calm and violence. There is something allegorical—not quite real—about the place that inspired Tolkien's Middle Earth and Wagner's *Ring.* Iceland was, in the Middle Ages, the literal location of hell; Jules Verne's explorers came here to find the center of the earth; and for the Nazis, its pure-blond racial clarity made it a kind of Aryan paradise (Auden quoted an unnamed Nazi as declaring, *"Für uns Island ist das Land"*). Iceland may be many things, but it is not your average country.

It is always difficult, even dangerous, to return to a world that has transported you, and epiphanies rarely repeat themselves. Yet I was determined to see Iceland outside the spell of its midsummer nights' dreams, in the lunar segment of its cycle. Last fall, therefore, I returned to the place I kept on dreaming about. Icelandair is the only carrier that flies to Reykjavík from the United States, linking its capital with Baltimore and now Orlando (as well as with New York). Keflavík is the only airport in Europe that has a duty-free shop for *arrivals,* which customarily was packed with Icelanders stocking up on beer. The most comfortable seats on Icelandair are in Saga class, and its stunning cabin attendants sometimes wear leather gloves. Many Americans know Iceland only as the place they were obliged to visit on what was, for years, the cheapest flight to Europe; now, ironically, Iceland is by some measures the most expensive country in the world (a fifteen-minute phone call from my hotel to Japan cost me $175).

Yet none of this prepared me for the biggest shock of all, when I stepped out of the airport: The whole place was dark. In all the time I had spent there in the summer, I had never seen it dark. And dark awakens something passionate and primeval in the land, some buried, burning intensity. Our bus bumped across a rainy emptiness, with here and there a few modernist blocks and eerie, red-lit geodesic domes winking in the blue-black sky: a high-tech, lit-up vision of surreal desolation. Reykjavík, at eight-thirty in the morning, was cradled in a northern silence. There is an extraordinary stillness to the place, as if it were held in suspended animation, its red roofs shining placid in the unpolluted sky. The overwhelming impression, on the tiny, empty street where I was staying, was of silence and of dark.

It is, of course, the changes that one notices most quickly when one comes back to any place, and it did not take me long to find that beer is now legal and that there are two TV stations, broadcasting even on Thursday. I saw an *I Was a Teenage Zombie* album amid the slabs of strange fish and the jars of bee pollen in the Reykjavík flea market (held every Saturday in an underground parking lot beneath the central bank); and Filipino women in flowing Islamic robes were walking down the street. The Holiday Inn has come to Reykjavík now, and the Hard Rock Cafe. There is karaoke too, and neon.

Yet again and again I felt I was in an Alice-like wonderland. Soon after arrival, I inquired about a day-trip (to Greenland); an eight-hour tour cost $460. I called for a cab and was picked up in a Mercedes driven by a hearty, shining matron. I walked to the Hotel Loftleidir for lunch and was treated to the sight of Anatoly Karpov, former chess champion of the world, sitting in a ring of light at one end of an auditorium, above a tiny chessboard, watched by eight old men in anoraks. Two hours later, I was being harassed by a Greenlandic dancer with black stripes down his face and a clothespin in his mouth that he kept pushing in and out at me.

By any standards other than Icelandic ones, Reykjavík is still a quaint and quiet place, as silent as a photograph. It resembles, like most of the settlements in Iceland, a kind of Lego town—rows of tiny, clean white boxes set out in geometric grids, with roofs of red and blue and green. Much of the country feels as if it were made for children—even the ponytailed boys and ring-nosed girls are pushing baby strollers—and Reykjavík might almost be a small child's toy, as clean and perfect as a ship inside a bottle. Iceland is famous for having no mansions and no slums, in much the same way that its language has no accents and no dialects: With a population smaller than that of Colorado Springs, uniformity is not hard to achieve. And because nearly all the houses are geothermically heated, the city, whose name means "smoky bay," shines silent in the smokeless air, as clear as if seen through panes of polished glass. Reykjavík is one place where it really is worth climbing the highest building in town to see the city, mute and motionless, laid out against the silver sea.

Yet it is not because of the capital but in spite of it that most visitors come to Iceland; desolation is what they seek and find. More than eighty percent of the country consists of nothing but ice fields, barren mountains, lava, and tundra. Huge stretches are as blank and inhospitable as anything in the Australian Outback. Such settlements as do exist look like suburbs in search of a city. A solitary farmstead here, a lonely lighthouse there, occasionally an isolated steeple: a small huddle of concrete inside a giant's rough paw. Nature adores a vacuum here. And the ground itself is like nothing so much as a geologist's textbook, a pockmarked mass of volcanic craters and hissing plumes of smoke till it looks as if the earth itself is blowing off steam, and the soil in parts is so hot that only a few inches down you can actually boil an egg. In Iceland, in John McPhee's happy phrase, "the earth is full of adjustments, like a settling stomach."

The largest glacier in Europe is somewhere in this nothingness (it is more than three times the size of Luxembourg), and the largest lava field in the world; the oldest parliament in Europe was set up on this youngest soil. Samuel Johnson used to boast of reciting a whole chapter of *The Natural History of Iceland* by the Dane Nils Horrebow. That was Chapter LXXII, "Concerning snakes." It reads in its entirety: "There are no snakes to be met with throughout the whole island."

The other factor that accentuates the bleak and weather-beaten beauty is the climate. In October, already a wild white quilt swaddles the countryside, and the sun shines silver over silver lakes. The view from a bus is identical to that from a plane thirty thousand feet above the Pole. Icelanders will tell you that because of the Gulf Stream that country has no extremes of temperature. Some years see no snow at all in Reykjavík, and the lowest temperature recorded in the capital in thirty years is minus fifteen degrees Fahrenheit. But the absence of extremes also means that it is never, ever warm. In summer, when I was here, people were complaining of a heat wave when the temperature hit a chilly fifty-four degrees.

In this unaccommodating world, it is not surprising that the people who come here are often as unorthodox in their way as the locals. Yet the country seems to bring out something pure in visitors, something a little bit out of the ordinary. The most luminous translations of modern Icelandic poetry into English, for example, were composed by a recent U.S. ambassador to Iceland, Marshall Brement, who has written beautifully of how Icelanders were the great European poets of the twelfth and thirteenth centuries and how, even now, on one night a year every member of parliament

must speak in rhyme. And though the island's attraction to photographers (Eliot Porter) and poets (from Auden and MacNeice to
Leithauser) may be self-evident, it seems to evoke something poetic in even the everyman. I once asked a young Danish student,
who had chosen to live here for a year, what was the most exciting
thing to do in Reykjavík. He thought for a long, long time. Then,
looking a little sheepish, he said, "Well, for me, I like walking at
night in the Old Town, seeing the old houses. Or, if you can go a
little bit out of Reykjavík, if it is cold, like tonight, you can see the
northern lights."

That kind of calm transparency is, inevitably, harder and harder
to maintain as the villages of Iceland get drawn into the shrinking
global village. For ten centuries now, the island has preserved its
own culture and Old Norse diphthongs by living apart from the
world, remote from changing realities. For centuries Iceland has
been a kind of hermit among nations, a private, inward-looking
odd-place-out of fishermen and visionaries and poets. The pur-
suits for which it has been famous are largely solitary ones made
to ward off months of winter dark. Thus the country boasts six
chess grandmasters and recently placed first in the World Contract Bridge Championship. The most famous Icelander in England, Magnus Magnusson, is, appropriately enough, the host of
a fiendishly difficult quiz show, *Mastermind* (when I looked up
the name in the phone book, I found fifty-three Magnus Magnus-
sons). Iceland is a kind of conscientious objector to modernity,
out of it in all the right ways and priding itself on being a sort of
no-man's-land in the middle of nowhere (and nowhen), a quiet,
neutral zone far from superpower rivalries.

Midway between Moscow and Manhattan, halfway between
medievalism and modernity, it had its two moments of ambiguous fame in 1972, when it was the site of the Boris Spassky–Bobby
Fischer chess championship, and in 1986, when it was the safe

house where Reagan and Gorbachev met and almost abandoned nuclear weapons. The miracle of Iceland is not just that, as Auden wrote, "any average educated person one meets can turn out competent verse" (and a kitchen maid he met gave "an excellent criticism of a medieval saga") but that the verse itself is devilishly complex. That tangled, palindromic, old-fashioned kind of rhyme has become almost a model for the country.

Now, though, increasingly that legacy is threatened. Scarcely a century ago only five percent of Icelanders lived in towns; today the figure is more than eighty percent. For almost nine centuries the population seemed scarcely to rise (it hit six figures only in this century); and by one account, as recently as 1806 there were only three hundred citizens in Reykjavík, of whom twenty-seven were in jail for public drunkenness. Today, however, 145,000 of the country's 259,600 people live in or around the suburb-sprouting capital. And the single fact of TV alone has inevitably cast a shadow over a world in which lighthouse keepers read sagas to fishing fleets and families waxed Homeric in the dark. Although the government has worked overtime to protect its culture (hence the longtime ban on Thursday TV, and no broadcasting in the month of July), its efforts have often been in vain: Iceland (which seems to lead the world in leading the world in categories) now boasts the highest number of VCRs per household in the world. In the Westman Islands, the rock formation that used to be called Cleopatra is now known by some as Marge Simpson, and the fishing crates nearby are decorated with portraits of the Teenage Mutant Ninja Turtles. Even young couples, in between talking of their holidays in Spain and their dreams of seeing the Pyramids, will tell you that purity is to be found now only in the countryside; that Reykjavík is dangerous and full of drugs; that people use the word *cassette* instead of its Icelandic equivalent.

Iceland is also more and more full of foreign faces and less militantly blond than even a few years ago. There is a Thai restaurant now in Reykjavík and a Thai snack bar (complete with a Buddha and a sign for Coca-Cola in Thai). There are Somalian refugees, adopted kids from Sri Lanka, and even immigrants from North Africa (whose children must—by law—be called Bjorn and Gudrun). In one factory alone there are ten "mail order brides," three of them cousins from the Philippines. None of this would seem exceptional except in a country where, until recently, many people could hardly imagine Somalia or Sri Lanka or even California. When I was here in 1987, I found myself an object of dark fascination to people who could hardly tell an Indian from an Indianan. Now, when I went to restaurants, I was greeted with a polite, unsurprised *Godan dag* in Icelandic.

A middle-aged matron invited me one night into her solemn, sepulchral parlor. The first things I saw when I entered were a book on the Gestapo and a picture of a sea blue sprite hiding inside a waterfall. Her grandchildren came out to stare at me, and when I explained that I was from India, they confessed they did not know if that was near Pluto or Neptune. Then I was asked what kind of music I would like to hear. Icelandic, I replied, and on came a blast of local heavy metal.

There is, in fact, a deafening strain of rock and roll in Iceland, and it is the voice of kids banging their fists against the narrow limits of their culture. With so few people in so vast a space, both elements are intensified, extreme: "Wild" applies as much to society as to nature here. Iceland, then, is an inspired setting for the Hard Rock Cafe. It is not just that the island used to have the two largest discos in Europe; or that its most famous recent export is the eccentric dance band the Sugarcubes ("I'd never been in a skyscraper place before," said their lead singer recently about her first trip to Manhattan); or even that Amina, the belle of Carthage, was recently performing there. It is, rather, that rock and roll is an almost primal statement of rebellion here, a spirit of release. It is the way the young advertise their impatience with the old ways and their hunger for the new. Garage bands are sizzling in Reykjavík, and local magazines are full of articles on such local heroes as Deep Jimi & the Zep Creams. The radio was blasting "Leader of the Pack" when I drove one night to Kringlan, the glittery new yuppie mall where the Hard Rock is situated and inside which blonds in dark glasses and boys in ties were clapping along to "The Wall" and shouting out, in English, "Unbelievable!" and "Give me five!"

It is easy to feel, in Iceland, that one is caught up in some homemade Arctic version of *American Graffiti*. The first time I visited the country, I could not believe the "cruising" rituals that filled even the tiniest places on every weekend night. In the small northern town of Akureyri, I watched a whole procession of Pontiacs, Range Rovers, and Porsches circling around and around the tiny central square until 4 A.M., teenagers hanging out of their windows, motorcycle gangs (called Sniglar, or Snails) revving up along the sidewalks, twelve-year-old boys crying out *Gledileg Jól* (Merry Christmas) in the golden evening light. But this was in the middle of the saturnalian summer, when everything is topsy-turvy—golf tournaments start at midnight, and three-year-old toddlers caper around till one in the morning each night (or one at night each morning). This is the time of midsummer madness, when people believe that rolling naked in the dew will cure you of nineteen separate ailments and that you will be granted a wish if you walk naked in the grass or cross seven fences, collecting a flower at each one.

When I returned to Iceland in the dark, though, I found that the same furious rites were taking place even in the freezing cold: bodies jamming the narrow streets of Reykjavík, "Jumping Jack Flash" pouring out their windows, the streets packed at 2 A.M., cars burning rubber in the parking lots. Reykjavík on a Saturday night is a reeling madhouse of people puking, people barking, people lying on the street, beautiful faces shining with illicit glee.

Sex? asked Auden of himself in *Letters from Iceland.* "Uninhibited." And that was fifty-five years ago! Iceland discos, it seems safe to say, are not for the faint of heart. "I started smoking when I was ten, gave up when I was eleven, started again when I was twelve," a hard-drinking girl of nineteen told me, while her friend started raving about her holiday in Bulgaria. Around us, various boys were burping, dancing on the table, and pursuing rites of courtship in which solicitations came well before introductions. "These men do not have any behavior," a young Danish boy standing near me remarked. "They are not even having a funny time." Later, I found there was a subtext to his complaint. "I went with four girls to the Moulin Rouge," he reported, "and all the men were blinking at me." After the discos close at 3 A.M., anyone who is not in somebody else's arms (and even some who are) staggers off to swim naked in one of the city's open-air pools.

Still, for all these odd eruptions there is a kind of innocence in Iceland—an innocence almost betrayed by that longing for sophistication—and it is one of those places that is difficult to dislike. Even now it seems to belong as much to Hans Christian Andersen as to Tolkien, and Peer Gynt's angels are as much in evidence as Axl Rose's. The most elegant hotel in Reykjavík puts a single lighted candle on its reception desk at nightfall. The waitress at the Shanghai restaurant is a classic Nordic beauty, with long Godiva tresses falling over her Chinese page boy suit. ("The good children do get ice cream as dessert," promises the menu, "with regards from Shanghai.") The telephone numbers here generally have only five digits, and a child's painting of a rainbow that I saw in the National Art Gallery had only four (not very vibrant) colors. Sometimes you're walking down the main street in the capital and, out of nowhere, you come across a statue of a bear, dukes up, above the legend BERLIN 2,380 KM. Everything's out of context here because there simply is no context.

Much of Iceland still has the phlegmatic, Spartan style of the laconic north. The best hotels in Reykjavík offer little more than a bed, perhaps a TV, and a Bible in Icelandic (with separate New Testament in German, French, and English); in rural areas, visitors generally stay in boarding schools. The museum in Akranes, the finest I saw in the country, offers a dentist's drill. On holidays, couples in cocktail dresses and suits munch on sheep's heads, ram's testicles, reindeer, and ptarmigan; Auden and MacNeice gnawed less happily on "half-dry, half-rotten shark." One Westman Islander told me that during the terrible volcanic eruption of 1973, he went with his grandmother to the harbor just in time to see the last fishing boat fleeing to the mainland. "Oh, well," the grandmother said as lava poured toward her, burying five hundred houses, "the last boat's gone. Let's go home and have a coffee."

Iceland has yet to lose this never-never quality. It is a cozy, friendly, Christmas tree kind of place: Even the chic black-leather girls who come into the cafés on Saturday afternoon are carrying bundles of babyhood in their arms. My old friend Kristin, now studying African dance, told me eagerly about her nine-year-old daughter's class in karate and how both of them kept strong with regular doses of "fish oil" (Icelanders, by some counts, are the longest-living people in the world). "Families are so important here," I said. She looked surprised. "They are not everywhere?"

And somehow, in the windswept silences so bare and broad that the mind takes flight, the close-knit purity of the people can work a curious kind of magic. Chill Lutheran bells awakened me one ringing Sunday morning, and I went out into the quiet, rain-swept streets, empty save for a few children, the smell of fresh baked bread, and an old crone in earflaps delivering the *Morgun-bladid*. From inside the most modern church in town, I heard choirs singing hallelujahs in the cool, severely tall, white nave. Hallgrímskirkja has the whitest, chastest interior I have ever seen, snowcapped islands misty through the windows behind its altar's cross. Across the street is the Einar Jónsson House, which opens up two afternoons a week to disclose the late artist's mythopoeic sculptures and Blakean visions of angels and ascents to heaven, all white but muscular and rugged.

And in the sepulchral silence and unearthly calm of Iceland, the religious impulse has room to stretch out and take wing and pick up light. The only thing I could find inside the reading pocket on an Icelandair domestic flight was a copy of the New Testament, and Van Morrison was singing "Whenever God Shines His Light" above the sober businessmen's breakfast at the Hotel Holt. The figure of Jesus in the Skálholt Church is one of the most haunting apparitions I have ever seen, a dim blue figure, hardly corporeal, faint as a half-remembered dream, emerging from the wall to look out upon an ice blue stained-glass window. One of my favorite Reykjavík restaurants is a medieval underground cavern lit entirely by candles, its waiters wearing friars' robes as they serve you panfried puffin in the dark. If countries were writers, Iceland would, I think, be Peter Matthiessen (whose very name and face suggest the elemental north): craggy, weathered, close to earth and sea, yet lit up from within by a high, ascetic charge. As I sailed through large caves near the Westman Islands, the ship's captain stopped the vessel, got out a flute, and started playing Bach toc-catas and "Amazing Grace." The high, angelic sounds echoed around and around the empty space.

Sometimes, I knew, the strangeness I found in Iceland existed only in my head. The flaxen-haired girls I took to be paragons of Icelandic purity turned out to be from Iowa or Essex. I did, finally, spot a dog one day, though whether he had—by law—an Icelandic name, I do not know. Every day in the lobby of my hotel I saw an old man marching up and down in red ceremonial costume, carrying a huge bell. When I asked an Icelandic friend what arcane custom he embodied, she, not surprisingly, shrugged—unaware that he was in fact the town crier of Lambeth, in London, sent here by the British Department of Trade and Industry.

Other times, though, I knew there was something going on in the chilly, haunted silences. After awhile the preternatural stillness of the treeless wastes can get to you and inside you, and you can feel a Brontëan wildness in the soil. With its uncommonly beautiful people, its island curiosity, its closeness to traditions and tales, Iceland resembles nowhere so much as Java, its spellbound air charged with an imminence of spirits. Cold winds whistle through rows of white crosses on the black moor outside Akranes. The distinctive feature of the Icelander, for Sir Richard Burton, was "the eye, dark and cold as a pebble—a mesmerist would despair at the first sight." From my bed at night I could see nothing but a white cross shining in the dark.

Something in Iceland arouses the most passionate feelings in me; it picks me up and will not let me go. On my first trip to the island, disoriented by the never-ending light, I stayed awake all night in my hotel uncharacteristically writing poems. But this time too, in the emptiness and dark, I could not sleep and found myself alone at night with feelings I could not scan, the wind so fierce outside my window it sounded like the sea. Sometimes it feels as if the forty miles or so that people can see across the glassy air here they can also see inside themselves; as if, in this penetrating emptiness, you are thrown down and down some inner well.

Sometimes it feels as if the land itself almost invites you to see in its changing needs a reflection of your own, and in the turning of the seasons, some deeper, inner shift from light to dark.

"Especially at this time of year, people have many different feelings here," a car mechanic named Olafur explained to me one night. "In the dark they have much time to think of God—and of other things in that direction."

1992

ICELAND'S HOT SPRINGS

The best of the country's famous hot spots

 It's the rare traveler who, upon arriving in this volcanic hotspot on the edge of the Arctic Circle, isn't moved by the landscape's raw, unearthly beauty. Best of all? You can experience it while taking a soak.

While the majority of this unspoiled country consists of ice fields and tundra, there are in fact some 250 geothermal areas producing more than eight hundred steam-billowing hot springs. Most visitors make the capital city of Reykjavík their home base and take charter buses to all other less-inhabited points throughout the country. There is only one major commercial road, Ringroad, which circumnavigates the island. Fortunately, long-distance charter buses and four-by-fours are common, and services can be arranged through hotel concierges in the city. One of the largest bus organizations, BSÍ, is based in Reykjavík and publishes a thorough timetable of departures and schedules for several outfitters that run countrywide explorations (bsi.is). Here are the hot spots most worth a visit.

BLUE LAGOON

Smack in the center of the lava field, the Blue Lagoon's unreal blue waters—runoff from a nearby geothermal power plant—attract locals and visitors alike. The silica-laden liquid, which ranges from 95 to 105 degrees, flows through a spacious main pool and three smaller hot tubs. The modernized lagoon, which underwent a facelift in the 1990s, now includes a cavelike sauna carved into the surrounding lava, changing facilities, spa treatments, and a restaurant and snack bar to keep soakers blissfully satisfied. Situated south of the Keflavík Airport, near Grindavík, the Blue Lagoon is serviced by a public van that makes pickups from hotels throughout the capital city (354-420-8800; bluelagoon.com).

LAUGAR

Just north of the Snæfellsnes peninsula in Western Iceland, on the Hvammsfjörður fjord, the town of Laugar is punctuated by several old baths, geothermal springs, and hiking trails. Here, look for remnants of the historical bathing pool used by Guðrún Ósvífursdóttir, a figure from Icelandic sagas. During the summer months, a hotel and small folk museum operate out of an old school building. It's also worth a visit to the Sælingsdalur Valley, whose springs once served as a stopping point for travelers making the journey back and forth from the Westfjords.

LANDMANNALAUGAR

Located near the outskirts of the Torfajökull volcanic district in the south, Landmannalaugar, which sits nearly two thousand feet above sea level, is one of Iceland's largest geothermal fields. Black lava fields and towering rhyolite peaks mark this desertlike landscape. Landmannalaugar anchors the Fjallabak Nature Reserve (english.ust.is), whose activities include hiking, swimming, and fishing for trout. Open daily, a soak in Landmannalaugar's simmering mineral-rich water is distinguished by its unusual flow, the result of a mixture of subterranean volcanic activity and the glacier-fed frozen waters on the surface. Midsummer draws the largest crowds, who flock to the springs for their purported healing properties.

HVERAVELLIR

Perched in the mountainous highlands between two glaciers, Hveravellir has both steam and water hot springs. With their natural jets of steam and silica-lined deep blue water, the pools resemble nothing so much as hot tubs. Bathing is permitted in one of the hot springs near the huts. Due to its remote location in central Iceland, a visit to Hveravellir is best made in the summer months, when the nearby accommodations, which include two sparsely appointed lodges and a campsite, are open. There are ample trails and several marked multiday hikes that weave through the area, the most famous being the route from Hvítárnes to Hveravellir, which takes two to three days (hveravellir.is).

REYKHOLT

The bucolic west coast hamlet of Reykholt, a UNESCO World Heritage Site, is home to a lively geyser, geothermal-heated greenhouses, and hot springs. The town was the home of Snorri Sturluson, a thirteenth-century saga writer whose eponymous museum is a worthwhile stop, as it provides an informative look at the history of Icelandic saga events and writings. Also of note is nearby Deildartunguhver, the largest hot spring in Europe, which draws upon the geothermal reserves from the surrounding Reykholtsdalur valley.

Gods, Kings, Mystics, and Mullahs

by

JAMES TRUMAN

Driving into Tehran from the ring of hills that encloses it, you descend slowly through the layers of smoke, smog, soot, dust, and floating debris that enshroud the city. It's an ominous welcome, but not without an eerie enchantment. In the late-afternoon light, as the high-desert sun begins to soften, you can picture a descent into a valley filled with the smoke of a thousand slow-burning brush-fires. Or, in a more Iranian image, as an approach to the ruins of a still-smoldering battlefield.

Tehran, the modern capital of Iran, has the feeling of a city under siege. Overpopulated and underserviced, it exists somewhere just a little shy of chaos. Officially the population is eight million, but most estimates start at twelve. Since 1979, when the Islamic Revolution, under the leadership of Ayatollah Khomenei, drew together the disenfranchised and the rural poor to overthrow the shah, the capital has been flooded with settlers from the provinces at a rate of several hundred thousand a year. Concurrently, Iran has undergone a population explosion: Khomenei had urged his followers to multiply, which they did so successfully that more than half the country's inhabitants are now under the age of twenty-five. This statistic is relished, and manipulated, by both sides of Iran's postrevolutionary divide: The religious hardliners—the mullahs—see a generation educated in the revolution's agenda. The reformers foresee the revolution's collapse amid soaring unemployment and a hopelessly overextended infrastructure.

The dance of power between reformers and hardliners is Iran's central (and openly debated) drama, played out in the governmental stalemate between the elected reformist president, Mohammad Khatami, and the supreme leader, Ayatollah Khamenei, Khomenei's successor (it's less confusing when spoken: *Kho-ME-nei* emphasizes the second syllable, *Kha-me-NEI* the last). I hadn't been in the country an hour before the nuances of the power struggle became apparent. Checking in to Tehran's Laleh Hotel—formerly the Intercontinental—I was interested to note the absence of the giant lobby banner that the guidebooks had warned about, the one declaiming DOWN WITH THE USA in English and Farsi. It had been hung shortly after the revolution, when all foreign-owned hotels were nationalized. I'd read that Khatami, mindful of his country's vanished tourism industry, had tried several times in the past six years to have it removed. Each time the conservatives had blocked him. So what had happened? Asking around, I learned that the president's people had recently scored a neat end run: They'd had the banner taken down to be cleaned, and subsequently managed to lose it.

I'd traveled to Iran with the thought of overlooking the country's politics and focusing on its history and natural beauty. This thought quickly disappeared, not least because Tehran itself is short on both history and beauty. A few hours in the National Museum of Iran began to illuminate the conjunction of politics and culture that has forever shaped Persian history. (Persia was renamed Iran in 1935.) The museum is divided into pre- and post-

Islamic collections, honoring the convulsive event of the seventh-century Arab conquest. But the larger story is of serial convulsions, and it begins to look like a miracle: how a barren desert sandbar was sequentially overthrown and ravaged by murderous invaders and rescued by saviors who revealed themselves as tyrants and by tyrants who turned out to be saviors, and how, through it all, a culture took root and continuously flourished, transforming everything it touched, even that which had come to annihilate it. The museum elegantly lays out this history of multiple renaissances, with the story ending in the decadence and lethargy of the late-eighteenth-century Qajar dynasty, when Persia, never colonized but widely exploited, fell off the political map. In their attempts to bring it back, the two twentieth-century shahs, Reza and Mohammad, would usher in Westernization, creating the bogeyman that eventually led to the Islamic Revolution.

I found myself thinking about the shahs that afternoon as I walked the wide avenues of Northern Tehran, where plane and poplar trees, kept alive by gushing roadside canals, shaded the pavement. I indulged in a leafy reverie about the romantic pursuit of reproducing the boulevards of Rome in the middle of a desert. Later, I read in Sandra Mackey's excellent book *The Iranians* that the trees were planted by Reza Shah's private militia at his personal behest. Each soldier was given a seedling, a watering can, and a warning: "The tree dies, you die."

A kind of fierce politesse permeates Iranian life. Formal greetings still rely on florid offerings of submission ("I sacrifice myself to you," or "May you step on my eyes"), and it's not uncommon to see two men stranded in a doorway, each pleading for the other to go through first. In their homes, to which any foreigner is instantly invited, Iranians are profoundly gracious and polite. Behind the wheel of a car, they are the opposite. Driving etiquette in Tehran is modeled after the chariot race in *Ben-Hur*. Cars hustle and swarm along the boulevards and freeways, ignoring signals, road signs, and traffic lights; the action intensifies at every corner, with each new opportunity to force another car into the dust. After an especially eventful taxi ride, I told the cabbie, who seemed to speak some English, that I'd never seen worse driving in my life. He pondered this for a few seconds, then replied with the sad pride of an Olympian who had just won the bronze, "I hear the Turks in Istanbul are actually much worse."

The reason for all this urgency is not clear. Iranians enjoy a Mediterranean attitude toward their work, and about thirty percent of the workforce is currently unemployed. The after-dark activities that usually quicken a city's pace—dating, drinking, dancing—are all forbidden. Entertainment was early declared an enemy of the revolution; to the mullahs, it suggested Western pleasures and a distraction from the prescribed doctrine of prayer and family life. The richly named Ministry of Culture and Islamic Guidance was established to oversee—that is, to prescribe—every aspect of the public's exposure to art. While I was in Tehran, the hot topic was a controversial new film that had just squeaked by the censors (though seven minutes shorter than planned). Made by a young woman director, *Women's Prison* follows the tumultuous relationships among a group of female inmates and their wardens in a Tehran jail, beginning in the year of the revolution and ending in the present. It was playing near the hotel, in a small, European-style multiplex, so I wandered over for an early-evening show. The last time I'd seen a film in this genre was in the company of some furtive-looking men in a Times Square fleapit, so I was surprised to see that the near sellout audience was well-heeled and mostly couples. The film is a bald allegory of contemporary Iran—the people versus the mullahs—made all the more startling by its allusions to prostitution, drug addiction, and lesbianism. "That was so radical," my Iranian companion marveled as we walked out. I asked him why. "That's the first time in twenty-three years that women have shown their hair in a movie."

This caught me by surprise. Walking around Tehran, one immediately notices that younger women have abandoned the chador. Wearing makeup, nail polish, sunglasses, and scarves set back on the crowns of their heads, they look more like fugitive film stars than religious pilgrims. The role of women in Iranian public life has also shifted dramatically: I was frequently (though erroneously) reminded that there are more elected women in the Iranian parliament than in the U.S. Congress, more women admitted to universities than men, and an increasingly large number of women CEOs running Iranian businesses. For all that, a woman is still forbidden to shake a man's hand in public. "It is slowly improving," my friend explained, "but it's too late. Alienating women was the mullahs' biggest mistake. In Iran, it is the mother who truly educates the child, and no matter what children are taught in religious school, the mother unteaches it in the home. Consequently, young people are very unreligious."

Later that evening, I met up with another face of the opposition, a member of Tehran's old ruling class. I was sitting in the living room of his well-appointed penthouse, up above the city's endless sprawl, when, with a renegade flourish, he produced a bottle of Scotch from a brown bag. This quickly facilitated the telling of his story: One of the three million Iranians who fled after the revolution, my host had wandered the world, settling in America for a few years, but had finally surrendered to his loneliness in exile and moved back to Tehran. "Things have changed, but not too much," he said with a shrug. "It used to be that we'd stay in to pray and go out to party. Now we go out to pray and stay in to party."

It wasn't the first time I'd heard this, nor would it be the last. It was a catchphrase of urbane resignation among Iranians in London and New York as well as Tehran. My host's real feelings, it turned out, were entirely different. "The country is basically ruined," he told me later in the conversation. "There is no pleasure, no culture, no imagination. There isn't even a good restaurant left." I asked him why he stays. "I have what I need," he replied. "I like the music, I have my whiskey, and I have my opium." It occurred to me that two of the three carry jail sentences.

We were sharing our third counterrevolutionary cocktail when there was a loud knock on the front door. I made a dive for the whiskey bottle, but he waved me off and ambled to open it. He returned unruffled a few minutes later. "No one cares anymore," he said. "The worst that can happen is you have to pay a bribe."

As the evening drew to a close, both of us glassy-eyed, he began to tell me what I understood to be an Iranian joke. He leaned across the coffee table and barked, "Why is America going to invade Iraq?" Not sure how to play along, I stumbled into a conciliatory explanation that I'd prepared for such an occasion, but my host cut me off. "No, no!" he exclaimed, delivering the punch line. "Why can't you invade Iran, instead?"

The desire to explore Tehran naturally cedes to the urge to leave. I was met at the airport by my guide, Ali. He told me that my intended guide, also named Ali, had been called away on a personal emergency and that he would be accompanying me around the country instead. The setup was so James Bondian that I automatically assumed Ali Two was a spy and Ali One was lying in a warehouse somewhere, bound and gagged. On the flight to Kerman, a southeastern city bordering the Dasht-e Lut Desert, Ali charmed me with tales of his school days in England and his fondness for Benny Hill. By the time we'd landed, I was buying his story—mostly because the thought of a spy school that teaches Benny Hill routines as a cover was too exotic to comprehend.

We checked in to the Pars Hotel, recently opened on the outskirts of town and built in the oil-rich modern style—awash in marble and glass and chrome. The old city center clusters around

the typical triumvirate of covered bazaar, mosque, and subterranean bathhouse, or *hammam*—the Middle Eastern proto-mall.
The seventeenth-century bathhouse, now a museum, is a delight.
In Iran, religious and secular architecture broadly overlap, so the
intricate tile- and stuccowork, vaulted ceilings, and brickwork
arches of the *hammam* suspend it between the everyday and the
devotional.

The country's relationship with its precious water resources
has always bordered on the religious. The first deities of ancient
Iran are widely believed to have been water gods; even today, one
has to drive only a few hours through the desert before the first
oasis sighting arrives like a triumph of the divine. In their elaborate gardens and bathhouses, Iranians have traditionally sought to
summon that same experience of grace, and make a community
around it. The rituals of the *hammam* were (and still are) egalitar-
ian: the men would come before 6:30 A.M., their changing rooms
divided by profession but not by class; thereafter, the women,
who would often bring picnics and make a day of it, enjoying
massages, mineral soaks, skin scrubs, and waxing. For all we know,
they might also have played New Age music.

In addition to its old city center, the reason to visit Kerman is its
proximity to Bam, the spectacular citadel-town founded in the
third century and inhabited until the late nineteenth century.
Looming up from the desert floor like a magnificent shipwreck, it
is built of the reddish sun-dried bricks and the straw-and-mud
compound that dominated construction in Iran for more than
two thousand years. There is poignancy in thinking of Bam as the
contemporary of Pompeii—the luxury and ease of the Roman
lifestyle in counterpoint to this walled-in, fiercely guarded desert
outpost of the early Persian empire. Waves of history enfold it: A
remnant of an ancient, pre-Islamic fire temple stands within a
mosque; in a thousand-year-old gymnasium, there are still plat-

forms for spectators and musicians above the pit where men rehearsed combat—until the day when Genghis Khan invaded and prohibited all military training (as an added precaution, he murdered most of the men of fighting age). The thick walls and watchtowers enclosing the town illustrate its always precarious position within striking distance of the Afghan border. The Afghan invasion of 1722 precipitated Bam's gradual decline; finally abandoned in the 1930s, it is now being slowly restored by the government.

Bam's location on the main highway leading from Iran into Pakistan and Afghanistan means a series of roadblocks and security checks, to ferret out opium smugglers. It's not uncommon to see trucks stripped of their cargo, or sniffer dogs surrounding a stopped bus. Fortunately, the word *turista* seems to hold the same magical properties that *VIP*—or *J.Lo on board*—might back home; our driver rolled down his window and said the word, and we were smilingly waved through. A short drive from Bam is the desert town of Mahan, with its twin attractions of a grand nineteenth-century garden built around stepped pools and fountains and, nearby, the exquisite shrine to Shah Nemat-ollah Vali, a fifteenth-century Sufi master.

In the garden, a handful of toughs blocked our entrance to the teahouse overlooking the fountains; the minister of culture was visiting. We sat below and watched him, a generic mullah in a black turban, puffing on a hubble-bubble. Iranian visitors milled around, seemingly unimpressed. Ali translated a comment he overheard, a rude remark about the minister's modest height. It was hard to imagine that we were in the vicinity of theocratic tyranny. At the Sufi shrine, we marveled at the brilliant turquoise dome commissioned by Shah Abbas I, whose forty-one-year reign (1588 to 1629) is held up as one of the golden ages of Persian history. In the line of charismatic potentates that runs from Darius the Great to the Ayatollah Khomenei, Abbas imposed himself as both spiritual guide and earthly leader. For a spiritual guide, he behaved rather curiously: Abbas established Shia Islam as Persia's unifying religion yet he himself delved into mystical Sufism and Buddhism. As an earthly leader, he was a more conventional despot. His death left a gap that was unfillable—in large part because he had murdered, blinded, or otherwise disposed of his potential successors.

These became the familiar elements of a day touring Iran: a glorious drive; a beautiful ruin; the retelling of a massacre; lunch; a palace with an accompanying story of a murder; a shrine or mosque of breathtaking, miraculous beauty; dinner. On most days, lunch and dinner kept closer company with the atrocities than the miracles. The signature dishes of Persian cooking, gently spiced and delicately balanced between the sweet and the savory, are made in the home. Restaurants are the province of the kebab, and the traveler quickly becomes a connoisseur of the form: when to order chicken and when to risk lamb; how to combine the flavors of basil, mint, and raw onion to make a more interesting experience; how to gauge the difference between the many kinds of Iranian bread and how to ask for *sangak,* the most delicious variety, which is baked over pebbles in a pizza oven.

In an exotic holdover from the past, every restaurant features a drinks trolley, which a waiter solemnly parks tableside for your perusal. Two or three times a day, we equally solemnly deliberated over our choice from the always identical options of Coke, Fanta Orange, and nonalcoholic beer. This is the meal's moment of pause; otherwise, Iranians eat as fast as they drive, but with more focused attention. The typical restaurant is lit with a ferocity that puts a Westerner in mind of a nighttime sporting event. When I questioned an Iranian about this, he nodded sympathetically. "I have heard about your restaurants," he said. "I am told the lighting is terrible."

The drive from Kerman to Yazd, several hundred miles of desert highway, was hypnotizing. The magic of the Persian landscape unfolded with a nobility that has captured foreign travelers, from Lord Curzon in the eighteenth century to Robert Byron and Vita Sackville-West in the twentieth. The desert plains, in tones of sand and ash and olive green, melted away into the distant bluish mountain ranges; in the flatness of the midday sun, the colors hovered and hummed like the panels of a Rothko painting. We were driving on a stretch of the old trading route into India. Every twenty miles—the daily range of a camel—we passed by a caravansary, the fortified desert hostels now abandoned and slowly decomposing like sand castles on a beach. In service for thousands of years, they were the backbone of merchant trade until the advent of the automobile and the rule of Reza Shah, who, seizing upon the camel as a detested symbol of all things backward, outlawed the animals. Some of the larger caravansaries are being restored as teahouses or hotels, while others slowly return to the desert. You can wander through them and conjure what now seems an impossible romantic picture: the caravan trains, sometimes three hundred camels strong, hauling through the desert, traveling at night to escape the summer heat, pulling in for shelter from the winter snows; the merchants transporting carpets, silks, and spices and, through their music and stories, dispersing Persian culture and history across the continent.

Marco Polo passed along this route on his way to China, and took time to note the appeal of Yazd. It's still a charming city, with an old quarter that preserves the architecture of medieval Persia. The fairy-tale skyline, a color of sun-scorched desert, is dominated by the gothic, stunted towers that are one of Iran's two great marvels of preindustrial engineering: These are the ancient *badgirs,* or wind catchers, that draw in even the faintest breeze and circulate it through a house, while simultaneously expelling the hot air. Ali is something of a *badgir* fanatic, and by the end of our first day in Yazd, I had become an expert in Iranian ventilation. Several large eighteenth- and nineteenth-century private houses have been restored and opened to the public; with their courtyard gardens, natural air-conditioning, and underground canals, they describe the vast enterprise and invention of a sophisticated desert society. The water flows into the canals via the other great low-tech marvel of ancient Persia—a series of man-made waterways, or *qanats,* which run beneath most of the country's inhabited desert, directing water from the distant mountain slopes to the farms and villages of the plains. Out in the desert, mounds of stones every few hundred feet denote another well that has been drilled down into the subterranean grid.

The Jameh Mosque, which dominates Yazd's old city, is among the most beautiful in Iran, with its towering minarets and perfectly preserved fourteenth-century mosaics. The patterned tile of turquoise and blue, which can look so strident in the display cabinets of Western museums, take on another life in the desert, resonant with the promise of comfort, refreshment, and survival. (In Persian, the word for blue is also the word for water.)

The symbol of Persia's first organized religion, Zoroastrianism, was water's complementary element, fire. We visited several still operative fire temples in Yazd, which is home to Iran's small but openly tolerated Zoroastrian community. I was curious as to how this ancient religion survived both the Arab conquest and the recent Islamic revolution, so we went looking for Zoroastrians to talk to. First we visited Taft, a Zoroastrian village outside Yazd. We wandered beneath hanging branches of voluptuously ripe pomegranates, watching farmers water their orchards of quince and apple and apricot trees. It is one of the delightful revelations of Iran that if you stand around long enough looking vaguely friendly, a stranger will invite you to his house for tea and snacks. Our first host was a young Zoroastrian farmer who, complicating my investigation further, told me that he learned to speak English while attending a Christian missionary school in India. He described Zoroastrianism as an agrarian religion, centered around the seasons and an agricultural calendar. Its fundamental belief, articulated by Zarathustra sometime before 500 B.C., posits life as an ongoing struggle between darkness and light, overseen by an omnipotent, invisible god. By establishing the dualities of good and evil, with the accompanying promises of heaven and hell, Zoroastrianism influenced not only Islam but also Judaism and Christianity. It was the state religion during the two great pre-Islamic dynasties, the Achaemenid and Sassanian empires.

On the outskirts of Yazd, atop a steep, barren hill, sit two structures known as the Towers of Silence, in which Zoroastrians would bequeath their dead to the elements, which came in the form of scavenging vultures. Dirt bikers were roaring up and down the hill when we got there at sunset, but they couldn't dispel the windswept melancholy of the place. Inside one of the towers, someone had spray-painted PINK FLOYD in large letters, possibly a mystical reference I didn't understand, and behind me I heard the first native English I'd heard in a week. I immediately invited the voices' owners, a distinguished-looking British couple, to join me for dinner.

A newly opened restaurant in a park spared us the gymnasium lighting. We ate our chicken kebabs beside a fountain under the stars, lounging on one of the traditional carpeted platforms that hover in the breezes a few feet aboveground. My dinner companions were Sir Michael and Lady Henrietta Burton, recently retired from the British ambassadorship of the Czech Republic. Previously, Sir Michael had served as undersecretary for Middle Eastern affairs, in which position he had been involved in trying to find a diplomatic solution to the fatwa declared against Salman Rushdie in 1989. His view of the present situation was sober. "Khatami has been a disappointment," he told me. "He's making a stand now, but it may be too late for him. At best he'll be Iran's Gorbachev—the real reforms will have to come from his successor. The crucial question is who that will be." Over ice cream— the sublime Persian variety, scented with cardamom and rose water—Lady Burton confessed an infatuation with the *hejab*. "No bad-hair days, no objectification, no pressure around gender," she explained. This was, quite unexpectedly, the overwhelming consensus among the foreign women I talked to in Iran. Having arrived from a New York summer, when the sidewalks become a Victoria's Secret runway and every man an objectifier, I'd been surprised by my own reaction to the absence of sexuality in public life. What at first felt like an imposition, and then a withdrawal, gradually softened into an invitation to experience sensuality less heatedly. One day, when a young Iranian man asked me, "Why are you Americans so obsessed with sex?" I found myself at a loss for words.

After dinner, I wandered through the streets of Yazd for an hour. It's guaranteed that any walk will at some point reveal the unexpected. That night, on an inauspicious road leading out of town, I stumbled across a giant amusement park full of families out on the town with their children. Neither familiar nor alien, it was nonetheless a wild sight: the women of Yazd riding the Tilt-a-Wheel, whooping and hollering and holding on to their children with one hand while the other was clamped to their heads, holding on to their chadors for dear life.

The road from Yazd to Shiraz, another hypnotic desert highway, took us through the small oasis town of Abarkuh, once a prosperous trading center and now notable for its crumbling thirteenth-century mosque. It was the eve of a public holiday celebrating the birth of Ali, the first imam and the cousin of Mohammed, whom Shiites hold to be his only true successor. The following day would be the anniversary of Iraq's attack on Iran in 1980, which began the eight-year war known in Iran as the "imposed war." The mosque was already festooned with military banners commemorating the dead; instead of the usual call to prayer, the speakers atop the mosque were blaring slow, looping, ecstatic dirges. It was the music that had been played hour after hour in the trenches before an attack, inspiring soldiers to dash out and get themselves blown to bits in Saddam Hussein's minefields. A handful of veterans hobbled up the stairs to the mosque as we sat and watched. It was an unbearably sad picture, with no escape clause: Iranians are fully aware that Europe and the United States supplied the munitions that killed hundreds of thousands of their soldiers; Westerners are equally aware that Khomenei sacrificed his troops with an almost medieval disregard for life.

Our next stop was Pasargadae, the birthplace of imperial Persia, where in 550 B.C. King Cyrus the Great defeated the king of Media (who happened to be his father-in-law) and founded the Achaemenid empire. The site, still not fully excavated, and subject to much archaeological speculation, is a windswept, grassy plain of several square miles, interrupted by the splintered ruins of several palaces, a temple, and the tomb of Cyrus. It operates now as a kind of antique drive-in: Families park their cars beside a ruin, have a quick look around, and then drive on to the next one. While there isn't a lot to see, there's something quite distinctive to feel. The ruins are as oddly situated as the Mayan pyramids, and emanate a similarly disembodied mystery; like the remnants of all epochal civilizations, they appear to have fallen to earth from another dimension.

Architecturally, the ruins of Pasargadae are a dress rehearsal for Iran's great wonder, Persepolis, built by Cyrus's heirs. The day we visited, a public holiday, visitors were swarming up the magnificent Grand Stairway (the prototype for every profligate ballroom and palace staircase built since). The complex of ruined palaces at the top, accessible through a succession of monumental carved-stone gateways, still has the power to enthrall—its confluence of beauty, vanity, and power seems as contemporary as, say, New York City. And yet the experience can be astonishingly intimate. On this busy day, a solitary guard stood in the middle of the ruins, blowing a whistle and maniacally flailing his arms as children clambered over the huge stone lions and fallen columns. Meanwhile, there was unimpeded access to the prize of Persepolis—and the Apadana Staircase with its thirty flawlessly preserved bas-reliefs of foreign delegations bringing offerings to the Achaemenid king. According to excavated records, it took twenty thousand workers to build Persepolis; historians are now certain that it was occupied for only a few days a year, in March, for the Persian New Year. From a modern perspective, it's the biggest vanity project in the history of the world. Two and a half millennia ago, it ceremonially merged the forces of earthly and divine power in the unassailable figure of the king, an arrangement—and an expectation—that has shadowed life and politics in the region ever since. Within this imperial grandeur may lie the psychological key to Persia's remarkable resilience to invasion, massacre, and suffering: From the earliest days of their civilization, Persians felt themselves superior to their occupiers. One can understand why Alexander the Great burned down Persepolis when he invaded in 330 B.C. And why in the early days of the revolution, Khomenei's clerics drew up a plan to bulldoze the remains.

From the pedestal in front of the Palace of Xerxes (adjacent to and, one notes, slightly larger than the palace of his father, Darius), there is a clear view down to a derelict encampment a few hundred yards away. It was here, in 1971, that the shah held court before the world's reluctantly assembled royalty and political leaders to celebrate 2,500 years of Persian monarchy. It was a bald attempt to inflate his own faltering regime with the grandeur of history, and it went awry. Famously extravagant (the food was airlifted in from Maxim's of Paris), the party became a rallying point for antiroyalists and broadened the movement to depose him. Thirty years later, the shah's royal pavilion still stands, wrapped in tatters of red and blue canvas. In close-up, it has the melancholy air of an abandoned carnival tent.

As we drove into Shiraz later that afternoon, the holiday spirit was blossoming. Public holidays are traditionally celebrated with picnics, and in this city of a million plus, space is apparently at a premium: There were picnickers camped out on the traffic islands, picknickers on the grassy highway meridians. Later that evening, in the park behind our hotel, we saw perhaps two thousand of them, in groups of ten or twenty, cooking, eating, drinking, and laughing in the warm early-autumn night. Family life, a central concern of Koranic law, is rarely on such public display in Iran. Following another day of imperial sightseeing, I was struck by the innocence of the scene. By chance, I ran into Sir Michael Burton, the British diplomat, who had just arrived from Yazd. "It's hard to think we're in the axis of evil," he said, sharing my wonderment. "And the funny thing is that if you went over the border into Iraq tonight, you'd see exactly the same thing."

According to Persian legend, or at least the guidebooks, Shiraz is the home of roses, nightingales, poetry, and wine. The modern city has extinguished the roses and nightingales, and the revolution did the same for the wine. But there are several beautiful mosques, and the extraordinary Shah Cheragh (King of Light) shrine, which houses the remains of the brother of the eighth imam. It is the smallest of three similarly bejeweled mausoleums (the other two being in Qom and Mashad) and the only one that will allow non-Muslims inside. More than a million fragments of mirror embellish its elaborate domed interior, making an Islamic marriage between Venice and India, the two furthermost stations of the old trading route. The effect is otherworldly, supernatural—

how the world might appear to a moth trapped inside a chandelier, or how God might look as a special effect.

The other great shrine in Shiraz is the resting place of the fourteenth-century Sufi poet Hafiz. The importance of Persia's mystic poets (Jaluddin Rumi, Omar Khayyam, and Saadi, also buried in Shiraz, are the other all-stars) is impressed upon every visitor. As illuminators of the everyday and escorts to the worlds beyond, they seem to combine the roles of philosopher, composer, romantic novelist, and shaman. It is whispered that in recent years, Hafiz has been outselling the Koran, although no one cares to discuss it. Sufis have forever been a challenge for the Islamic establishment. A mystical outgrowth of Islam, Sufism nonetheless refutes much of its doctrine, including the core Koranic belief that God cannot be directly experienced by man. Sufi rituals—most famously, those of the whirling dervishes—insist upon a profound fusion of the human and the divine. Hafiz appears to touch upon the Sufi relationship to Islam in this poem: "The Great religions are the Ships, / Poets the life Boats. / Every sane person I know has jumped Overboard." During his lifetime, Hafiz was successively celebrated, disgraced, exiled, and memorialized. His books are now appreciated as an Iranian version of the *I Ching:* Opened randomly, the poems are believed to answer the reader's deepest-held questions. His shrine, a modest structure built in the last century, is enclosed by an attractive walled garden and teahouse, but the atmosphere is missing the grandeur of other sacred sites we visited. Over tea, it occurred to me that death was not Hafiz's masterpiece; he is among the few celebrated Persians who did not die a martyr.

A week into the trip, I was ready to break with the program. Although this involved a modest amount of bureaucratic wrangling—all travelers have to register their itineraries—by mid-morning, we were leaving Shiraz for the high Zagros Mountains. The first few hours were uneventful, as the desert plateau slowly ceded to the approaching hills. At lunchtime, we passed through our first mountain village. From the car window, I noticed a crowd of men painting a large American flag on the road surface. It was the first anti-U.S. sentiment I'd encountered, and I was unsure how to respond. A few miles from town, we stopped to admire some Sassanian-period bas-reliefs cut into the rock face. They represent the by-now-familiar military victories of various kings over the Romans: For instance, King Shapur I on his horse, the emperor Gordian dead beneath his hoof and the emperor Valerian on one knee in subjugation. The capture of an actual Roman emperor was one of the great coups of the Sassanian army. Valerian was obliged to spend the rest of his life under house arrest in a palace built for him in the nearby citadel of Bishapoor; history records that he was utterly miserable and longed for Rome.

Standing in the ruins of his palace, crushed by the sledge-hammer of midday heat, I felt fairly antagonistic myself, and convinced Ali to escort me back to town to converse with the flag painters. By the time we got there, the American flag had been supplemented by the flag of Israel. The crowd had dispersed, but three toughs with military haircuts were hovering around. Ali gingerly approached them to start a dialogue. Their spokesman, a red-faced fellow with a spark plug neck, demanded assurances that I was not a journalist. Satisfied, he explained that there would be a parade later, and that troops would march on the two flags. I asked him what his personal feelings were toward America. His red face turned crimson, and he let fly with something that Ali translated as "America is the great oppressor. It oppresses every country in the world. You are the world's great oppressor." Then he was finished. The scene was highly familiar from CNN—anti-American agitator delivers inflammatory sound bite—but without a new story to cut to, he and I were left staring at one another, bewildered as to what should happen next. Finally, his friends led him away, and Ali whispered in my ear, "Basiji. Let's go." This seemed like a good idea. These Basijis were the untrained, often adolescent recruits that Khomenei used as revolutionary martyrs—which is to say cannon fodder—in the Iraq war. Their continuing role is as a rural militia entrusted with protecting the revolution. Along with the better-trained Revolutionary Guard, they are the muscle behind the hardliners.

As we started to haul up the mountain roads, thoughts of Basijis faded. We were moving into the Iranian wild west, the land of the nomads. We stopped for the night in Yasuj, a mountain settlement that hums with the unruly energy of a border town. On main street we saw Mongols, Afghanis, and Turks, and it seemed like everyone was just passing through. Nomadic towns were a legacy of Reza Shah, an attempt to rein in the lawlessness of the mountain tribes. Instead, the forced settlements created poverty and deadly disease. The poverty endures. The attempted solution in Yasuj, decreed by the supreme leader himself, was the building of a large, modern hotel, the Azadi, to attract business-men and tourists. Six years old, the hotel is already decrepit. As you might expect, nomads are not natural-born hoteliers. At din-ner, the waiter handed us a menu listing an impressive twenty dishes. By the time we ordered, five minutes later, seventeen of the twenty had migrated off the menu. Staffing problems in the kitchen, he explained. The next morning, when I asked the man-ager to find the porter who'd helped us with our bags the night before, he looked up, shrugged, and without much surprise said, "Gone."

The drive through the hills and down to Isfahan is one of the most beautiful in Iran. The procession of plains and mountains, fertility and barrenness, unfolds like an elemental drama of living and dying. The valleys, sage green and burnt umber, red and gold, are a changing patchwork of sun-bleached rock and lush oases of clover and rice, sunflowers and wheat, framed by groves of oak and walnut trees. In the simple, irrigated squares and rectangles of these cultivated oases, you can see the origins of the Persian garden, and also a model for the enclosed, open-air courtyard of the Persian mosque. The fanfare of blue tile and mirrored mosaics that dances before the eye in the mosque or shrine surely consecrates the wonder of the oasis. Likewise, the landscape illuminates one of the more otherworldly Persian innovations—the elaborate stepped moldings known as stalactites, which sometimes decorates domes and recesses. In the hard sunlight of early morning, the mountains take on the same honeycomb formations, mysterious and imposing.

The last golden age of Persian Islamic architecture occurred in the early seventeenth century under Shah Abbas I, who built his royal capital in Isfahan. Like most sophisticated cities, Isfahan is routinely referred to as the Paris of its region, and its combination of formal spaces and romantic architecture in fact gives the comparison some merit. The sprawling Zayandeh River divides the city, and the antique stone bridges that traverse it are a wonder of organic engineering. While traffic and pedestrians scuttle across the upper levels, the lower layers, with their lovely open-air teahouses, consummate the Persian love affair with water. It is possible, and accepted, to sit cooling one's feet in the water while waiters hop across the stone pedestals planted in the river, delivering tea, ice cream, and hookah pipes stuffed with scented tobacco. While we were reclining in the teahouse beneath the most famous of Isfahan's bridges, the Pol-e Khaju, we were momentarily bothered by a band of young beggars, the first I'd seen in Iran. After a waiter came by to shoo them away, they sat at a table, ordered tea, and paid their bill before wandering off. No one seemed to find this peculiar.

The centerpiece of Isfahan is the vast Emam Khomenei

square, created in the early seventeenth century by Shah Abbas to accommodate his palace and two magnificent mosques. The square, now a garden, once held a giant polo field, and the palace's elevated terrace was the royal box, from which spectators observed the games and, on occasion, public executions. Two flights up from the terrace, sequestered on the top floor, an exquisitely ornate music room hints at the pleasures of palace life. Then as now, music occupied an ambiguous position between the profane and the sacred. In the nearby Chehel Sotun Palace, built by Shah Abbas II, murals show court musicians entertaining royal visitors; in one panel, a group of dancers strike temptress poses, their breasts daringly revealed through sheer tops. Iran's hard beauty begins to soften in Isfahan. Perhaps its most Parisian aspect is the note of sensuality that glides beneath the surface—even the surrounding mountains, a distant, milky lavender, have a velvet softness. Approaching the monumental Eman Mosque, the city's Notre-Dame, I noticed for the first time that the familiar combination of thrusting minaret and voluptuous dome speaks of earthly as well as divine union. The Emam Mosque is a textbook masterpiece—the apotheosis of the art and science of Islamic architecture. Across the square, the smaller Sheikh Lotfollah Mosque may be Isfahan's true treasure. I found myself wandering back at different times of day to catch a new effect of light on the domed sanctuary interior, whose arrangement of glazed and unglazed tile, blue and lemon and pale rose, shone and glowed in ever-shifting counterpoint. Two weeks of intensive mosque immersion had begun to initiate my Westerner's eyes: Far from being hieroglyphic riddles, the wild colors and patterns emerged as explosions of life, molecular and biological, caught in a single moment of perception. One surrenders to it without sentimentality or storyline.

I'd been hoping to sit down with a mullah before leaving Iran, but the ones I'd encountered so far hadn't displayed much chattiness.

En route to Tehran, in the town of Kermanshah, we loitered outside the local madrasah (theological school) and soon fell into conversation with a handsome young cleric, Ashrafi, who agreed to discuss Islam with the foreigner. He insisted that this be over dinner at his house, after he had led evening prayers at the local mosque. His home was a modest pair of rooms, off a communal courtyard in a quiet back alley of the city, that he shared with his wife (most mullahs, even ayatollahs, are married). The room we sat in—on the floor, in traditional style—was littered with recent wedding presents: a still bubble-wrapped washing machine, a tiny TV, a chest of drawers, and, most implausible, a large Mickey and Minnie Mouse floor rug that served to invalidate most of my questions about anti-Western hysteria in the Muslim world.

Ashrafi patiently laid out the fundamentals of Shia Islam: the codes of personal ascetism, social responsibility, and humility before God that form the core of Koranic governance. He discreetly sidestepped the question of whether religious devotion and political power can coexist. He was born at the time of the revolution and educated in the politically charged theological schools of the post-Khomenei era, yet his interest in politics seemed oddly remote. It may have been self-censorship, but it more closely resembled exhaustion—coupled with the almost certain knowledge that his generation of clerics would not be running the government. His vision of the future held the wistful yearning particular to Shia Islam—the belief that the twelfth imam, the last successor to Mohammed, who disappeared in the year 873, will imminently return as a prophet of peace. This conviction seemed to permeate many aspects of Iranian culture: Indeed, it makes life possible at the fraught intersection of certainty and hopelessness.

At dinner, a kebab-free feast of minced lamb and rice, cooked by the mullah's invisible wife—we were joined by a friend, a crippled veteran of the Iran-Iraq war. He told the story of working as a teacher and heading off to the front to fight during school holidays. On his fourth trip he was gassed, on the fifth he took a bullet in the spine. Now confined to a wheelchair, he professed nothing but gratitude for being able to serve. Such resilience is hard to quantify: In a friend it looks like heroism, in an enemy fanaticism. I asked whether he'd be happy if the United States removed Saddam. He shook his head vigorously and answered with an epigram: "The cat doesn't catch the mouse in order to bring it to God."

I asked my host what relationship he would like to see between Iran and the United States. He paused for a moment and then answered slowly: "Iran and America were once close, and you turned away from us. And then we turned away from you. This has made our relations difficult." I found this a little flat and was surprised to see everyone else in the room nodding their heads with pleasure. Ali, who had been translating, explained that the mullah's answer had been a series of double entendres describing the act of sodomy. He leaned toward Ali to make sure that I had fully understood the meaning and, smiling broadly, finished with "Please tell your people that we will always prefer to face America."

I spent my last night in Iran with a group of Ashrafi's contemporaries. The children of Tehran's cosmopolitan elite, they volunteered to show me a good time. This involved driving madly around Northern Tehran, from party to party. Each one began the same way: We entered a private house, exchanged formal Iranian greetings, and then the girls removed their *hejabs* and coats to reveal tight jeans and sexy tops. A bottle of vodka was produced, the music went up, and the lights went down. The music was vaguely Arabic, but it was made in Paris, and the dancing was similarly international. I struck up a conversation with an attractive young medical student who told me that she'd spent a week in jail the previous year after the police raided a party like this. Like the characters in *Women's Prison,* she'd shared quarters with murderers and prostitutes. I asked if her parents were angry, and she looked surprised. On the contrary, she said that they sympathized and had pulled strings to get her out. All around us that night, the drinking and partying was a family activity: The grown-ups were more wasted than their children.

On the flight to London the following morning, the steward pointed out the mountains on the western horizon, looming above the morning mist. We agreed on their beauty, and I made a comment about the Iranian landscape, to which he cheerfully replied that we were actually looking at Iraq. But I couldn't get too excited—this current showdown began to seem like just the latest installment in a continuum of conflict. I was reminded of a conversation I'd had with a man who invited me to his house just outside Yazd. Like most Iranians I met, he was educated and worldly without ever having left his country. At one point, I asked him where outside Iran he would most like to visit. "Sweden or Switzerland," he answered. "I very much admire their culture."

Somewhat cynically, I responded with some variant of, "Huh?"

"Yes," he explained. "Their culture of neutrality."

2003

READING IRAN

The essential books

 **1.** Roy Mottahedeh's *The Mantle of the Prophet* (Simon & Schuster, 2000) tells the true story of a young cleric's boyhood, intellectual journey through the seminaries of Qom, the Iranian Revolution, and beyond. Gorgeously written and laced with insights into the world of Shia ayatollahs, Mottahedeh's classic still offers the most textured, accessible account of religion's role in Iranian society and the 1979 revolution.

2. In *Daughter of Persia* (Crown, 1992), Sattareh Farman Farmaian recounts growing up in a 1920s Persian harem as the daughter of a wealthy Qajar prince. The tumults of her story, from founding Iran's first school of social work to battling tradition in her personal life, illustrate the breadth of challenges Iranian women faced in the twentieth century.

3. Ryszard Kapuściński's collection of atmospheric snapshots of the Islamic Revolution, *Shah of Shahs* (Random House, 1985), captures the chaos and psychological turmoil of the Iranian society at its moment of great transformation. A brilliant work of literary journalism at its best, *Shah of Shahs* chronicles how the shah's court, busy jaunting to Europe for lunch, failed to notice the perversity of its decadence, as well as the imminence of its demise.

4. *Persepolis* 1 and 2 (Pantheon, 2003) is Marjane Satrapi's enchanting comic-strip-as-memoir that spans her girlhood during the

Iranian Revolution through her adulthood during the dark days of the Iran-Iraq war. Her story is told with wrenching candor and irrepressible wit, and the stark black-and-white images render her story especially powerful, turning a young girl's ghastly encounter with dictatorship into a universal tale of spirited survival.

5. Anahita Firouz's *In the Walled Gardens* (Little, Brown, 2002), a rare English-language novel by an Iranian writer, explores class tensions on the eve of Iran's revolution. Sophisticated and engaging, it is the story of an ill-fated love affair between an aristocrat and a revolutionary, set against the backdrop of a graceful world of privilege destined to collapse.

6. In *My Uncle Napoleon* (Random House, 2005; originally published in 1973), Iraj Pezeshkzad weaves an epic farce around an eccentric Iranian patriarch jointly obsessed with family honor and the conviction that Iran is run by the invisible hand of the scheming British. The latter is a constant source of paranoia fixed in the Iranian psyche, and Pezeshkzad's charming satire of this ruinous cultural tendency, told alongside a tender love story, has made his *Napoleon* the best-loved Iranian novel of the twentieth century.

7. A collection of contemporary Iranian poetry and prose, in translation, Nahid Mozaffari's *Strange Times, My Dear: The PEN Anthology of Contemporary Iranian Literature* (Arcade, 2005) showcases how Iranian writers, in the tradition of their Eastern European counterparts under communism, have resisted political repression through creative forms of expression. The strength of the compilation lies less in the translations than in the stratagems artists use to evade censorship—a practice that until now the West has observed mainly through Iranian cinema.

8. *All the Shah's Men* (Wiley, 2003), Stephen Kinzer's suspenseful account of the 1953 American coup that overthrew the democratically elected government of Prime Minister Mohammad Mossadegh, is required reading for anyone wishing to understand the hostility between Iran and the United States that persists to this day. Paced and told like a spy novel, the reconstruction traces how the unintended consequences of such interventions continue to haunt American policymakers.

9. *Zoroastrians* (Routledge, 1979), by Mary Boyce, is an accessible introduction to the three-thousand-year-old religion that originated in Iran and shaped its civilization and cultural rituals in ways that are apparent everywhere today. If the central drama of Iranian culture is the interplay between an ancient, Zoroastrian past and the invasion of Islam in the seventh century, then Boyce's work offers perhaps the richest context for deciphering Iran's current-day contradictions.

10. *Iran Awakening* (Random House, 2006) is the memoir of Shirin Ebadi, the only Iranian Nobel Peace Prize winner and a figure known throughout the world for her work defending women and children, as well as her resistance to Iran's harsh Islamic penal code. The country's first female judge, Ebadi recounts being demoted to a clerk by a revolution she supported, and the struggles she faces living and working for change under the Islamic regime.

The Glory
That Was Not Rome

by

ROBERT HUGHES

 I had only the vaguest interest in the Etruscans when I first went, twenty-five years ago, to live in what had been their country—the Tyrrhenian coast of Italy.

From Rome north to Grosseto, the coastal flats rise to a long low tableland, which farther inland gathers up into the foothills of Italy's spinal mountain chain. The town where I lived, Porto Ercole—then a fishing village, now a congested resort—is set on Monte Argentario, a spectacular and leonine mass of rock that heaves out of the sea a hundred miles north of Rome. It is almost, but not quite, an island, attached to the coast by only two thin curves of natural land and a causeway that carries the road from Orbetello. These strips enclose lagoons from whose flat shimmer in the early mornings one could see Orbetello rising like a tawny little mirage low to the water. On the seaward cliffs of the Argentario, the Spaniards—for this was a Habsburg enclave in the sixteenth and seventeenth centuries—built a string of castles: Forte San Filippo, Forte La Rocca, Forte Stella. These are all condominiums and private palaces now, but in the midsixties they were long abandoned and you could picnic on their ramparts, looking down the tremendous fall of blue air to the islands of Giglio and Giannutri floating in the heat haze, with nothing but stone, lizards, and silence for company, feeling part of a world that giants had built and then abandoned. The heights of Monte Argentario were clothed in *macchia* and pine forest, their recesses full of wild boar. Its beaches were secluded and, except in high summer, empty. The huge marina, which disfigures the Feniglia beach and destroyed most of it, did not exist. The ruin of the Italian coast by land and water, an accomplished fact by the eighties, was thus far incomplete. There were still a few fish in the Tyrrhenian Sea. At night, from a tiny balcony, I would see the boats with their acetylene flares rounding the mole of Porto Ercole in search of sardines.

In fact the Argentario, much as its few resident *stranieri,* or foreigners, fretted about overdevelopment, was still quite unspoiled in those days, and sizable tracts of it still are; while the mainland behind it, where southern Tuscany met northern Latium, was entirely so. The "cultural" resources of Porto Ercole were meager (it only entered art history once, when Caravaggio died there of malaria in 1610, on the run from the authorities), but one soon found out that all the coast around it, and the hills behind, were seeded with antique presences—the burial place of a pre-Roman civilization. For this was the *terra Etrusca,* speckled on the map with the names of ancient settlements and necropolises that went back to the seventh century B.C. It would become sacred ground for me, and its names still irresistibly evoke the wild thyme and thistles on the tumuli, the iron-colored tufa and the cool dampness of old tombs, the gray bloom on the swollen surface of black bucchero ware, the stone effigies of dead magistrates, the illegible inscriptions, the damp, tangled autumn valleys, and the quiet, almost unguarded provincial museums— Tarquinia, Cerveteri, Vulci, Veii, Norchia, Tuscania, Viterbo,

Volterra, and a dozen other places on the Etruscan itinerary, encountered many times, with many side turnings, on my rusty Lambretta in that first flush of Italian discovery.

The Etruscans are, so to speak, beginners' antiquity. Not for the professional archaeologist, of course, for whom they present a whole array of exquisitely knotty problems. But for the amateur, the semi-ignorant traveler, they are easy going, for the simple reason that—compared with the Romans or the Greeks—so little is known about them. Consequently, in Etruscan Etruria one does not feel quite the shame at one's own ignorance that attends a tour of Roman Rome: the sense that, because one has not read Virgil and Horace in Latin (or perhaps not at all), and cannot say, without consulting a guidebook, when Augustus was born or what buildings other than the Pantheon his backer Agrippa constructed, and does not know the names of the Antonine emperors or who the Dioscuri were or what the lex talionis was, one has no business being there.

With the Etruscans it is different. They were among the first of a long line of cultures Rome subjugated and destroyed in her outward march of conquest. Theirs were the unconsulted ruins below the ruins. No embarrassment attaches to not having read their poets and historians for the simple reason that no Etruscan poetry or history survived. Their temples cannot move you to awe since they no longer exist and, when they did, were hardly more than decorated sheds of wood and terra-cotta that sat lightly on the landscape. No Etruscan character stands out from the mist as Augustus or Caligula, Brutus or Julius Caesar, Cicero or Seneca, Virgil or Horace or Vitruvius do. There is no flesh of character on the bones of Etruscan history. A hundred years ago, schoolboys who had to memorize Thomas Babington Macaulay's *Lays of Ancient Rome* would recite the name of the semilegendary Etruscan chieftain against whose army Horatius kept the bridge: "Lars

Porsena of Clusium / By the Nine Gods he swore / That the great house of Tarquin / Should suffer wrong no more." But Lars Porsena is only a name, and who does Macaulay by rote today? Of the Etruscans' laws, political organization, religious ceremonies, and social customs we know little—compared, that is, with the immense corpus of information that survives about the Romans; and the fabric of what is known is still being unpicked and resewn by scholars.

Hence the popularity of the Etruscans in modern times. As Churchill said of the Russians, they were a mystery wrapped in an enigma. Greece and Rome were clear. All nineteenth-century Europe had inherited their writing, their architecture, their laws. The overarching metaphor for all later imperialism—French, German, but especially British—was the Roman Empire. *"Tu regere imperio populos, Romane, memento"* ("You, Roman, remember to rule the people with power")—Anchises' mandate to his son, Aeneas, Rome's legendary founder, was also the motto of Clive of India, Pitt, Palmerston, Rhodes. The classical revivals of the Renaissance and the eighteenth century had turned Greek and Roman cultural forms into unassailable prototypes. They represented a past that was no longer mysterious, but continuous and, above all, as authoritative as a Victorian father.

But the Romantic impulse kicks against authority. It prefers mystery to history. It wants to make up the past for itself, without the disapproving gaze of dons to tell it where it goes wrong. It prefers losers to winners and "outsider" cultures to "central" ones. Rome meant ponderous columns, the tramp of legions, the weight of law, the enfilade of stone gods and Caesars in museums. Although ruined, it was cataloged and textualized to the last fragment. But the Etruscans were unknown, and no English schoolboy was ever flogged for misconstruing an Etruscan text. Etruria, for travelers in the late nineteenth and early twentieth centuries, meant nature as culture, a wild coastal landscape with hidden tombs; it meant fragile pots, delicate gold ornaments buried in the earth, incomprehensible inscriptions, the echo—no more—of vanished flutes and sistrums caught by imagination's ear in the offshore Tyrrhenian wind whispering above the breastlike tombs of Cerveteri and through the blond grass of Tarquinia's long sunstruck ridges. Nothing of its people, except a few sarcophagi, their features blurred by time, stood above the earth.

It was an idea of antiquity fundamentally different from the marmoreal past of Winckelmann and Canova, one whose relics had gradually fused with the landscape, becoming one with its wildness, its strangeness. As the great Etruscan scholar Massimo Pallottino wrote in 1957, the Etruscan landscape seemed to merge "in one indissoluble impression of beauty both natural characteristics and the traces of human activity: rocks, plants, ancient and medieval ruins, almost as if the handiwork of history . . . had gradually reverted to nature's living womb."

And there are Etruscan places where this impression is vivid to the point of eeriness. One is Norchia, a little-visited ravine a dozen miles from Tuscania that, even at midday in early July, seems as deserted as it must have been fifty or a hundred years ago. Here tombs were hewn from the tufa face of the canyon, and they include two large ones designed like Doric temple facades, pediment and all, still bearing—among the wild profusion of brambles and myrtle—the remains of carved figures and animals, with faint traces of ancient paint and plaster. The other tombs that have turned the cliff face into a megalithic dovecote of the dead are cruder and simpler, no more than a slot of darkness surrounded by a roughly sculpted doorframe. At first, it is hard to tell whether they are nature or culture. Inside there is nothing, not even a sarcophagus: only spiderwebs and the smell of damp. The ravine gathers the sun's heat like a parabolic mirror, the dust of the track hangs in the air among the asphodels, your eyes sting with sweat, and a kite circles, uttering its thin *eee-eee* of alarm. You feel like looking over your shoulder at something that cannot be there. Haunted, it seems, by midday ghosts from the Iron Age, Norchia is one of the spookier places in Italy. Tombs like these, stumbled on in the wild, must have been the source of the cult of the grotto in the late Renaissance. The strangeness of this experience is recorded in Ariosto's romantic sixteenth-century epic *Orlando Furioso,* when the hero, Orlando, riding through a forest in search of his love, Angelica, comes upon such a tomb:

> *Scende la tomba molti gradi al basso,*
> *Dove la viva gente sta sepolta.*
> *Era non poco spazioso il sasso*
> *Tagliato a punte di scalpelli in volta:*
> *Ne di luce diurna in tutta casso,*
> *Benche l'entrate non ne dava molta.*

Over the centuries, Etruscan remains have been dug up, plundered, taken apart, patched into newer buildings, buried again, overgrown with scrub. Dense bush hides the necropolises of Tolfa and of Monterano on the Mignone River, inland from Cerveteri. Around Tuscania, Viterbo, and Pitigliano the provincial roads wind through cuttings in whose strata, every few hundred feet, the gaping hole of a tomb is exposed, now converted into a chicken cave or a storage grotto. Stone coffins, their portrait lids long lost, become cattle troughs. On the Colle di San Pietro, outside Tuscania, stands a superb Romanesque church long desecrated, a Christian edifice built over a Roman acropolis that, in turn, sits on an Etruscan one: Its crypt is a forest of Etrusco-Romanesque columns, no two the same, dug by thirteenth-century workmen from the layers and reused, while many of the carvings patched into the facade are Etruscan images turned to Christian purposes. Forgotten, obliterated, the Etruscans sank so far into their rich earth that they became a kind of raw material for their remote descendants. Even in the sixties, every *tombarolo,* or tomb thief, I met—mostly the sons of local farmers—regarded the more portable Etruscan relics as a kind of cash crop, something inherent in the soil they owned, like mushrooms or truffles. Today, to the annoyance of archaeologists, they still do.

English travelers discovered the Etruscans in the nineteenth century. The man responsible was George Dennis, at the time a clerk in Queen Victoria's excise office. Between 1842 and 1847, Dennis made several tours north of Rome, by shanks' mare and hired mule, through the Etruscan countryside. He had the essential qualities of the nineteenth-century traveler: indefatigable curiosity and disregard for comfort. Which was just as well, since the low-lying Maremma region in those days was malarial, the inns in the backcountry towns of Latium and southern Tuscany were as rare as churches were abundant. "Here and there a withered bush at a doorway shows that wine may be had within; but as to an inn, except on the great highways—God save you! You might as well look for a railway station." But to research his great work, *The Cities and Cemeteries of Etruria,* Dennis trudged for hundreds of miles and wormed his way into hundreds of tombs, many of which have since disappeared, producing one of the best travelogues in Victorian literature, a plum pudding of a book stuffed with firsthand observations and recondite local curiosities. (I have been to the Villa Lante, that masterpiece of Renaissance gardening in Bagnaia, near Viterbo, perhaps a dozen times, but until reading Dennis I never suspected the existence of the Sasso Menicante, a huge and mysterious rocking stone atop the mountain behind the villa, which Dennis measured and found to be twenty-two by twenty by nine feet, weighing more than 220 tons, "yet easily moved with a slight lever.") He was not a short-winded writer, but he could carry the reader along in his spate of Romantic enthusiasm for the grotto, the ruin, the fragment, the evocative landscape. One does not easily forget his descriptions of the necropolis behind Tarquinia, of the bridge over the gorge of the Fiora at Vulci, or of the now-inaccessible "Grotto of the Column" at Bomarzo, where "the single pillar in the midst, more simple and severe than any Doric column, the bare, damp walls of dark rock, the massive blocks of masonry, the yawning sarcophagus with its lid overthrown, and the dust of the long-forgotten dead exposed to view—the deep gloom never broken but by the torch of the curious traveler—all strike the soul with a chill feeling of awe, not unmingled, it may be, with some admiration of the good taste which constructed so appropriate a home for the dead." (There is something quintessentially Victorian about that last clause.)

The most read book on the Etruscans in English—perhaps in any language—is much shorter than Dennis's and one of the lesser works of a greater writer: D. H. Lawrence. It is cast in the form of a passionate threnody for a civilization more "natural" than anything he could detect in modern Europe. Lawrence visited Tarquinia, Cerveteri, and other parts of Etruria in 1927, in the early stage of Mussolini's dictatorship. He was enchanted by the wilderness of Etruria, especially by the painted tombs he visited in the necropolis of Tarquinia, with their scenes of ritual, dancing, feasting, and sex. "It is as if the current of some strong, different life swept through [the Etruscans]," he wrote in *Etruscan Places*, "different from our shallow current today; as if they drew their vitality from different depths that we are denied. . . . Behind all the dancing was a vision, even a science of life, a conception of the universe and man's place in the universe which made men live to the depth of their capacity." Mussolini's Rome might be possessed by the anachronistic hope of becoming ancient Rome again, acquiring its authority and empire; to Il Duce, the ancient Romans were the precursors of the Italians in their new age of the biplane and the machine gun. And so they were for Lawrence too. The Roman destruction of Etruria, he thought, held lessons for the twentieth century, which, coupled with his worship of the élan vital that he saw in every painted tomb and pot, inspired his most indignant flights in the Etruscans' defense: "Those pure, clean-living, sweet-souled Romans, who smashed nation after nation and crushed the free soul in people after people, and were ruled by Messalina and Heliogabalus and suchlike snowdrops, they said the Etruscans were vicious. . . . Myself, however, if the Etruscans were vicious, I'm glad they were. To the Puritan all things are impure, as somebody says. And those naughty neighbors of the Romans at least escaped being Puritans."

For Lawrence, the Etruscans, more than any other ancient people, were Nature. Their culture was arcadian, ever fresh, innocent. They embodied spontaneity: "Because a fool kills a nightingale with a stone, is he therefore greater than the nightingale? Because the Roman took the life out of the Etruscan, was he therefore greater than the Etruscan? Not he! Rome fell, and the Roman phenomenon with it. . . . The Etruscan element is like the grass of the field and the sprouting of corn in Italy: it will always be so."

The Etruscans were a kind of Rorschach blot on which Lawrence could project his own poetic ideas about vitalism and instinct. No documents existed to contradict him. And that has always been part of the Etruscans' allure. No original written sources on the Etruscans have survived; and early writing about them was filtered by a basically hostile culture—that of their conquerors, the Romans. Not only was their story written by their victors, but most of that was lost, too. Not a word remains of the history of the Etruscans written by Verrius Flaccus around 1 B.C. or of the slightly later one penned by the emperor Claudius, that stuttering and sympathetic intellectual, in the first century A.D. The Etruscans had interested earlier Greek writers, who puzzled about where they had come from, some saying that they had come to Italy by sea from Lydia and others that they were native to Italy. But as far as anyone knew—until the late eighteenth century, when some rudiments of ordered information began to emerge from the wholesale looting of Etruscan sites—they might as well have dropped from the moon and then gone back to it.

If the "problem" of Etruscan origins is thorny, that of their language is thornier still. Though they were two thousand years closer to the Etruscans than we are, the Romans thought their language an insoluble mystery. All attempts to connect the angular chicken scratches of Etruscan with surviving Indo-European languages (Italian and Greek were tried first, and later, with mounting desperation, Finnish, Albanian, and even Basque) have utterly failed. The trouble with Etruscan is that, although it can be read letter by letter, there is not much to read. There are about ten thousand inscriptions, ranging in date from the seventh century B.C. to near the birth of Christ, all of which have been read, but reconstructing a whole language from these names and brief stereotyped phrases is as flatly impossible as piecing English together from gravestones. Apart from these, the total canon and corpus of Etruscan literature is about the size of a longish editorial in the *New York Times*. There are three hundred words on a tile found in Capua, dealing (apparently) with funeral ceremonies, and a couple of dozen lines on some gold sheets found in 1964 during a dig at Santa Severa, which was once the harbor of Cerveteri—and that is nearly all. The longest known Etruscan text was found, by a bizarre fluke, written on the bandages of an Egyptian mummy that turned up in the Zagreb National Museum. It is 1,300 words of a book of ritual, though nobody seems to understand completely what it says. On the other hand, we may not be missing much:

> *ceia hia etnam ciz vaci trin velthre*
> *male ceia hia etnam ciz vacl ais vale*
> *male ceia hia trinth etnam ciz ale*
> *male cia hia etnam ciz vacl vile vale*

In any case, people *like* lost languages: They are never banal, as found ones so often are. Aldous Huxley was well aware of that when he had Mr. Cardan, in *Those Barren Leaves,* rhapsodizing to his companions in a tomb in Tarquinia: "Latin and Greek have a certain infinitesimal practical value. But Etruscan is totally and absolutely useless. What better bias for a gentleman's education could possibly be discovered? It's the great dead language of the future. If Etruscan didn't exist, it would be necessary to invent it."

Nevertheless, the Etruscans created the first civilization in Italy. It was at its zenith when Rome was nothing more than an infant straggle of huts beside the Tiber. It took the form, not of an empire with power centralized in a capital, but of a loose confederacy of city-states, each resembling a small Greek polis, which spread all over Tuscany, Latium, and parts of Umbria. This area, loosely known as Etruria, was bounded on the north by the Arno, on the south by the Tiber, to the east by the foothills of the Apennines, and to the west by the sea that bears the name of its settlers, the Tyrrhenian (*Tyrrhenoi* being the Greek for Etruscans). Practically every major city and provincial town in this area—Florence, Arezzo, Cortona, Perugia, Orvieto, Viterbo—has an Etruscan settlement under its foundations. And in fact, the limits of the Etruscan confederacy at its height—around the fifth century B.C.—stretched even farther than that: north to the valley of the Po and as far south as Capua and Naples. It embraced places that, today, are merely names on a map, spots that failed completely to sustain life after Etruria succumbed to Rome and the plains of the Tyrrhenian coast began to decay into wilderness.

One such settlement, enormous in its day and mere farmland and river gorge now, was Vulci. It is one of the most evocative sites in Etruria. A Roman highway ran through it and was carried on a vaulting single-span bridge of stone across a chasm where the river runs far below. Later, Roman engineers built an aqueduct into its parapet. It leaked, and over the centuries the water produced an extraordinary stalactite, a ragged curtain of calcified salts that hangs down twenty feet from the bridge. This, and the frowning castle of reddish black tufa next to it—now the Vulci museum, filled with pots and bronzes from the huge necropolis beyond it, the courtyard decorated with the rusted iron spikes with wooden handles that have been confiscated over the years from tomb-robbing *contadini,* or peasants, who used them as probes to find the hollows beneath the soil that indicated virgin tombs—is the only sign of old habitation. Even on a sunny day it is a funereal place, though less so than when Dennis first saw it from muleback a hundred and fifty years ago. "Can it be," he reflected then, "that here stood one of the wealthiest and most luxurious cities of ancient Italy—the chosen residence of the princes of Etruria? Behold the sole relics of its magnificence in the stones scattered over yonder field on one side and in the yawning graves of the vast cemetery on the other . . . the one desolated, the other rifled—both shorn of their glory! The scene is replete with matter for melancholy reflection, deepened by the sense that the demon of malaria has here set up his throne, and rendered this once densely populated spot 'a land accurst.'"

The earliest traces of Etruscan settlement in Italy—bronze helmets and safety pins, ash chests, urns, and the remains of wooden huts, dating from the ninth century B.C.—were excavated in 1853 near the village of Villanova, outside Bologna. Since then, the strong primitive artifacts of the Iron Age Villanovan culture have turned up all over Etruria. But their style changed quite fast because the economic base of Etruscan life was shifting from settled farming to trade.

Ancient Etruria was rich in minerals. Not for nothing are the hills between the coast and Siena called the Colline Metallifere, the "metal-bearing hills." They were full of veins of iron, copper, lead, tin, and zinc. The area around Volterra, in particular, is one vast copper mine. Etruria became the source of essential metal for the cultures of the Mediterranean—the Phoenicians, who planted colonies in Sardinia and western Sicily in the eighth century B.C.; and the Greeks, whose galleys came probing westward to set up their own beachheads on Ischia and by the Bay of Naples around 760 B.C. From there, they could trade with Etruria. Bronze, an alloy of copper and tin, was the universal substance of ancient metallurgy. Armor, caldrons, sculpture, jewelry, and tools of every kind were made from it (and harder blades and spearpoints from iron).

The Etruscans' mineral lodes were as vital to the economy of the ancient Mediterranean as the oil deposits of the Middle East are today, and their economy grew fat on mining and trading the ores. Populonia, on the coast just northeast of Elba, was a metal-processing center—the Ruhr of the ancient world. In exchange, the Etruscans demanded (among other things) gold and Greek artifacts, which is why their tombs, from the sixth century B.C. onward, were crammed with red- and black-figured Hellenic pottery, foreign gold- and silverwork, ivory objects, and even ostrich eggs brought all the way from North Africa.

They also absorbed foreign technologies. Villanovan pots had been thickly molded or coiled masses of clay; the Greeks showed Etruria how to throw thin-walled pots on the wheel, how to smelt and cast bronze objects instead of hammering and riveting them together out of sheets and rods, and how to make granular gold jewelry of dazzling finesse. After the Persians conquered Ionia (the Aegean coast of Turkey) in 546 B.C., its Greek craftsmen emigrated to Italy and found work turning out luxury objects for the wealthy citizens of what had become by then the "League of the Twelve Peoples of Etruria"—Tarquinia, Veii, Cerveteri, Vulci, Roselle, Perugia, Vetulonia, Chiusi, Volsinii, Arezzo, Cortona, and Volterra.

In turn, Etruria exported its own creations (versions of Greek pottery, and especially bronze objects) all over the Mediterranean. And they exported even more of them to the afterlife, burying thousands of vases, tripods, weapons, bracelets, pins, frescoes, and even whole war chariots in their tombs, with which the earth of Etruria was honeycombed.

By about 500 B.C., the Etruscans were at their peak of military reach, economic power, and cultural sophistication. Their biggest cities, such as Tarquinia, are thought to have held as many as thirty thousand people—an enormous population by ancient standards. They dominated Italy by land, and their fleets of sailing galleys controlled most of the western Mediterranean. But then Rome began to stir.

Actually, the foundation of Rome, much as later Romans disliked the fact, had been inextricably bound up both culturally and politically with the Etruscans. The early kings of Rome—such semilegendary figures as the Tarquins—were Etruscan, and even the famous *Lupa,* the bronze figure of the she-wolf suckling Romulus and Remus, which stands in one of the Capitoline Museums and is the symbol of Rome's foundation myth, is actually an Etruscan bronze from Veii. Most of the emblems of Roman political power—the purple toga, the fasces, and even the ivory-inlaid throne of magisterial authority, the *sella curulis*—were Etruscan legacies. The most important link of all was religious. The Etruscans, said the Roman historian Livy, were "a nation more devoted to religion than any other, and all the more so because they excelled in practicing it." And Etruscan religion became Roman religion: Having absorbed the Greek gods, it handed them on—a jumbled, anthropomorphized pantheon—to Rome. Their thunder god, Tin, became Jupiter; Uni turned into Juno, Marisl into Mars, and Menvras into Minerva. The famous Sibylline Books, the sacred prophetic texts kept in the Temple of Jupiter on the Capitoline Hill and consulted only by an elite group of priests, were given to Rome by one of its seventh-century Etruscan kings, Tarquinius Priscus. Roman soothsayers' claims of foretelling the future from the sound of thunder and the flash of lightning (fulguration), the behavior of birds (augury), or the markings on the guts of sacrificed animals (haruspicy) came out of the "Etruscan discipline" and its efforts to divine the gods' will through portents. A special college of Etruscan priests was maintained in Rome long after the Etruscan confederacy broke up, rather as German scientists would be imported to America to head up the space programs after World War II.

The Etruscans' decline began with the rise of Rome. In 510 B.C. the Romans threw out Tarquinius Superbus—Tarquin the Arrogant—their last Etruscan king, and proclaimed a republic. And though the Etruscan armies promptly marched on Rome and almost reconquered it (an event recounted by Macaulay's verses about Horatius at the bridge), they could never reestablish their grip. Little by little, the fifth-century Romans moved north into Etruscan territory, conquering the Etruscans and cutting off their land access to their southern dominions. Then the Greeks, sensing their moment, attacked the Etruscan fleet off Cumae, in 474 B.C., and sank it. As the old sources of Etruscan trade withered, other enemies moved in—Gallic tribal armies plowed south through Etruria in the early fourth century B.C., even as the Romans were striking north. In 396 B.C., Veii became the first city of the Etruscan confederacy to fall, and by the third century B.C. it had been followed by all the southern cities of the confederacy, including Cerveteri and Tarquinia. The northern city-states, such as Volterra and Chiusi, Arezzo and Perugia, held on longer, and the last Etruscan city did not succumb until 40 B.C., when it fell victim to the armies of Augustus. But it was as though, after Veii went, the Etruscans' resistance was foredoomed to crumble: Their loose political structure could not stand against the ruthless, centralized thrust of Rome. The siege of this once-impregnable city, perched on a high tor and girdled with stone ramparts, took ten years, and (legend says) the Roman commander Furius Camillus dug a tunnel through the living rock and broke upward through the floor of the temple of Uni (Juno) on the acropolis.

Practically nothing remains of Veii today: First the Romans carried off its terra-cotta gods, and then, over the centuries, local peasants—remote descendants of Romans who settled there after the Etruscan defeat—cannibalized its walls for building stone, so that even in the 1840s one reads George Dennis lamenting, "Every time I visit Veii I am struck by the rapid progress of destruction.... The site has less to show every succeeding year ... before long, it may be said of Veii, 'Her ruins have perished.'"

And so they have, but some of the former contents of those ruins remain in the museums of Italy, of which the greatest in terms of its Etruscan holdings is the Villa Giulia in Rome. The Villa Giulia is the essential starting point for any Etruscan journey. The thoroughgoing traveler might also want to visit the Palazzo dei Conservatori (one of the Capitoline Museums) and the Vatican's Museo Gregoriano Etrusco, both of which contain wonders—especially the Gregoriano, which received much of the Etruscan booty dug up throughout the Papal States. But the Villa Giulia gives you the fullest look at the material culture of the Etruscans, from their Villanovan beginnings to their final collapse. For the casual visitor it is too full. It would take weeks to really look at all the objects and images in its thirty-two galleries, and for the non-Etruscologist the parade of more or less identical black bucchero pots and bronze utensils soon palls.

But as in any great museum, the masterpieces stand out from the mass. Among them are two terra-cotta sculptures. One, in room seven, is an effigy of Apollo made in the sixth century B.C. for the roof of a temple in Veii and unearthed in 1916. When the god emerged from the earth, the archaeologist—Giglioli by name—was so overcome with emotion that he flung himself into the trench and kissed Apollo on his archaically smiling lips: And one can see why, because this figure, striding forward with such intent energy, radiates life through its austere stylization. This is the implacable Apollo of the Greeks at Troy, not the soft musical creature of the Renaissance. The other work is sixth century B.C. too: a terra-cotta sarcophagus bearing the life-size effigies of a husband and wife, found in pieces in an already plundered tomb at Cerveteri around 1900. Arrested in movement, the woman's hand raised as though on the point of speech, her husband's arms encircling her in the ghost of a caress—probably they were both holding eggs, the Etruscans' symbol of rebirth after death—the sculpture has an uncanny presence; your impulse is to step forward and say something to these young people who died 2,500 years ago. Their intimacy is spellbinding, their dignity complete. There is not a slack moment in the undulating rhythm of line and volume that carries your eye around the whole mass. No archaic sculpture, one feels, has a more elegant relation of parts to the whole.

The sheer size and pervasiveness of the Etruscan cult of death is concentrated, boiled down to its residue, in the museums of Italy. How many hundreds of bronzes, Greek imports, ash chests, and black bucchero pots of every conceivable type and pattern lie unconsulted in their basements for every dozen that are on view in the glass cases? The sum is beyond estimation. I remember, a few days after the flood that ravaged Florence in November 1966, picking my awkward way in waders through the basement of the Archaeological Museum, which had become a tidal mudbank of thousands of Etruscan buckles, fibulae, helmet fragments, figurines, mirrors, studs, and fragments of pottery (dug up from tombs, patched together, now broken again and awaiting a more difficult form of archaeological salvage). The inrushing water had collapsed the floor of the building and sucked everything out of its glass cases into the stacks below. You would have needed a clam rake to make sense of the place then, and nobody knows what disappeared into the pockets of the cleanup squads.

But if you want a quick view of the Etruscan funeral industry, the place for it is the Museo Guarnacci in Volterra. Volterra has always been known for its stone souvenirs—the local alabaster trade is famous. Even so, the museum's collection of ash chests is a surprise: hundreds and hundreds of much the same miniature coffin, each box bearing on its face an emblem or a mythological scene, each lid bearing a sculptured effigy of the dead—*portrait* is too strong a word. Volterra must have had scores of workshops turning these out, to pattern. Much of this material has a slightly native, dumpy, staring charm akin to that of rustic eighteenth-century tombstones, though it is mythologically more elaborate; after half a dozen galleries of it, one's attention wanders off. And then it will snap back for something isolated and remarkable, like the fantastically elongated bronze of a youth—Giacometti pushed to the nth degree, stiff and threadlike—which was made in the sixth century B.C. for ritual purposes that are now unknown and was christened *L'Ombra della Sera,* "The Evening Shadow," by the Italian writer Gabriele D'Annunzio.

Who knows how many such things have disappeared over the centuries? The plundering of Etruscan tombs has been going on for five hundred years, its tempo increasing with time. One sixteenth-century bishop of Tarquinia ordered the local peasants to bring him any metal they dug out of the fields. A few years later he presented six thousand pounds' weight, three *tons,* of Etruscan bronzes to Rome's church of San Giovanni in Laterano, which was being rebuilt. Every ounce of this mountain of pagan trinkets was melted down and recast into ornaments for the church. As an act of vandalism, this ranks with Urban VIII's decision to tear all the bronze facings off the Pantheon and give them to Bernini to cast his famous *Baldacchino,* with its candy-stick columns, in St. Peter's. Very little that was of Etruscan origin had any cultural authority as far as the seventeenth or eighteenth centuries were concerned. Tomb robbers were only interested in gold and in the Greek pots that Etruscan nobles had buried with them. These, with the advent of neoclassic taste in the eighteenth century, were of growing value, and landowners sought them out. Everything not gold or identifiably Greek was discarded or smashed so as not to depress the antiquities market. George Dennis, on his visit to melancholy Vulci in the 1840s, saw work gangs under orders from the Princess of Canino—Lucien Bonaparte's rapacious widow—rifling through the burial mounds, crushing the Etruscan black bucchero ware underfoot, and then hastily filling in the plundered excavations so as to lose no grain-growing surface on the fields for that summer's crop. The bucchero, the foreman told him, was "cheaper than seaweed" and not worth keeping. It was a form of Etruscan strip-mining. Horrified, Dennis became one of the first people to plead for what one would now call relational and contextual archaeology—based on the axiom that the whole site, and not just a few "treasures" dug from it, is what counts and must be preserved. "Facts . . . are now unnoticed, and unrecorded. We see in the museums of Europe, from Paris to St. Petersburg, the produce of these Vulcian tombs, and admire the surpassing elegance of these vases and the beauty of the designs . . . but they afford us no conception of the places in which they have been preserved for so many centuries, or of their relations thereto." Among the plundering landowners there were, he admitted, a few "whose views are not bounded by moneybags," such as Lucien Bonaparte himself, but in general "the mercenary character and barbarism of Italian excavations are notorious."

Dennis called for government supervision of the *scavi.* He was whistling in the wind, and not until the twentieth century would the Italian government make any serious attempt to protect its Etruscan heritage. Even so, there has never been enough money or manpower to do it properly, although things have improved a lot in the last twenty years: According to Francesca Boitani, the superintendent of Etruscan archaeology for southern Latium at the Villa Giulia, the rate of theft peaked in the 1960s and has leveled off—or possibly fallen somewhat—since then. Nevertheless, if you know the right people, a phone call will bring the local *tombarolo* to your house with a cardboard carton in the back of the Fiat filled with chipped trophies—a black clay kylix with handles like the ears of a startled hare, a Campanian pot—all wrapped in pages from the *Cronaca di Grosseto*. And from that humble level the trade goes up: There has never been much doubt, for instance, that the Metropolitan Museum's Euphronios krater, bought at a world-record price in the early seventies and allegedly from a private collection outside Italy, was in fact found by tomb robbers in Etruria and smuggled out of the country.

The trade also goes down because, despite the abundant supply of minor Etruscan material, there is also a flourishing business in fakes: Each year the new bronzes are laid down to mature, wrapped in the urine-soaked straw that before long will give them a passable enough imitation of the crusty green patina of two thousand years to fool some lucky Americans in Rome's Porta Portese market. (One enterprising bar owner near Tuscania, with whose relatives I went on a fruitless tomb-robbing night twenty-five years ago, had a small trench full of such freshly minted effigies at the back of his house, and would irrigate it after dinner. *"Bisogna pisciare sugli dei,"* he would say, heaving himself up from the table: "We have to go piss on the gods.")

Under the present laws, any traveler found leaving Italy with Roman or Etruscan antiquities in his luggage faces stiff penalties. But this only works at airports, where bags are X-rayed—the people who look for bombs also keep an eye out for bronzes and pots.

In any case, it only stops amateurs and souvenir hunters. No serious smuggler would take his loot on a plane. It goes out by road to Switzerland or by boat to France. But because the major sites of ancient Etruria have been excavated and picked over by now, the losses—allowing for a truly exceptional piece here and there—cannot be as great as they were in the eighteenth and nineteenth centuries. Nor can the finds.

So nothing is in the tombs and everything is in the museums. But the tombs—those empty houses of the dead—must be seen anyway. For painting, the tombs in Tarquinia are without equal. The most interesting for architecture are in Cerveteri, known to its Roman conquerors as Caere and to the Etruscans probably as Kaire or Kisra.

Hire a car and drive up the coast from Rome. (Lawrence did it by train, but there is no reason for you to follow his every move.) If you are in a hurry, take the autostrada. If not, follow the old Via Aurelia that meanders more narrowly along the coast, laid over the stone blocks set down for the Roman legions: It and the Via Cassia, inland from Rome to Siena, are among the most ancient paved roads in Europe. Either way, Cerveteri (assuming good traffic) is no more than an hour from the center of Rome.

Not all of it can be visited. The original Etruscan town—where, Livy recorded, young Romans in the fourth century B.C. used to be sent "to be taught Etruscan, as today Greek is taught"—has all but vanished. But you can go to the necropolis of Sorgo, where in 1836 two amateur archaeologists, a priest named Regolini and an army officer named Galassi, armed with permits from the Papal States dug down and discovered long, corridorlike chamber tombs, with a steeply pitched stone ceiling, containing the treasure in granulated gold and amber—bracelets, necklaces, and a magnificent embossed pectoral—that had been buried with some Etruscan noblewoman and is now the core of the Vatican's

Museo Gregoriano Etrusco collection. The Regolini-Galassi find was one of those events, like the discovery of the Laocoön or Tut's tomb, that helped shape the taste of its day.

However, the main part of Cerveteri is the Banditaccia cemetery, a long necropolis on a ridge where the Etruscans, between the eighth and the fourth centuries B.C., placed their dead in tombs constructed beneath huge mounds. One walks in ruts worn in the tufa by the heavy wheels of Etruscan carts. Some of the mounds are raised on circular stone walls with carved bands; the sepulchral chambers, some of which contain half a dozen branching rooms, were constructed of stone, with beds and chairs for the dead and roofs that mimic the arrangement of beams and coffering in a wooden house. Then the earth was filled in and rounded off. Thus, the cemetery city looks like a landscape of soft, enormous breasts and beehives—maternal and consoling, with hundreds of wombs (long vacated by the Etruscans) to return to, however briefly.

But whatever Etruscan places you may visit, Tarquinia is the essential one. It is thirty miles up the coast from Cerveteri.

According to one myth, which may have some trace of a historical basis, Tarquinia was founded on an existing Villanovan settlement by Demaratos, a rich Greek immigrant from Corinth who landed on this coast in the seventh century B.C. with a complete retinue of artisans, potters, and painters. From these newcomers, the primitive Villanovans learned to improve their arts. Demaratos married a local noblewoman; their son, Lucomo, went south and became the fifth king of Rome, taking the name Lucius Tarquinius Priscus.

Fact or not, what this legend points to is the lost importance of Tarquinia: how it preceded Rome and ruled over it in the years of its dominance, during the seventh century B.C. No sign of that remains today. Tarquinia is a market town, a lot better off than it was twenty years ago, but deeply provincial. Only from the museum can one intuit some of its former cultural scope; it seems barely credible that this place could once have been the chief city in central Italy. No ruins exist aboveground, because Etruscan temples were of wood and terra-cotta, and whatever the Romans left of them has long since gone to dust. There are beautiful things in the late medieval Vitelleschi Palace that became the town's museum: the pair of marble winged horses from the temple of the Ara della Regina; a superb collection of Greek and Etruscan ceramics and bronzes; frescoes salvaged from tombs; and on the ground floor the stone sarcophagi, all of essentially the same type, with the life-size figures of fleshy Etruscans displaying their magisterial bellies and gripping their paterae, or round funerary dishes, as they raise themselves on one elbow like diners disturbed at a banquet. These have a time-coarsened, realistic power, but they do not prepare you for the real core of Tarquinia, which is the tombs.

There are thousands of tombs in the Monterozzi necropolis, which lies a little way outside the town on a long ridge of tufa above a vast panorama of shore and sea. Nowhere else in Etruria do Curzio Malaparte's words seem so true: "The real Etruscan cities are the necropolises. The cities of the living were only suburbs of those of the dead. . . . The Etruscans felt that they were destined to die, in the way that other people felt destined for power and glory. You could say they were born old and died young. Their existence was like a funeral march towards youth, towards a state of incorruptibility." And nowhere else in the ancient world of the Mediterranean do the dead seem so vivid. Only a tiny slice of the Monterozzi necropolis is open to the public, but everywhere on the hill one sees the little shedlike structures with iron doors that mark the entrances to excavated tombs. Some of them, like the labyrinthine complex known as the Tomb of the Ogre, actually abut on the present-day cemetery of Tarquinia, whose stands of dark, funerary cypresses thus mark two and a half millennia of more or less continuous burial.

Not all of the tombs have been excavated—most of them, in fact, were located with echo sounding devices, under a program set up by the engineer Carlo Lerici in the 1960s, and then left alone. But approximately a hundred and fifty of the known tombs that have been dug into contain wall paintings ranging in date between the sixth and second centuries B.C. Of these, about fifty can be visited, although only half of them have lights and stairs and no more than two or three are open on any given day. (The exposure of the paintings to fresh air, light, vibration, and human breath has to be kept down, and it is flatly impossible to gear Tarquinia to the demands of mass tourism—which does not matter, since mass tourism happily ignores Tarquinia.) This is the greatest corpus of flat painting from the ancient world still in existence: By contrast, all that we know of Greek painting between the eighth and fourth centuries B.C. is based on vases, for not a single panel or mural has survived.

The Etruscan paintings are abundant and historically pure—they have not been faked and overpainted by "restorers," as have the Minoan frescoes at Knossos in Crete—but they cannot be "done" in a casual visit to the necropolis. You have to choose. Given the choice, I would take the sixth-century Tomb of the Augurs first, with its linear profile scenes of gesturing priests, thickset and ruddy, and its struggling athletes and gladiators. Not because one can know exactly what rites are honored in it—what the priests are invoking, or why the captive with his head wrapped in blindfolds has been set with a stick against a dog, which bites his thigh and makes the blood run—but because of the strength of the paintings themselves, with their firm bounding lines and their earthy vivacity of color: ochers, reds, the black of hair, beards, and tunics, set against the creamy ground. Death receded from this underground cell long ago, leaving nothing but the intense life of the paintings; death, one is persuaded, lies on the other side of the red-painted door studded with bosses that occupies one of the walls.

One would also want to visit the Tomb of the Baron (about 510 B.C.) for its frieze of horseback riders and solemnly erect cult figures; the Hunting and Fishing Tomb, for its delightful (though, alas, badly damaged) scene of an Etruscan slinger on a rock, taking aim at a flurry of sacred ducks while fish leap from the water; and the Tomb of the Lionesses, named for the pair of big spotted cats—an Eastern import—that occupy the shallow pediment on the end wall, between a checkerboard ceiling and a two-part frieze, the upper band showing dancers and a pair of musicians flanking an enormous wine jar, the lower depicting dolphins leaping, in sinuous rhythm, in and out of the waves.

Often, one has no idea whom the figures represent, although names are occasionally scratched in Etruscan beside them. But because the epic literature of early Greece spread to Etruria, the scenes on the walls can be familiar. In the tomb of the Bulls, the central scene is of an armed man lurking behind a fountain as a horseman approaches. He is Achilles, waiting in ambush for Troilus, the beautiful youngest son of Priam, king of Troy, in order to kill him and thus frustrate a prophecy that Troy would never be taken by the Greeks if the boy reached the age of twenty.

A secondary version of the Homeric legend has it that Achilles was in love with Troilus but killed him anyway. This may connect, in some way now obscure to us, with the famous *po'di pornografia* on the tomb wall above the Achilles fresco that Lawrence enthused over. On the left, a red Etruscan man is rogering a white Etruscan woman, watched by a bull with a human face—the same immemorial white Maremma bull with the spreading horns that one sees in the fields of Etruria to this day. The beast seems calm and benign. On the right, however, another Etruscan is buggering his companion, a somewhat paler man—the pallor signifying passivity, lack of virile force—while another bull, seeing this, lowers his horns and charges in outrage. Apart from the thoughtless homophobia of ancient Etruscan bulls, surely a fit subject for protest and deconstruction by the gay community of modern Tarquinia (if there is one), it is hard to know what these scenes are doing in a tomb. The moral, if any, is that if you picnic in an Etrurian field, you should be careful what you do alfresco afterward.

The mood of the tombs changes with time. Those of the sixth century reflect a basically untroubled assurance that the wealthy Etruscan could, indeed, take it all with him—wives, dancers, horses, furniture, gold, pots; that the feasting and rituals would go on after death as they had in life. But by the end of the fifth century, driven perhaps by a sense of crisis (shrinking power, military defeats), the Etruscans saw a different and pessimistic underworld full of terrors. And their tomb frescoes begin to record the great change in European eschatology: the birth of hell.

So it is with the most recently opened of the Tarquinia tombs, that of the Blue Demons, found in 1985 after Lerici's survey of the Monterozzi necropolis was finished. It was very deep—about twenty-five feet down in the tufa. Guided by echo sounders, the archaeologists drilled a hole through the roof and lowered a probe with a fish-eye TV lens. There were the frescoes. Today, with a guide, one goes down a sequence of rough wooden ladders into the resonant rock chamber with its faint images, eaten by two millennia of fungal spores. The tomb was sacked (when, no one knows; *tombaroli* nearly always get in before the archaeologists), but the thieves did not damage the paintings. The artist's hand remains, faded but vivid, in the subtle, naive twists of the brush in delineating a toe or the beaky thrust of a demon's nose. The colors are ochers, umbers, earth reds, and lapis lazuli, that rare blue which, in the ancient world, had to be imported from Egypt.

On two of the walls one sees the "old" scheme of Etruscan death—a procession, a party. First, a cortege going to the tomb, with a chariot drawn by two spotted leopards, musicians with flute and lyre, a table laden with vases. Then, the funeral banquet with guests on their dining couches—all men, except for the central couple, who must be the dead man and his wife.

The third wall, however, reflects the coming of "new" doctrines connected with the Orphic mysteries at the end of the fifth century: a gloomy, cruel afterlife, ancestor of the Christian hell. On the far left, half obliterated, is the boat of Charon, ferryman of the river of the dead. Small figures are propelling passengers toward it, and on the right are two demons, both blue—one brandishing a pair of bearded snakes, the other winged. They have hooked noses and, if you look closely, sharp teeth, all the better to eat you with. The one with the wings, a malignant angel, has traces of red on his mouth, the blood of the corpses on which he has been feasting. He is, literally, a *sarcophagus*—a "flesh eater"—the Greek word, which, purged of most of its awful meaning, would come in later centuries to apply simply to burial coffins. The faded state of the fresco does not make him any milder. Indeed, the effort of decipherment has pulled you into the image, and it is with some relief that you scramble up the ladder into the world above.

There, on the burial ridge, the grasses are dry and tawny, speckled with wildflowers and high clumps of thistles; small dust devils spin along it, and far below, there is the Tyrrhenian, shining like blue silk through air washed by the *maestrale*. Somewhere around here, according to the legends of Tarquinia's foundation, a plowman saw an apparition rise from the broken soil. It was Tages, a spirit with an adolescent's face and the wisdom of a god. He gathered around him a group of Etruscans whom he taught to become haruspices (diviners, priests), and thus the art of foretelling the future by reading the guts of fresh-killed animals was born. Tages also disclosed the secrets of geometry, surveying, and the construction of canals before vanishing, as mysteriously as he had appeared, into the earth. The plowman's name was Tarchon, the son (or brother) of the hero, Tyrrhenos, for whom the sea is named. He founded the twelve cities of the Etruscan League and spread among his people the mysteries of divination that Tages had revealed. Moonshine, of course; deep myth. But on issuing from the tomb, you think for a moment that it might have some kind of truth.

1991

ETRUSCAN ESSENTIALS

Seven sites worth visiting

 As D. H. Lawrence wrote in *Etruscan Places,* "We know nothing about the Etruscans except what we find in their tombs." Luckily, Italy's vast necropolis offers some tantalizing clues. Most of the important sites are north of Rome and many can be seen in day trips from the capital. Alternatively, make Viterbo your base, as it offers easy drives to Cerveteri, Tarquinia, Tuscania, Vulci, and Norchia. Before starting your excursions head to the Museo Nazionale di Villa Giulia (National Etruscan Museum), a papal palace from the sixteenth century that houses one of the most priceless collections of art and artifacts from the period—the former contents of the tombs. Highlights include the sixth-century B.C. bronze sculpture of Apollo (from Veio), and a bride and bridegroom coffin (Piazzale di 9 Villa Giulia, Rome; 39-06-320-1951).

TARQUINIA/MONTEROZZI

One of Etruria's most important sacred cities sits some forty miles outside Rome. This former metropolis once rivaled Athens in size and population. Many of Monterozzi's six thousand tombs are decorated with wall paintings depicting the period (from feast days to battle scenes, and of course, sex) in vivid color. Usually only a handful of these are open at a time, but because they date from various eras, you'll be well able to see the differences in their artistic styles—don't miss the Tomb of Augurs with its famous mural of the door to the underworld. The on-site archaeological museum (Palazzo Vitelleschi in Piazza Cavour; 39-076-685-6308) has fantastic findings, including an exquisite terra-cotta winged horse dating from the fourth century B.C.'s Ara della Regina.

NORCHIA

Thirteen miles northeast of Tarquinia is this much-less-visited and melancholy site, where you might find yourself completely alone exploring the tombs sculpted out of tufa in the overgrown cliff face. Two of the best-preserved still show the remains of carved figures and animals.

CERVETERI/BANDITACCIA

This huge complex of beehive tombs in the former site of the ancient town of Caere (and about a twenty-minute walk from its modern incarnation, Cerveteri) were erected between the seventh and third centuries B.C. and now contain re-creations such as stone beds and chairs—from the former city dwellers' homes (their gold jewelry, vases, and *bucchero,* the black ceramics particular to the Etruscans, have long since been spirited away to various museums). This is a rather unmanned operation, so you'll find yourself clambering in and out of the various tombs without interference. The Regolini-Galassi tomb is a particularly good example of the influence of Oriental design during the 600s B.C., though sadly it is closed to most visitors. The museum (Fortress of Palazzo Ruspoli), in an old castle on the main piazza, is also worth a stop. Nearby, the port of Pyrgi has the remains of two temples dedicated to the goddesses of Uni and Asarte.

VULCI

On the border between Lazio and Tuscany and about fifty miles northwest of Rome, this now-uninhabited and haunting spot houses the remains of a second-century villa, an Etruscan temple, and the remaining two doors of the city walls. Make a stop at the museum to see the pots and bronzes found in the tombs nearby.

VEII

For years, the bronze Lupa, the wolf figure that the Romans claimed for their foundation myth, now housed in the Capitoline Museums, was thought to have been recovered from this Etruscan site, the first city to fall to Roman foes. The Lupa's provenance has since been disproved, but Etruscanphiles will still want to see one of the greatest cities of the period, only eleven miles north of Rome. Just this past summer, a repentant tomb raider led authorities to discover one of the richest finds in Etruscan archeology here, the Tomb of the Lions, whose beautiful paintings of migrating birds date back to a century earlier than those at Tarquinia.

VOLTERRA

For a quick history of Etruscan funerary, head to Museo Guarnacci (15 Via Don Minzoni) with its collection of urns, each with its own effigy. The Giacometti-like *L'Ombra della Sera* ("The Evening Shadow"), an incredible elongated bronze statue from the third century B.C., makes it worth the trip.

TUSCANIA

On top of the hill of Saint Peter just west of Viterbo, the tufa tombs here are particularly interesting for their houselike designs, including one with a colonnaded portico.

Bella Capri

by

SHIRLEY HAZZARD

Who can say why the shape of a legendary place—hill, harbor, headland—should in itself strike us as significant, a destination? In a region whose volcanic forms never appear random, the island of Capri, lying at the horizon of the Neapolitan gulf, has grand inevitability—as if "planted there on purpose," as Joseph Addison observed three centuries ago, "to break the Violence of the Waves that run into the Bay." Among the neighboring islands of Ischia, Procida, Nisida, and Capri, only Capri can be seen from the Naples shore: at times a mere outline of greater peak and lesser, at night a small galaxy of far-off lights. On days of glassy clarity or impending storm, the island will draw forward, however, in astonishing detail of white houses, clock tower, and wooded uplands, the whole supported on vertical strokes of limestone. Even when screened entirely by mist or mainland smog, Capri is a presence, a reference to a happier, and stranger, life: a foremost example of the suspense generated by islands as they lie, enigmatic with distance, in their separate silence.

It is the privilege of travelers in Italy to visit not only the modern nation but also the land of other ages—an advantage that Italians themselves, seized with current crises, are seldom quite free to enjoy. Knowledge that the silhouette of Capri has floated, just as now, before the gaze of immemorial onlookers excites our own awareness. And, when one of the region's dramatic equinoctial storms makes the island inaccessible for days, we look with eyes of the past across the seventeen miles of ocean that long kept Capri and its people remote—distinct in dialect, customs, convictions—not only from Naples but from all the world.

Not long ago I came across the ferry ticket from my first crossing to Capri, in the spring of 1957. Throughout a winter spent working in Naples, I had looked out daily to the island, learning something of its moods and lights and its melting, gouachelike colors, intending at last to touch its shores. Today's tourists, moving in the fast lane, miss that setting of the scene, the extended waiting that gives scope to dreams and ensures that arrival will be no trifling matter. On a fine Friday morning in spring, I went to the port of Naples, where, in the shadow of the great dark castle— "the Male," as it is locally known, in tribute to its overt power— the white steamers sailed, as they do still, for the islands. My ticket records that this occurred on the nineteenth of April, that I traveled by fast boat (*linea celere*), and that I paid 950 lire for the round-trip (less than one-tenth of the present one-way, half-hour fare by hydrofoil). In those years there were no hydrofoils or helicopters to the islands of the Neapolitan gulf, the boats themselves were few, and passage to Capri by *linea celere* could take close to two hours, depending on the temper of the sea. Other steamers, moving with less celerity, called at Sorrento en route, adding considerably to the trip. None of these journeys seemed long, nor did one feel that time might be better spent.

Most leisurely of all sailings, then, to Capri was an afternoon boat carrying mail to that tip of the Sorrentine peninsula known

today as Punta della Campanella—a long, steep, sparsely inhabited headland, treeless and nearly roadless, that stands across a
three-mile strait from Capri. In antiquity, this promontory was
consecrated first to the Sirens and subsequently, following Greek
conquest, to Athena, who was, Norman Douglas reminds us, "a
parvenue in these lands of the Sirens." In later ages, Athena presided there by her Roman name, and her spur of rock, the mainland point nearest to Capri, is still, on occasion, referred to as
Cape Minerva.

Minerva's ground has long since been combed of its littered
small antiquities, and the exact site of the temple has never been
established. But to the ancient world it was an absolute landmark, looking, on the one hand, to Capri and, on the other, down
the Amalfi and Salerno curve to a southern shore, discernible
only on clearest days, where stand the temples of Paestum. It is a
setting—even now, when crisscrossed by tankers and coastal
boats—for heroic departure and high romance; and it is no surprise to find Goethe, at Naples in 1787, noting a common occur-
rence, the passage of the regular frigate for Palermo, in these
words: "With longing, I watched her spread sails as she passed between Capri and Cape Minerva and finally disappeared. If I were
to watch a person I loved sail away in this fashion, I should pine
away and die."

That, then, is the approach: the old, congested, clamorous
town of Naples opening on its vast and lovely bay; the crossing,
past Homeric scenes, to the island, whose features are slowly
disclosed—an interval in which we leave our knowing mainland
selves behind and become accessible to destiny.

The last stage of the journey is marked by a stretch of water
famed for turbulence and known as "the Mouths": Le Bocche. In
the first century after Christ, the philosopher Seneca watched
from the thronged waterfront of Naples while a fleet of mail boats
advanced through the Bocche, and identified the Alexandrian

ships by their topsails—all other vessels being required to haul down their upper canvas in those waters. The Bocche are no respecters of persons or of genius. In 1851 Gustave Flaubert wrote of his visit to Naples: "I was set on going to Capri; and very nearly remained there—in the deep. Despite my prowess as a boatman, I thought my last hour had come, and I confess I was worried and even afeared, much afeared. I was within an inch of annihilation."

In the lee of the island, the sea is calm, deep, and deeply colored. The pale, dramatic cliffs are reddishly weathered. Above the bright boats and houses of the port, the town of Capri clusters like a Casbah in the saddle between two green heights. There are shouts, sounds, and seaside smells; there is animation. There are people—porters, boatmen, purveyors of souvenirs; and a solid, cheerful dame selling peaches or figs: in short, the Capresi, who had not until now figured in one's expectations. Even in the pandemonium of Easter or August, these people of the Marina Grande maintain the fundamental calm of persons accustomed to providing first—and last—impressions, and to supplying, unjaded, that essential element of welcome, reassurance.

The brief ascent from port to town passes—whether by road or funicular—between lemon groves and vineyards and walls overgrown with flowering vines. Even an abominable little stretch of busy road that, crammed in summer with tourist buses, precedes the town of Capri, appears merely as a last, confirming test, analogous to the Bocche. One walks away from this on a broad terrace that looks over the bay and is itself overlooked, in turn, by the Anacapri slope and the rock face of Monte Solaro, crowned by the high, solitary rockbound little church of Santa Maria a Cetrella. On fine days here—and fine days are frequent—the air and light are pure, and the island appears as a great garden risen from the sea. Every pleasure is intensified, rather than beclouded, by the dark, reminding form of Vesuvius, imponderable on the Naples shore.

One feels straightaway that this beauty is not banal. Although much silliness occurs here, the island itself is not inane. Nor is it innocent, amenable to the sunshine phrases of resort brochures. There is something formidable about Capri. In the nineteen-fifties, W. H. Auden wrote from Ischia of "sheer-sided Capri who by herself defends the cult of Pleasure, a jealous, sometimes a cruel, god"—and in fact the island exerts a mastery over its visitors. With this, antiquity has much to do, and the mystery intrinsic to places of ancient fame. What has been so long in the making cannot be abruptly dispelled.

As yet, Capri retains some glimmering of an earliest identity, acquired before the era of the Romans—before that time, two thousand years ago, when all this region became a resort and, for cultivated Romans, a means of revisiting Hellenic life. Naples and its surroundings were then already a survival from the Greek world—having, as Gibbon relates, "long cherished the language and manners of a Grecian colony." Though nearby islands came to be dominated by fortresses and prisons, Capri was the chosen residence of emperors, whose mighty constructions, assimilated now like natural formations, remain encrusted on height and shore. The ports and porticoes of the Romans, their palaces and cisterns and watchtowers, still dictate, even in ruin, the island's temperament and command its attention—as do the massive blocks of Greek wall and the perpendicular Phoenician Stairs, five hundred rock-hewn steps that fall plumb from mountainside to sea.

In the summer of A.D. 14, the dying Augustus revisited his Capri villa for the last time, and from Capri, in later years, his heir Tiberius ruled the world. The name of Tiberius, variously rendered, prevails on the island today, denoting districts; naming wines, walks, hills, dogs, hotels, and restaurants. (A statue of the Madonna, placed on the summit of the imperial villa that Tiberius named for Jove, was lately exploded by a bolt of lightning. The future of her outsize bronze replacement, set on the same pedestal by a U.S. Navy helicopter, bears watching.)

The little piazza of Capri, the Piazzetta, was once the cloister of its presiding church—that "queer bubbly *duomo*," D. H. Lawrence called it, that stands on its own elevation above the square. At piazza level, the crypt of the church has long since been hollowed out to create an indispensable café: the Bar Tiberio. Here, from May through October, the crowds surge and circle, while the Capresi pass among them, intent on the business of an island that now depends exclusively on tourism. With the coming of November, a month of brilliant mornings and chill, early dark, the piazza grows empty at evening, resembling by midnight nothing so much as . . . a deserted cloister.

Is Capri spoiled? Given the facts of its modern life—the unchecked onslaught of summer crowds, the rapacious speculation in building, the neglect or mutilation of its monuments—Capri should indeed be spoiled. That so much beauty lingers—ravishing along the quiet paths and farthest walks, and on the long western descent of Anacapri, with its olive groves and molten sunsets—is another of the island's mysteries, abetted by precipitous cliffs unfavorable to "development." I do not know how long this extraordinary rock can preserve its character—can shed, each autumn, the glossy bosoms and bottoms of expensive summer days and produce again its nights of supernatural silence, interspersed as they are with grand nocturnal storms in which every declivity and grotto reverberates and the face of the mountain flares with lightning all night long. Capri is a microcosm of the planet itself, and its expectations are bound up with those of all the earth. For myself, I expect to arrive, throughout my lifetime, in this beloved place with the same joy—hoping that on certain evenings a smudge of candlelight will testify, as ever, to a solitary presence on the mountaintop, at a still-remote Cetrella.

1991

Capri's best walks and views

 The combination of Capri's legendary beauty and its proximity to the mainland makes it an irresistible magnet for day-trippers, but if you are fleet of foot and willing to walk off the main tourist track, you'll also find some of the most spectacular views in all of Italy.

Shoulder season is the best time to visit Capri—April, May, September, and October are the months to book—though even in the winter the temperature hovers around fifty degrees (many hotels and restaurants close from November to March).

Catching a boat from Naples is easy: A forty-five-minute hydrofoil from the Molo Beverello dock is the quickest ride, while a *traghetto* (ferry) takes twice the time but is half the price (call 39-081-551-3882 for schedules for both). For Sorrento departures, go to the dock right by Piazza Tasso for the twenty-minute hydrofoil ride (39-081-807-3024), or from Positano to Capri, book in advance with Alicost (39-089-871-483). Once there, these are the vistas most worth a walk:

- Walk or take a chairlift (the station is right by Piazza Vittoria) from Anacapri up to Monte Solaro; at 1,932 feet, this is the highest point on the island, and, arguably, the very best views—you can even see the island of Ischia in the distance (the station is at 10 Via Caposcuro).

- Villa Jovis: The best way to get here is via a forty-five-minute hike from Capri town, following villa signs along

Via Croce and Via Tiberio. At the top, the whole of the Gulf of Naples provides the spectacular backdrop; on clear days, you'll see the Gulf of Salerno as well. After, head to "Tiberius's Leap," where—after touring the ruins of the emperor's pleasure palace—you'll be able to enjoy the jaw-dropping perspective into the sea. During Tiberius's time, it was the last thing disobedient servants and unwanted visitors would see before being thrown from the precipice (Via Tiberio).

• Hotel owners are smart about their real estate, hence their proprietorship over some of the island's best vistas. But you don't have to stay over to enjoy them. Stop for lunch or an *aperitivo* at Hotel Caesar Augustus: the thousand-foot view takes in Mount Vesuvius and Sorrento; Hotel Villa Brunella, with its fabulous perspective of the Marina Piccola and Capri town; and La Scalinatella, overlooking the ocean and pretty gardens. You'll understand why guests like to look at these views for weeks at a time.

• La Scala Fenicia (the Phoenician Stairway) might be the world's best natural StairMaster (complete with incredible views down to the Marina Grande and up to the rock of Capodimonte). Until 1874, the climb up the stone steps—which were lovingly restored in 1998—was the only way to get from Capri to Anacapri.

• At Da Gelsomina alla Migliera, a family-owned trattoria built into the cliffs under Monte Solaro, the beauty of the view is matched by the pleasure at the lack of tourists, most of whom don't bother taking the thirty-minute hike to get here—and don't know that they can book a car (72 Via Migliera; 39-081-837-1499).

- Don't miss the sunset from Villa San Michele, the former home of a Swedish writer and doctor that now houses a museum. But the collection of art doesn't compare to the views of the Bay of Naples from the bucolic botanical gardens (Viale Axel Munthe, 39-081-837-1401; sanmichele .org).

- A *passeggiata* from Via Camerelle (the island's high-end shopping stretch) to the lookout point on Via Tragara (in front of Hotel Punta Tragara) provides an unbeatable combination of beautiful people and natural beauty.

Treasures of the Popes

by

JOHN JULIUS NORWICH

My first visit to the Vatican, in February 1956, was impressive indeed: a private audience given to my mother and me by Pope Pius XII in person. I well remember the invitation—really more of a summons— inscribed in fine copperplate beneath the insignia of the Triple Crown and Crossed Keys; my mother was referred to by name, I simply as "The Son"—which, in the circumstances, I found distinctly flattering. On reaching the papal apartments we were received by a black-cassocked, pink-buttoned *monsignore* and led through an apparently endless succession of staterooms, each of which appeared to belong to a different century: One room was occupied exclusively by Swiss Guards, resplendent in that glorious slashed costume of red, blue, and orange stripes, designed— whatever the guides may tell you—by neither Raphael nor Michelangelo; the next, by people dressed as we were; a third, by several immensely tall army officers in braid-encrusted uniforms that were pure nineteenth-century Ruritania; a fourth, by a dozen or so elderly gentlemen in inky black doublets and hose and white ruffs, for all the world like Hamlet's father's court in a rather old-fashioned repertory production. In the last room we were ceremonially handed over to a bishop, who told us to wait while he informed His Holiness of our arrival; fortunately he left the door very slightly ajar, and peeping through the crack I was astonished to see a pool of purple on the floor as he prostrated himself on the ground before his master.

In we went, and a tall, emaciated figure advanced across the carpet to meet us, his scarlet slippers almost incandescent beneath his snow white soutane. Carefully briefed in advance, we had been assured that the Holy Father spoke perfect English; this, however, proved something of an exaggeration. After a few halting words of greeting, he left most of the going to us, only occasionally interjecting a positive comment ("Very fine, very fine") or a negative one ("Very difficult, very difficult"), from which it soon became clear that he had not the faintest idea of what we were talking about. Not surprisingly, the conversation began to flag. We had been warned to bring some religious object for him to bless; all my mother had been able to find was a glass cross containing locks of hair belonging to King William IV, his mistress—the enchanting *comédienne* Mrs. Jordan—and five of their illegitimate children, from one of whom I am descended. "Don't let me tell him the story," she had implored me earlier that morning; but tell it—out of sheer desperation—she did. "Very fine, very fine," murmured His Holiness, and blessed the object without hesitation. He then asked me whether I had any children and whether they were boys or girls; on learning that I had one of each, he handed me a white rosary for my daughter and a black one for my son and blessed them, too. (Sometimes, we were told, he forgot the second question and absentmindedly murmured, "Black or white?" instead; this had on occasion given rise to misunderstandings.) Finally—and not, we felt, a moment too soon—there arrived a white-tie-and-tailed photographer. The camera flashed; and the audience was over.

Seven years later the telephone rang on my desk in the Foreign Office with the news that I was to serve as general dogsbody to the Duke of Norfolk at the coronation of Cardinal Giovanni Battista Montini as Pope Paul VI—at which ceremony, as the senior Roman Catholic of England, the Duke was to be the Queen's personal representative. This second visit to the Vatican was even more memorable than the first: three days of functions and festivities, reaching its climax with the coronation mass itself, which was held—since it was July and, even by the standards of a Roman summer, stiflingly hot—outdoors, on the steps of St. Peter's. A reception for the Commonwealth cardinals, given by the British Legation to the Holy See on our first evening, set the scene magnificently: In those days—as today, for all I know—any cardinal attending such a gathering would be in full scarlet-and-magenta robes and preceded by two men carrying enormous lighted candles; the effect, particularly on the dark skin of Cardinal Gracias of Bombay (who spent most of the evening with the Duke talking about cricket) and the immensely tall Cardinal Rugambwa of Tanzania, was breathtaking.

I remember too another, still more splendid reception given by the Vatican itself in the Borgia Apartment (of which more later). As we queued on the stairs in the hundred-degree heat, the British Minister tapped me on the shoulder and whispered, "Watch the drinks, they're lethal." Assuming this to be a reference to the Borgias' distressing habit of poisoning their guests, I laughed learnedly and thought no more about it. A few minutes later we were ushered into the first of that gorgeous enfilade of rooms, in which a long table groaned under the weight of immense wineglasses, each of them filled to the brim with an almost colorless liquid that I took to be dry white wine. Parched and sweltering, I fell on the nearest, drained it at a gulp—and very nearly collapsed. It was a dry martini—one of the most powerful I have ever known. As I struggled for breath, I saw the Minister grinning at me. "Told you so," he said.

The coronation itself began in the late afternoon. By the time it ended, three or four hours later, night had fallen: Gradually the lights had come on, including floodlights for the great facade of the Basilica. The official foreign representatives—including the Duke, and with me as his humble attendant—had been given places of honor directly behind the cardinals, who were now all in white, with outsize white miters; to our right the whole Piazza was thronged with people, the crowds stretching halfway down the Via della Conciliazione toward the Tiber. Unseen choirs sang, hidden organs boomed, little bells tinkled, and at last the Triple Crown (unfortunately, a remarkably ugly modern one that looked like a huge bullet made of gunmetal—the gift, we were told, of the people of Milan) was lowered onto the papal head, and the new pontiff broadcast a brief message in several dozen languages to the world's faithful. My last memory of the evening is seeing him enthroned on the Gestatorial Chair under its waving ostrich plumes and carried, swaying dangerously, through a forest of up-raised hands clutching little white skullcaps. He would seize the nearest, place it for a second on his head, then return it and seize another, and another, and another. After a few minutes of this, one felt, his arms must have been dropping off; but several hundred of his flock would possess an object that had been worn, if only momentarily, by the Holy Father himself and that they would treasure for the rest of their lives.

It was then that I felt, in a way I had never felt before, the full majesty of the Papacy. This elderly, undistinguished-looking little man with the bald head and the huge ears was the successor in direct and unbroken line to Saint Peter himself—who had been chosen by Christ as the Rock on which the Church was to be built; who, if tradition was to be believed, was himself crucified (upside down, at his own insistence) within yards of where I was sitting; and whose tomb, discovered as recently as 1949, lies in the Vatican Grottoes immediately beneath the Basilica. What other human being, I asked myself, enjoyed such prestige or exercised such immense spiritual authority over some 900 million people? What other institution could boast nearly two thousand years of history and still pack so powerful a punch?

All these things—the prestige, the authority, the history, and the punch—are most perfectly illustrated by the Basilica itself. Like all successful churches, it knows the value of drama. This begins long before we even reach it, with the approach across the Piazza between the sweeping arcs of Bernini's colonnade, and increases steadily as we pass the obelisk—moved here from Nero's Circus in 1586 by Sixtus V, who thus set a fashion for obelisks— and mount the broad, shallow steps to what in any other major ecclesiastical building would be the west front but which, in fact, faces east. (It is one of the eccentricities of St. Peter's that it is built, liturgically speaking, back to front, with the altar at the west end.) Yet even now we are not entirely prepared for what lies ahead. The first object of St. Peter's is to impress, and it succeeds. That vast space, those gigantic fluted pilasters that look as if they could hold up the universe, that extraordinary barley-sugar *Baldacchino* (Bernini again, with his great bronze sunburst in the apse behind it), the sculptures, the mosaics, that immense gilded dome soaring up to heaven—everything comes together in a single explosion of glory so tremendous that you can almost hear the trumpets. Here, unmistakably, is the Church Triumphant.

It is not a lovable building; but then, the Roman Catholic Church has seldom (if ever) been a lovable institution. Many people—particularly British and Americans, in whose native lands the full-blown Baroque is relatively unknown and thus almost invariably misunderstood—find it almost shocking: This, they argue, is not a house of God, like Durham or Chartres; it is merely a drawing room for his ministers. As it happens, they are wrong: Despite today's tourist hordes, there is as much genuine devotion in the world's second-greatest Christian shrine as in any religious building on earth. But sanctity lies, like beauty, in the eye of the beholder; and it is hard indeed for people brought up to expect places of worship to be Romanesque, Gothic, or eighteenth-century classical—let alone anyone with the faintest of Low Church leanings—to feel entirely at ease amid such shameless opulence.

Although the decision to replace old St. Peter's (which had already stood for almost a thousand years and was beginning to crumble) was taken by the first of the great Renaissance popes, Nicholas V, in 1450, nothing much was done for another half century; it was only on April 18, 1506, that the formidable Julius II laid the foundation stone for the great new Basilica, entrusting the work to the leading architect of the day, Donato Bramante. But Julius died in 1513, Bramante a year later, and Raphael—whom the architect nominated as his successor—in 1520; and work was interrupted yet again by the Sack of Rome, by German and Spanish troops, in 1527. At last, on January 1, 1547, the seventy-one-year-old Michelangelo was summoned by Pope Paul III to take charge; and St. Peter's was to prove perhaps his greatest achievement—one on which he labored, refusing all payment, for the last seventeen years of his life. Most of the interior architecture we see today is his, including the basic plan in the shape of a Greek cross (the nave was lengthened early in the following century), the giant Corinthian pilasters, and, crowning all, that breathtaking dome—which he never saw, since it was still uncompleted at his death.

Michelangelo's St. Peter's is the work of an old man; but in the first chapel on the right—now, sadly, behind a toughened glass screen since an attack by a lunatic some twenty years ago—stands the greatest monument to his youth, the *Pietà*. There are several other superb sculptures in the Basilica—Arnolfo di Cambio's bronze statue of Saint Peter, its right foot worn and polished by the kisses of the faithful; Bernini's tomb of Alexander VII and Pollaiuolo's of Innocent VIII; even Canova's monument to the last of the English Stuarts—but none of them can bear a moment's comparison with this sublime masterpiece, carved when the young genius was just twenty-four.

But the Basilica need not be seen only at floor level. There is a stunning view downward from the top of the dome, from which we can also go out onto the "panoramic loggia" and gaze down over the Eternal City. Alternatively, we can descend to the Vatican Grottoes and another group of papal tombs—including that of John XXIII, always covered in flowers. More fascinating than either, however, is what is known as the Pre-Constantinian Necropolis. It was discovered only in 1940, when engineers digging out the tomb of Pius XI accidentally hit on what proved to be a part of a Roman mausoleum. The new pope, Pius XII, immediately ordered a full-scale excavation, and nine years later there was revealed a complete cemetery of the first and second centuries A.D., together with a rudimentary tomb that there is good evidence to believe may be that of Saint Peter himself. (What the poor Galilean fisherman would say of the extravagant building above him that bears his name has for centuries been an irresistible subject for speculation—though my own guess is that he would be absolutely delighted.) The necropolis can be visited only by special permit (obtainable through the Ufficio Scavio on the south side of the Piazza), but this is well worth the trouble.

And so to the Palace and Museums. I find, after a good many visits over the years, that my favorites in the Vatican are not so much individual objects but intrinsic parts of the Palace itself. Unlike most of the contents of the Museums, all these rooms (or suites of rooms) were inspired or commissioned by one or another of that magnificent succession of Renaissance popes who reigned between the mid fifteenth and mid sixteenth centuries. The names of these tremendous pontiffs crop up again and again as we go through the Palace and Museums, and since they were not only among the most colorful in the whole history of the Papacy but also did more than anyone else to restore Rome to her ancient glory, it might be a good idea to introduce the most important of them, very briefly, here.

First was Nicholas V (1447–55), the best and most enlightened of all the Renaissance popes. A passionate lover of the arts and sciences, he founded the Apostolic Library and restored many of Rome's ruined churches; it was he who had the original idea of rebuilding St. Peter's and the Vatican Palace. His successor, Calixtus III, was the first pope of that Spanish house of Borgia which was later to become a byword for papal infamy; but apart from making one of his nephews cardinals—the future Alexander VI—he did no serious harm and can at least claim the credit for annulling (unfortunately rather too late) the sentence on Joan of Arc and declaring her innocence.

Next came Pius II (1458–64), whose life is so sumptuously illustrated by Pinturicchio's paintings in the Piccolomini Library of Siena Cathedral. An indomitable traveler (he got his toes frostbitten in Scotland) and compulsive writer, Pius's works include not only a brilliant autobiography but—surprisingly—a love story, *Euryalus and Lucretia.* His second successor was Sixtus IV (1471–84), who created—and gave his name to—the Sistine Chapel and Choir, restored countless churches all over Rome, broadened streets, paved piazzas, and spanned the Tiber with a fine new bridge, the Ponte Sisto; in other respects, however, he was a worldly and ambitious ruler who enriched his family and embroiled himself deeply in those endless intrigues that made up so much of Italian political life.

After the brief and unremarkable reign of Innocent VIII came the second Borgia pope, Alexander VI (1492–1503), who was to make five of his family cardinals (and was said to keep a whole harem of young girls and boys in the Vatican for nocturnal orgies) but who also rebuilt much of the ancient city. Then—following a few months under another nonentity—came Alexander's sworn enemy Julius II (1503–13), as much a soldier and statesman as he was a pope. Julius was succeeded by Leo X (1513–21), the thirty-eight-year-old son of Lorenzo de' Medici ("the Magnificent") who will always be remembered for his exultant words to his brother when he became pope—"God has given us the Papacy, now let us enjoy it"—and who was to prove one of the greatest patrons of the arts that even papal Rome ever produced. Finally, after the Dutchman Hadrian VI and another Medici patron who took the name of Clement VII (1523–34), there was Paul III (1534–49), who boasted at least four illegitimate children but in whose reign Michelangelo painted the *Last Judgment* in the Sistine Chapel and assumed responsibility for the completion of the Vatican Palace and the new St. Peter's.

The earliest of the really great masterpieces in the Palace is the Chapel of Nicholas V. In all Italy there are few things lovelier than this tiny room. Painted by Fra Angelico between 1447 and 1449, it is suffused with the spirit of the early Renaissance, a world of purity and simplicity and innocence that seems infinitely far removed from that of the darker, sterner century which was to follow. Next in date comes the Borgia Apartment, so called because it was chosen by Alexander VI for his own personal use on his accession in the fateful year of 1492. Its decoration he entrusted to a certain Bernardino di Betto, called Pinturicchio, who had been assistant to Perugino in the Sistine Chapel some fifteen years before. The first two of the six rooms are relatively austere, but Room IV (Alexander's former study, which is dedicated to the sciences and liberal arts), Room V (which portrays the lives of the saints and carries a strong Egyptian flavor), and Room VI (the pope's dining room, which explores the mysteries of the faith) are—with their richness of color, exuberance of stucco, and extravagant use of gold leaf—as sumptuous a celebration of the glory of a single family as can be found anywhere on earth. Alexander himself appears in the fresco of the Resurrection, affecting a degree of piety that was conspicuously absent from his life; his infamous son Cesare Borgia stands nearby, together with the brother he murdered; the pope's daughter Lucrezia appears in Room V, inappropriately disguised as the virgin saint Catherine of Alexandria; while, again and again, the splendid ceiling features the bull and crown that were the Borgia emblems. Only Room VII, the so-called Sala dei Pontifici ("Room of the Popes"), though by far the largest of the series, is something of an anticlimax. Its ceiling collapsed in 1500, nearly killing Alexander—who was in the room at the time—and largely destroying the original decoration, which was replaced by lesser artists under Leo X.

Immediately above the last Borgia rooms are the Raphael *stanze*. Essentially, these consist of the four rooms that were used as the official apartments of the warrior-pope Julius II (1503–13)—he who commissioned the Sistine Ceiling—and his ten successors until Gregory XIII (1572–85). In the previous century the rooms had already been frescoed by a group that included Piero della Francesca and Andrea del Castagno; to Julius, however, such painters seemed boring and old-fashioned. He first decided to call in a new team consisting of Perugino, Baldassare Peruzzi, Sodoma, and Lorenzo Lotto; then, in the autumn of 1508, he heard Bramante speak of a prodigiously talented compatriot of his from

Urbino, a young genius of twenty-six named Raffaello Sanzio. Raphael was summoned to Rome, shown the rooms in question, and given carte blanche.

Only the two central *stanze* are entirely by his hand. The first, the Stanza dell' Incendio—named after the great fire of 847, which, we are told, was quelled when Leo IV made the sign of the cross before it—has a ceiling by Raphael's master, Perugino, while much of the painting is the work of his pupils Francesco Penni and Giulio Romano; the same pair were also almost entirely responsible for the last *stanza,* the curiously disappointing Sala di Costantino, which was completed only in 1524—four years after Raphael's death at thirty-eight. The Stanza della Segnatura, on the other hand, betrays the hand of the master at almost every stroke, at the same time providing a typically Renaissance combination of the sacred and the profane, in which the Triumph of Religious Truth is contrasted with the Triumph of Philosophical and Scientific Truth on the opposite wall. This latter fresco depicts the two greatest philosophers of antiquity, Plato—almost certainly in the likeness of Leonardo da Vinci—and Aristotle, surrounded by other ancient masters, many of them also portraits, including Michelangelo as Heraclitus and Bramante as Euclid, on the collar of whose tunic the painter has signed himself with the letters R.U.S.M., for Raphael Urbinus Sua Manu ("Raphael of Urbino, by his hand"). The painter and his friend Sodoma stand modestly together in the right-hand corner.

Raphael was also responsible for three of the four frescoes in the third room, the Stanza di Eliodoro, all of which are concerned with the intervention of providence in the defense of the Church. That which gives the room its name illustrates the story—little known except to those who know their way around the Second Book of Maccabees—of the expulsion of Heliodorus from the Temple in Jerusalem; the other subjects are Saint Peter's delivery from prison, the miraculous mass at Bolsena (at which the host began to bleed, thus allaying the doubts of the officiating priest about transubstantiation), and the meeting of Leo the Great with Attila the Hun (when the pope persuaded the barbarian to advance no further on Rome). Only the last is less than satisfactory; first, because it is largely the work of assistants and, second, because Leo X, on his accession in 1513, decided that it should be made an allegory of the Battle of Ravenna of the previous year, at which he himself had been present. In practice this meant giving his own features to the figure of Saint Leo, despite the fact that he had already been cast as one of the attendant cardinals. Thus— since nobody bothered to change the latter portrait—the first Medici pope now appears twice in the same picture.

Beyond the last room, the Sala di Costantino, runs the long gallery that is always known as the Loggia di Raffaello, although the master's direct participation was probably limited to the overall plan and sketches of the first eight of the thirteen bays. The series begins at the far end with the Creation and continues through forty-eight scenes from the Old Testament and four from the New; but what gives the gallery its charm and freshness is the lovely lighthearted stucco decoration (by Giovanni da Udine) and the grotesque figures on the walls and pilasters, inspired by those that had recently been discovered in the Golden House of Nero and other ancient Roman ruins. In all Rome there is nowhere more joyful than this, nowhere—if one could only share it with just a few friends rather than a thousand tourists—one would rather spend a hot summer afternoon.

And so, finally, to the Sistine Chapel. Although Michelangelo's ceiling frescoes echo many of the subjects in the Raphael Loggia, they introduce us immediately to a sterner, nobler world. Opinions differ as to the success of their recent cleaning and restoration by the Japanese. To some, the new brilliance of color has come as a revelation; to others, the restorers have removed not only the centuries-old grime and soot but a good deal of the mystery and magic as well. You must decide for yourself. Remember always, however, what so many people forget—that there is more to the Sistine Chapel than its Ceiling, and that there are other great painters represented there besides Michelangelo. The walls, frescoed for Sixtus IV between 1475 and 1480, are themselves an art gallery of the early Renaissance, with glorious work by Perugino, Botticelli, Ghirlandaio, and Rosselli, to say nothing of Pinturicchio, Piero di Cosimo, Bartolomeo della Gatta, and Lucia Signorelli. Thus the Chapel would have been world famous even if Julius II had not called on Michelangelo to paint the Ceiling some thirty years later, in 1508. It took him four years. The result was nine monumental panels telling the story of the Book of Genesis from the Creation to the Flood, supported by naked youths (so-called *ignudi*) of uncertain significance, with prophets and sibyls below them.

But even this was not the end. Nearly a quarter of a century later, in 1536, at the age of sixty-one, Michelangelo began work on the western end of the Chapel. His *Last Judgment* was unveiled on October 31, 1541, twenty-nine years to the day after the unveiling of the Ceiling; but during those years the painter's world had changed out of all recognition. Papal Rome had watched in impotent dismay as the baleful influence of Martin Luther and his heretical Protestant doctrines spread relentlessly across much of northern and Central Europe; in 1527 the Sack of Rome had provided still further confirmation of the wrath of God. Was this the penalty exacted by the Almighty for the confident humanism of the early Renaissance? It certainly seemed so. By the 1530s a new austerity was in the air—grim, militant, and unforgiving. It is known as the Counter-Reformation, and Michelangelo's *Last Judgment* (at the time of this writing unfortunately shrouded in scaffolding) illustrates it to perfection. The clean-shaven figure of Christ, pitiless and inexorable, raises his right arm as if it is he personally who has struck the blow that has sent the damned spinning down to their eternal perdition. We are a long way from the "Gentle Jesus, meek and mild" of our childhood; here there is no gentleness or love, only bitterness, anger, and terrible power.

The Vatican, with its total area of just 109 acres, is not only the smallest but, in terms of art, far and away the richest independent state on earth. No single article—no single book, even—can hope to cover all the treasures it contains. The astonishing variety of its collections—quite apart from the world-famous Chiaramonti and Pio-Clementino museums, there is an Egyptian Museum, a Papal-Historical Museum, an Etruscan Museum, a Missionary-Ethnological Museum, even a *Profane* Museum, to say nothing of the superb art gallery (the Pinacoteca, with its roomful of Raphaels) and one of the greatest libraries in the world—cannot be attributed to any one pope or even a group of them. Its possessions have been acquired over nearly two thousand years and in every conceivable way: by accident, by design, by inheritance, and by pure good luck. They have been bought and borrowed, begged and bequeathed, seized and stolen; paid in tribute or given in homage to saintly popes, demanded in ransom and extorted as blackmail by villainous ones. The result, inevitably, is a hodgepodge—but a hodgepodge that has been touched by magic.

1992

Walking the Vatican

A tour of the museums

Rome in the fifteenth century looked more like a stinking, sprawling, crumbling poorhouse than the center of Christendom: centuries of cow dung and garbage covered what remained from imperial days; thieves, pilgrims, and beggars loitered in pestilential streets. As late as 1510, Martin Luther described rubbish twice the height of a soldier's lance stacking up along the Tiber. At the same time, the stern German was appalled at a papal fund-raising tactic: the sale of indulgences. For a few coins tendered here on earth, sinners could reduce future time in purgatory.

But those of us who visit Rome these days will probably be quite positive on the subject. For a great many of those coins went right into financing St. Peter's and other papal projects dedicated to re-asserting papal prestige after many years of schism and decline. We see this in the Vatican itself, whose bastioned walls incorporate one of the greatest art collections in the world, spread out in fourteen museums. Many of the most stunning contributions were made by a procession of popes so venal, so corrupt and decadent, that they could have done with a few indulgences themselves. But for us what matters are the antiquities they saved from destruction and the paintings and buildings they commissioned. As the historian J. H. Plumb once wrote: "To the sensual, warlike popes who ruled from 1471 to 1521 Rome owes a great deal of its present beauty." Here, then, is the only walking tour of the Vatican you'll need.

Most people, of course, come here to see the Sistine Chapel, and are they ever annoyed that this is achieved by walking through some of the longest corridors and halls in Christendom. There is no direct route. After you have surrendered your ticket, take the escalators (or the spiral ramp) up to the glass-covered Cortile delle Corazze (Courtyard of the Cuirasses), now the new entrance to the museums. Here you will find the granite base of the **Column of Antoninus Pius** in the back of the Courtyard of the Pinacoteca, which is directly in front of you. The column was erected shortly after his death in A.D. 161 and honors the Roman emperor and his wife, Faustina, who both rise to the heavens tucked aboard the wings of an angel-like genius. As his name suggests, Antoninus was one of Rome's less venal and vicious emperors; Edward Gibbon, the chronicler of Rome's decline and fall, gave him a gold star. But all that goodness didn't help the cause of art, which was slowly degenerating into sclerotic stiffness, just like the empire; you can see this in the stumpy soldiers with their interchangeable faces.

From here, take a left. Do not follow the crowds up the Simonetti staircase; proceed instead into the vast Cortile della Pigna—the great big bronze pinecone left over from a Roman fountain. In medieval times the pinecone aroused great wonderment among the locals, who thought it must be a thing of magic. Take a left at the pinecone's mysterious, modern companion, that bronze apple-like thing cluttering up the court's center (**Arnaldo Pomodoro's *Sphere with Sphere***), and head into the Chiaramonti Museum. The **marble head** by one of the doors shows the idealized (and enlarged) features of Augustus Caesar, of whom you are about to see a more human-size representation. This is the famous ***Augustus of Prima Porta,*** which stands in the Braccio Nuovo, or New Wing, built in the nineteenth century and just down the hall on your right. The light-flooded gallery alone is worth a visit—a lavishly marmoreal, faintly funereal space so chilly to behold that it takes your temperature down a few degrees, never mind the broiling heat outside. Here the emperor stands, raising the arm that may have once held a lance, on his breastplate a crisp report of a battle won against the Parthians. The statue, found in 1863, takes its name from the estate of the odious Livia, Augustus's wife.

Ignoring countless portraits of the misshapen bullies, psychotics, and mass murderers who followed Augustus to the throne, you'll next come upon friendly **Father Nile** on the left, resting from his labors on a sphinx and a cornucopia. The babies crawling on his body further the image of fertility.

There is no way out, so you must loop back into the Chiaramonti, heading toward the stairs and into the Vatican's Pio-Clementino Museum, avoiding all signs for the Egyptian Museum with its skimpy collection. The Pio-Clementino is home to many of the Vatican's major sculptures, and here at the top of the stairs, through the Belvedere Atrium, is the first, **an athlete** tidying himself up with a scraper after rigorous exercise. As are so many statues in the Vatican, this is a Roman marble copy of a Greek bronze from the fourth century B.C., probably by Lysippus. The Romans were gifted at many things, particularly plumbing, but when it came to sculpture, they turned to the Greeks for inspiration.

So it is with ***Apollo Belvedere,*** which takes its name from the azalea-filled octagonal court. The original Greek bronze by Leochares no longer exists, though it could hardly have been more poised than the Roman copy from the second century A.D. Placed here by Michelangelo's patron, Pope Julius II, the *Apollo* came to signify beauty incarnate. Antonio Canova, for example, never lifted his chisel without a vision of the nude deity nudging him on in his slavish daily struggle to emulate the antique. ***Perseus,*** his dull masterwork, is in the Canova cabinet across the courtyard.

A separate niche contains the **Laocoön** group, perhaps commissioned by Augustus Caesar, who liked to link his name with those of Homeric heroes. Laocoön and his two sons are shown writhing in the horrible embrace of two fat serpents. The goddess Athena sent these to punish the priest for having warned the Trojans of the wooden horse left behind by the Greeks. Only Aeneas listened, and escaped to found the city that Augustus made grand.

You are now in the **Room of Animals,** a marble zoo that looks like a warehouse for Romans eager to decorate in those pre-Boehm, order-by-mail days. The prize is the pointy-eared beastie in the room on the left, looking down from the ledge with a satisfied expression that says, "I've been *bad*!" If the galleries to the right are open, take a quick detour to admire the elegantly draped figure of **Ariadne** in the niche to your left.

The marble chunk stopping the traffic straight ahead is the **Belvedere Torso.** Just what the complete statue looked like in the first century B.C., with all its appendages intact, is impossible to say. But there is no doubt that the expressive powers of this fragmented pent-up mass of muscle were not lost on Michelangelo, who intentionally left unfinished the immensely affecting sculptures of his later years.

How unfortunate that all of the hideous bronze gilt of *Hercules* in the Sala Rotunda survives and so little of the *Belvedere*! But such are the vagaries of preservation. Nothing much remains, either, of Nero's Domus Aurea, or Golden House, an immense two-hundred-acre estate that was decorated by an ancestor of Cecil B. DeMille. The **porphyry basin** in the Sala's center gives an idea of its buffoonish scale.

Never mind Nero's most earnest efforts, Christianity survived to become the favorite religion of the emperor Constantine and, eventually, of the Roman Empire. We are reminded of his conversion in the fourth century in the cross-shaped next room. It contains the **sarcophagi** of his daughter Constantia and his mother,

Helena, a tough old bird who spent her declining years chasing down the True Cross in the Holy Land and was sainted for her efforts.

Chockablock with urns, statues, herms, and the massive light fixtures that give it its name, the **Gallery of the Candelabra** leads us into another numbingly long gallery, this one devoted to tapestries. The most eccentric is the *Supper at Emmaus* toward the end. The artist who designed it was far more concerned than usual to get another, apparently quite satisfactory meal—the one being consumed by the hulking cat and dog near the wine cooler.

Now there is a daunting sight: the **Gallery of Maps,** almost six hundred feet long and a navigational nightmare with its massing tour groups, annoying makers of miniatures, and souvenir stands hawking postcards, disposable cameras, guidebooks, and mousepads.

There is no need to go into the Apartment of St. Pius V; just follow the crowd into a large room filled with Polish tour groups huddling admiringly in front of a florid battle painting featuring a dead maiden exposing a large nipple. This is the **Sala del Sobieski,** named after a Polish king who helped defeat the Turks in the seventeenth century.

Neither can you linger in the Room of the Immaculate Conception, which leads, via an outside balcony, to the Raphael *Stanze* and the Room of Chiaroscuri. Here you'll get a look at the tiny **chapel decorated by Fra Angelico** in the mid-1440s. What a keenly observant eye the devout friar brought to the richly varied costumes and people wearing them: Note the soldiers knocking firmly on the door, fetching Saint Stephen for his martyrdom.

One gift shop later, you re-enter the Vatican's most magnificent rooms—the *stanze* decorated by Raphael for Julius II. It was Julius who did much to restore the reputation of the papacy and Rome after the cheerfully dissolute reign of Alexander VI (the fat father of Lucrezia and Cesare Borgia). So much did Julius detest the Borgia pope that he refused to move into his vacated apartment and ordered up this new suite from the young Raphael.

These are not big rooms, but in terms of ambition and imagination they are absolutely stunning. Look at the startling light suddenly illuminating the prison as an angel arrives to rescue the sleeping Peter. Note that Peter, the founding father of the church—the first pontiff, in fact—wears the face of Leo X, who was never one to shrink from extravagant gestures and connections. In 1506, two years before he began his apartment, Julius laid the cornerstone of the new St. Peter's, a project of such unnerving scope that it wore out a number of architects, beginning with Donato Bramante.

In the **Stanza della Segnatura,** once Julius's study and library, Raphael attempted nothing less than to illustrate the concepts of truth, beauty, and goodness. In one fresco he depicts Parnassus, where the arts reign supreme; in ***School of Athens,*** he gathers the philosophers of the ancient world, paying tribute to his own day by giving the noble truth-seekers the faces of friends and colleagues. Bramante puzzles over his compass in the costume of Euclid. And there, dressed as Heraclitus, is Michelangelo, his great rival, who was working in solitude behind closed doors on the Sistine Ceiling.

Yet if you press on into the next room, dominated by the cleaned and sparkling **Room of the *Fire in the Borgo,*** you think Raphael must have sneaked a look. The nude fellow hanging on to the wall for dear life looks as if he migrated from the Sistine Ceiling.

Now a terrible error is possible. Note that the paths part in a dingy little hallway. Ignore the signs to the Borgia Apartment and the Sistina, thus avoiding the modern Christian art gallery. Instead, take the signs to the Cappella Sistina and the Vatican Library, leaving the Borgia Apartment for another day and homing

in ever so slowly on the **Sistina.** Now you pass through the Sobieski Room again and go down the stairs on the left. Soon,
booming loudspeakers are telling everybody in many tongues to
be quiet and refrain from photography. And there it is, the Chapel, crowded with folks chatting about their lunch plans and taking pictures with their cell phones. Anyone who has waited for the
New York subway at rush hour in one-hundred-degree heat will
be well prepared for the experience. How things have changed: In
the early 1960s you could come here and find maybe a dozen people inside, sitting down on benches in the center looking at the
frescoes with mirrors.

Working alone (but unlike Charlton Heston, not on his
back), Michelangelo spent four years embellishing the monstrous
135-by-45-foot span with his singular vision of the Creation, of
stars and planets, plants and animals, Adam and Eve. Ignore the
shrieks, mostly from nonspecialists: The most recent cleaning did
no damage. It just peeled away a lot of soot and long-held notions
of the brooding genius and his somber palette.

The effect is like removing a pair of dark sunglasses at the
door, with dusty colors giving way to a cheerful array of pastels:
mauves, salmons, pale greens, and yellows. Note the green robe
and peach cloak swathing a sibyl who is studying an orange-red
book with bright white pages, her head wrapped in an elaborate
light gray scarf. More important, you can finally see the trompe
l'oeil architectural effects, so important and essential for creating
the spaces in which the figures live.

Escape is now possible—if you go past the grill and take the staircase on the right leading to St. Peter's. It is an exit route reserved
for special groups, though no one seems to check.

But soldier on if you wish to see the stunningly painted library Sixtus V built in the sixteenth century or the Vatican's painting gallery, the Pinacoteca. En route, note the odd **wooden**

gadget, invented by Bramante to produce the lead seals used by the Vatican. Why lead? Because it was a sign of humility, and the popes, as we have seen, were humble at heart.

Take a loop into the picture gallery, whose entrance is right near the cafeteria. It is modestly sized and rarely crowded, though some very famous **angels** hover in Room 4. Melozzo da Forlì painted them in the fifteenth century, using his particularly hypnotic blends of green and purple and unusual blues. The corpulent pope in the large group portrait was one of the most architecturally active of popes, **Sixtus IV,** who built the Sistine Chapel and is here seen glumly celebrating the founding of his new library—eventually replaced by the one we have just seen.

Down the hall is a ***Madonna and Child*** by Perugino and a monumental ***Transfiguration*** by his pupil Raphael. But the real treasure here is the shimmering ***Miraculous Draught of Fishes,*** one of the tapestries designed by Raphael for the Sistina. The richness of the silk and wool, embellished with silver gilt thread, and the liveliness of the detail—in some Roman restaurants today you can eat the fish that are flopping about the boat—remind us of why tapestries were held in the highest esteem centuries ago.

Around the corner is a sad sight: Leonardo da Vinci's ***St. Jerome,*** left unfinished by the master and just about ruined by clumsy restorations. And yet what an extraordinary pathos still seeps through the brownish smudge. On the opposite wall, the greedy-looking bon vivant from the fifteenth-century Spanish School is the Borgia pope Alexander VI.

The octagonal hall straight ahead presents an interesting visual battle between two large and imposing paintings from the seventeenth century: Poussin's ***Martyrdom of St. Erasmus*** and Caravaggio's ***Deposition from the Cross.*** Both of them are about suffering and death, yet the modes of expression couldn't be more different. Caravaggio makes the darkly lit events seem real and tragic; Poussin stays firmly in the academic tradition, even adding a couple of *putti* to keep us distant—if somewhat curious: Just how many more feet of small intestine can be pulled from the saint's abdomen and wrapped around the nearby log?

Our tour is over, but as you exit into the sunshine, you come upon yet another museum. This is the unbelievably hideous Gregorian Profane Museum, built in the 1960s by, sad to say, the Vatican's own architects. The sight of innocent sculptures held in place by steel vises and racks that look like torture instruments is too much on an empty stomach.

The Vatican Museums are open weekdays and Saturdays from 10:00 A.M. to 1:45 P.M. (but note that the ticket office closes at 12:30); in March through October from 10:00 to 4:45 (last admission at 3:30). Admission is seventeen dollars except the last Sunday of the month, when entrance is free (9:00 A.M. to 1:45 P.M. year-round). The Vatican café has a full self-service cafeteria with various stations (including a salad bar) and a pizzeria and coffee bar (39-06-6988-1663; vatican.va).

Eight Ways of Looking at a Garden

(or, the Art of Setting Stones)

by

NICOLE KRAUSS

1. EVERY GARDEN BEGINS WITH A QUESTION

It's Sunday morning in the heart of Tokyo. Leaving the subway station, we pass the last customers stumbling out of the bars in Bunkyo-ku, looking surprised to find all the neon doused by misty gray daylight. Two turn the corner and disappear inside a pachinko parlor that's just opened, slipping back into the darkness. It seems impossible to believe that somewhere in this tangle of streets strung with electrical wire lies a garden from the seventeenth century. Yet here it is, a small sign bearing the garden's name, Rikugi-en. The smell of the new cedar gates is intoxicating. My husband and I go in. The first thing we hear is silence, and the second thing is a crow. The first thing we see is harder to say. There are no neat rows of trees, no symmetrical hedges, no flowers planted in repeating patterns to guide the eye like a lazy schoolchild. The garden offers only suggestions. Why not look there at the craggy shape of that cherry tree which resembles an old woman? Or down at the unexpected design of the flagstones that form the path under your feet? Or the sudden flick of an orange carp beneath the water, where maple leaves float like tiny green hands?

We have come to Japan in part because we've had the brilliant idea of turning the patch of nothingness behind our Brooklyn house into a Japanese garden—only we don't know how. On our first morning in Rikugi-en, stopping every few steps to stand in hushed silence, we discover the problem of where, and how, to look: Everywhere our glance falls there is something interesting—the natural sculpture of an upright stone, the reflection of a bridge, the pattern of lichen on a lantern—but no single view allows us to immediately make sense of the garden as a whole. It refuses to reveal itself in any way except detail by detail. And so we learn our first lesson: Subtle, unpredictable, elusive, a Japanese garden prefers questions to answers. This discovery is both a victory and a setback, because although we have determined something about the nature of Japanese gardens, we have also realized that understanding them is going to be more difficult than we'd thought.

2. THE ART OF SETTING STONES

On a bullet train to Kyoto, I read a book on the history of Japanese gardens. The buildings outside tear past with a speed that is at once exhilarating and sickening. Focusing on the task at hand, I assemble a story to tell my husband, who is asleep across from me. It goes like this: In the imperial court of the Heian period, in the twelfth century, a beautiful poem could mean getting promoted to a higher post, while a mismatched color in your kimono ensemble could mean the end of your political career. It was in this atmosphere of heightened aesthetics—where elegance and refined taste meant everything and attention to the smallest detail was essential—that gardening was first raised to an art in Japan. Inspired by the Buddhist idea that all realms of being are transient, the Heian aesthetic was defined by a bittersweet sorrow born of the evanescence of life, which led to *awaré,* an intense emotion felt in response to beauty. It was during this period that the *Sakuteiki,* a gardening treatise which outlined principles and techniques still followed in Japan today, was written. It begins with the words *Ishi wo taten koto,* "The art of setting stones," a phrase that in four words suggests just how different a Japanese garden is from a Western one, whose treatise, if there were one, might begin with the words "The art of laying lawns." The *Sakuteiki* warns that a poorly arranged garden can invite disaster, while creating the right garden will ward off evil. But despite the many rules it lays out, the *Sakuteiki* also instructs that a garden is a form of self-expression and should reflect the creator's taste and spirit. Though over the course of the next thousand years Japanese gardens evolved into many forms—branching into stroll gardens, Zen gardens, and, in the final years of the medieval era, tea ceremony gardens—the basic spirit of the art remained unchanged. The Japanese garden is born of the meeting between the beauty of nature and those receptive to it; as the scholar Teiji Itoh writes, "A beautiful mind is essential to the creation of a beautiful garden."

3. A ZEN GARDEN WITH NO ONE IN IT

We arrive in Kyoto, city of two thousand temples, with enough daylight left for a walk. We cross the bridge on Shijo Dori, passing through Gion, the city's old district, where after dark, geisha and their teenage apprentices will emerge in full makeup and kimonos, hurrying through the narrow streets in wooden clogs to meet their clients. Saved from the World War II bombings that destroyed so many of Japan's old cities, Kyoto feels worlds away from the sprawl and modern skyscrapers of Tokyo. With its temples, gardens, and shops nestled between contemporary buildings, Kyoto hangs in the balance between old and new.

Eight Ways of Looking at a Garden

It's raining as we pass under the massive wooden gate of Nan-zenji, a temple built in the thirteenth century. In mid-October, the tips of the maple leaves have already begun to turn; in another month they will go up in a flame of red. Because of the weather and the lateness of the day there are few tourists, and after changing into a pair of slippers and padding down a dim wooden corridor to the porch overlooking the temple's famous Zen garden, we're surprised to find ourselves alone. Like most Zen gardens, this one is to be contemplated from the edge, not entered. Designed in 1600 and guided by the principle of *yohaku-no-bi*, or "the beauty of extra white," the garden consists of mostly empty space: a long rectangle filled with raked white gravel. The exception is an irregularly shaped island of moss at the far end where a number of large stones, rounded azalea bushes, and three trees have been set in an arrangement that seems, the more we stare at it, to possess profound meaning. The largest stone echoes the shape of the mountain behind it in the distance, creating an elegant rhyme. The garden's original name was Toranoko-watashi, "young tigers crossing the water," and if you squint at the stones in a certain way, they do take on the humped forms of animals leaping across the waves. But what about the precise placement of that tree, what is the meaning behind that? Or the rounded forms of that clump of bushes that seem so significant? Is it possible to break the garden down into its elements, since the enigma lies in their combination? What is accidental, we find ourselves wondering, and what is deliberate? Are we really to believe that the original meaning of the garden, if there was such a thing, has been preserved through four hundred years of weather and pruning, and if not, why are we sitting here, staring speechlessly?

What's clear is that the beauty of the Zen garden, which offers no easy conclusions, is magnetic. By the time we leave, it's already dark.

4. A Garden That Can Fit in Your Pocket, or a Garden That Goes On Forever

In Japan, where 127 million people live cramped in an area smaller than the state of California, we discover that there are gardens everywhere: on terraces and in restaurants, inns, temples, and courtyards. Wherever there is a patch of outdoor space, there is a tiny garden. So it makes sense that people tend to think of a Japanese garden as an act of miniaturization—nature compressed to fit in a small space. But standing in the gardens of the imperial villa of Shugakuin, in Kyoto, we begin to feel that the true secret of a Japanese garden is not that it makes itself so small but rather so big: It seems to draw the world into itself, never giving up the chance to claim the beauty of the distant mountains to the north and west, to which it is connected by a bridge of sky. There is a word for this—*shakkei,* or borrowed view. A Japanese garden can imitate the rocky shore of an ocean, a mountain precipice, or reedy wetlands though its natural surroundings may be the opposite. In this way, re-creating distant lands or folding into itself the world beyond, a Japanese garden appears to have no sense of its smallness. Sometimes its aspirations even seem cosmic—as in Tokai-an, in Kyoto, which is composed of a certain stone surrounded by gravel raked in concentric circles and stones placed like revolving planets, or the garden of A-Un in Ryogen-In, a medieval temple also in Kyoto, where two stones sit at either end of a raked expanse, representing the inhale and exhale, heaven and earth, or, as the temple's leaflet suggests, "the truth of the universe."

5. What if Your Bathroom Were Outdoors, Your Walls Were Made of Paper, and Grass Grew in Your Living Room?

If the boundary between the Japanese garden and the world is always being blurred, so is the boundary between what's inside and what's out. Walking one rainy evening down a corridor in the Fukuzumi-Ro, a charming, rickety nineteenth-century inn in Hakone, I keep thinking that the rain is somehow falling inside. It is only when I look closely that I see that a panel has been removed from the screen dividing the interior corridor from a courtyard garden with mossy stones and a pool full of carp, allowing the sound of rainfall to float in. Unlike Western houses, where the only contact with nature is visual—through glass windows—a traditional Japanese house is connected to the garden through openings created by freely sliding panels, or shoji. The house usually also has a veranda that is roofed but can be completely open on one side.

Early one morning, walking through the Itoh family mansion outside Niigata, now part of the Northern Culture Museum, we stand in the large open space that served as the main room of the house. Outside, we see an exquisite garden with streams, pools, falls, and no fewer than five teahouses, and yet there seems to be no way out. We stand with our noses pressed up against the windows, looking out, until the old caretaker comes by to check on us. He speaks no English and we no Japanese, so all we can do is point outside. At last his face lights up and he hurries over to the wall of glass and removes an entire panel. Then he hands us each a pair of clogs and gestures for us to go out. It rained that morning, deepening the green of the moss and leaving the stone paths glistening. Winding around bends, crossing streams by way of elegant flat stones, stopping to listen to the sound of falling water or to take in the patina on a laver, we follow the paths up and down through the many levels of the garden, each few steps adding a new, magical experience. When we finally go back in, the caretaker replaces the panel, and the entrance to the garden becomes, once again, a secret.

In his slim elegiac book *In Praise of Shadows,* Junichiro Tanizaki mourns the loss of traditional Japanese toilets, which stood apart from the main building in a grove "fragrant with leaves and moss," and where one could sit gazing out on the garden, half inside, half out. In each *ryokan* where we stay, our room has a view onto a small garden that usually contains a tiny waterfall and is lit at night so that it becomes a theater of soft shadows, the wind rippling leaves in and out of the dark. One night at the Hiiragiya *ryokan* in Kyoto, I am awakened by a howling storm and get up to go to the bathroom. Picking my way through the dark, I see on the paper screen wall the silhouette of a tree in the garden being tossed madly by the wind. It is like watching a cross between a silent film and a Japanese ink drawing, something universal and intimate, the perfect marriage between outside and in.

6. A Garden That Can Stop Time

But the endlessness a Japanese garden can convey is not only inspired by its flirtation with infinity; it also has to do with the element of time. The Heian fixation on the transience of life never really vanished. It's still evident today, in the Japanese passion not only for the seasons but also for taking photographs, for obsessively memorializing each moment before it passes out of one's hands. The Japanese respect for change comes from the Buddhist idea that to observe the mutability of life is to be reminded that one is also part of that changing nature, an awareness which leads to peace of mind. Many of the great advances in the art of gardening were made by Zen priests who saw it—just like eating, meditating, cleaning—as a spiritual discipline. For them, all work in the secular world reveals the Buddha; or, to put it differently, meditating on the changing world is part of the process of achieving eternal peace.

The garden is a canvas on which time enacts its changes, and so each design carefully considers how the garden will look under a blanket of snow and in spring blossom, during the deep green of summer and with autumn foliage. But even more than that, almost every Japanese garden contains metaphors for the passage of time. In the heavily symbolized world of kabuki theater, the movement of an actor through space is a movement through time. Similarly, in stroll gardens such as Kenroku-en, in Kanazawa, or Tokyo's beautiful Koishikawa-Korakuen, or the smaller, perhaps even more exquisite garden of the city's Nezu museum, it's the pathway itself, and the act of strolling, that represents the passage of time. Often, I find myself looking down at my feet as we walk through these gardens. In the beginning, it is because the stones are uneven or because the pattern keeps breaking its rhythm. But soon I begin to take pleasure in the beauty of the placement of the stones, which controls not only my pace but also where I pause to take in a view.

Another temporal metaphor in most Japanese gardens is running water. Among the kinds of waterfalls for which the *Sakuteiki* provides instructions are the Twin Fall, Off-sided Fall, Sliding Fall, Leaping Fall, Side-facing Fall, Cloth Fall, Thread Fall, Stepped Fall, Right and Left Fall, and Sideways Fall. There are also descriptions of how to properly pace a stream so that it moves neither too fast nor too slow, and how, in *karesansui,* or "dry mountain water" gardens, to arrange stones to look like a stream or to rake gravel to look like ripples. In Shinnyo-in, in Kyoto, a river of large cobblestones all placed with the same orientation between two banks of moss creates the look of a crashing torrent, frozen as if by an instant ice age. Perhaps it is here, in these sand and stone gardens, that the Japanese have come closest to stopping time. Or maybe the opposite is true: Maybe it is here—where the subtlest change (the flutter of leaves in a breeze, or a bird winging across the sky) registers like an ink stroke on an empty page—that the evidence of time passing is most stark.

7. A MOSS GARDEN DURING A TYPHOON

In order to visit Saihoji, the Moss Temple in Kyoto, it is necessary to write for a reservation weeks or months in advance. It's raining on the morning we're scheduled to visit, but we think nothing of it: It's been raining for days, and we have grown to love the different sounds rainfall makes on the hundred kinds of surfaces found in a Japanese garden. The owner of the Hiiragiya, an elegant, soft-spoken woman whose family has run the inn for six generations, warns us that a typhoon is coming up from the south and will hit after lunch. Two members of the staff wait in the inlaid stone entryway with our shoes and two large umbrellas. They wave us off. When we get to the end of the street, I turn around and they're still waving.

The wind has picked up and it's pouring by the time the taxi deposits us in front of the temple gates. A monk in a black robe checks our reservation papers, then motions us down a path that runs beside a long, straight wall. On the other side, we can see the treetops of the moss garden, designed in 1339, but the garden itself remains hidden. As if to build our anticipation, we're asked to kneel at a small desk in the temple and copy out a sutra with ink and brush before we're allowed to go any farther. We finish as quickly as we can, so that we will have a few minutes alone in the garden before the rest of the group catches up.

In our first moments within the walls, we sense that we've arrived at the most beautiful place in all of Japan. Under the cover of our umbrellas, we peer out at an enchanted world, like something out of a fairy tale. Over a hundred species of moss blanket the ground under the trees, and in the center is a pond, built in the shape of the Chinese character for the heart. An old wooden boat floats, half-sunk, tethered to a tree. The rain falls silently, as if on velvet. We climb the stone steps to the upper *karesansui* garden and come to the rock where Muso Kokushi, the monk who designed the garden, used to sit in meditation. "It is easy to feel a little sad as one accepts its quiet, delicate beauty," Teiji Itoh writes, and by now I understand that the sadness which comes from seeing something beautiful arises in part from the knowledge that neither you nor it will last.

8. A VIEW FROM THE BATH

Barely back home a week, I am sitting in the bath, reading one of the books we bought on Japanese gardens. "In 212 B.C., when the first emperor of China, Qin Shi Huang, burned all the books and buried the scholars alive," I read, "he issued a special decree exempting those on the cultivation of trees." I glance up and look down at the yard, strewn with dead leaves now, in the middle of November, at the small magnolia tree we planted when we moved in two years ago. It's already twice as big, growing according to its own design. If this were Japan, it would already have a scaffolding of crutches around it, guiding it (or "torturing it," as a Japanese friend of ours suggested) into an ideal shape. Maybe it would be easier to leave things as they are—plant tulip bulbs, a hydrangea, a few flats of annuals come May. Anyway, having seen the most beautiful gardens in all of Japan, I've come to understand just how much work it would require not only to design one but also to care for it. For some, like the seventeenth-century hermit whose garden, Shisen-do, we fell in love with in Kyoto, it is a life's work.

But then my mind is wandering again, and I begin to remember countless views I looked out at from countless Japanese baths: the tiny illuminated garden at the Dairo-an inn on the grounds of the Northern Culture Museum, the river rapids outside the window of the Fukuzumi-Ro in Hakone, the mist-covered mountains and cedar forests from the bath I took in Koyasan, the miniature paradise outside the window of the Yama No O inn in Kanazawa. And then, the next thing I know, I'm imagining myself out in the yard, raking gravel in perfect concentric circles.

2005

A GARDEN GUIDE

Beauty, the Japanese way

 True Japanese gardens have been designed with an appreciation of all seasons in mind, but they are perhaps at their most poignant on the cusp of change—in April, when the blossoms appear, or in November, when the leaves turn. Allow plenty of time to stop, look, and reflect, or you'll miss the subtleties. Pause, too, at teahouses along the way to refresh yourself with a cup of whisked green tea and *wagashi,* a Japanese sweet.

TOKYO

The capital's gardens are a peaceful and enchanting escape from its noise and neon. **Koishikawa-Korakuen,** an Edo-period stroll garden influenced by Chinese Confucianism, has an exquisite Full Moon Bridge. The plum (or *ume*) grove blossoms in February, the irises in spring (1-6-6 Koraku, Bunkyo-ku; 81-3-3811-3015). In **Rikugien,** a *kaiyu* ("many pleasure") garden designed at the end of the seventeenth century, are eighty-eight landscaped scenes evoking famous Japanese poems (near Komagome Station; 81-3-3941-2222).

KYOTO

You'll have to choose just a handful from the city's hundreds of gardens. To see the moss garden of **Saihoji,** it's worth the effort to request a reservation in advance; include your name, address in Japan, occupation, age, the number of visitors, three possible days you can visit, and a return-reply envelope (56 Kamigaya-cho, Matsuo, Nishikyo-ku; 81-75-391-3631). At **Tofuku-ji,** after visiting the four Zen gardens of the Hojo, or Abbot's Hall, walk through the Valley of Maples to the garden in front of Kaisando Hall. It's dry stone on one side, green and hilly on the other; the harmonies and echoes are complex and exquisite (81-75-561-0087; tofukuji. jp). Explore at least one of the glorious imperial villa gardens— either **Katsura** or **Shugakuin.** The reservation process for all imperial sites in Tokyo and Kyoto is outlined online (81-75-211-1215; kunaicho.go.jp). The country's most celebrated rock garden is **Ryoanji**'s (near Ryoanji-michi Station; 81-75-463-2216), but the one at **Nanzenji** seemed both warmer and more profound (81-75-771-0365; nanzenji.com*).* If you do make it to Ryoanji, see the nearby Kinkakuji, rebuilt after it was burned down in 1950 by a fanatical monk, an act that inspired Yukio Mishima's book *The Temple of the Golden Pavilion.* At Daitoku-ji, a huge complex of temples, visit **Ryogen-in,** with its five small Zen gardens, and **Ko-rin-in** (a fifteen-minute walk from Kitaoji Station; 81-75-491-0019). In a part of Kyoto that still feels like a village, **Shisen-do** is the former hermitage of a monk who was both a scholar of Chinese classics and a well-known landscape architect. The garden is built along a stream, with a backdrop of towering maples that turn scarlet in autumn (a five-minute walk from the Ichijoji-Sagarimatsu bus stop; 81-75-781-2954).

KANAZAWA

Take one of the most celebrated strolls in the country at **Kenro-ku-en,** in the city center. "Combining the six features of a perfect landscape garden" (spaciousness, seclusion, antiquity, artifice, abundant water, and panoramas), it was built more than two hundred years ago for the most powerful feudal family under the Tokugawa Shogunate. Arrive early—it opens at 7:00 A.M.—to

avoid the crowds (81-76-234-3800; pref.ishikawa.jp/siro-niwa/
kenrokuen/e). Smaller and less famous, the garden at **Nomura
Samurai House** is a miniature paradise of streams, waterfalls, and
stone lanterns with a cherry granite bridge and a four-hundred-
year-old myrica tree (1-3-32 Nagamachi; 81-76-221-3553).

Jinn City

by

EDMUND WHITE

I went to Petra in January with three Parisian friends, and we were so silly as to pack swimsuits. The Middle East, or at least Jordan, sounded suitably warm. Moreover, I remembered a grade-school teacher who'd assured us that the Nativity paintings by the old masters had got it all wrong; Baby Jesus had been born amid sultry breezes and palm trees.

Well, let me assure you, Baby Jesus was *cold*. We were in the same general area as Bethlehem and we were nearly snowed in. If I were a true aesthete, I'd say I had never heard anything so moving as the sound of hail falling on the wild tulip leaves that cover the vast valley of Petra. And it's true enough that it was a lovely sound, a light crepitation, as though someone were delicately untwisting dozens of expensive candy wrappers in an adjoining room.

Petra is one of the wonders of the ancient world, which an English poet, John William Burgon, once celebrated as "a rose-red city half as old as time." For several centuries, from 312 B.C. to A.D. 106, it was the capital of the Nabataeans, a shadowy people who grew rich through the spice trade and once ruled an empire that extended as far north as Syria and as far south as the Arabian peninsula. Very little is known of the Nabataeans, who seemed to have been too busy making money and building palaces and tombs to have left behind adequate descriptions of themselves or their purposes.

The Romans conquered Petra in A.D. 106, paved everything, and added a large, ugly amphitheater. They stayed on until the Empire divided; the Byzantines continued to rule Petra until about A.D. 600. Soon the sands began to drift over the valley, and two major earthquakes leveled all but one of the freestanding buildings, leaving intact only the five hundred or so temples, houses, and tombs that the Nabataeans had carved directly into the living rock.

By the twelfth century only a few monks still inhabited the mysterious site. Then even they disappeared, and Petra was forgotten by the outside world for six centuries—until 1812, when Johann Ludwig Burckhardt, a Swiss explorer disguised as a bedouin, rediscovered the grandiose ruins.

I'm not much of a hippie, but Petra exudes such a powerful magic that it can make anyone sound like a throwback to the sixties babbling about "strange vibes" and "mystical energy."

We had already spent a week in Syria, slogging through mud and snow, traveling over fifteen hundred miles in a rented car, seeing and smelling and hearing extraordinary things. We'd wandered through the ruins of Apamea under a rainbow while sheep lazily trimmed the grass beside us and shepherds plagued us to buy "ancient" coins. We'd happily got lost in the miles and miles of covered souks in Aleppo, where a jovial old man taught us the art of carving woodblocks with intricate designs to be used in printing fabrics, and where we strolled through the metalworkers' district, in which every man and boy was banging giant caldrons into shape—the noise sounded like a particularly clangorous moment in *Das Rheingold*.

Best of all, we'd driven through the desert in the pouring rain. (Did you know it rains in the desert? I mean *buckets*.) We didn't see anything or anyone for hours—and then the weather cleared and we entered the ancient oasis city of Palmyra, with its mile-long royal processional route that starts at one end with the temple to the god Bel, passes a theater, baths, and an agora, and ends at the palace where Queen Zenobia reigned. We were virtually the only tourists on a cold, clear day.

So we were inured to miracles. Through the night we drove south from Amman, the capital of Jordan, down a four-lane highway across the desert toward the port of 'Aqaba. Suddenly we swerved off onto a sinuous two-lane road that rose into the hills. The fog became pea soup, and we took turns running in front of the car, hooting and flapping our arms to indicate the route. For a moment the weather lifted to reveal the moon glittering on miles of frost-blanched olive trees. We became slightly hysterical from our close calls on corkscrew mountain curves. I decided the wraiths of fog were jinns, deliberately barring the way to Petra.

But we made it. The Forum Hotel, a new, quietly luxurious place run by the Inter-Continental chain, welcomed us warmly. The next morning we rushed to the visitors' center, where we rented four horses and found a chatty, intelligent guide with perfect Detroit English, despite his never having left Jordan.

To enter Petra, where, fortunately, all cars are forbidden, you must ride a horse or walk through the Siq, a mile-long crevice that was formed when a mountain split in half. Horses' hooves strike pebbles, and the hollow sound reverberates off the sheer walls. Dogs bark in the distance. At some points the pass is no wider than two yards, yet the rock face on either side is as high as a forty-story building. Strange swirls of colors flow together, as in that moment when chocolate is first stirred into a batter. Giorgio, the Italian cook who accompanied the poet and artist Edward Lear to Petra in the nineteenth century, had said: "Oh, Signore, we have come into a world where everything is made of chocolate, ham, curry powder, and salmon."

As one forges deeper and deeper into the Siq, signs of ancient habitation spring up—a fragment of a triumphal arch that once spanned the ravine; squat roadside altars; carved steps leading off to nowhere; a continuous horizontal ledge that once housed terra-cotta freshwater conduits; traces of the roads the Romans paved. The rigid, rectangular facade of a temple wavers, drifts, bulges, as though seen through a passing wave. The porphyry colors of tombs are edged in snow.

At every turn you're hard-pressed to distinguish between natural and human creations. The rock formations have been so sculpted by floods that they often threaten to turn into Mount Rushmore faces, or they look like those slightly corny hands Rodin fashioned in marble, whereas the antique columns and pediments have been so effaced by wind and water that they resemble the natural wonders of the Grand Canyon. In fact, one often thinks of old Westerns here. Picture an Indian chief standing on top of a mesa—but one carved like a Chippendale breakfront—and you'll get something of the feeling of Petra.

As we neared the end of the narrow, gloomy Siq we spotted the Khazneh, or the Treasury—or rather, we saw a sunstruck, rose-colored carving of a running goddess. Then we emerged into full sunlight, and there was the immense building crowding down on us, most of its details as shockingly crisp as the face on a new dime.

This 135-foot-high building, with its two stories and its noble Corinthian columns, was named the Treasury by the bedouins, who made up the story that an Egyptian pharaoh had secreted his treasure in the eleven-foot-high urn that surmounts the central kiosk. For years horsemen shot at it with arrows or bullets, hoping to break the piñata and spill the gold. The only result was to scar this one element of a structure otherwise remarkably intact. No one knows the real function of the Khazneh, but it may have been a temple to Manathu, the patron deity of Petra.

Architecturally the most striking feature is the broken pediment of the upper story. On either side a slanted roof, supported in each case by two sturdy columns, rises and abruptly breaks off, although the eye naturally fills in the missing lines of ascent; they join in an imaginary apex just above the urn. This broken-pediment style (which will remind New Yorkers of the top of Philip Johnson's AT&T Building) is the most important innovation of the Nabataeans—that, and their shameless eclecticism, for like the good merchants they were, they hunted and pecked everywhere and integrated the decorative bits they'd discovered in Egypt, Assyria, and Rome, as well as the Syrophoenician and Hellenistic worlds.

As we pushed farther into the valley, the strangeness of Petra overwhelmed us. Everything here is improbable—the remoteness, the mineral force, and especially the bizarre juxtapositions of color, which sometimes look like watered silk, sometimes like batik, sometimes like old rag rugs. Annabelle, a young French designer in our group, asked an artisan in the valley to fill up test tubes for her, each with a different-colored sand. He came back with twelve hues, ranging from sulphur yellow to basalt black and including the red sand of the valley floor and a dark purple sand, which resembled grape Kool-Aid granules before you add the water.

It was so cold that Mohammed, our guide, tied us into our newly bought kaffiyehs, those red-and-white (or black-and-white) tasseled scarves that Americans associate with Arafat but which every man wears in this part of the Arab world. We needed to bundle up, since Mohammed was leading us eight hundred steps up to Ed Deir—the Monastery—so named because it served as a monastery under the Byzantines, although it had been built centuries before as a temple by the Nabataeans.

Mohammed was extremely tactful; he knew just when to pause for "a view," so we could catch our breath without being made to feel out of shape. And he was practical and kind about my nearly paralyzing vertigo. I would never have thought myself capable of scrambling so high. As though to mock my fears, a black-and-white baby goat gamboled all the way up alongside us, spilling over the rocks. A goatherd of eight ran past with bare feet in the snow in pursuit. Beside us a cataract spun glass, or was it merely crystalline water?

Breathlessly we reached the top, walked down a path, turned a corner, and confronted the Monastery, the largest rock-cut monument in Petra and the ultimate expression of its powerful structural aesthetic. Again a broken pediment crowns the building, but this time all distracting ornamental details have been eliminated to emphasize the boldness of the massive forms. The central kiosk is crowned by a carved mandarin's hat as large as a merry-go-round.

As soon as we descended, Mohammed led us right back up a neighboring mountain to the High Place of Sacrifice, an ancient site containing a stone altar with a drain for catching blood. Perhaps to make us shiver still more, Mohammed said the Nabataeans may have practiced human sacrifice. We looked down over thirty-five square miles of greater Petra, a whole world of incised and hollowed-out stone, where everything faintly resembled the dentures and molds in a dental lab.

Here we saw the most imposing ensemble of buildings at Petra—the Royal Tombs. The largest is the Palace Tomb, so named because it is a copy of Nero's now-vanished palace in Rome. Next to it, in a line, are the Corinthian Tomb, the richly colored Silk Tomb, and the Urn Tomb. The facade of the Silk Tomb is particularly striking because of the whorls and bands of color that cross it like the magnified grain in a cross section of . . . well, redwood.

Mohammed built a fire out of branches he had gathered. We

took turns fanning the flames with a strip of plywood, and soon we were warming up over cups of mint tea. The only other tourists we saw all day now came huffing up the path, a Japanese couple and an American couple, representatives of the two most irrepressible nations of travelers. We shared our tea and picnic lunches with them.

In biblical times religious sacrifices (more often of sheep than of human beings, although the story of Abraham and Isaac suggests they could be interchangeable) were always carried out in such high places. The altar at Petra is the most celebrated. At the very edge of the promontory, where the cliff plummets down to the valley (and where my knees turned to jelly), a moon goddess is carved into a small altar no larger than a chair. The goddess, who wears a crescent in her hair, faces the spot where the moon rises on the eve of the Nabataean high holy day in the spring. This is a place where people have worshipped since the Nabataeans' predecessors, the Edomites, first settled Petra in 1300 B.C. To see this sculpture, with the goddess's face still expecting the moon to rise in the same place, gave me a sharp sensation of the sacred.

To be honest, I've always preferred a pantheon of beautiful, childish nature gods and goddesses to the solitude and abstractness of a single angry Jehovah; I guess I prefer the nursery to the study. In the Bible we read that the ancient Hebrews hated the Edomites. The cause of this enmity isn't exactly clear, although apparently the Edomites forbade Moses to cross their territory on his way to the Promised Land. In revenge, the Hebrews later drove ten thousand Edomites over a cliff—possibly this very one, I thought, as I succumbed to a new wave of sickening vertigo. Mohammed herded me back to the fire and another cup of tea.

Perhaps the Hebrews felt that their sterner religion was threatened by Petra, where every outcropping of stone looks carved and every carving looks natural, where every turn of the path inspires an urge to pray to some strictly local spirit. Certainly for us every gust of snow and even the distinctly audible noise of a donkey munching tulips far, far below filled us with superstitious affection for the jinns of the place, which were quite possibly devils.

1989

VISITING PETRA

How and when to see the ruins

 While Petra works as a long day trip from Amman or the Red Sea resort of Aqaba, you need to spend at least one night here to experience the site properly. Be prepared for lots of walking. Saddle horses and horse-drawn carriages can be hired in either direction for the three-quarter-mile trip through the Siq, and donkeys and camels can take you a few hundred yards farther into the inner valley, but most of the complex is accessible only on foot. A leisurely round-trip walk through the Siq to the main monuments of the Treasury, Roman Theater, and the lower Royal Tombs will take about four hours, and a hike up to the High Place of Sacrifice or the Tomb of Aaron requires four strenuous hours more from the inner valley floor. Spring or fall, when temperatures rest in the comfortable seventies, are the best times to visit.

The security gate to the Petra complex opens by 6:30 A.M. Try to arrive early to watch the wind- and water-carved rocks change color as the sun rises and to beat the 8:00 A.M. tour group rush hour. You must first purchase an entrance ticket from the Visitors Center, which is also the place to obtain a map or hire friendly, colorful, and competent local guides (962-3-215-6020). Bring a small backpack to carry bottled water, which is sold on site from Bedouin-run stalls or from the restaurant at the end of the paved Roman road below Petra's small archaeological museum. You might also bring a small flashlight to illuminate the rock chambers and some money for souvenirs, which provide income for members of the Bedul tribe, who used to raise goats and live among the caves, but who were evicted and relocated to a cinder-block village after UNESCO declared Petra a World Heritage Site in the mid-1980s. While it is no longer possible to camp overnight in the caves or linger alone after sunset, the Visitors Center arranges guided night tours with a Bedouin storyteller Thursdays in high season and on other nights if enough people sign up. Discovery Travel and Eco-Tourism, an Amman travel agency, can arrange permits from the Ministry of Antiquities for private night hikes and candlelit dinners in the Siq and in lesser-known gorges including Little Petra, a two-mile-long defile bearing traces of Nabataean carvings five miles from the main Petra complex (from the United States: 713-377-8046; from Amman: 962-6-569-7998; discovery1.com).

Jordan's 1994 peace treaty with Israel launched a hotel construction boom in Wadi Musa, the town just outside Petra, which now has a broad range of accommodation. Opened in 1996, the Mövenpick Resort Petra has an Arabian-themed interior and a convenient location steps away from the Visitors Center (962-3-215-7111; moevenpick-hotels.com). On a ridge above the Mövenpick, the Crowne Plaza Resort Petra has chalets and large suites suitable for families, as well as an unheated outdoor pool with dramatic views of the surrounding mountains (962-3-215-6266; ichotelsgroup.com). A ten-minute shuttle ride from the site entrance, the Taybet Zaman Resort occupies a former nineteenth-century Bedouin mountain settlement and retains the feel of a village with freestanding stone chalets linked by candlelit paths (962-3-215-0111).

Petra is a two-and-a-half-hour drive from Amman or ninety minutes from Aqaba on recent, well-marked highways. Hotels can arrange rental cars or private taxi trips to Petra, where a car is unnecessary once you arrive. The national JETT bus company also offers air-conditioned Petra service (962-6-566-4146).

Beauty and the Beast

by

SIMON WINCHESTER

 I suppose I shouldn't have been all that surprised when shortly before noon one Philippine morning, somewhere about a mile and a half up the side of a volcano, my guide and the porters announced that they were quitting and ran away.

It was getting pretty frigid this close to the summit of Mount Mayon, and like most Filipinos, my guide—who confessed to having gone on a bender the night before, drinking locally made gin until dawn—was quite unused to the cold. Besides, everyone was soaked to the skin, the gales were plainly terrifying them, the black cliffs were rain-slick and extremely vertiginous, and the volcano was just then starting to emit ominous (but as it happens, quite routine) puffs of sulfurous gas.

So when Elmer, the previous night's party animal, cried out to me, "Sir, we are dying here!" and began shivering and chattering his teeth uncontrollably with what looked like gin-induced hypothermia, then started to scamper back down the mountainside, I was dismayed—but not altogether astonished. No sticking power, I muttered darkly, along with one or two other stronger imprecations, and turned back up toward the top, teeth set into what really was a most inconvenient, unexpected, and freezing-cold gale.

Mount Mayon is said to be the most perfectly conical volcano in creation, a classic of its kind, a type specimen of the volcanic art. It has a base that is a flawless circle, eighty miles around, and from which it rises with a spare and unwavering elegance to a point that stands eight thousand feet above the sea. The angle of repose of its andesite ledges is a gem of geologic symmetry. A good map will show its contours as a series of perfect concentric circles, like a spider's web, a dartboard, or an archer's boss.

From a distance the sight is unforgettable, especially if the weather is fine, the tropical sky a deep, clear blue. Dark green jungles cloak the volcano's lower slopes; temperate forests, grasses, and bamboos in a range of paler shades limn its upper reaches; black and smoking rocks, streaked yellow with sulfur, are then riveted onto its final few hundred feet. The mountain towers over the surrounding rice paddies and cornfields and the grazing livestock, and mariners who sail across the Pacific into the Albay Gulf say they can see its peak from a hundred miles and more. Mayon is a landmark, a source of much pride to the villagers and townspeople above whom it towers; and though it steams fitfully and has an unfinished look to it, in consequence it remains, in fair weather or foul, breathtaking in its simple perfection.

Yet Mount Mayon—its name comes from the Bicol dialect word for beautiful—is also terribly dangerous. Not because it is difficult to climb, though its cliffs and slippery rocks can badly injure those who are foolish enough to try, but because it has the irritating habit of exploding, prodigiously and without warning. It did so in 1993, and more than seventy farmers tending their tomato plants inside a deep ravine known as the Bonga Gully were killed.

Elmer said he had been on the mountain that day, trying in

vain to lead three Germans and an Israeli to the top. He shuddered theatrically at the memory. "All four of them got away—by running," he'd warned me the day before our own climb. "But then I saw other men, the farmers, who were caught in a hot wind. They were roasted dead, like chickens on a spit. They had no chance. The hot wind can go faster than any man, you know. It is quite silent. It just races down and cooks people. They were"—and I swear that at this point he seemed to lick his lips— "done to a crisp."

All of the world's landscape is, ultimately, the product of geology. That much is almost too obvious to state. The type of rocks, their ages, the way each sits in relation to its neighbors—all of these simple factors determine as absolutes the shape of the land, what crops and foliage grow on it, what creatures live on it, and exactly how. Geology, like mathematics, is one of the core realities of the universe, its laws underlying all that we do and are.

What is a little less apparent, though, is that the earth's surface comes in two essential forms. There is first the landscape that has been created by old geology, where the forces of creation are long dead, where the landforms are the product of events that happened in the very distant past, and where no new events seem likely. And then there is the landscape that comes from new geology, which shows that the planet is still in the throes of creation, where the geology is still alive and at work, where the earth can still be seen to be flexing its muscles.

By muscles, we mean essentially two things—earthquakes and volcanoes, both of them almost casually destructive means by which the earth demonstrates its ultimate mastery over everything that lives upon it.

There are more than thirteen hundred potentially active volcanoes in the world. And while not all of these have yet been explored and analyzed and classified in detail, and though there is still no foolproof way to tell which of them is going to erupt, how impressively, and when, a simple axiom holds: Although there is such scenery and grandeur around the edge of the Pacific as to make the heart stop, all of this beauty and magnificence conceals a terrible and, what's worse, a quite unpredictable danger.

For where live geology reigns, dreadful things can happen. Japan's Mount Fuji, for example, is inexpressibly lovely—but the forces that made it so also devastated the city of Kōbe 300 miles away three years ago. San Francisco charms everyone who visits— and yet what made all the pretty hills is the selfsame geology that wrecked the city in 1906 and will likely do so again one day. And the perfect symmetry of Mount Mayon lulls onlookers into forgetting that the lava flows and gas surges that made it so perfectly symmetrical can roast a man to death in ten seconds flat. Man dies in places like this because, once in a while, the earth chooses to remind us that it is still very much alive.

And in the main, the world appears to come most dramatically alive where the geology is newest, where the volcanoes and quakes are most numerous—around the long and ragged edge of the Pacific Ocean.

More specifically still: Most of the world's truly great volcanoes exist and have long existed—and most of the true seismic and tectonic spectaculars take place and have taken place—in Asia. These stupendous seismic events are a phenomenon of the entire Pacific Rim but are not evenly sited along the so-called Ring of Fire. They are concentrated on the rim's western side, on its Asian arc. They lie along the chain of island-states that begins with Sumatra in the tropical Indonesian west; they continue through the seismically active islands of the Philippines (where there are at least twenty-one big, active volcanoes) and end in Hokkaidō in the frigid Japanese north.

More than anywhere else on earth, these five thousand miles of islands are where beauty and the beast most dramatically coexist, where you can see the most breathtaking scenery and at the same time enjoy, suffer, or derive vicarious pleasure from the risk that something—and who knows what? who knows when?—may happen. The world's most beautiful and most symmetrical volcanoes are there, but if you choose to visit them you risk, as Elmer's German and Israeli partners risked, the possibility of being bombarded by hot boulders, swept into newly torn crevasses, licked by gusts of flame, drowned in lava, or sucked up by some terrible pyroclastic wind, roasted and done to a crisp.

Yet these days none of this seems to be much of a deterrent. Quite the reverse, in fact. As ever more travelers continue to weary, as they say they do, of the more conventional destinations, so volcanoes, at least in Asia, appear to be nudging their way into becoming a new kind of travel business. And there is also a mood developing toward this kind of mountain, a new appreciation that has been spawned by a rash of books which argue that volcanoes are ultimately benevolent, giving us fertile soils and moisture and doing far more good than their destructive, fearsome reputation deserves. Volcanoes are hero-mountains, goes the new thinking; they should not be shunned so much as they should become the subjects of pilgrimage and reverence.

It is not an entirely new phenomenon. People have long been fascinated, if wary. You could always find a boatman to row you out to clamber up the remains of the great volcano of Krakatoa, between Java and Sumatra (although a visitor was killed there five years ago), or you could hire a strong young boy to take you up Mount Bromo on East Java. There have always been men like Elmer, fit and wiry-legged fellows who hang out at the local bars near the big exploding hills, available to anyone who wants to come and climb.

But now the scale of the business and the personalities involved have changed. A new band of entrepreneurs appears to be springing up, enthusiasts who believe that volcanoes can offer the kind of challenge and spectacle that will lure even the most jaded of Westerners, will reinvigorate both the body and the spirit.

A former U.S. Air Force maintenance man by the name of Rusty Kitchin is one of this new breed—a man who is currently betting that today's travelers are made of stern enough stuff to be beguiled by the combination of beauty and danger. He believes that there are enough sensible and thoughtful new adventurers who will figure that the risk of personal catastrophe is measurably small, and a risk that will in any case be well offset by the experience of seeing one of these mountains firsthand.

So he has settled in the Philippines and is among the first to open a small guiding company—leading people to the top of what is perhaps Asia's most notoriously dangerous volcano: Mount Pinatubo.

When I arrived in the Philippines, I had been planning simply to try to reach the top of Mount Mayon—it is the sort of breathtaking peak that once seen (even in a small black-and-white snapshot in Volume 7 of Britannica) demands to be climbed. I had long wanted to climb Mount Pinatubo, too. So when I saw Rusty's advertisement in a Manila magazine, it seemed a good idea—since I wasn't in a hurry—to try his mountain as an appetizer. I tracked him down in the lobby of the Swagman Narra Hotel in Angeles City, handed over a fee for his services and those of a couple of porters, and at dawn the next day we set out.

"We're off to see the belly of the beast," he said jauntily as we swung onto a track leading up the lower slopes. "Six hours and you'll be able to have a swim in it."

In the summer of 1991, Mount Pinatubo had a thousand feet blown off its summit, as if a crude giant had sheared it off with egg scissors. Huge flows of mud and ash and hot water, known as lahars, had cascaded down the volcano's flanks and had spread unchecked for dozens of miles. Villages were submerged; hundreds died; a landscape was changed and ruined.

We walked first across the strange moonscape of one of these lahars, now frozen into peaks of compressed ash, chalk white, and fringed with new grass. The cliffs are a hundred feet high and razor-edged. The flow forms a huge, impenetrable maze that only Rusty and his local Filipino guides know how to navigate: Only the course of an old river, the O'Donnell, suggests an entryway. We trudged up it, weaving past immense towers of ash, for hours.

There were clouds swirling across the tops, and once in a while a shower; and when the view improved, we could see a rainbow over the buildings of the air base below. We passed a sweet spring, then another of hot, sour water that steamed and left a crust of chemicals along its bank. There was a small grove of trees, a patch of blue flowers, and then the canyon closed in—but only for a while, because suddenly the vista opened up and we found ourselves standing on the lip of the crater lake itself, a lake so new that it appears on none of my maps, formed when the dome of the mountaintop had been blown off.

We clambered cautiously down a sheer cliff face toward a dark sand beach and stepped gingerly into the water. It was hot—not scalding, but like a pleasant bath—rich with chemicals, and had a faint but luminous green tinge. We swam in it: The solutes buoy one up, like in the Dead Sea. My skin turned a strange color for a while but suffered no obvious harm.

Some days before, two of Rusty's porters had lugged an inflatable canoe up the track, and within moments I was out on the lake in it, paddling for the far side. I wanted to go where I could see a suture line, with clouds of steam venting from the shore. As I paddled closer to it, the water became hotter until it was far too hot to touch, and the canoe started to melt and sag in an alarmingly rubbery way. Close to the steam vents, which now roared deafeningly, the water was boiling, and the little craft tossed as though it were in a kettle. Small gobbets of sulfur were spat into the air, and soon the bow glistened with bright yellow crystals.

And then there came a deafening crack from up ahead, and a massive slab of black cliff dislodged itself, as though the mountain had shrugged it off its shoulder: A vast rain of rock plunged into the lake, frothing the surface and setting the canoe rocking even more alarmingly. Further, the heat was now making the boat sag still more dangerously, and my seat was uncomfortable and scalding; and what with the noise and the choking air, it seemed prudent to paddle back to cooler, calmer waters.

Probably bottomless, a visiting geologist said of the lake. One of the entrances to Hell, said Rusty, more poetically. He and his porters insisted over lunch that they will make a business out of bringing travelers to this most extraordinary of sights. "You feel like one in a million up here," Rusty said. "I mean, who else comes up to see a green and boiling lake, to paddle through a mess of steam jets, to watch a whole side of a cliff crash down a thousand feet?"

But that, I said, is just the problem. The volcano hissing and crumbling and steaming away in the background has to be a powerful reminder of the old caution that man proposes, but God disposes. "Sure," said Rusty, ever the optimist. "But so long as he carries on disposing nicely, we'll be okay. I have faith in him, you know. You have to, sitting under a volcano."

The next day, after taking a perfunctory side trip to what is said to be the world's lowest volcano, the island-in-a-lake-in-an-island-in-a-lake complex known as Taal (where a spectacular eruption in 1965 killed two hundred), I flew to Legazpi City in southern Luzon to make my long-awaited attempt on Mayon. I had been there three times in the previous decade: Twice we started too late to finish the climb in a day; once we were beaten back by bad weather. This, I reckoned, was my last chance.

The pilot took a long and lazy descent around the mountain, spiraling down from the summit over the slopes where we would be struggling the next day. The evening was still, with not a cloud in sight. The great mountain cast a five-mile shadow over the rice fields, and at the top coughed yellow smoke gently from what seemed, from this height, a small, untidy throat, like a hungry fledgling's. As we landed, the mountain turned purple in the twilight, and a small shower of sparks danced at the summit, reminding us that it was very much alive. It was then that Elmer told me of the bodies he had seen and of his terrified charges running ahead of the pyroclastic gales.

We rose at four and drove through pitch darkness to a hut where we collected our porters—two men who emerged blinking and sleepy, smoking hand-rolled cigarettes, and hefted our bags onto their backs. Like the hungover Elmer, they wore plastic thongs on their feet; they had on ragged shorts and T-shirts. It was cold just before dawn, and I felt I needed my Patagonia fleece.

The guidebooks insist that it takes almost eleven hours to make the summit—two and a half to Camp 1, four to Camp 2, another four to the final ridge. But we must have been a great deal fitter than the average guidebook reader, since we took no more than ninety minutes to reach Camp 1.

But what we saw ahead was dismaying: An anvil-shaped mass of cloud was scudding in from the east, blotting out the rising sun and, worst of all, spreading itself like a skirt over the lower slopes of the mountain. The gullies and ravines ahead began to fill up with a thick mist, and from time to time gusts of wind blew patters of rain down, cooling us after our hearty prebreakfast walk—which was nice, but ominous.

We stopped for ten minutes, ate mangoes and chunks of bread, and drank noisily from a stream. Then we set off again, up one of the radial gullies that reach down from the summit—a mile-long pathway of cliffs and river-smoothed andesite that sloped upward at an ever-increasing angle.

It was murder to climb—slippery, steep, wet, deceptively long. Once in a while the porters took us into the forest, clapping their hands to keep away snakes. On the whole, however, it was just a constant slog upward: wet, bruising, wearying. We made Camp 2 after another two hours—we were well ahead of the plan, having taken a total of three and a half hours to achieve what the book insisted would take six.

The going above Camp 2 became steadily worse—ever more cliffs, ever more steep gullies, rocks made ever more slippery by the rain. And then the smell of sulfur started to pervade everything, and there were strange yellow-rimmed cliffs that, if you peered over, seemed to be the edge of a giant nothingness. "Crater," said Elmer helpfully, and I kept well away from the lip.

To his credit, he and his men soldiered on for another half an hour, up another three hundred feet. We passed two young men from Belgium, both on their way down, the look of failure about them. "Too windy," one shouted. "Too dangerous. And we felt movement. A bucking in the ground—as if it was going to explode."

I gulped but trudged on. By the time we reached the part where the slope became truly steep, where the ground became friable and broken, the wind was howling and knocking us flat each time we emerged from behind a sheltering wall of rock. By the time we were at the point where the book said "it is most advisable to be roped together," the porters had clearly had enough. They conferred in whispered Tagalog and then turned away.

"What's happening?" I cried.

"Sir, we are dying here!" shouted Elmer. He was soaked and shivering and looked terribly frightened.

"Eruption?" I shouted.

"No, sir," he replied. "Just too dangerous. We wait below. You go on."

And so I did, painfully, one handhold after another, one foot after another, hiding below the cliff every few moments for shelter. And slowly, like a great gray tombstone, the summit ridge eventually appeared out of the gloom, and I found my way to its center, keeping well away from the edges and from a certain and unpleasant death in that sulfur-rimmed crater.

A gust blew me, staggering, to the very lip, and I had a momentary feeling of vertigo, staring down into the glowing heart of the volcano. But I recovered, and with the fumes now half-choking me and the gale buffeting me, I found myself at the narrowest point of the ridge, a precarious and tiny black boulder from where all the rock faces and surfaces at long last pointed down.

It was eleven-thirty in the morning. To reach the summit, at 7,943 feet, had taken five and three-quarter hours. There was no view, nothing of which to take a photograph, no reason at all to linger. So I simply turned back the way I had come, and slipping and sliding and falling until I was bruised and cut and bleeding, arrived back at Camp 2. Elmer and the porters were there, hiding in a cave.

Then there came a rumbling from above and a strange shaking deep in the ground, as though some giant were stirring in his sleep, turning over, grunting, acting restless. It was time to head down, I thought. The sun came out. We were off the lower slopes by five and taking a cold San Miguel at the Trinidad hotel in Legazpi by the time twilight fell and it turned to dark.

The next morning the air was clear and still once more, and the mountain gleamed in the morning sun. There was not a cloud in sight, and besides a slight wisp of yellowish smoke drifting

from the very summit, no indication that the mountain was anything other than it looked—serene, perfect, beautiful. The hotel
receptionist, waiting for my credit card to clear, said she expected
Mayon to erupt again next year. "But you really never can tell,
which is what makes it so exciting." And she smiled.

1998

Volcanoes Explained

What you need to know about volcanoes:
plus, where and how to see the world's most active

The Protocol

Locals recognize the idiosyncrasies of active volcanoes: If they tell of hearing or feeling ominous grumbles, get well clear. The magnificence of these slumbering monsters is matched only by their dangerous sense of caprice. (In descending order of danger, volcanoes are classified as active, meaning that they are known to erupt; dormant, meaning that they are not currently erupting but have the potential to do so; and extinct, meaning that they have a history of erupting but are not likely ever to do so again.)

If you are on a mountainside when a volcano erupts, beware the active lava flow. In Hawaii and at Etna, the flows will be fiery; in places like the Philippines, however, they may be black and slaglike on the surface but molten a few inches below—and stepping onto what looks like a solid crust could plunge you into red-hot lava.

If an eruption produces the scalding rock-filled winds known as pyroclastic flows, stay at least sixty miles from the volcano's cones. Pyroclastic flows move fast and kill either by blast or by heat.

If there is any local indication that a volcanic dome is changing its shape, keep your distance: The handful of tourists who die each year in volcano accidents around the world do so after straying onto exploding domes.

If, as on Mount Pinatubo, there are water-and-ash streams, or lahars, run like hell. These have a nasty habit of increasing in volume and speed.

Poisonous and suffocating gases may be produced close to a

crater or from the tiny piped exits known as fumaroles. The poisonous gases—hydrogen sulfide and sulfur dioxide—usually smell distinctively foul, and you'll *want* to move away (always make sure you have an escape route). Carbon dioxide is odorless, however, and heavy enough to remain in a pocket—and can choke you to death in minutes. If you see dead animals or bones in a crater, you could go the same way if you take the same path.

If rock and lapilli bombardments start up, immediately find a cave to shelter you until the eruption subsides.

And take care in an obviously geothermal area where there are mud pools and geysers. Crusts that are formed here can look deceptively solid (and alluringly pretty): Plunging through a crust and ending up neck-deep in boiling mud can really take the shine off your vacation.

Following is a rundown of the volcanoes most worth a visit in the Philippines, Indonesia, Japan, Russia, and the Hawaiian Islands.

PHILIPPINES

There are twenty-two active volcanoes in the Philippines. The most easily accessible are Mount Mayon and the notorious Pinatubo, both in the southern part of the principal island of Luzon.

The closest town to Mayon is the port city of Legaspi, which is well served from Manila by air and bus. Mountain guides, though not always reliable, are available. Start your climb before dawn to ensure that you'll make it up and back in a day.

INDONESIA

Indonesia has 173 active volcanoes, most on the suture line where Eurasian and Australian plates collide along Java, Sumatra, and Bali.

The most famous is Krakatoa, now called Anak Krakatau

("Child of Krakatoa"), where on August 26, 1883, what was likely the greatest eruption in recorded history took place—its death roar, reckoned the loudest sound ever, was heard from Ceylon to Australia. The island lies between Java and Sumatra and is accessible only by boat.

The twin peaks of Merapi and Merbabu, near the southern Javanese city of Yogyakarta, attract visitors because of the lovely sunrise between them each day. Both are active—the eruption of Merapi in 1006, it is said, prompted the Hindu raja of Java to flee eastward and bring Hinduism to Bali.

Bali's sacred Mount Agung, ten thousand feet high, last erupted in 1963, killing almost two thousand. The climb starts in the village of Besakih. Stay at one of the many small hotels around Lake Batur.

JAPAN

Japan claims 108 volcanoes, of which the best known is Mount Fuji. Its last eruption was in 1707, and it can fairly be expected to remain quiet—a good thing, since hundreds of thousands of people get to the top every year. The trails are open in July and August.

Mount Usu, on the northern island of Hokkaido, has spawned sinister-looking upstart mountains in recent years, including the thirteen-hundred-foot Showa Shinzan, which rose out of a wheat field in 1943 after a series of earthquakes. There is a cable car up Usu itself, but exploring the neighboring peaks is a good way to remind yourself of the bizarre power of vulcanicity. Stay at any of the hotels around the pretty Lake Toya.

Sakurajima lies in Kagoshima Bay, off the southern island of Kyushu, and erupts more or less constantly. Its three peaks can be reached from several places on the road around its base. Tiny oranges grown in groves at the foot of Sakurajima sell for a small fortune in Tokyo markets.

RUSSIA

With Kamchatka, the dangling peninsula off far eastern Russia, now getting easier to reach by air and sea, its twenty-nine huge active volcanoes are becoming increasingly accessible. The most famous is the Bezymianny peak, which can be reached by charter helicopter (quite inexpensive) from the regional capital, Petropavlovsk-Kamchatsky—the headquarters of Russia's Pacific atomic submarine fleet.

HAWAII

After 70 million years of volcanic activity Hawaii still has five active volcanoes, including two of the world's most active. The 13,680-foot-tall Mauna Loa, the world's largest active volcano, last erupted in 1984, and Kilauea, where the mythic volcano goddess Pele made her eternal home, has been erupting continuously since 1983.

Located thirty minutes southwest of Hilo on Hawaii's Big Island, these volcanoes compose part of Hawaii's three-hundred-thousand-plus-acre Volcanoes National Park (nps.gov/havo). Adventurous backpackers can hike the park's Mauna Loa summit trail in about two days, holing up for the night in the Pu'u 'Ula'ula cabin at 10,035 feet, or in the Mauna Loa cabin at 13,250 feet. Visitors preferring a two-hour trek can traverse verdant rainforest and a mile-wide crater on the Kilauea Iki trail. Those who left their hiking boots at home can loop around the Kilauea caldera by car on the scenic Crater Rim Drive.

The Red Danube

by

GREGOR VON REZZORI

Ten years ago I went to Bucharest for a few days. As I headed toward customs at Otopeni Airport, I was met by a huge woman, a kind of Mother Russia personified, with a Mongolian fur cap engulfing her apple-cheeked face. Steaming in her army great coat like a hot samovar, she was ten inches taller than me. She had stuck her fur-lined mittens in her leather belt next to the pistol holster. Sternly she asked me for my passport. Handing it to her, I said in Romanian, "I was born in this country and it's the first time I've returned in forty years." She threw her arms around me, heaved me into the air, and kissed me on both cheeks. *"Bine ai venit, feciorule!"*—"Welcome, little son!" (I was in my sixties then.)

This time, as we waited to take the plane from Bucharest east to Tulcea, near the Soviet border, the entrance to Băneasa Airport was blocked by another woman, smaller than my greeter from ten years ago but of the same cannonball solidity. It was May, and she wore a summer uniform: a white blouse with black shoulder straps studded with two buckles and a star in sparkling brass, a stiff black skirt, black stockings and shoes, and, on her thick peroxide-bleached hair, an officer's cap with a black patent leather peak that cast a masklike shadow over her eyes. Behind her back an alarming operation was being carried out: A policeman was smashing his truncheon into the thick glass of one of the airport doors. The noise was horrifying. Big shards crashed to the floor and broke into a heap of daggerlike splinters. Someone must have cracked the pane, perhaps with a bulky piece of luggage, and the wardens of public safety wanted to protect passengers from injury. When the philanthropic destruction was completed, our guardian angel stepped aside. Our way to the check-in was clear.

Not really the check-in, though. A line of policemen stood behind a barrier ready to submit the passengers to a rigorous examination. One asked for our documents, another for our tickets, a third searched our clothes and bodies for weapons. A group of particularly grim-looking fellows made us open our luggage piece by piece and started fumbling among our belongings, pulling out such suspicious objects as binoculars and electric shavers for meticulous scrutiny. Deep down at the bottom of a bag, one of them found our supply of cigarettes. He gave me an incriminating look. It is by no means forbidden to bring cigarettes into Romania, but he made a face as if he had just discovered a major conspiracy. "Keep a package for yourself," I said to him. "They were meant to be given away. I don't smoke." With a magician's skill he made the package vanish from sight. Then, with a side-glance to a colleague next to him, he said, "He too has seen them." The colleague nodded sternly. "Well," I said, "let him have some too." The colleague helped himself with equal skill. "What about my comrade who checked your documents?" he asked. I said, "He shouldn't smoke. He looks as if he has a heart condition. I can see that. I'm a doctor, you know." They laughed and let me pass.

———

We had our trip arranged beforehand by a travel agency—an advisable thing to do when touring Romania. The tourist office had delegated a licensed guide to steer us through the vicissitudes of airplane embarkation. She had watched the scene. "I am ashamed of my fellow countrymen," she said in Italian, which she spoke as fluently as French and English. "Oh, don't be Robespierre-ish," I replied. "This doesn't happen only in Romania. Besides . . ." I was about to explain to her—the Romanian—her own people's character: that mixture of arrogance and generosity, violence and kindheartedness, baseness and humor, slyness and childishness— all that made them unpredictable and never banal. I was about to tell her that apparently things had not changed since I had left the country in 1938; that perhaps they would never change, given the country's past, its millennia of turbulence, the perpetual necessity to adapt to invaders, conquerors, oppressors. But was I right? I felt as if I myself belonged to a past as remote as that of the waves of barbarians that had come out of the vast open spaces of the East and swept westward along the Danube into the plains of Wallachia and over the Carpathians into Transylvania and farther on into Hungary, up to the walls of Vienna: Goths, Gepidae, Slavs, Bulgars, Magyars, Huns, Petchenegs, Cumans, Turks. Fifty years of modern technology and mass-media brainwashing might well have changed what had formed over twenty centuries of perilous exposure and backwardness. I decided I'd better keep my opinions to myself. I thanked our high-minded guide for her readiness to help and shaking her hand slipped into it a pair of silk stockings, which she too made vanish from sight.

The flight from Bucharest to Tulcea takes forty-five minutes. Our plane was small and shaky. Breakfast was served in the shape of full tumblers of Romanian cognac. I looked for the Danube below us but could not see it. We landed bumpily on a strip in a vast field. When we taxied toward the airport buildings, we saw that they were guarded by heavily armed soldiers.

The road from the airport to Tulcea winds through flat hills covered with vineyards. Only five people, two men and three women working the soil by hand, were visible in miles and miles of parallel rows of vines. We wondered how much time it would take them to rake, weed, and water such immense acreage. And what about the actual harvesting? I expressed my worries to the man sitting next to me on the bus, who looked like a local. He said dryly, "It's a long way to the harvest. We are only at the end of May."

The harbor of Tulcea came into view, looking small and very maritime. A few freighters, much larger than you would expect to find on a river, floated at anchor. Desperately in need of paint, they had a patina of rust that bespoke adventurous passages to re-mote shores, although they probably never got out of the Black Sea, into which the Danube empties.

A small tourist boat waited for us at the pier to take us to the hotel at Crişan, in the middle of the Danube Delta. We had a photographer with us, a young Frenchman called Hugues, who thought—or pretended to, for he liked to tease us—that Bucha-rest was the capital of Hungary and that the mouth of the Dan-ube was the Dardanelles. As I am never quite sure about young people's knowledge of Eastern Europe's geography and history, I gave him a briefing.

He nodded distractedly. In fact his attention was fully ab-sorbed by a group of German tourists who filled the boat to the brim—not so much by their number as by their bulkiness. They were in high spirits, handing around unlabeled bottles of pale wine that they swigged lustily. Two Romanians in token national costume—their embroidered shirts and blue-yellow-red sashes in strange contrast to their cream-colored slacks and Adidas sneakers—also came aboard. They were armed with an astonish-ing variety of musical instruments and instantly began to dis-play their virtuosity on each one of them. Their repertoire—from

"The Blue Danube" to "La Paloma"—was small; therefore they repeated it over and over. Each time they played on a different combination of instruments: fiddle and accordion, flute and cymbal, bugle and guitar. The climax was the usual one in any performance of Romanian popular music: the "Ciocîrlia," a phonetic transcription of a lark's ascent into the sky and its fluttering up there. It is a particularly demanding piece on whatever instrument it is played, and it bores itself into the listener's ear with the devastating persistence of an ichneumon fly. The Germans enjoyed all this immensely. They waved their bottles, clapped one another's shoulders, and assured one another at the top of their voices that they were having a very good time indeed.

Beatrice, my wife, got a bit annoyed. I said to her that the drab waters on which we were now proceeding quickly downstream had carried many a wondrous craft since the Argonauts: Phoenician boats, Hellenic triremes, Roman galleys, Byzantine ships, Genoese caravels, Venetian galleons, Turkish caïques, and, in recent times, tugboats, barges, and motor ships. For the Danube has been one of the most frequented European waterways since time immemorial. The 1,676 square miles of its delta not only have no match among the wildlife territories of the Continent— Tulcea is the gateway to this miraculous last bit of relatively unspoiled nature in Europe—but also are, and always were, sprinkled with groups of the strangest peoples: Turks and Caucasians, Gypsies and Moors, Bulgarians and Wallachians, Russians and Serbs. With its innumerable channels, rivulets, brooks, swamps, lakes, marshes, and lagoons, the Delta was, by its nature and throughout the centuries, a realm of outcasts, the ideal hiding place for all sorts of delinquents, brigands, deserters, runaway convicts. In the beginning of the twentieth century the Lipovans, members of a religious sect driven out of czarist Russia, settled on the banks of the main branches as fishermen and still make up the greater part of a population of about forty thousand. The recent invasion of package-tour tourists, I said with feeble conviction, can only add to the exoticism of the area.

In the meantime, what surrounded us was anything but exotic. We were sailing down the middle one of the three main branches of the Danube that lead to the Black Sea. Doubtless the other two are more spectacular. The first—Braţul Chilia in Romanian—wider and deeper than its brothers—swings around in a flat curve to demarcate the frontier with Russia. The second, Braţul Sfîntu Gheorghe, meanders in the south through boundless areas of reeds, swamps, and woodlands before reaching its destination. Ours—Braţul Sulina—is the shortest. It aims in a straight line directly for Sulina, Romania's largest harbor after Constanţa.

For a long time, the only eye-catchers on its banks were rusty cranes and dredgers that jutted up out of the boscage like skeletons of prehistoric monsters. But the deeper we penetrated the Delta, the lusher the vegetation on the banks became. The land behind seemed to take a step back and widen; occasionally mallards paired off and crossed overhead. We were nearing the fabulous sites where, sixty and more years ago, my father used to hunt to his heart's content. He never ceased to talk about the unbelievable abundance of birds of all kinds; the thousands of teal, mallards, sheldrakes, herons, cranes, swans, pelicans, flamingos, and whatnot in the reeds and ponds; the wild boars, stags, wolves, foxes, and otters in the marshes and woods. I began to watch the banks through my binoculars. Every black-headed gull that darted to the water to catch what it thought might be a morsel—but was just the cork of the umpteenth bottle the Germans threw overboard—I took to be the advance guard of the swarms of winged and beaked, shrilling and chirping beasts that would soon arise from behind the trees that lined the bank and darken the sunlight. But nothing in particular happened. After about three hours, when the musicians had mastered the "Ciocîrlia" on harmonica and bagpipe and finished their program with "La Paloma" on the same instruments, we arrived at Crişan.

Crişan is built up around a small village of some twenty-odd flat cottages of wood and clay, each in its tiny garden behind a high wooden fence. They lie in one row along the channel, separated from it by a well-worn path and a seam of chamomile and blue thistle growing on the riverbank, among which old boats rot peacefully. The fences, joined in a straight line behind which only the roofs of the cottages and the tops of rosebushes and hollyhocks can be seen, are mulberry blue and olive green and rust and azure and egg-yolk yellow, faded in the sun. Behind the cottages are gardens with cabbages and carrots and orchards with apple trees and currants; and beyond that yawns the vast space of marshes, rivulets, and lakes where swans and cormorants and the great crested grebe brood. The air carries the smell of the sea, a few miles away.

The Hotel Lebăda (Swan) lay across the channel opposite the old village, on a spit of land formed by the Braţul Sulina and a dead branch of the river's old course. It was a futuristic combination of a Swiss chalet and a Neolithic lake dwelling, with a compound of small cabins for those guests with a special taste for camping. We didn't give more than a glance to our rooms, which were small, dull, functional, and clean. We were too impatient to set off and see the wildlife. This turned out to be more difficult than we had imagined.

The receptionist—purser and concierge all in one—was a pretty girl who spoke a few words of French and English. Putting them together, she said that we did not belong to a group for which sight-seeing tours on a barge could be arranged. Therefore we would just have to wait until we could join one. She suggested the Germans with whom we had just arrived. But they, she said, were now having a picnic with folk music; afterward they would rest and, presumably toward evening, set out for their trip to see the sunset. When Beatrice said that everything that had to do with tourist groups was a nightmare anyway, the girl said, "*Pour vous, madame!* For us they are sheer bliss." She became more manageable when I said that the deutsche marks could be matched by a few American dollars. Well, she said, she might be able to arrange for a rowboat to take us around in the immediate area; for a motor launch or any of the large state-owned boats, we would need permission from the state authorities in Tulcea. This was a blow, but for the moment we gladly accepted the rowboat. While waiting for it we would have something to eat.

The dining room was huge, a sort of winter garden with curtains that looked like brocade but weren't. We had a fish soup, stewed fish, and fried fish with some slimy white mash that the waiter told us was rice. Could we have some potatoes, please? Potatoes? The waiter smiled. No, there were no potatoes. There was no pudding, either. Would there be some fruit? Oh no, there was no fruit. Coffee? No, there was no coffee. We gave up. Our oarsman turned up, a tall fellow with a nice face who resembled the late Danny Kaye. He was a Ukrainian from the village on the other bank. Fishermen? Yes, but some worked in factories, too. We asked what factories. There were some around, he said evasively. His name was Gheorghe. With steady strong strokes he rowed us upstream to the left bank and into a narrow channel. On both sides the reeds were impenetrable. Willows, gnarled like oaks, dipped their leaves into the still water. The silence was perfect, underlined by the occasional croak of frogs. The soft thump with which they plopped their gaping heads into the water when our boat approached was the only sign of wildlife.

Hugues had his cameras ready. Every now and then he took a shot of some picturesque turn of our watercourse—not an easy task, for our boat was swaying like a dugout canoe at the slightest movement. But Gheorghe rowed it masterfully, and we eventually came to a lake, peaceful and empty. When I asked Gheorghe where the birds were, he said there had been too many foreigners who'd shot them. I felt guilty for my father; but it sounded like somewhat of an exaggeration that he and his ilk could have ruthlessly decimated all those hundreds of thousands of ornithologists' delights. Not even Gheorghe himself seemed totally convinced. There were some left, he said, thanks to the protection they enjoyed under the laws of the socialist republic. But for the moment the birds were busy sitting on their eggs.

He took a deep breath, scratched his head, and recited a litany of protective laws for the local flora and fauna. We assured him that we had no intentions of violating any of these prohibitions. But was shooting forbidden entirely? we asked. Absolutely, he assured us, except that the head of state, Comrade Ceauşescu, was a great shot himself, so there might be some exceptions. We hoped there wouldn't be any. The peace was perfect. We would have hated a shot to disturb all those millions of birds that were sitting quietly on their eggs.

We came to another, bigger lake. It must have been shallow, for a log stuck out in the middle, with a cormorant sitting on it. Then we saw the swans. There were six of them, majestically circling a small bay on the other side of the lake. At the same time, a grebe shot out of the mirrorlike water, turned its crested head around in a full swivel, and vanished as mysteriously as it had appeared. The day was fading. Gheorghe rowed us back by another channel. In the hall of the hotel the Romanian staff was watching Russian television. I took Gheorghe to the bar and we drank some Ţuica—a light and delightful plum brandy. Hugues, whose cunning charm had seduced the entire staff, turned up with a bottle of whiskey. We had fish for dinner—and no potatoes. At nine o'clock we were fast asleep.

Thunder woke us up at half past five the next morning. The leader of the German group was banging his fists against our door. He soon realized his mistake. A simple mix-up of the room numbers, he shouted with a hearty laugh. His group was leaving at six. We blessed their departure. The morning was spent negotiating for a motorboat to take us deeper into the wildlife reserves, nearer those eggs all those birds were sitting on. Beatrice had studied a map that indicated a large maritime sandbank of high interest for naturalists, a place called Letea, near which there was a forest of the same name, a renowned and protected Monument of Nature. Gheorghe had told us that the main breeding ground of pelicans in Europe was there.

But the assistant to the top manager declared that going to Letea was out of the question. Not even the top manager himself could give us the permission. It had to be issued by the competent authorities in Bucharest. The only thing he, the assistant manager, could do for us was to procure the motorboat, provided that we paid for it in dollars. It could bring us to the village of Mila 23, where there was the slim chance of finding a fisherman with a longboat who could row us a bit nearer to Letea. That too would be illegal, but not as much as disturbing the brooding birds with the noise of an engine.

Mila 23 is a famous settlement of the Lipovans. It seemed absurd to go there, for the sandbank and forest of Letea, where we were headed, lie in the opposite direction. But our boatman said there was no other way to get there, except by a very bad track from Sulina. To use it, we would need a tractor. Besides, he added, the interest naturalists take in Letea was not so much for the pelicans, which are found in the south near Caraorman, as for the eighteen hundred species of insects that find the sand dunes an ideal environment—particularly the largest of flies, *Satanas gigas*. They would not waste their time sitting quietly on their eggs. But it didn't matter anyway, as no one would take us near them.

Our boatman's skepticism proved justified. The men who sat on
the terrace of a pub facing the landing place in Mila 23 stared at
us blankly when we asked about the pelicans, as if we were speaking to them in Chinese. It wasn't because they were descendants
of Russians. They didn't look it anyhow. No high boots, no Tol-
stoy beards, just checkered shirts and denims. It took us a while to
grasp that they were actually paralyzed with drink. It was high
noon and we felt hungry, but the pub was closed. I asked one of
them where they had got their bottles from; on the table were
dozens of empty and half-full ones. When the meaning of my
question finally sank in, he managed to answer by pointing his
index finger in slow motion at a house with a roof of corrugated
iron next to the pub. It was a little shop.

The woman behind the counter had a lovely face, strong,
cheerful, and motherly. When we asked her if we could buy something to eat, she smiled and shook her head. The wall behind her
was handsomely decorated with pyramids of tins on shelves. We
couldn't see what they contained, but we presumed it was edible.
But when we pointed at the tins, she shook her head again. At the
far end of the counter sat a large basket full of eggs. They looked
wonderfully fresh. Those eggs were not for sale; on the contrary,
they were brought in by the villagers. Every household where
chickens were kept, we were told, had to deliver 250 eggs a year to
the state. When there were more, the villagers could barter them
for other goods. Had the drunks on the terrace bartered surplus
eggs for their bottles? No, wine was to be had for money. We
bought a bottle. While I was counting the change she had given
me back, she took out from under the counter half a loaf of freshly
baked bread and six eggs from the basket. Without a word she
shoved them toward us. No, she did not want us to pay for them.
It was a present to welcome us to Mila 23.

We wanted to have the eggs boiled, but where? A man who

came out from behind the pub beckoned to us and took us inside by a back door. He led us into a large saloon with colorfully painted walls. A young man sat at a table eating fried fish. Our guide just took the plate away from under his fork and put it on our table. "Eat," he said. "It's good fresh fish." We shared the wine with the chap from whom he had taken the fish. He didn't mind at all giving it to us, he said. They ate fish day in, day out, anyway. The eggs, which we had given to the other man to boil, never turned up again. We had some cucumbers instead. No potatoes.

The weather was fine, and we strolled into the village. As in Crişan, the houses were lined up along the river, but here the hinterland was laced with lagoons, canals, and trenches. Venice must have had a similar beginning some fifteen hundred years ago. Dwellings were mainly built of wood and covered in reeds. Fishing nets were hung out to dry on high poles. Fences too were of reeds or wickerwork, turned mahogany with age. Graves with slanted crosses were scattered about a small spit of land in front of a clay building painted bright azure with white window and door frames. Children played there with a bearded fellow whom we thought to be as drunk as most of the other villagers but who turned out to be a particularly friendly village idiot. There were fresh flowers in front of quite a few of the crosses. A woman in an apron came out of the house and told us that thirty-four people had been buried there recently. We asked if there had been a epidemic. No, it was a normal toll for the winter. Hugues liked the place so much that he said he would stay overnight and join us at Lebăda the next morning.

Our boatman must have felt a bit guilty that we had seen no wildlife, for he took us up the other waterway and through a few more lakes as near to Letea as we could go. We got a whiff of the Delta's immensity. Vast flats and open spaces often cause a certain restlessness. Not this unbounded proliferation of floating plants clinging together in an infinity of green tints under an open sky. It was both cheerful and calming. It offered itself like the palm of the hand, the waters glittering through the thickets of reeds and water ferns and marsh thistles or gleaming in clean sheets of rivulets and lakes. We crisscrossed it the whole afternoon. Of course, there were also various kinds of water birds, neglecting their duty to sit on their eggs; but they had ceased to be the main target of our expectations. Our minds were stilled. The willows, ashes, and elders that bordered the canals were like majestic elms along the allées of an old park. B. and I came back to the Hotel Lebăda and happily had fish for dinner—without potatoes.

Hugues came back in the morning from Mila 23 as loaded with exposed film and tales of adventures as a honeybee is loaded with pollen. He had avoided sharing a bed with one of the drunkards by staying up all night in the pub teaching the others to sing the "Marseillaise." B. and I had not been idle either. We had spent the previous evening telephoning some friends in Bucharest to help us get permission to see a bit more of the Delta's Natural Reserves and Monuments of Nature. As at least four members of the hotel staff were attentively listening in on our line, we did some hearty name-dropping, with the result that, in the morning, the head manager himself became enormously attentive and promised to procure a tractor that would take us from a point on one of the lakes near Caraorman to the famous forest there.

The weather had changed. Large clouds gathered over the sea of reeds, and it became quite cold. The pretty girl at reception said thoughtfully, "It may rain in the afternoon. A weather to make love." A group of tourists who looked Austrian but were Swiss arrived at the hotel to the sounds of "Ciorcîrlia." We braced ourselves with parkas and raincoats and set off for Caraorman.

More canals. More, and even vaster, marshes. More lakes.

The world seemed flatter here, less lush. Then out from the reeds rose what gave us a better explanation for the scarcity of birds than their perpetual brooding. On a totally deserted building site covered with rubble and dust and all sorts of rusty machinery stood the remains of a gigantic industrial plant in—obviously interrupted—construction. It looked menacing in a hopeless, desolate way—an abandoned fortress of progress—evoking echoes of the unfulfilled dreams and promises of this century.

A tractor that must have been built in the first decade of Soviet Russia's industrialization waited for us on the pier. Two men stood by it: the tractor's driver and his elderly friend. They were chattering with three urchins from a nearby village, which looked gray and dreary. While we were driving toward the forest, I asked the older man about the factory. What was it for? Better: What was it meant for? Processing fish? Well, sort of, he said vaguely. Maybe in the future. At present all construction has come to a standstill. He and the urchins jumped off the tractor while we were passing the village. The telegraph poles were crowned with nests of storks.

The forest of Caraorman was deep and green and silent as a forest should be. On the way—the tractor rocking on the scarcely recognizable track—we had picked up a family of five, two couples and a newborn child. They were Romanians who had come for a holiday. We stopped deep in the woods and picnicked, sharing our food and wine with them in the shade of some mighty oaks. The baby was so firmly swaddled we feared it would choke or in the end turn our deformed, like a Chinese lady's foot. But it seemed quite happy, patiently sucking its pacifier while flies promenaded over its face. We forgot about the factory. The scenery was idyllic, and Hugues took many pictures while cuckoos called out of the depths of the wood. "How long will you be staying?" we asked our Romanian friends as we parted. "Forever."

They lived nearby. Both men were working in another factory. "Are there many around?" we asked. Quite a few; and there would be many more in the future, they said proudly.

Back in our boat, our boatman gave us the complete tour of canals, rivers, rivulets, and lakes. The weather had cleared up again. As if nature seemed to want to disprove any theory about a possible disturbance of fauna and flora by factories and other forms of industrialization, we saw rare birds at every bend: great white egrets and spoonbills, avocets, lapwings, grebes, and many others. Then, in the middle of a broad canal lined with rusting tubes, we met the pelicans. The encounter was so unexpected that Hugues hastily grabbed the wrong camera to photograph them. There was no film in it—or so he told us then, just to tease us. To comfort us, Gheorghe took us to his parents' house in the village of Crişan. We had dinner with his family: a stew of fish and delicious fresh potatoes. "Take some more of them," his eighty-year-old mother encouraged us. "They're full of vitamins."

1988

OF CASTLES AND COUNTS

Exploring Romania's architectural heritage

 Romania is a rare amalgam of cultures, incorporating Ottoman, Venetian, German, Slavic, and Romany influences. The result of an often volatile past, this mélange is most evident in Romanian architecture, or, more specifically, the numerous castles and fortresses strewn about the landscape.

"Dracula's Castle," perhaps the best-known attraction in Romania, draws busloads of tourists into Bran, a small town about eighty miles north of Bucharest in picturesque Transylvania. However, true fans of the mythical bloodsucking prince know that the real villain who inspired the myth, Vlad Tepeş (1431–76)—more popularly known as The Impaler for his favorite method of murder—was imprisoned in the fourteenth-century fortress atop a bluff for just four days (or so legend has it, anyway). This proto-Dracula was a cruel but heroic leader of medieval Wallachia, later part of the united Romania.

Beyond the Dracula myth, Transylvania is actually far less frightening than Bram Stoker would have you believe. In fact, its brightly colored villages are pretty and festive, recalling the towns of the old Austro-Hungarian Empire. This makes sense—ethnic Germans and Hungarians still make up a good portion of the population, although many have emigrated since the fall of communism, leaving their quaint abodes behind to squatters. Sixteen miles southwest of Bran, the city of **Braşov** is a great example of such a town. It has the nation's best baroque city streets and a richly historic center with architecture dating back to its medieval Saxon origins.

Dracula aficionados should also visit the prince's tomb near the choir of the fifteenth-century **Snagov monastery,** on a tiny island in Lake Snagov, twenty-five miles north of Bucharest. The church, a little gem of Byzantine architecture whose interior is decorated with precious frescoes, is itself worth the short trip to the lake, which is now lined with the villas of the country's new rich.

Poienari Castle, built for Vlad by his prisoners, sits 1,480 steep steps up the Cetatuia Mountain (this hike isn't for the faint-hearted). From its peak, you can look down into the Arges Gorge and imagine Vlad's condescending perspective. Two and a half miles south is the charming village of Arefu, home to the descendants of Vlad's followers.

Nestled in the Prahova River Valley, at the foot of the Bucegi Mountains, Sinaia gained prominence in the late nineteenth century when the Hohenzollern king Carol I, the first German king of Romania, chose it as the site for his summer residence. With tall spires reaching toward the sky, the brooding, neo-Gothic **Peleş Castle** is reminiscent of Mad King Ludwig's Bavarian creations. Copies of antiques and great paintings, and extravagant furnishings in mother-of-pearl, walnut, and leather fill the interior. Nearby, the simpler seventeenth-century **Sinaia Monastery,** which served as the temporary summer home of the royal family during the castle's construction, stands in contrast. On display are original frescoes as well as the first Romanian translation of the Bible, from 1668.

Between 1899 and 1902, Czech architect Karel Liman built a smaller castle adjacent to Peleş for King Ferdinand, Carol's successor. Today the art nouveau–style **Pelisor,** or Little Peleş, is a museum showcasing turn-of-the-century Viennese furniture and Tiffany glassware, the work of Viennese interior designer Bernhard Ludwig.

Romania's most striking religious architecture takes the form of painted monasteries dotting **Southern Bucovina,** in northern Moldavia near the Ukrainian border. With astonishing polychromatic walls, gloriously covered in frescoes, these rustic structures resemble the icons inside Orthodox churches and have been declared World Heritage treasures by UNESCO. The outdoor Village Museum on the shores of Lake Herastrau has a life-size retrospective of this phenomenon.

West of Bucovina, across Prislop Pass, is the valley region of Maramures, home of Dacian people traditionally known for their intricate woodcarving. The **wooden churches** of the Mara Valley are striking inside and out, with colorful interior frescoes and tall steeples (built without metal nails). Interestingly, although they were painted mainly in the eighteenth century, about two centuries after those of Bucovina, they appear more sophisticated and modern.

In Romania, all roads lead to its capital. **Bucharest** is a fascinating city where brash new mega-constructions coexist with tree-lined back lanes whose nineteenth-century oriental villas recall the region's past as a satellite of the Ottoman Empire. After Romania became independent in 1877, this wealthy trading center drew French architects of the Beaux Arts school, who imparted an eclectic (though charming) pomposity to the city's most prominent structures, making a stroll through the center an appealing experience. Like in Transylvania, the memory of Vlad the Impaler permeates the capital. The old Citadel in Bucharest was his principal castle, built in 1456. Today, it is a ruin in the historic center, its pebbled walls barely discernible behind tall apartment buildings.

Without a doubt, the most famous building in Romania is one formerly occupied by another notorious monster—the late dictator Nicolae Ceausescu. Nearly one-fifth of Bucharest's historic districts were destroyed to make room for the **Palace of Par-**

liament during the late 1980s. Ironically named "Palace of the People," it is a vivid reminder of Romania's dark communist past. At 3.7 million square feet (and a thousand rooms), the sprawling behemoth is the second largest administrative building in the world after the Pentagon, and probably the world's most quintessential expression of postmodern kitsch.

Portrait of the City as Genius

by

ROBERT HUGHES

I became a Barcelona groupie, as near as I can re-
call, in the spring of 1966. I hardly had a word of
Spanish, let alone Catalan, but I did have one
friend who turned out to be the key to the city:
the last of the Catalan dandies, the sculptor Xavier
Corberó, a wiry bantam of a man with a blade-
like gypsy nose, a wild, cackling sense of humor, and an aptitude
for carving marble into the most refined shells, wings, and demi-
lunes. Corberó's ambition, which he shared with a number of
young Catalans—writers, economists, doctors, architects, embryo
politicans—was to help Barcelona recapture some of the luster it
had had back in the 1880s, a half-century before their birth: in 1966
a moment forgotten by everyone but the Catalans themselves.

It seemed an impossible idea, at a time when Franco had
banned the Catalan tongue, when most critics viewed fin-de-siècle
Barcelona as an eccentric footnote to French Art Nouveau—and
Art Nouveau itself as a freakish style fit only for hippies. People
knew Picasso had lived in Barcelona as a young man, and that
Salvador Dalí and Joan Miró were Catalans. They even thought

of Antoni Gaudí as a Surrealist architect (an idea that would have horrified Gaudí himself), but the names of his peers, like Domènech i Montaner or Puig i Cadafalch, were left out of the history books. Anyway, hadn't Barcelona lost whatever juice it might once have had? Why should it "matter," except as a flea market, given that Manhattan was the center of the world?

None of this seemed to deter Corberó and his friends. He lived in a dark, rambling *masia,* or farmhouse, preserved along with the rest of a rural lane, south of the city in Esplugues de Llobregat. Esplugues means "caves," and indeed the place seemed riddled with catacombs dating back to Roman times. Corberó kept thousands of bottles of excellent wine in them—not racked but dumped in heaps, the labels half-obliterated by mold and rats. In this labyrinth, given the booze and other more controlled substances, the Spanish hours, and a floating population of polyglot houseguests that included a number of strippers from the Crazy Horse in Paris, one was apt to lose track of time and place alike; but most mornings I would manage to lurch out into the white-gold Catalunyan light like a disoriented bat and head for the city, there to study—if that was the *mot juste*—the works of Gaudí and his circle, to riffle through the boxes of prints and cards and old photos in the dark, narrow bookshops in the Barri Gòtic and then, at three in the afternoon, to have lunch.

The meals of my conversion took place in the fish restaurants that stuck like wooden fingers out to the beach at Barceloneta, the triangular, warrenlike grid of dock housing that occupies the northern end of the port. They all had much the same layout. One walked past the open kitchen, with its haze of smoke from the roaring grills and the crackle of sea-things dumped with a flourish into tubs of boiling oil; past the gargantuan display of ingredients, the round trays of *cigalas* each stiffly arched on the ice, the mounds of red shrimp, the arrays of dentex, sea bass, squid, minuscule sand dabs, and toad-headed anglerfish, the tanks of live rock lobsters, *palinurus vulgaris,* named for Aeneas' drowned helmsman. One sat down as near the doors to the sea as possible (not always an easy feat, since the lunch crowd usually swelled to ten or twelve). One struggled with the Catalan menu.

Fried baby eels arrived, like white spaghetti in boiling oil; raw gooseneck barnacles, known as *percebes,* and *parrilladas,* oval steel platters crammed with six or eight kinds of grilled fish. The long, noisy room was full of families, three generations represented at each trestle table, from elderly patriarchs with seamed faces and Orwellian nailbrush mustaches to mayonnaise-smeared infants gumming their first squid. Beyond the glass doors, it seemed that half the working population of Barcelona was spending its lunch-time on the beach. No matter that the sand was grayish-brown and littered with plastic. This was a populist paradise, like Reginald Marsh's drawings of Coney Island in the 1930s or the Bondi Beach I had left behind in Sydney in 1964. Barceloneta presented a spectacle of democratic pleasure very unlike other parts of the Mediterranean I had come to know. This, it dawned on me through the wine and the hubbub, was because the city around it was in essence a citizen's town. Barcelona has always been more a city of capital and labor than of nobility and commoners; its democratic roots are old and run very deep. Its Consell de Cent (Council of a Hundred) was the oldest democratic political body in Spain. On it, artisans and laborers had equal votes with landowners and bankers. Catalans were fervent trade unionists at a time when most other Spaniards were bowing to the throne. The independence of Barcelonan working-class character was summed up in a cabaret song about the girl from Sants, the quarter between Montjuïc and the sea, where the big calico mills once were. "Sóc filla de Sants, / tinc les males sangs i les tares / de la llibertat / que m'havien dat els meus pares": I am a daughter of Sants, and I've got the bloody-mindedness and the blemishes of the freedom my parents gave me.

I loved the signs of this spirit with the naive intensity that (fortunately or not) is reserved for one's twenties. Slowed by two or more decades, I still do. But of course, there are plenty of other reasons for one's homages to Barcelona, ones that bear more conventionally on tourism. The place is an architectural marvel, not only for its Gothic churches and palaces, but for its early modernist ones. Paris, Vienna, and Barcelona were the three queen cities of fin-de-siècle culture; we know all about the first two but much less about the third.

On either side of 1900, Catalan *modernisme* produced a rich, tolerant urban texture, a humane and generous face for architecture that seems not just a century but a world away from the miseries of the "glass box" and the trumpery, fast-quote, inflated corporate PoMo that has flooded American cityscapes in the last decade. No other Mediterranean city I know has Barcelona's mixture of contemporary élan, richly eccentric history, strong local pride, and resistance to blanket "development," with the issue of Catalan independence threaded through it all. It evokes loyalties and produces disappointments. "This is the *omphalos*," declares Margarita Obiols, one of the young administrators of city planning in the Socialist government at the town hall. "Barcelona is the center of Mediterranean culture today." Boosterism? Well, yes and no.

If one sets down one's impression that Barcelonans tend to be sharp, sardonic, and more open to the outside world and its values than most Spaniards, doubtless someone can produce enough stupid, literal-minded, and insular Catalans to make the opposing point. Yet a great port does something for its people. Harbor cities are eclectic, mutable, open to influence. As marts of commerce and ideas they breed relativity and skepticism, a taste for naysaying together with a tolerance of the outsider and the misfit. This, along with its mercantile traditions, is why Barcelona could develop the only "modern" culture in Spain, why it bitterly resisted Franco—and why, especially after a few drinks, Catalan intellectuals are apt to revile Madrid.

The flavor of the place is strong. Partly it comes from the city's practical roots in the domains it mediates, agriculture and the sea. It is perhaps the last great European city in whose food markets, particularly the Boquería, just off the Ramblas (in Catalan, Les Rambles), one can get the feeling Paris lost with the closing of Les Halles—that the real Middle Ages, in their clamor, provinciality, closeness, and scatological humor, marginally survive.

By the same token, the Catalans have always been a seafaring people. The souvenirs of that tradition are preserved as a maritime museum inside the Drassanes, the array of magnificent fourteenth-century vaults on the seafront that once rivaled the shipyards of Venice. Everything, seemingly, is there, from lobster pots and Roman anchors to a rebuilt version of the great red galley, manned and officered by Catalans, in which Don John of Austria swept to victory over the Turks at Lepanto and changed the entire political future of the West. (My own favorite object in the museum, however, is a carved wooden emblem from a seventeenth-century ship, which reads, with heroic disdain for the odds, ES NECESARIO NAVEGAR, NO ES NECESARIO VIVIR. One remembers this when one steps outside and looks at the statue of Columbus at the end of Les Rambles, high on his column; alas, because of the shape of the Catalan coastline, he is pointing toward Libya.) The attitudes to the sea expressed in the urban fabric of Barcelona remain what they were. The Mediterranean is a workplace, not a playground. The port puts no premium on a harbor view. The luxury flats are all up in the Eixample, on either side of Passeig de Gràcia; only workers live on the water.

The city has changed, of course. Some aspects of Barcelona in the 1960s have either contracted or vanished altogether—but not the fundamental ones. Prices have shot up. Some landmarks have gone: a remarkable whorehouse, for instance, in (I think) Carrer

Sicília, which reportedly gave Jean Genet the idea for the house of illusions in which his play *The Balcony* is set. One of its rooms simulated a moving train, with sound effects and a diorama of the Pyrenes unscrolling creakily past the window, and every year one of Franco's ministers was said to appear from Madrid, his brief-case bulging with cash, and commission a sort of Cecil B. DeMille spectacular at whose climax he, as the penitent sinner, would as-cend the palatial staircase lined with girls in cotton-wool wings, toward his ritual absolution by Christ and Mystical Union with the Virgin. Drugs and AIDS have hit Barcelona with a deadly im-pact, and the Plaça Reial, a stately arcaded square that is one of the architectural delights of the city, is now Drug Central, the do-main of inert junkies, dealers on motocross bikes, and vulpine transvestites in Dolly Parton wigs, hooking to feed their habits. It is recommended (to adopt the proscriptive tone of early Baede-ker) that the visitor have nothing to do with Catalan whores, for even if the girl in his arms does not turn out to be a boy, he is still apt to find an array of self-mutating Afro-Catalan viruses installed in his immune system next morning. All great ports demand the tax of elementary street-smartness from their visitors, and Barce-lona, a courteous city but one with a permanent underclass of drifters, geeks, and manky predators, is no exception.

Nor is a city whose population soared from about 2.5 million in the early 1960s to 4 million by 1980 immune from the equation that people mean cars. Barcelona is one long traffic jam, with (thanks to the siesta) not two but four rush hours a day. Cars mean noise, a fact that seems to have been lost on most Catalan hotel keepers, who tend not to provide double-glazing; you can be driven nuts by the roar and honking of a thousand SEATs and the howl of low-caliber motocross bikes, the kids' favorite, climb-ing up through the gears. From July to October, your eyes sting. The pollution is worse than in Los Angeles. From the top of

Tibidabo, the old mountain funfair served by a funicular, you can look down on the city below and see nothing but brown smog stretching out to sea, with only Gaudí's towers of the Sagrada Família piercing the murk like drippy wax candles. But then the next morning a wind will spring up and the whole grid looks washed, virginal, new in the sunlight—the Los Angeles effect, with the difference that the city to which it happens is more than two thousand years old.

Barcelona is a palimpsest—a sheet inscribed with one urban text after another, written across and between the lines. Its first recorded inhabitants were there by 300 B.C.: the Laietani, an Iberian Bronze Age people. Julius Caesar took it in the first century B.C., and Augustus gave it full colonial status under the pompous name of Colonia Faventia Julia Augusta Pia Barcino. Almost all of it lies buried under the Barri Gòtic, the old Gothic quarter that was built over the original walled nucleus of the Roman city. Four Corinthian columns, no more, of a large temple of Augustus stand in a medieval courtyard at 10 Carrer del Paradís; Barcelona's two seats of government, the *Ajuntament* (town hall) and the *Generalitat,* face one another across the Plaça Sant Jaume, which must have been the original center of the forum.

The most visible legacy of Rome was the *muralles,* the walls of the fortified city, which stick out from the medieval fabric here and there like old bits of jawbone; one can still trace them in a morning's walk. One section is the Carrer d'Avinyó, a cranky street that descends to the port more or less parallel to Les Rambles; it enters modern cultural history by containing the brothel whose women Pablo Picasso immortalized in 1907, along with his mania for El Greco and his fear of syphilis, in the precocious masterpiece whose convulsed surface provoked Cubism—*Les Demoiselles d'Avignon* ("The Girls of Avinyó Street"). It is now a seedy boardinghouse, and no plaque commemorates its role in the birth of modernism.

After the Romans left, wave after wave of invaders arrived—Visigoths, Moors—then stabilization at last under the Christians by the thirteenth century. By the fifteenth century the Barri Gòtic had most of the buildings that give it its present architectural grandeur. New walls were made, to secure an expanded city that was gobbling up the *horts i vinyets,* the farms and vineyards on its outskirts. Inside the second girdle of *muralles* were such buildings as Santa María del Mar with its apse of towering octagonal shafts, the heroic bones of building, plain as a gray limestone cave, its ogival vaults spanning the widest space in all Gothic architecture; the immense cathedral; the Saló del Tinell, beneath whose diaphragm arches Queen Isabella received Columbus upon his return from America; the Monastery of Pedralbes, the church of Santa María del Pi, and dozens of private or semipublic palaces—a concentration whose historical density resembles Venice's.

Some parts of the Barri Gòtic still seem to be caught in a time warp. One spring evening in 1985 my wife, the Corberós, and I had wandered off to a restaurant in the Barri Gòtic, where the table expanded to include the young Socialist mayor of Barcelona, Pasquall Maragall, and some of his staff. Maragall has a face at least as well known in Barcelona as Ed Koch's is in New York, and though more of an intellectual and less of a flesh-presser he is an accessible man, and genuinely popular. He is on TV a lot. He attracts controversy. He got the 1992 Olympic Games for Barcelona. Hence no Barcelonan, one supposed, could fail to recognize him, at least by name. Many plates of snails later someone suggested that we all go to a palace around the corner from the town hall, whose owner, the widowed Marquesa de Sant Mori, was having some friends in for drinks.

We arrived, a dozen of us by now, and clambered up the long flight of stone stairs from the Gothic courtyard. One of the Marquesa's daughters started on the introductions. Who are your friends? she asked Corberó. "Well," said Xavier, "to begin with, you know the mayor, of course." A small wrinkle crossed Sofia's brow. *"El alcalde de donde?"* she inquired. ("The mayor of where?")

The Mayor of Where has Spain's most aggressively modern city to run, not just a Gothic time capsule. By the end of the eighteenth century the city was the textile capital of the Mediterranean; it breathed industry while the rest of Spain was still choking from feudalism. Cloth mills created immense wealth for their family owners, like the Güell family, later to become Gaudí's patrons. They also created Spain's first industrial proletariat. The new money was condensed in building up Les Rambles, the promenade to the sea that was the social spine of eighteenth-century Barcelona.

The crucial modernization began in 1859, with the Plan Cerdà. Ildefons Cerdà, a Catalan engineer, was a visionary of urban design—the inventor, one might also claim, of the grid city. Look at a map and you will see the warren of streets and alleys in the Barri Gòtic suddenly turn, above Plaça de Catalunya, into a regular array of identical blocks. This modular city, spreading its cells east and west of Passeig de Gràcia, is called the Eixample, or Extension, and Cerdà planned it, thus becoming the father of modern Barcelona. Cerdà's plan, breaking out of the Gothic cincture, was born out of his own utopian and mildly socialist convictions, and out of the desire to show what rationally planned capitalism could do. It worked superbly, allowing for all the variety and texture a growing city needs. It became the civic pattern behind the Catalan Renaixença ("Renaissance") of the late nineteenth century, whose most coherent symbol was the International Exposition held in Barcelona in 1888.

The exposition marked a new phase in Barcelona's image of itself. It was the one modern city in Spain, the sole "European" community. Other Spanish cities were encumbered by reactionary values; Barcelona saw itself as liberal, innovative, and even revolutionary. For 1888 as for 1992, Catalunya wanted to be known as Spain's open door to the rest of Europe, a separate state by whose standards of progress Madrid would look arthritic. The Catalan Renaixença at the end of the nineteenth century was not exactly a political movement like the Italian risorgimento; few Catalans hoped for a formal secession from Madrid. It was a middle-class cultural movement with strong ties to traditional folkways, bringing Catalan back as a literary language. In music, with the encouragement of patrons like Lluís Millet, there was a surge of interest in Catalan folk song—the very old coexisting with the newest of the new, a passionate adherence to Wagner. Architects and decorators set out to show what the vast resources of Catalan craftwork could do, especially in wrought iron, stained glass, and ceramics. They were acutely conscious of the Catalan Gothic past, and obsessed with the task of reviving its exuberance, intricacy, and structural daring. Hence the paradox of "exposition culture"—it used medievalism as a sign of modernity, and turned the "provincialism" of Catalan roots and language into the base of an international vision.

The fair building that caught most of the limelight in 1888 was Domènech's Gran Hotel Internacional. A five-story, steel-frame building sheathed with brick and tile, it stretched five hundred feet along the waterfront and housed two thousand visitors a day. Domènech finished it in fifty-three days flat—a feat no builder could hope to rival today. It was torn down after the fair, but its memory remained a powerful stimulus to younger architects: Puig i Cadalfalch, for instance, spoke of it as "my first vision of that great Barcelona for which we are all working."

Other buildings from the fair remain—Domènech's playful yet didactic Café-Restaurant, for instance, and the soaring Umbracle, or Palm House. But the grandest expression of the spirit of '88 is surely Domènech's Palau de la Música Catalana, which rises like some spiny, tessellated sea beast amid a bubbling of domes and a blaze of mosaics on the upper Carrer Sant Pere just off the Via Laietana. It was built (largely by popular subscription) between 1905 and 1908 as a place where both Barcelona's newly gathered folk songs and classical music from all over Europe could be performed. In its decoration, the Palau expresses three themes. The first is Catalan identity, so that it swarms with effigies of Saint George, patron saint of the city, and is bathed in the light of red-and-yellow stained glass, these being the colors of the Catalan flag. The second is flowers, suggesting the budding of an indigenous culture; even the ceiling of the Palau is covered with immense ceramic roses, each the size of a cabbage. The third is choral music, which receives its apotheosis in the stained-glass portion of the ceiling, a huge, glowing rectangle that bulges into an inverted bell with radiating figures of angels singing together in Paradise. Forget Tiffany: This is *the* masterpiece of Art Nouveau stained glass, the last ecstatic outpouring of a tradition that now can scarcely be revived on such a scale, and can never be surpassed. A grid burgeoning with roses, the Palau is one of the great buildings of the world, not just of Barcelona, and (though its musical programs can include such oddities as Negro spirituals sung in Catalan) you must buy a ticket to wallow and gloat in its full decorative effect.

Most key buildings of the Renaixença stand in the Eixample, on or around the Passeig de Gràcia. This great street, the Champs-Elysées or Park Avenue of Barcelona, begins where Les Rambles end, at Plaça de Catalunya. Like Les Rambles themselves, it is consecrated to strolling—even the long, gently sloping pavement beneath your feet has period charm, being made of hexagonal blocks embossed with marine motifs of squid and nautilus designed by none other than Gaudí. (This was the idea the city echoed when it invited Miró to redo the pavements of Les Rambles.) The flamboyant wrought-iron streetlamps are Gaudí's, too, and the sidewalk benches—both, alas, rusting and spalling now. Passeig de Gràcia was the social stage for the high bourgeoisie, as

Les Rambles were for the workingman. It was all grace, furs, sidelong glances, saluting canes—a residential street, whereas now it is mainly banks, hotels, and shops, and has lost some of its character as a result.

Nevertheless it has some splendid blocks, one of which is known as the *manzana de la discòrdia,* "the apple (or block) of discord," because it contains three competing buildings by three geniuses of turn-of-the-century Catalan design: Domènech i Montaner's Casa Lleó Morera (1905), Puig i Cadafalch's Casa Amatller (1898–1900), and Gaudí's Casa Batlló (1905–07). Domènech's exquisitely intricate fusion of Gothic and Hispano-moresque motifs was badly mutilated in the sixties by the luxury leather-goods firm of Loewe, whose showroom it now is; in revenge, one should look but not buy. Three doors up, at number 41, Puig's Casa Amatller is virtually intact—an older palace remodeled in an even wilder mix of native Catalan Gothic that culminates in a tile-clad, stepped Dutch gable. Then, right next to it (number 43), the climax: Gaudí's Casa Batlló, with its undulant front, its second-story windows like tense, open fish mouths, its swelling and breaking balconies, and the lovely drift and sparkle of broken-tile mosaic (blue into green into pale gray and buff) up the facade, preparing you for the zoomorphic hump and fold of the roof, like the back of some old sea beast off a portolano chart.

Then, four blocks farther up and on the opposite side of Passeig de Gràcia, at number 92, is the most famous of its buildings, Gaudí's Casa Milà (1906–10): gray, ponderous, heaving, like an elephant's erotic dream fixed in stone. La Pedrera—"the stone quarry," as it is nicknamed—turns out to be in terrible shape when you look closer. But the Caixa de Catalunya, a bank known for its vigorous cultural programs, has bought it and plans to return its apartments to their former organic splendor. Many stories are told of the difficulties tenants had with Gaudí's rooms, to whose convolutions no normal furniture would adapt. My favorite concerns a Mrs. Comes i Abril, who complained to the crabby genius that her grand piano, try as she might, would not fit what was to be the music room. Gaudí visited her and attentively looked at every part of the salon, gravely nodding his silver head. "Who plays this instrument?" he asked at last. Señora Abril said that she did, a little. *"Miri, toqui el violín,"* said Gaudí, abruptly. ("Look, play the violin.")

Across town, the Sagrada Família (the Expiatory Temple of the Holy Family, to give its full name) remains more problematic. It is Gaudí's most famous building, but the least authentically his. Gaudí took it on in 1884 and worked on it for forty years, between other projects like the Palau Güell and the superb, but also unfinished, Parc Güell. When he died in 1926 he had finished the crypt, part of the walls, and one facade—that of the Nativity, with its four tapering spires and the deliriously teeming portals.

But the tempo of work was lost with his death. Moreover, by the outbreak of the civil war the Sagrada Família had come to symbolize everything the Catalan Left most hated about the Catholic Church. During the civil war the anarchists sacked it. All Gaudí's drawings and models were destroyed. Today no one really knows how the finished temple was meant to look. The intended details and finishes—the living, unpredictable skin of Gaudí's work—can never be authentic, since he made many of them up as he went along.

The Sagrada Família is now the world's largest architectural question mark, and perhaps most Catalans and visitors prefer it to remain that way.

In the meantime, to sense what Gaudí could really do with a church one should set aside a morning to visit the Colònia Güell, an "ideal community" at Cornellà, half an hour's drive from Passeig de Gràcia, which Gaudí designed for the textile workers employed by his patron, Eusebio Güell. Its focus is the chapel, which takes the forms of Catalan Gothic and reinvents them. Gaudí's columns (each a "found object," a natural organ pipe of gray basalt) cant at wild angles to meet the thrust of the roof, and the complex logic of the ceiling ribs and the shallow, thin vaulting—membranes of tiles laid edge to edge—gives the brick an organic tension, a pure springing of curves and multiplicity of textures, that fairly ripples through the building.

The architecture of the Renaixença was greater than the painting, although fin-de-siècle Barcelona had some brilliantly gifted artists, such as Santiago Rusiñol, the sculptors Josep Llimona and Pau Gargallo, and Ramon Casas. The latter's bravura charcoal portraits form (like Nadar's Parisian photographs) an unequaled record of the cultural life of their time. The main gathering place for artists, writers, composers, and culture groupies was the café Els Quatre Gats ("the Four Cats") in the Barri Gòtic; like the magazines that Casas and the young Picasso contributed their drawings to, such as *Pèl y Ploma,* it closed long ago, although some of its decor, like Casas' large canvas of himself and a friend in plus fours puffing along on a tandem bicycle (then an archsymbol of modernity), is preserved in Barcelona's Museum of Modern Art. What cannot easily be evoked is the febrility of the time, the volatile character of Catalan political life that spilled over into its cultural loyalties, the sympathy of artist for anarchist, the milling crowds and the thrown bombs. With our present fixation on terrorism, we are apt to forget how commonplace it was in Europe at the turn of the century. An anarchist's bomb that failed to explode is preserved in the Museum of the City of Barcelona—a relic of an attack on the Opera House, the Gran Teatre de Liceu, that left twenty dead. It looks almost elegant, like an old-fashioned naval mine: round, polished, about the size of a grapefruit, and bristling with detonator horns.

Never having been an imperial power, Barcelona has no great storehouse of imperial acquisition, no museum like the Louvre, the Prado, or the National Gallery in London. But its local museums are still rewarding, especially the Museum of Catalan Art up on the hill of Montjuïc, which contains the world's best collection of twelfth-to-thirteenth-century Romanesque frescoes, rescued from abandoned churches in the Catalan countryside. To spend a morning with them is to realize the perfect continuity of modern and ancient in this culture. The metallic linearity of their style, the scalloping rhythms, the sawing of line into color, the schematic clarity and the wild, lyrical distortions of bird, beast, and saint, are revived in early Miró—just as the massive, stony rotundity of the folk pottery on the floor above would be reborn in his later sculptures.

Picasso, of course, has a museum of his own in a Gothic palace (15 Carrer Montcada, in the Barri Gòtic) whose absorbing collection is founded on his gift to Barcelona of his juvenilia, from the days when he was a hungry young affiliate of Els Quatre Gats. The Museum of Modern Art, in the Parc Cuitadella, is more regional than international—and no less intriguing for that, despite its "provincialism"—while the Miró Foundation, in Montjuïc, has regular international shows. But the city's most eccentrically charming collection is its *"museu sentimental,"* the Marés Museum, housed in another fifteenth-century palace in the Barri Gòtic. It was all put together by one man, Federico Marés, who is ninety-five and until fairly recently was the head of the Barcelona School of Fine Arts. He had a moderate salary and no inherited wealth, but he built this collection by sixty years of rummaging in flea markets and back-street shops: room after room of glass cases, full of early cameras, fans, corsets, parasols, revolvers, walking sticks, matchboxes, cigarette cases, folk art, and devotional sculpture. Marés was a penniless Morgan, an entranced pack rat; one imagines him buried among his suitcases and etuis, a frail little pharaoh in a rusty-black suit.

In such places one realizes how intensely nostalgic Barcelona can be—and the question, up to the death of Franco in 1975, was whether in cultural terms it could bounce back and become more than a shadow of its *belle époque* past. I remember the evening in the Opera Club on Les Rambles when this was borne in on me. The club, a fossil of the Liceu's ritual days, a capsule in which time stopped three generations ago, was designed by Oriol Mestres in 1903. Ramon Casas decorated its rotunda with a cyclorama of *boulevardier* life, including two hatted-and-veiled girls in a 1903 de Dion-Panhard that seemed to plunge at you out of the dim wall, and whose headlights shone when the ancient doorman twisted an equally ancient switch. It was the Tut's tomb of the *belle époque,* and Corberó and I were alone there. We solemnly ate our omelets, drank our wine, smoked our puros, played billiards, drank some distinguished brandy, and left without glimpsing so much as one member. The evening seemed emblematic. And it represents the image of Barcelona that its present civic government is trying to reverse.

Maragall, the mayor, has his enemies among conservatives, but there is no doubting the depth of his belief in Barcelona's future. He is out to earn the kind of historical niche gained by his predecessor Rius i Taulet, who set the 1888 exposition rolling and convinced half of Europe that Barcelona was the only vibrant city in Spain. As did the 1880s, the 1980s have brought to Catalunya a surge of speculation about cultural renewal through a mix of regionalism and modernism. How do you make Catalan identity *interesting*? First, the argument goes, by keeping it—which means, by retaining the Catalan language as the social matrix of the place.

Some factions take this to extremes: Academic separatists, for instance, want to ensure that all university lectures are given in Catalan, a project that (since most Spanish intellectuals and teachers cannot speak it) would condemn the University of Barcelona to instant provincialism. But the moderate point, Maragall insists, is that Catalan is not a difficult language, even though outsiders think of it as an utterly hermetic tongue, like Basque. Any foreigner with French and Italian can read a Catalan newspaper more easily than a Spanish one.

As with the language, so with the physical form of the city. *Urbanism* is the buzzword, and Maragall describes his task as "stitching the city together, mending the urban fabric piece by piece," rather than indulging in the kind of grandiose abstract planning without regard for neighborhood that has done so much to wreck other European cities. One peseta out of every ten in the civic budget goes for urbanism, mostly restoration and recycling of old buildings. The city's main advisor on this—an energetic, bull-shouldered man who may one day be remembered as fondly as Cerdà himself—is the architect Oriol Bohigas, who is also Barcelona's leading historian of modernist design. But with the 1992 Olympics, larger schemes were added. The design opportunities of the Games were turned over, not to Catalans alone, but to a roster of the world's leading architects: Arata Isozaki from Japan, Richard Meier from America, Gae Aulenti from Italy, The pet project of city hall is the clearing of the waterfront, thus giving Barcelona's sea back to its public—a project whose scope compares with the building of the Eixample a century ago.

But all that is on paper. The main urban-renewal program a visitor sees today is a growing string of "oases" across the city. These involve, in equal measure, landscape design, the retuning of buildings and plazas, and new sculpture by leading artists, mostly Spanish and American—among them, Claes Oldenburg, Ellsworth Kelly, Roy Lichtenstein, Beverly Pepper, Antoni Tàpies, and, posthumously, Joan Miró. Each artist works with an architect, for cost, and for a specific place. It is shaping up to be the largest and best public-sculpture scheme of the twentieth century.

The sites are under the care of another urbanist, Josep Anton Ace-billo, who waxes dogmatic and lyrical (a highly Catalan combination) about their social meaning. "You can see in Barcelona what makes Spanish democracy different from other European kinds, or what you have in America. It's the influence of urban restoration on local pride. By the time we've finished, this will be the greatest Mediterranean city in terms of living culture, as it ought to be. It's not just a matter of having a leftist government. Hell, the Italians have *communist* governments in Umbria and Tuscany, but they can't agree about restoring one square, let alone fifty. . . ."

One of these projects is an old friend of the history books: Mies van der Rohe's German pavilion for the 1929 World's Fair, one of the chief canonical buildings of the International Style, now meticulously reconstructed on its original site at Montjuïc. To stroll through its exquisite spaces, in which the refinement of Japanese teahouse architecture is mirrored in onyx, marble, sheet glass, and stainless steel, is to realize how great a figure Mies was in the twenties—and what corporate sins have since been committed in his name.

The sites are not meant as "monuments" in the old sense—bronze generals gesturing from bronze horses. After forty years of Franco, Catalans were understandably fed up with that kind of public sculpture. The actual popularity of some of these schemes is fairly nebulous, but people seem to like and respect them. At least the kids in Plaça de la Palmera spend more time playing handball against Richard Serra's concrete arcs than spraying graffiti on them. Josep Llimona's 1910 monument to the liberal-socialist mayor Bartolome Robert is one of the masterpieces of *modernista* sculpture, but it was dismantled (though not destroyed) in the Franco years; it is set up once more in Plaça de Tetuan. Its sweeping and generous forms give focus to the plaza, the gray stone base with its hollowed sea caves evoking the maritime essence of Barcelona, the Rodin-like figures above thrusting into the air. But at the same time it is *used*: People sit on and in it, brass taps dispense drinking water—it is as much maternal as official.

The new sculptures tend to leave out the oratorical distance of monuments. Corberó's array of carved marble blades and fins in the Plaça de Soller—a lake-apparition with faint echoes of the Trevi Fountain—completes rather than dominates the square and the lake. And the largest sculpture so far, the last big work of Joan Miró, could not be less authoritarian: a lunar, massive torso twenty-four meters tall with a horned cylinder of a head, ponderous but also silly in its dignity, a mooncalf dropped from Brobdingnag. Its bovine appearance neatly refers to the bullring behind it. One realizes that a city that can have such a beast as its main emblem of modernity has not shed its power to enchant. But then, nobody could accuse Barcelona of losing that.

1987

Barcelona's New Masterpieces

The city's art and architecture: The best of the new guard

Mies van der Rohe Pavilion, Montjuïc

After the pavilion designed by Bauhaus architect Mies van der Rohe as the German contribution to the Universal Exhibition of 1929 was reassembled in Montjuïc from 1983 to 1986, Barcelona recovered its innate fascination with avant-garde architecture. The building is a stunner, too—its interlocking planes of white marble, green onyx, and glass constitute a powerful less-is-more retort to such other local idioms as the *modernista* (Spanish art nouveau) Palau de la Música and all of Gaudí's work. Note the matching patterns in the green onyx panels and the visual play between the black carpeting inside the pavilion and the reflecting pool outside (Avenida del Marquès de Comillas s/n, Montjuïc; 34-93-423-4016; miesbcn.com).

Richard Rogers's Hesperia Tower Hotel

Coming in from Barcelona airport, you can't miss Sir Richard Rogers's Hesperia Tower Hotel, a campy sixties space-age building with a flying saucer–like panoramic restaurant atop a slender tower. It's not only a great preview of the superb contemporary architecture you'll find all over town, but shows off the degree to which Spanish business has embraced the fact that cutting-edge buildings lead to great publicity (144 Gran Vía; 34-93-413-5000; hesperia.com).

Fundació Joan Miró, Montjuïc

Architect Josep Lluís Sert, who spent the Franco era as dean of architecture at Harvard, celebrated his return to Catalonia by designing one of the world's great museums. This appealingly light building of white walls and arches contains a collection of more than 240 paintings, 175 sculptures, and all of Miró's graphic work, along with 8,000 drawings. Originally part of the 1937 Spanish pavilion at the Paris World's Fair, it includes an Alexander Calder fountain at the entrance to the sculpture collection (Parc de Montjuïc; 34-93-329-1908; bcn.fjmiro.es).

BARCELONETA AND THE PORT DISTRICT

The redesign of Barcelona's waterfront, an astonishing urban makeover on scale with Haussmann's transformation of central Paris during the nineteenth century, was the centerpiece of the 1992 Olympic games, an event that called the world's attention to the city's proud and carefully deliberated emergence from the intellectual and political stagnation of the Franco years. It also implicitly represented the rebirth of Catalan identity, since both the language and the culture were fiercely repressed following the Spanish Civil War. This is a great area in which to stroll, since few cities in the world meet the sea with such a display of handsome contemporary architecture, landscaped walks, and provocative street sculpture. Acres of warehouses and outdated port installations were razed to create the glittering waterfront, and, more controversially, the working-class neighborhood of Barceloneta, once a popular place for a quick dip in the Med and a seafood meal, was completely rebuilt.

MONTJUÏC TELECOMMUNICATIONS TOWER, MONTJUÏC

Santiago Calatrava's beautiful and highly iconoclastic telecommunications tower was completed in 1991, on the eve of the 1992 Olympics, and has since become one of Barcelona's most recognizable landmarks. From a distance, the 427-foot tower looks like a white marble sculpture inspired by a fishbone. In reality, the architect intended for it to be seen as a kneeling figure posed on a base of broken glazed tiles, an homage to Gaudí, Barcelona's most famous architect. The tower's orientation means that the shadow of the central needle on the circular platform functions as a sundial. Part of the Olympic Ring complex in Montjuïc Park, it can be reached via the Funicular de Montjuïc, or take Metro lines 1 or 3 to the Espanya station.

MUSEUM OF CONTEMPORARY ART OF BARCELONA, EL RAVAL

Though local art critics dismissed Richard Meier's stunning white MACBA (Museu d'Art Contemporani de Barcelona) as a grandiose exercise of style over substance when it opened in 1995—its permanent collection *was* rather puny at the time—locals have since warmed to this exciting, light-filled building, an example of the best new Mediterranean architecture from another city-by-the-sea, Los Angeles. MACBA has subsequently earned its credentials as an important part of the city's cultural scene with a series of superb exhibitions and also set off the gentrification of the historic El Raval quarter (1 Plaça dels Angels; 34-93-412-0810; macba.es).

MERCAT SANTA CATERINA, CIUTAT VELLA

The renovated Santa Caterina Market where Enric Miralles and Benedetta Tagliabue of EMBT Arquitectes Associats created a huge, undulating polychrome canopy roof for a formerly shabby neoclassical-style nineteenth-century market building is contemporary Catalan design at its best—it wears its modernity boldly, and successfully, but fuses well with the city's existing urban fabric. The roof is covered with a vivid mosaic of 325,000 hexagonal brick tiles whose various colors are meant to reference the produce sold in the market. Tip: Have lunch at the bustling Cuines Santa Caterina, a stylish new brasserie inside the market building with an international menu (16 Avenida de Francesc Cambó; mercatsantacaterina.net).

Torre Agbar, Poblenou

Visually similar to Sir Norman Foster's "Gherkin" tower for the Swiss Reinsurance company in the city of London, French architect Jean Nouvel's sleek 466-foot-high glass building with a polychrome facade resembles (depending on whom you ask) either a huge corncob or a giant phallus and has challenged a long-standing local aversion to skyscrapers by dramatically changing the city's skyline. The headquarters of the local water authority, it broke new ground when it opened in 2005 as the city's most ecologically correct building—all the construction materials are recyclable and an ingenious system of forty-five hundred louvered windows eliminates the need for air-conditioning. The building's skin is its most striking feature—the red, blue, and green colors of its aluminum facade shimmer through glass slats and change constantly in the sunlight (Plaça de les Glòries Catalanes, Poblenou; torreagbar.com).

Edifici Fòrum, Poblenou

Located on a triangular site at the end of the Avenida Diagonal, one of the city's main arteries, the Forum was inaugurated in 2004 as part of the Universal Forum of Cultures. The centerpiece of the largest urban redevelopment project in Barcelona since the redevelopment of the waterfront and Barceloneta for the 1992 Olympic Games is the striking blue Edifici Fòrum, a conference center designed by architects Herzog & de Meuron, who refurbished London's Tate Modern. Intended to make a major ecological statement about the importance of sustainability in urban planning, treated water from the adjacent sewage-treatment plant cascades over the black stone roof and the semitransparent parts of the facade. The complex also includes a marina, a large plaza, a water sports complex, and an artificial island (Plaça Llevant).

La Rambla del Raval, El Raval

Some of Barcelona's most innovative architecture is very subtle. In 2001, several blocks of dilapidated housing in the heart of the Raval, the city's densest neighborhood (the name Raval derives from the Arabic word *rabad,* or suburbs, a reference to the fact that much of the area huddled up against the convents and libraries that were built here after the Arabs were driven out of Spain), were demolished to create a new palm-lined *rambla,* or open square that would give some lungs to the neighborhood. It's since become one of the most animated spaces in the city, lined by cafés and restaurants and filled with a multiethnic mix of strollers who come to inspect Fernando Botero's *El Gat,* a huge sculpture of a cat, and take in the open-air weekend market. If Barcelona is the most innovative city in Europe, El Raval is its utopian laboratory, a place where the liberal, ecological, cosmopolitan, pacifist personality of the city is proudly, almost aggressively, shown off. Indeed, it's hard to find another urban neighborhood in Europe, especially such a motley one, that lives, a little street crime notwithstanding, in such social harmony.

Street Art

Barcelona is one of the most interesting cities in the world for street art, a long-standing local tradition that was goosed up again as part of the sprucing-up done for the 1992 Olympic Games; city planners shrewdly saw bold new open-air sculpture as a way of adding a breath of modernity, visual wit, and humor to existing urban landscapes. A quick and edgy hit list of the city's best recent street sculpture begins with Roy Lichtenstein's *Barcelona Head,* one of the city's best-loved urban icons, at the intersection of Passeig Colom and Vía Laietana. Not far away, at the Pla de Palau, Ulrich Rückriem's untitled sculpture known locally as "Four

Wedges" is a rather more somber monument that consists of two pairs of matching granite. At the Plaça del Mar, Juan Munoz's *A Room Where It Always Rains* is a cerebral piece typical of what pleases locally—a rather arcane but intriguing slotted bronze cage that references Pirandello's *Six Characters in Search of an Author.* Continuing up the beach, one encounters Rebecca Horn's wistfully charming *The Wounded Star,* a rectangular pile of rusty steel cubes that's a sly reminder of what was lost when the city's dazzling new waterfront doomed seething, friendly Barceloneta—the boxes are intended to reference the (now nonoperative) lighthouses and impromptu seafood bars that once made this part of the city so popular. Nearby, at Carrer de L'Almirall Cervera, is Jannis Kounellis's nod at the waterfront's hoary and very ancient commercial past—seven scales hung from a steel beam charged with sacks of coffee. James Turrell's *Deuce Coop* at 23 Carrer del Comerç in the Born district is similarly abstract, but more ethereal—the "sculpture" is created with light, and so is best viewed at night. On the waterfront, don't miss Frank Gehry's metallic fish in front of the Arts Hotel (19-21 Carrer de la Marina) and Claes Oldenburg's charming *Mistos,* a huge matchbook that's become a local favorite and is a Metro ride away in Montbau; it's a tongue-in-cheek reference to the lighting of the Olympic flame in 1992.

HOTEL HABITAT

One of the most spectacular new buildings of the past twenty-five years, the Hotel Habitat in L'Hospitalet de Llobregat, designed by Enric Ruiz-Geli with Cloud 9 and Acconci Studio and Ruy Ohtake, is an eleven-story, 135-room hotel that is set back on its lower three and upper three levels with rooms and stairwells that protrude from its facades. Its most distinctive feature, however, is its external "tent," or skeleton, of five thousand LED-photovolatic hybrid cells, each of which has an electronic clock that tracks sunrises and sunsets. Each cell lights up at night to reveal the energy that has been collected during the day, glowing red when the least amount of energy has been captured and white when the cells have been fully stocked.

Coming Soon: Museu de la Mobilitat

After the Guggenheim Museum in Bilbao and the Hotel Marqués de Riscal in La Rioja, architect Frank Gehry will make his mark on Barcelona with a new multifaceted project at the railyards in Sant Andreu La Sagrera. The project will include a high-speed train station, a three-mile-long park, eighty-five hundred new apartments, office space, and a transportation museum.

Pilgrim's Pride

by

WILLIAM DALRYMPLE

There were wildflowers everywhere: meadows of knee-high clover dotted with foxglove, cowslip, and patches of red campion. It was early still, and the fields were deserted. My pack was light, the grass was soft underfoot, my spirits high. It was going to be a fine day, I told myself; if only I knew where the hell I was. But whatever way I turned my map—upside down, around in circles, on its side—there was no escaping it: I was completely and utterly lost.

I had walked for two hours through the meadows of the foothills of the Pyrenees before I found the Basque farmer. Bereted, overalled, and jowly, he was leaning on his staff at the edge of a beechwood, watching a pair of collies drive his sheep swirling into their pens.

"I'm looking for the way to the Spanish border," I said. "I'm trying to get to the abbey of Roncesvalles by nightfall."

"Where 'ave you come from?" he asked suspiciously.

"The foot of the pass—St-Jean-Pied-de-Port."

"And how did you get *there*?" he asked. He was not a man to be put off easily.

"From Oloron," I said. Then, proudly, I added: "I walked."

"You started your journey in Oloron?" he persisted.

"Not exactly."

"Where from, then?"

"Toulouse."

"YOU 'AVE COME FROM TOULOUSE?" he asked, raising his voice. "BY FOOT?"

"Yes," I replied, feeling suddenly rather pleased with myself.

"Pourquoi?"

"I am on a pilgrimage," I said. "I'm going to Compostela."

"Compostela? In Spain?"

The farmer shook his head.

"You are a priest?"

"No."

"A monk?"

"No."

"A seminarian, perhaps?"

"No."

"Then why are you going on *pèlerinage*?"

"For a holiday," I said. "For a change."

"You are doing this," continued the farmer, a look of increasing amazement spreading across his face, "you are doing this for pleasure?"

"I suppose so," I said, my spirits beginning to fall somewhat.

"Then," said the farmer. "It is quite simple. You are a madman."

"Honestly, I . . ."

"A sane man," continued the farmer with almost De Gaullian finality, "does not walk across Spain for pleasure."

"No?"

"*Non*. I live next to Spain and I should know. Your footpath is on top of that hill. Good day."

There were a number of occasions during the following weeks

when I wondered if the Basque farmer could have been right: Perhaps you do have to be a little dippy to elect to walk several hundred miles across the mudbake of the Castilian plains when you could equally well hire a car. And, of course, every long-distance walk has its bad moments: the blisters, the squalls of rain, the sprained ankle, the closed hotel at sunset.

Yet looking back now, for every moment of despair there were a hundred of ecstasy. You can never forget those beautiful Spanish evenings—a soft breeze blowing through the poplars, the irrigation runnels bubbling by your feet, the gnarled old olives creaking in the breeze, and a church tower—the destination that night—dividing the horizon ahead. The journey to the tomb of Saint James at Santiago de Compostela—a journey that in the Middle Ages was undertaken by more than half a million pilgrims every year—was, according to the sixteenth-century traveler Andrew Boorde, "the greatest journey an Englishman mae goe," and much the same remains true today.

For the Camino de Santiago, the great pilgrim's road, is still a magnificent route, a five-hundred-mile-long footpath leading through some of the most stunning and unspoiled scenery in the world. If you choose to make the pilgrimage in the authentic manner, by walking it or riding it on horseback, you still take the old original track, along which tens of millions of other pilgrims have passed before you, a road whose cobbles have been rubbed as soft as sea pebbles, rutted by Roman carts, polished by passing horseshoes. You see exactly the same sights, feel the same pains, as generations of previous pilgrims—men like John of Gaunt and Saint Francis of Assisi, women like Chaucer's formidable Wife of Bath. In a very real way you become part of the road's history.

But equally, if you have neither the time nor the energy to take medieval transport and elect instead to go by bicycle or in a car, the modern asphalt road will still let you see some of the most extraordinary churches, sculptures, and objects of religious art to come out of the European Middle Ages. And you will still stay in some of the world's most intriguing and ancient hotels, from simple medieval inns, whose furnishings can hardly have changed for five hundred years, to the Hostal Los Reyes Católicos in Santiago, a sixteenth-century Spanish Renaissance palace now magnificently restored into what is arguably the most elegant hotel in Europe. Either way, on foot or horseback, bike or limousine, taking the road to Compostela is as fine an introduction to both Spain and medieval European culture as any traveler could wish for.

Like all the best things, the pilgrimage to Santiago began with a dream. Or, rather, two dreams.

The first dreamer was Charlemagne, the Holy Roman emperor who in the late eighth century reunited most of Europe in the Carolingian Empire. It is said that in the year before his death he had a vision of a starry road in the sky that crossed France and Spain and reached toward the end of the world; and he heard a voice saying:

"This is the path of Saint James and I am that apostle, servant of Christ, son of Zebedee, brother of John the Evangelist, whom Herod slew, appointed by God's grace to preach His law: Look you, my body is in Galicia, but no man knoweth where, and the Saracens oppress the land. The starry way signifies that you shall go at the head of a host and free that land, and after you, peoples in pilgrimage will follow until the end of time. . . ."

So Charlemagne led his host to Spain, vanquishing the Saracens and following the Milky Way into the misty wastes of Galicia. When he came to *"Finis Terrae"* (from the Latin for the "end of the earth"), he walked straight out onto the waves. Then a boat appeared, the same mystical boat that centuries before had carried the body of Saint James from Palestine, and it took Charlemagne out into the open ocean. There, he stood on the prow and hurled his spear into the deep.

Thus northern Spain was freed from the Moorish yoke. But for all these Carolingian heroics, the body of Saint James still lay undiscovered in its resting place. And for that discovery to be made, a second vision was necessary.

It was given to a hermit named Pelagius, who lived a life of prayer and austerity in the damp mountains of Galicia, eating only honey and wild grasses. One day Pelagius was tucking into a plate of delicious greenery when all of a sudden he saw a new star appear in the sky, accompanied by fragments of strange celestial music. He reported this vision to Theodomir, his bishop, who in turn called out the local people, who armed themselves with picks and shovels. In a deserted place in the hills, directly underneath the star, the stone tomb was discovered in a dank and echoing cave. Within it lay a body, its head intact, sweetly perfumed; and on the ground lay a letter:

"Here lies Santiago, son of Zebedee and Salome, brother of Saint John, whom Herod beheaded in Jerusalem. He came by sea, borne by his disciples. . . ."

A small church was built on the site, and from the beginning it attracted pilgrims. Later the church became a monastery, and a town grew up around it. The town was named Santiago de Compostela, St. James of the Field of the Star.

Of course, modern academics will have none of it. Saint James never came anywhere near Spain, they say, either in his life or after his death. The story is probably a clerical fraud dreamed up by the monks to attract donations; or if not, it was simply the result of a monastic muddle, with some ignorant scribe who was copying out the Acts of the Apostles confusing the Latin for Jerusalem (Hierosolyma) with the Latin word for Spain (Hispania). What's more, so the academics contend, the name of Compostela has nothing to do with stars and a lot to do with a derivation from the Latin *compostum*, from which we get the phrase *compost heap*.

Even the tradition of pilgrimage, they argue, is simply a mem-

ory of some orgiastic pre-Christian bondage cult that used to organize illicit visits to nearby Cabo Finisterre, where cult members
got up to no good among the menhirs and dolmens on the seashore. It is from this cult that Saint James inherits his emblem, the
scallop shell: Long before the Vatican converted scallops into the
emblem of Christian pilgrimage, worn by every footsore traveler
to Santiago, the shell was the Roman symbol for the vagina and
the emblem of the pagan love goddess, Venus. It was worn by
devotees of esoteric classical cults in altogether different contexts
and, so it seems, for altogether different purposes.

The modern pilgrim is free to choose whichever of these two
versions he cares to believe: the dull and scholarly or the romantic
and mythical. For myself, I was quite happy to suspend my critical faculties for the duration of the pilgrimage, and at the end I
said a prayer at what I like to believe was the tomb of Saint James.
Moreover, I walked the road with a *coquille St-Jacques*—a pilgrim's
scallop shell—around my neck. Although (disappointingly) it did
not elicit any indecent propositions from beautiful Spanish girls
au fait with Roman erotic symbolism, it did awaken in every village I passed through a deep reservoir of old-world goodwill
toward itinerant pilgrims. After twelve hundred years, you would
have thought that the novelty of passing pilgrims would have
worn off in villages along the route; yet, strangely, it is not so.

Old men out in the fields polling their olive trees would stop
what they were doing and politely bow to you; village priests
would offer you their blessing and ask you to pray for them at the
tomb of Saint James. In village bars, the owners would round off
my bills to a convenient decimal. One hotel owner solemnly presented me with a bar of chocolate: "*Hombre!* My son is your age,"
he said, holding me in a firm Iberian grip. "He did the pilgrimage
last year. Now he is in Salamanca, studying for the priesthood."

Most remarkable of all was the hilltop village of Cirauqui, a
little to the south of Hemingway's beloved Pamplona. Even from

afar, the village looked different. The widows had done their best to make the place cheerful: put cages full of birds—canaries and cockatoos—out onto the windowsills and loaded their balconies with snapdragons and nasturtiums. The village had red-tiled roofs and whitewashed walls, and as I sat in the shade of the village church, beginning my picnic lunch, I was abducted by a gray-haired, prickly-chinned old lady and carried off to her house with cries of *"peregrino"* (pilgrim) and "Santiago."

Like every other house in the village, it was wind-worn and crumbling; above its door was hung the escutcheon of some long-extinct don. Inside, the furnishing was dark and frugal: A solitary picture of a bleeding Sacred Heart hung on the wall, and there was a strong scent of beeswax polish and mahogany. I sat down next to her sleeping husband in the kitchen, and while her grandchildren climbed all over me, course after course of an enormous peasant lunch was put on the table. A vast salad, soaked in local olive oil, was followed by a huge plate of ham and eggs, suspended in a welter of tomatoes; this was followed by a succession of other courses, including a strange confection of morels, and brought to a close by bowls full of ripe Castilian fruits. The feast was washed down by wine from the old lady's own small vineyard.

"You do have an awful lot of grandchildren," I said, as twelve of them tumbled among the remnants of the meal.

"There are ten more at school," she replied, beaming proudly.

After the lunch was finally finished and the dishes cleared, the old lady sat back and asked me where I was from—Germany perhaps?

"Scotland," I said.

"Where is that?"

"Near England."

"England . . . *Londres*," said the lady vaguely. Then her face lit up. She rose and indicated that she wanted me to follow her. I was led into the pitch darkness of her shuttered bedroom. She scuttled off into a corner, returning with a magazine cradled lovingly in her arms.

"*Londres,*" she said, opening the pages at a much-thumbed center spread and pointing to a picture of an elegant blond. "*Londres,*" she said. "The city of Lady Di."

Of course, it was not always like this. Hospitality varied from place to place.

In the Middle Ages, the pilgrim who braved the heights of the French Pyrenees would be rewarded on reaching Spain with the medieval equivalent of the New York Hilton. The monks of the abbey of Roncesvalles would wash his feet for him on arrival; he would be offered an actual bed in a heated dormitory; free meals would be offered during the period he was resting there; a picnic would be given to him for the next part of the journey; and if all this proved too much for the amazed traveler, he would be given a decent burial, in consecrated ground.

Today the monks at Roncesvalles—whose monastery was founded specifically to look after pilgrims—are too busy flogging knickknacks to tourists to take much interest in modern pilgrims. Having read about the provisions made for medieval pilgrims, you come down from the cold gray mists of the Roncesvalles Pass expecting great things. And indeed, there is still a dormitory—but it is very cold, entirely without linen, and, far from having your feet washed, there is no provision even for hot water. You are not fed nor provided with a picnic, and you are thrown out at nine o'clock the following morning.

To make matters worse, the villages around Roncesvalles are some of the most inhospitable in Spain. The houses are shored with buttresses and pierced with windows no wider than a lancet; their stones are rarely smaller than the average-size coffin. Half farm, half castle, half church, the houses of Navarre are old and solid and easily defensible. They are deserted but for packs of howling, wolflike dogs and hobbling, black-clad windows: It is as if some terrible plague had descended and carried off the men, the children, and the cats. Torn posters cover the village walls. There is no sound but for some ill-oiled door creaking on its hinges in the wind.

Medieval writers often took a dislike to these villages too. Aymeric Picaud, a bigoted Benedictine from Poitou, wrote what is still the most amusing guide to the pilgrimage route in the mid twelfth century A.D. In his writings he is rarely polite about anyone unfortunate enough not to have been born French, but he reserves his worst venom for the Navarrese, the inhabitants of this area:

"They dress as badly as the Scots," he writes, "are as full of wickedness, but are dark in colour, ugly, debauched, peverse, perfidious, disloyal, corrupt, drunken, experts in every kind of violence; they are ferocious and savage, dishonest and false, impious and impolite, cruel and querulous, incapable of decent sentiments, and experts in all vices and iniquities."

The first week of the trip had been dogged with rain and thick Pyrenean mists. In Navarre, however, the sun was scorching. The midday heat quivered over the vineyards, driving me off the track and into the narrow shade of the roadside cypresses. One afternoon I decided to take a siesta in a haystack. I was exhausted: That morning I had risen early and walked from the last conifers and pastures of the hills to the olive groves and cornfields of the plains. It was hot, and I lay down and enjoyed the new sounds and smells: almond blossoms and buzzing flies, rock roses and blue columbines, the grating of amorous grasshoppers and the woodland cackle of a golden oriole.

I had been dozing for no more than half an hour before I was awakened by the unlikely sound of chanting male voices. Two dark, burly men were heading toward me with enormous backpacks on their shoulders. They were each holding something in their right hand, and as they drew closer I could see that these were rosaries. The chant was the Roman Catholic prayer, the Hail Mary, in Italian.

Oscar and Giuseppe were pilgrims from a village near Turin. Giuseppe was a farmer; Oscar had just been laid off by Fiat. Both had sons training for the priesthood, and Giuseppe had a brother who was a Trappist monk; both had undertaken the pilgrimage out of strictly religious reasons. They joined me on my haystack, and Giuseppe took off his shoes. His feet were red and swollen; one sported a pustule the size of a small football.

"You will cripple yourself if you walk with feet like that," I said. Giuseppe grinned, pulled a toothpick out of his shirt pocket, and began to pick at his molars.

"Seriously," I said, "you should rest them, at least for a day or two."

"We must cover at least forty kilometers a day," he replied. "We have less than three weeks to get to Compostela. I have to get back for the harvest, and Oscar needs to look for a job."

"If you are in a hurry, you could take a bus for a bit of the route," I suggested.

"No," replied Oscar firmly. "This is a pilgrimage."

"What difference will it make?"

"I need a job and I am going to ask Saint James for one. If he knows what I have suffered, he will not refuse me."

Oscar was dressed in sneakers, jeans, and T-shirt, indistinguishable from a million other twentieth-century Europeans. But his beliefs were those of a medieval peasant. Carrying a backpack two or three times the weight of my own, he had already walked more in that week than I had in the previous two; and the pain he was inflicting upon himself and his friend was quite deliberate. After the polite, lukewarm piety with which I had grown up, I found the robust faith of the Italians strange—and oddly attractive. Their approach to the pilgrimage would have been quite familiar to Aymeric Picaud, and maybe even to Chaucer's Wife of Bath.

I walked with the Italians that afternoon, scrambling along the track in an effort to keep up with them. We trudged from village to village; sometimes the road sank into the ground, as if cut down by some fast-flowing river, down into a tunnel of overgrown scurvy grass and wild poppies. Dry-stone revetments held up the vine terraces above. Below, the walls were like a section of an archaeological excavation—dotted with shards and skulls, an old pilgrim's charm perhaps, the discarded rubbish of a millennium of travelers.

Up in the open again, church towers were rarely out of sight, and we descended down paths corkscrewing through shallow hills along avenues of poplar and cypress. Sometimes our footsteps would fall in time with the dull thud of mattocks on dry earth, as villagers turned the soil around their vines.

The Italians and I tramped on long after darkness had fallen. All became quiet but for our muffled footfalls in the white dust of the track, luminous now in the light of the moon. I was very tired and longed for the lights of Puente la Reina, our destination. But we did not get there until after ten o'clock.

We were taken in by the Fathers of the Reparadores and given bare bunks in their pilgrims' hostel. There was no food and no hot water, but the Italians did not seem to mind. They kissed the pictures of Il Papa on the wall and hung their rosaries on the bars of their bunks. Their only grouse was that the monks refused to give them Holy Communion until the next morning.

When I awoke at eight o'clock, the Italians had long gone. I thanked the monks and made my way to a bar, where I ate breakfast. Then I headed off along the old cobbled track, alone again.

As I walked I wondered how far Oscar and Giuseppe were representative of the pilgrims who had walked the road over the centuries. Certainly, many of the modern pilgrims whom I talked to were motivated as much by the wish for a holiday as by any religious urge, and there is evidence that quite a lot of medieval pilgrims must have felt the same way. Andrew Boorde, who left us the fullest English-language account of the journey, was certainly no saint. He was very skeptical about the relics he saw at Santiago and, moreover, ended his days in London's Fleet Prison, accused of living with three women simultaneously.

Nor do other records give the impression that the medieval pilgrimage was all piety and long faces. Those who could would travel in some style. They brought their own musicians with them and passed along the road in a litter, or palanquin, serenaded by viols, tabors, and harps, interspersing visits to the more attractive shrines with visits to tournaments and other noblemen, allowing time to try out Spanish delicacies—Galician shellfish or the fine wines of La Rioja.

The poorer classes, then as now, traveled in groups, drank a great deal, and made a lot of noise:

> "They will ordain beforehand to have with them both men and women [including those sorts of women] who sing wanton songs; and some other pilgrims will have with them bagpipes; so that every town they come through, what with the noise of their singing, and with the sound of their piping, and with the jangling of their bells, and with the barking of dogs after them, they make more noise than if the king came their way, with all his clarions and many other minstrells. . . ."

One thinks also of Chaucer's pilgrims, crooks virtually to a man, what with the corrupt Miller, the lecherous Wife of Bath, the worldly Prioress, and particularly the loathsome Pardoner selling relics that were supposedly the ossified remains of great saints but were in fact "pigges bones." It was people like this who gave pilgrimage an increasingly bad name as the Middle Ages progressed, and at whom the famous saying was directed: *Ir romera y volver ramera* ("Go a pilgrim, return a whore").

And yet it is undoubtedly true that when mass pilgrimage first became popular in the eleventh century, it was inspired first and foremost by devotion: People really did believe in saints' relics, that they had a spiritual power and could act as divine gobetweens in the quest for personal salvation. Today when we read of the warehouses full of "true" relics stored up by monasteries across medieval Europe—those gallons of the Virgin's Milk, forests of fragments of the True Cross, jars full of Our Lord's Breath, and even His Holy Foreskin—the collections seem more comic than anything else. But to the simple Christians of the Middle Ages, relics held out the promise of an authority superior to man's and were, as a second-century Greek writer put it, "more valuable than refined gold." Moreover, people believed that the places in which relics were kept were invested with magical properties—the ability to heal earthly sickness and wipe clean a soul besmirched with sin—and many were prepared to travel vast distances to experience those powers.

My pilgrim friends Giuseppe and Oscar spoke with the authentic voice of early medieval pilgrims. But at the end of another day's walking, I saw a work of art from the twelfth century that to me expressed the feelings and fears of medieval pilgrims better than anything I had ever previously seen or read.

The church of San Miguel in Estella is a great fortress of a building and is reached by a massive, almost Wagnerian flight of steps. Inside, it is as dark as night. Narrow, arrow-slit windows emit only the minimum of light; above, massive masonry vaults groan under the weight of stone; it is cold and empty and silent but for the tread of feet on flagstones. It is an awesome sight—yet nothing affects one so much as the great north portal, emblazoned with some of the most frightening sculpture I have ever seen.

It is flanked by a line of martyrs who grimly grip the instruments with which they were tortured. With their severe expressions and hanging-judge eyes, they look as intolerant and autocratic, as stiff and as Spanish, as a line of *guardia civil*. Their beards appear to have been crusted with fixative, their clothes coated with plaster of paris. They point at their scrolls as if passing sentence. If these are the men who are going to be the jury at the Last Judgment, you think, the sentences are going to be far from lenient.

Yet the martyrs are nothing compared with Christ, sitting Enthroned in Majesty at the center of the tympanum. He is as still and unmoving as the eye of a hurricane. Yet around him swirls a typhoon of cherubim and seraphim, holy women and beasts of the Apocalypse, bunches of grapes and man-headed animals, Babylonian griffins and coiling snakes—the images becoming ever more anarchic the farther removed they are from the calming influence of Christ. It is a simple and effective idea: Without God, life becomes gruesome and Hell-like; moreover, there is another idea implicitly linked to the first. In the twisting, tortured forms of the self-devouring man-beasts, evil is shown as a kind of human insanity, a mental condition. Hell is not so much heat and torment as a kind of terrible apocalyptic bedlam.

The vision is deeply troubled, harrowing, and pessimistic. The portal shows the nightmares and forest fears looming large in the psyche of medieval man. It shows him tortured by doubt in this world and living in continual fear of damnation and hellfire in the next. At the end of the day, it was that fear that led men to leave the comfort and safety of their homes and take to the pilgrimage roads in search of divine forgiveness. It was fear, not hope, that inspired the first pilgrims to Compostela.

After Estella, you head through low, hilly country to Burgos, one of the most windswept cities in Spain. There you enter a wasteland.

For the following two weeks the pilgrim passes through

strange deforested plains—bleak, flat, austere, and desolate—
wearying both to the feet and to the spirit. It was always an empty
and inhospitable area, although today the traveler is unlikely to
see what once was a common sight: a pack of wolves descending
to devour the bodies of pilgrims.

It takes at least a fortnight's walking before you come to León,
where you are rewarded for your labors by a night in the Hotel
San Marcos—one of the great hotels of Europe: once the headquarters of the Crusader Knights of Saint James, now a flagship of
the Spanish Parador chain. It is a great palace of a building, its
magnificent frontage decorated with one of the finest pieces of relief carving to have come out of the Spanish Renaissance. Inside,
it is restored with perfect taste and furnished with medieval tables
and chairs. You wake up unable to believe you are really staying
here: It's like finding yourself taking rooms at a great Oxford college furnished with the finest exhibits from the British Museum.

From León, you pass briefly through more clement Mediterranean regions, full of vineyards and olives, until you move up
into the hills of Galicia. For me, a Scot, it was a kind of home-
coming: Suddenly I was back among Celts, back among the rain
clouds, back in a country where the rocks blossomed with strange
gray lichens.

The change from the olive groves of Castile was very sudden.
In the morning at Villafranca I had still been in the heat of the
plains. But at Herreria, I had turned left off the road and immediately crossed some invisible barrier. Suddenly the dust turned
to mud, and soft mosses began to creep up the dry stone walls,
overloading the bows of the trees and hanging heavily off the
branches. There were dripping hawthorns and muddy detours
through thickets of yellow broom. Hens pecked about in dense,
damp grass.

The people changed too: The narrow Castilians gave way
to thickset farmers in knitted cardigans and flat caps; in the bars

they ate in silence, cutting up their chops on wooden plates with knives that looked as if they had been stolen from some abattoir. They drank wine from tumblers, and the air was heavy with woodsmoke, cigarettes, and the primeval charcoal stink of grilling meat.

The women also seemed to thicken out: As I passed through muddy farmyards I would be watched by silent, broad-bosomed matrons in aprons and pinnies. They would be carrying meal out for the hens, shepherding their children in for supper, or sternly calling their dogs to back away from the pilgrim. Sometimes I would meet them carrying in fodder for the cows, their faces lost under great mountains of hay.

That evening, as a strong gale was blowing up the mountainsides, I reached Cebreiro, believed by some to have been the site of the Grail Castle, and a near neighbor of the legendary Château Merveil, the fortress of Klingsor the Necromancer. As heavy rain lashed down, I sought the shelter of its church, the very embodiment of Chapel Perilous, small and dark, with granite walls and a slate roof. For an hour I stood shivering in the porch, waiting for the rain to stop, watching the water dripping off the eaves into a puddle.

Later, reading sitting up in bed while the rain pattered on the window, I discovered that the chapel had been the site of a famous miracle. One day during the Consecration, a doubting priest had been confounded when the altar wine had actually turned into blood. I wondered whether the stories of the Grail had thus emerged from confusion of the words *San Greal* (the Holy Grail) and *Sang Real* (the Royal Blood)—or whether it was the area's Celtic past that had led to its becoming linked with the Grail myths. For long before it ever became adopted by Christianity as the chalice used at the Last Supper—a development that took place only in the twelfth century—the Grail had a long history in Celtic myth as the Horn of Plenty, the emblem of Ceridwell, the

Sow Goddess, and it was sought after long before Arthur, by Gwynn ap Nudd, King of the Faeries and Lord of Glastonbury.

The Grail has always been a mesmeric subject, breeding wild speculation and unanswered questions, and that night I went to sleep dreaming of Bors, Galahad, and Perceval setting sail in Solomon's magic bark for the land of Sarras.

The monks were in their fields, planting cabbages with the air of old Edwardian gentlemen playing croquet. There were fifteen of them: plump, elderly men in matching blue overalls and wide-brimmed straw hats, and as they raked the earth and carefully placed the cabbages in neat lines, the abbot shouted encouragement from his seat on the side of the field; you knew he was the abbot because he was wearing a heavy pectoral cross and bright green Wellington boots. When the cabbages were in place, the abbot squatted down on his hams to make sure the line was straight, as if sizing up the angles before sending his ball flying firmly through the hoop.

Father Domingo, the guestmaster, detached himself from the clerical chain gang and came to meet me at the side of the field.

"*Peregrino?*" he asked.

"*Sí.*"

"Follow me," he said; and together we headed toward the monastery gates, I with my staff, he with his rake.

After several weeks on the road, my pilgrimage had achieved a certain rhythm. Apart from those occasions when I would splurge on grand hotels like the Hotel San Marcos, I would usually try to stay in the old pilgrims' rest houses, which in turn would usually be housed in an abbey or a monastery. Every morning I would leave the shelter of the abbey walls and pass out into the hazards of the world: not the bandits, wolves, and plagues faced by the medieval pilgrim, perhaps, but the no-less tiring uncertainties of rain, wind, blisters, and sprained ankles. By evening

I would be back in the charge of another guestmaster, twenty miles on along the road, conducted by another hooded figure through a flagstone cloister garth to the bare shelter of another pilgrims' dormitory. The following morning there would be Mass, breakfast, and the open gate in the monastery wall.

I was educated by Benedictine monks in an English public school in Yorkshire, an experience that was enough to put anyone off monasticism for life. Yet on this journey I grew to love the monasteries I passed by: They seemed marvelous towers of solid ivory, abodes of faith, wisdom, and learning marked out from the outside world by their calmness, their lack of haste. Each monastery had a different quality to recommend it. One might distill an unusual liquer, some rich brew flavored with wild herbs and derived from a medieval recipe carefully guarded in the monastic library. Another might make strong goat's cheese, or pottery, or have cloisters carved with tangling Romanesque vine scrolls. But Samos, with its troops of cabbage-farming monks, was probably the most ostentious of all the monasteries I stayed in: as grand as a palace and as huge as a barracks.

It was a wild Baroque extravagance, all volutes and broken pediments, lined with Corinthian pilasters and reached by a great double staircase. Inside, the cloisters enclosed an area the size of a field, planted with palm trees and dominated by a lapidary fountain supported by a family of thrashing reptilian behemoths. There were goldfish in the pond and, nearby, a plague to the blessed memory of Generalissimo Franco. In the church a monolithic statue of Alfonso of Castile towered over the body of a decapitated Moor; the head, only recently severed, still gushed scarlet gore over the pedestal.

The atmosphere was anything but prayerful, yet Vespers, the most beautiful of all monastic liturgies, managed to transform even this monstrous edifice into something profound and moving. A bell was ringing; incense wafted down from the *coro*. The tread of monastic footsteps echoed from dome to semidome and around the apse. The monks, in habits now, passed up the aisle, black breviaries in their hands. There was a spin of cassocks and a creak of misericords:

> *"De profundis clamavi ad te, Domine,*
> *Domine exaudi vocem meam . . ."*

The music, Gregorian chant, was contemporary with the founding of the abbey and dated from the late sixth century; the same music had been sung on the same site while Picts still painted their bodies and Irish kings still ruled from Tara, while Arabs besieged Constantinople and the Venerable Bede was writing on a rickety desk in Jarrow:

> *"Exaudi nos Domine,*
> *Miserere mei Deus, miserere mei . . ."*

The lights were turned out, the thuribles extinguished, and the Great Silence began.

In medieval times, the pilgrim to Rome came down from the heights of Tuscany to be rewarded with a view of the city's magnificent walls, looping over the seven hills. The approach to Jerusalem was an equally suitable climax to so long a journey: that last wonderful stretch of road up from Emmaus threading up through the pine trees and oleanders.

In comparison, the first view of Santiago was always unremarkable; even the Romans seemed to have been unimpressed, for the river you cross is named Lavacolla, derived from the Latin for "arse wipe." Yet to arrive at any destination that you have longed for has its rewards. I was in a fairly bad way. I was unshaven, and none of my clothes had been washed for a week. I smelled. More seriously, a blister on the ball of my right foot had gone bad and I had a pronounced Quasimodo limp. Just to arrive, just to cease walking, seemed enough.

The outskirts of Santiago seemed strangely deserted. It was only when I neared the towering cliff face of the Cathedral that the crowds thickened, and then they did so dramatically. Suddenly police cars were everywhere, and so were policemen, keeping the crowds back with metal crowd gates and machine guns. I asked a passerby what was happening. The king, Juan Carlos, was about to arrive in Santiago. Where was he staying? In the Hostal Los Reyes Católicos. The same hotel at which I had a reservation.

I was within seconds of perfectly mistiming my entry to the hotel. Having fought my way through the police cordon, waving my reservation slip, I limped up to the door of the parador seconds before His Majesty. Smooth functionaries in gold brocade had time to secrete the embarrassing specter away in a corner and hide his stinking rucksack. There was a fanfare of trumpets, and the king entered the magnificent hostel, originally built by his predecessor, King Ferdinand, for the shelter of pilgrims. On this occasion, understandably enough, they were rather less welcome. At breakfast I found an ally in the waiter:

"These kings," he said, disdainfully. "They make such a mess. We get so many of them here."

I laughed, thinking he was joking. But he was quite serious.

It was midafternoon before I had exhausted the novelites of my hotel room: baths, linen sheets, a laundry service, even a bidet in which, in the absence of any more suitable use, I soaked my aching feet. Washed, shaved, and scented, with a fresh change of clothes, I headed out into the square to finish my journey.

The hotel was still surrounded by limousines and their attendant hordes of chauffeurs, policemen, and photographers. But the area in front of the great Cathedral, built on the site of the original small church, was now empty but for a small group of pilgrims like myself. A Belgian bicyclist was dancing a small jig on the Cathedral steps. Another pilgrim, a young bearded Spaniard whom I had previously met near León, appeared to have virtually expired beside the portal; one old lady dropped a coin on his lap as she passed.

Inside, the Cathedral was almost pitch dark. Rolling Romanesque arches thundered forward on massive feet toward the shrine—a huge baroque construction that filled the space normally occupied by the *coro*. It was an extraordinary object, a forest of wooden pinnacles and stalactites, dominating the nave like some hugely enlargd cuckoo clock, the image of Saint James filling the little cavity normally reserved for the bird. Yet in the night blackness of the nave, the shrine took on a strange quality of gilded magnificence. We pilgrims queued up beside a staircase, waiting to be admitted into the space behind the statue, as excited as a group of children waiting for a ride on a fairground roller coaster.

For the pilgrims of the Middle Ages, the bones of Saint James were the supreme relics of Europe, the most powerful miracle workers and sin cleansers in Christendom. Even Aymeric Picaud, the author of the twelfth-century pilgrim's guide normally so rude about all things Spanish, was forced into awestruck admiration:

> "His whole body is there . . . divinely illuminated by heavenly carbuncles, endlessly honoured by divine fragrant odours, decorated with the brightness of celestial candles and unceasingly honoured by angelic adoration. . . ."

We pilgrims clutched our staffs, burly young men hobbling forward like old women. One by one, we climbed the stairs up into the darkness and there threw our arms around the statue, hugging it close. What should have been a hugely embarrassing exercise was, in the circumstances, oddly moving. The statue was cold, hard, and solid, yet it felt quite natural to squeeze it as enthusiastically as if it were your girlfriend, and it responded to the cuddle with a satisfactory rattling noise.

Then the stairs led down again, down, down, deep down into the crypt, to a dim, bare, round-arched, flagstone space furnished with a single kneeler. Here I knelt before a grille and looked forward. A few feet away, through a narrow passage, a small chamber was lit with dazzling brilliance. There, encased in solid silver, sat the reliquary that contained the bones of the saint.

Logically, I knew it was a fairly slim chance—though far from impossible—that the bones were those of the fisherman Jesus first picked up beside the Sea of Galilee, James the son of Zebedee and Salome. But irrespective of their identity, I felt that the bones had been imbued with sanctity and importance through the pain of the tens of millions of pilgrims throughout the ages who had traveled thousands of miles to pray at the kneeler at which I now knelt.

So, despite having long dropped the habit, I did pray there, and the prayers came with a surprising ease. I prayed for the people who had helped me on the journey, the priest who had blessed my stick, the innkeeper who had refused payment, the monks who had given me food, and the cobbler who had mended my torn shoes. And then I did what I suppose I had come to do: I prayed for my fiancée and for the success of my forthcoming marriage, now only a few weeks away.

Then I got up, climbed the steps, and walked back, under the great incense-darkened vaults of the nave, under the triple portal and the old rose window.

Outside it had begun to rain.

1992

A PILGRIMAGE HOW-TO

Five hundred glorious miles through Europe

 To go on pilgrimage implies walking, and the great majority of pilgrims to Santiago de Compostela have always walked the Camino de Santiago; it remains one of the great footpaths of the world—free of cars, leading through superb countryside, and well signposted. Four paths go through France: from Paris, Vézelay, Le Puy, and Arles; they join at Puente la Reina near Pamplona, Spain. The Pyrenees are pretty inhospitable from November to February, and the plains around León are too hot in July and August. Medieval pilgrims traditionally set off in March or April; and April, May, and June are still the best walking months.

Those who prefer to concentrate on the Spanish section of the journey can fly to Toulouse and take public transport to Saint-Jean-Pied-de-Port on the Franco-Spanish border. From there, Compostela is a three- to five-week journey, depending on whether you aim to travel a sensible fifteen or a breakneck twenty to twenty-five miles a day. Although so long a walk seems a daunting prospect, fifteen miles a day is far from impossible, and many quite elderly people manage it.

By bicycle, the journey can be done at a leisurely pace in two to four weeks. By car, it takes about twelve hours, but allow ten days if you are to see even a fraction of the sights.

Two items are essential: a staff and a scallop shell, the latter the symbol of Christian pilgrimage. On the road they are like membership badges to some exclusive club and enable you to strike up instant friendships with other pilgrims.

Several companies organize walking tours of the pilgrim

route as well. The Tourist Office of Spain (spain.info) has information. Also, for details about the hostels and monastic guest rooms along the route that are open free of charge to pilgrims on foot or on bicycle, contact the Confraternity of St. James in England (44-20-7928-9988; csj.org.uk). The organization's site also offers valuable information about the history of the pilgrimage and how to get a pilgrim's passport.

Where the Wild Things Are

by

PHILIP GOUREVITCH

I don't speak Swahili, and the young man standing in the arrivals area at Dar-es-Salaam International Airport and holding a piece of cardboard marked MR. PILHIP doesn't speak much English. "No problem," he keeps saying, as he ushers my wife and me to a battered old Corolla and drives us to the domestic terminal down the road. "No problem." This is the extent of his communication, and it makes me uneasy. Over the years in Africa, I've learned that when someone denies a problem repeatedly without being asked, it's best to assume that something's amiss. Sure enough: It turns out the six-seater Cessna that was supposed to carry us into the bush of southern Tanzania for a week's safari is stuck out there, having collided with a giraffe during takeoff. The passenger at the time—a former Enron executive—was unharmed, as was the pilot. (Questions about the fate of the giraffe are met with silence.) And so—"No problem"—a much smaller Cessna awaits us instead, a tiny contraption, like a child's toy. A man stands beside it, sweating heavily in the midday sun, which has also softened the tarmac underfoot. "I am Mohammed," he explains, "and I am your pilot."

In the air, suddenly buoyant, the plane handles like a kayak, nosing along in skittering, mildly nauseating jerks and lunges. Beneath us, Dar-es-Salaam (Dar, as everyone calls it), a drab port city disfigured in the 1970s and '80s by the dismal poured-concrete architecture promoted by Tanzania's Socialist-bloc patrons, shrinks into its haze of diesel exhaust and cooking fires. As we fly south and slightly westward, leaving the Indian Ocean coast behind us, the tin-roofed shantytowns on Dar's outskirts give way to more dispersed settlements, encircling kraals for cattle amid ragged patches of trees and messily arranged fields. Then, abruptly, desert takes over. The sand is striped, in places marbled, with fat bands of beige broken by fingers of chocolate brown and washes of black. Even the occasional tree, parched and leafless at the peak of the dry season, looks to be made of sand. The earth is uninhabited here, most likely uninhabitable, and it appears to go on this way forever.

This isolation is why we've come, of course. Somewhere in the sandy wasteland below runs the border of the Selous Game Reserve, the biggest wildlife sanctuary in Africa. Covering an area greater in size than Switzerland, it is almost entirely undeveloped and in large parts barely explored. In the famous northern Tanzanian parks—the Serengeti and Ngorongoro Crater—as in their Kenyan cousins like the Masai Mara, the abundance of game is matched by a proliferation of tourists. But in all the immensity of the Selous (pronounced *se-LOO*), a tract of wildly varying ecosystems—river and desert, forest and grassland, rocky canyon and rolling hilltops—there are blessedly few humans and only five safari lodges. Each has just a few beds, so that most of the reserve remains nearly as untamed and untraveled as it was at the turn of the last century, when the man who gave it his name, the great white hunter Frederick Courteney Selous, first beheld it. In fact, the place is even wilder now, since the Africans who originally made this bush their home have since been moved off in the name of conservation, and a visit to the Selous today is still, as the writer and explorer Peter Matthiessen described it a quarter of a century ago, when he trekked through with a party of naturalists, "the ultimate safari into the last wilderness." As it happens, one of the outfitters of that expedition, Richard Bonham, an acclaimed game tracker and ornithologist, went on to establish the finest camp in the Selous, Sand River Lodge, which is where we're headed. Sure enough, just as the desert desolation below appears absolute, vegetation returns, now denser than ever and ferociously green.

Streaks of water gleam through the foliage; the course of a river announces itself, then lakes, as we descend from the bottoms of the clouds to just above the treetops, startling a trio of drinking elephants. The shapes define themselves more swiftly now— hippos here, crocodiles there. A flash of white is an egret, a weird long shadow leads to a giraffe. We are flying low, in circles, cutting figure eights over forested hills and watering holes and a golden web of dry riverbeds: the famous sand rivers, whose meanderings create a disorienting labyrinth. Delighting in the sights as we bank this way and that, I imagine we are being treated to an air safari and marvel that anyone can find his way around such a tangled landscape even with this bird's-eye view. Then I hear Mohammed muttering, "No problem," and I realize that we are lost.

The air in the cockpit is cool, but Mohammed is streaming with sweat again, staring in bewilderment at the terrain below. For a second I think I see a road down there, two tire tracks in red dirt, but the thread is quickly swallowed by the bush and never emerges. There are two fuel gauges on the instrument panel: One has been on empty since takeoff, and the needle of the other has dropped from the half-full mark to well blow a quarter. I'm thinking about how—damn it—I really wanted to make this trip by train.

Dar is the northeastern terminus of the old TAZARA rail line that slices west and south through the continent—across Tanzania, through Zambia, and into South Africa, all the way to Cape Town. The train still makes the journey several times a week, with a couple of whistle stops in the Selous, and the ticket costs just ten dollars. All trains have romance to them, and this one provides a rare chance not to be removed from the normal life of Africans, as happens on most safaris. Riding the TAZARA rails allows you to have it both ways—remaining in African society even as you enter the African bush, measuring your transition from one world to the other—and it was the prospect of crossing such a swath of Africa by train that originally lured me to this part of Tanzania. But every time I tried to buy a ticket, I was rebuffed and foiled. I kept being given different schedules for the train, then I was told that it only ran once a week, then that it didn't run at all anymore. I found out too late, when I was already in Africa and had booked this flight, that none of this information was true. The train is real and it runs, and now here we are, in the air, burning fuel, with no idea where we are, and with a pilot whose lips have begun moving without making sounds, suggesting a man deep in prayer.

My wife, wedged in amid the luggage behind me, still assumes we're on course. She's gazing out the window—at the patterned sand, the greenish swamps studded with palms, the weird and wondrous upward-yearning branches of baobab trees—and she's grinning. When I catch her eye, she mouths a big "Wow," which reminds me that while we may be lost, there's nowhere I'd rather be. I'm even getting good at identifying the animals from above, but I can't make out a tawny shape crouched in the shade of a giant tree. Suddenly I get it and start shouting, "There—a truck!" In fact, there are two trucks parked at the edge of a long dirt lot that can only be an airstrip. Mohammed sees it too now. "Of course, exactly, no problem," he says, and swoops down, making an initial pass to check that the runway is clear of giraffes or whatever before wheeling around and bringing us back to earth.

———————

I have never seen, never even imagined, a landscape like this—at once fiercely alive and utterly parched, a jumble of rocky hillocks clung to by bare, sinewy trees. It has been months since the last steady rains, and bouncing away from the airstrip on the back bench of an open Land Rover I see that the ashy soil is littered with the bleached bones of old kills: Cape buffalo, impalas, hippos, warthogs. It feels like we've stumbled onto the set of *Waiting for Godot*. I am used to being surprised in Africa—in fact, the continent's reliable capacity for surprise is largely what keeps drawing me back—but in the past, when I've gone there as a reporter, my trips and my surprises have been determined by human dramas: political upheavals, spasms of terrible violence, revolutions, peace deals gone bad, great human displacements. Arriving on the scene of these traumas was always a jolt, and at the same time I came equipped with a vocabulary for what I was seeing. Now, in this other Africa of unpeopled bush, I lack the precise language to describe it—and as the Land Rover carries us down from the arid hills to a floodplain spotted with grazing game, my notebook fills with lists of new names for this new world, a sort of found poem of flora and fauna.

First there are the trees: leadwood, pod mahogany, rain trees (so-called because spittlebugs lay their eggs beneath the bark and their spittle drips), doom palm (brachiate, candelabralike, multiple trunks), a paperback acacia (laden with weaverbird nests), ebony trees (scraggly) a long-pod cassia, sausage trees (named, ever so accurately for their fruit), wild sage (a sweet, sun-warmed smell), a toothbrush tree (whose shoots are used by locals for cleaning teeth) wrapped by Indian tamarind trees. Then come the birds: little bee-eaters, fish eagles jeering like gulls in a harbor, a pelican, three spoonbills, a white-faced whistling duck, a common sandpiper, a purple-crested touraco, a gray hornbill, a yellow-billed stork, an Egyptian goose, a goliath heron, and, in the forked trunk of a big tree, the massive nest (nearly a hundred pounds of woven twigs and branches) of a hammerkop. Then comes the game: a pair of giraffes running in their stiff-hipped, slow-motion gait and a herd of impalas (the females all pregnant and soon to give birth with the coming of the rains), several strolling hippos, a troop of yellow baboons, a trio of zebras clambering up a rocky slope—and, on the road's shoulder, lying tuskless, the skull of an elephant, an astounding boulder of bone.

Finally, there is the name of the source of all these names, our guide and driver, Ernest Okeyo. The lodge is barely a fifteen-minute ride from the airfield, but Ernest has treated us to a two-hour driving safari before delivering us to our lunch. I'm not hungry and feel like I could keep driving and looking forever—until we come over a rise and see where we'll be staying, at which point I'm struck by a strong sense that I might be content never to go anywhere else again. The lodge occupies the high shoulder of a sweeping bend in the north bank of the Rufiji River. Its main hall and guest cabins—an architects' extravagant fantasia on the theme of traditional African huts, with low curving stone walls and high-vaulted thatched roofs—stand open to the air and the immense views over the river, like a collection of deep and deeply cozy porches. Ours is perhaps a hundred feet from the main dining terrace, yet it is a perfectly private roost, with two heavy armchairs positioned irresistibly at the front as if on the prow of a ship. And the vista, up the Rufiji and across it, does make us feel as if we are sailing. The river is wide here, spread lazily between giant sandbars, and the current drives hard against the bank at our feet. But from the chairs, and better yet from the bed—an immense four-poster draped in gauzy mosquito netting, like a house within a house—the water's surface has a glazed tranquillity that belies the turmoil of the lives it contains and sustains.

—————

In this age of extreme sport and extreme travel, to push on against ever greater obstacles and resistance has become an end in itself for many people, who mistakenly regard sitting still as doing nothing. But why come all this way to remain always in transit and never arrive? At Sand Rivers there is no set program for guests; each day can be shaped as one wishes, and as we finish lunch, the resident manager of the lodge stops by to suggest a variety of possible excursions for the afternoon. But this is where we want to be, perched at the river's edge, watching the comings and goings of a troop of giant elands on the far bank, and some time later a lone giraffe, then upriver on a different sand spit a family of elephants settling in for a long drink. And always there are the hippos wallowing and yawning in the shallows and the sluggish, sinister forms of massive crocodiles gliding among them.

For a while, we float nearby—in a swimming pool built out over the river's edge in the shade of an ancient baobab tree—and the safety and serenity of the scene, assisted by some good whiskey from the always-open self-service bar, lull us into an unguarded sense of oneness with the natural world, a feeling perfectly conveyed by the spectacle of a skimmer darting over the river made pink by a pyrotechnic haze of sunset bursting through a scrim of silken clouds.

So it comes as a jolt a little while later to find ourselves crouched in the dark in the bushes while a one-tusked rogue elephant kicks through our camp. We didn't hear the elephant coming, and we can't see him. But the alarm of the watchman who is escorting us to dinner is palpable. He's armed only with a flashlight and has no illusions about its inadequacy as he aims the beam in the direction of a tremendous crashing noise and herds us, scampering, to our meal: lamb curry and chapati, followed by barbecued fruit with chocolate sauce. (The excellent food is particularly remarkable because the cooks are Africans who don't like to eat what they serve us—preferring rice and beans—and so cook strictly by the book, following the manager's instructions, much as if they were mixing concrete.) When we finish and stand up, the watchman is back at our side. "No problem," he says, but he is still walking on tiptoe and at great speed as he ushers us to our bed.

The elephant is gone, but the night is hardly quiet. This is the hippos' time. All day, they lie submerged in water, waiting to come ashore and graze after dusk, and the crashing and splashing ruckus they make when they return from feeding is the sound of a large truck being driven off a cliff into a river. All night, they bellow and snort and gurgle and fart at a terrifying volume—directly under our pillows it seems. Several times, waking abruptly to an especially jarring outburst from the hippo chorus, I imagine that I'm back in New York City, listening to garbage trucks hoisting and emptying Dumpsters in the street below.

Although they are hopelessly cumbersome-looking creatures, hippos can charge at great speed, and despite being practicing vegetarians, they kill more people in Africa than any other animal, trampling their victims or biting them in half. Most hippo attacks occur on dry land and in the dark, when people inadvertently come between the animals and deep water. But that is small comfort in the morning, when we rise early and join Ernest for a boat safari up the Rufiji. After all, Ernest tells us that hippos can move at twenty-five miles an hour underwater—about five times faster than the motorized rowboat we're in—and on every side of us the beasts are surfacing, nostrils wide and spraying mist. But this time, when Ernest says, "No problem," his tone of unconcern is so authentic that I believe him and am soothed. After all, whatever the lurking submarine menace may be, there is an almost Edenic sense of order and grace to the scene as waterbucks and Thomson's gazelles emerge from the underbrush for their morning drink to the wild, strangled screaming of a low-flying squadron of hadedah ibis.

As we go on, the river narrows; its sandy banks tighten, turn rocky, and lift into a deepening gorge. This is leopard territory, and Ernest tells us to scan the banks. He boasts thirteen leopard sightings on the river in the past few months, and he's serious about his quest for a fourteenth, but I'm more interested in how the hunt for one thing leads one to notice so much else. A huge Cape buffalo tossing its great horns emerges from the bush. Around the next bend, we come upon a huddle of twelve elephants drinking—six of them quite young and small, with short, stiff trunks. We watch them shuffle off, single file, into the forest. Farther on, we find a troop of blue monkeys playing on the rocks, and a sandbar strewn with elephant droppings, which reveals—on closer scrutiny—two perfectly camouflaged lionesses, one sprawled in the sun, the other sitting on her haunches, watching us watching her.

"To me, this is the heart of Africa," Rick Bonham, the founder of Sand Rivers Lodge, told Peter Matthiessen a quarter of a century ago when they explored the Selous together. "This is how it used to be. The place is stacked with game, even if you can't see it . . . and what you do see, you have all to yourself. In the parks, there's always a minibus parked next to it." This sense of the Selous's authenticity is still the essence of its appeal. In the great open East African grasslands of the more visited game parks, you can spot animals from a long way off—and the exhilaration of seeing them in great numbers and with great ease can be considerable even when there are a good many other people around. But there, you can never fully escape the feeling that you are in a giant zoo, albeit with you in the cage (the minivan or Land Rover) while the animals roam free. A week ago, in Kenya, my wife and I were parked in a ring of vehicles around a pride of more than a dozen lions that were busily polishing off a buffalo kill. Now, drifting down the Rufiji River on the way back to base camp with the engine shut off, we see only a solitary lioness, but the thrill is greater, not only because we have her to ourselves but because she is more alert to us, more wary—in a word, wilder.

Of course, it's one thing to enjoy a predator's wildness from a boat, and another thing entirely to encounter such an animal at close range on foot, as a young Australian couple—Melinda and Ben—assure us at lunch. "Walking safaris" between tented camps are the specialty of Sand Rivers, and the Australians had just completed a four-day trek with the lodge's then head guide, a massive and massively bearded white Zimbabwean named Dean. He had carried a rifle every step of the trip, and even without it, he looked like he might be able to scare off most predators just by puffing out his chest, roaring, and charging. But Melinda had experienced her hike through the bush as one long paroxysm of terror. Save for brief naps during midday lunch breaks, when Dean and Ben were awake and watching, she had not slept the whole time—spending her nights riveted by every rustling bush, every snapped twig, every animal grumble or gurgle. She had resorted liberally to gin in the evenings to put herself down, but without success. Encounters with an aroused buffalo, which threatened to charge, and a frisky lion, which reared up before them, left her clinging to Dean and imagining the advent of some other murderous beast at every turn. To be sure, she keeps saying that her walk in the Selous was the best experience of her life, but somehow Ben is more convincing when he says it sure is nice to be back at the lodge.

Melinda leaves me wondering whether I should get a head start on the gin—imbibing it preemptively, as it were—since in the morning my wife and I will be setting out on foot for several days. But our guide for the trek, a Scotsman who calls himself Santa, assures me that won't be necessary. Santa is a stocky twenty-nine-year-old with carrot-red hair. His real name is Guy, but since his birth on Christmas Day nobody seems to have called him that—and besides, his family business back in Scotland is a Christmas-tree farm. Before coming to Sand Rivers, he had been a professional hunter in Tanzania, a line of work his father had also pursued as a young man in Africa. Santa had given it up for the same reason his father had: The money was awful. That night, he maps out the route for our expedition, a hopscotch walking and driving tour of the rocky heights, sand rivers, and lakes in a radius of about ten miles from the lodge.

It's a pleasure to be on foot in the morning air. As a New Yorker, I'm used to walking more each day than I have in ten days of driving, flying, and boat safaris—and the physical and psychic stretching out into the landscape feels long overdue. We start early, when the air is still cool. Ernest drops us off on a high plateau, and we set out on a loop through dry, wooded brush—thorny acacias and magnificent baobabs—leading down into a rocky canyon, where Santa hopes to find one of the leopards that eluded us on the river. But the joy of walking is counterbalanced by the fact that it means seeing less, because you are enclosed in the bush, watching your step, and because walking over dry leaves and twigs and loose rocks makes a tremendous racket of just the sort that sets off any wild creature's fight-or-flight response.

Santa, rifle in hand, wears the flimsiest of tennis shoes—barely better than slippers—and tiptoes ahead of us, squatting to study droppings and tracks, or stopping to kick at the dust and examine which way the wind is blowing. After several hours of scrambling through parched, thorny bush in steadily intensifying heat, we haven't seen a single living thing—not even a bird—and when we find our way back to the Land Rover, Ernest is shaking his head. Every other self-respecting life-form, he reminds us, is sleeping in the shade at this time of day.

Santa is only mildly chastened. After a sandwich in a cool glade by the riverbank, we are off again and haven't driven far before we come upon a big male baboon straddling the middle of the road, barking angrily—a loud, hollow-throated *rwa-huh! rwa-huh!*—at a thicket of undergrowth on the right shoulder. Santa concludes there's a leopard in there, and he's nearly as excited as the baboon, which is pawing the ground, pacing and barking, and barely seems to notice us. He's fixated on the bush, which is so tangled as to be impenetrable by the human eye, and Santa explains: "Leopards eat baboon, but a big male like this will scrap with them." He inches the vehicle forward, and the baboon backs off, scrambling up a tree, still barking as he watches Santa check his rifle to see that it's loaded. "Could be a lion," he muses as he slips into the bush to have a look, "but that baboon was very angry."

Leopard? Lion? For now the coolest cat to behold is Santa himself, creeping silently with coiled, sinuous steps into the snarl of vegetation. A full minute passes without a sign of him, and then another. The baboon is still barking, tirelessly staring at the spot where Santa vanished. Then suddenly the branches fly apart, and Santa is back. "Bloody thick in there," he says, as if it had only just occurred to him that the leopard he couldn't see might have been watching him. I'm delighted to be in this man's company, but I can't help sympathizing with Ernest, who has refused to go on walking safaris since one of his best friends was gored to death by a Cape buffalo while trying to protect his client from the charging beast.

Through the hot afternoon, as we drive through woodlands and wetlands, my notebook again fills with the names of things seen: a pygmy mongoose, emerald-spotted wood doves, golden palm weavers, a Bohn's bee-eater, an immature tawny eagle, and, near dusk, a stand of splendid umbrella-shaped tamarind trees, decked in delicate red flowers and bursting with a flock of trumpet hornbills. Coming upon a posse of juvenile giraffes—goofy grins twisting their big protuberant lips, their little horns tufted like old-fashioned shaving brushes—Santa explains that mother giraffes are famously careless and are forever losing track of their babies, so the abandoned youngsters band together and follow the rare responsible mother. "A giraffe crèche," he calls it and then goes on to describe how when bull buffalo grow old and their horns knit together over the crowns of their heads like a barrister's wig, they become vicious and ornery and are forced out of their herds, to live their final years as lonesome and troublesome rogues. These tales of solitary animals—strays and exiles cut off from their kind to wander the bush—clearly touch Santa, who himself exhibits the almost militant self-sufficiency and easy gregarious-ness characteristic of men who construct their lives around a need to inhabit true wilderness.

As the light begins to fade, a breeze springs up and Santa steers us around the edge of a lake studded with the dark skeletons of dead leadwood trees, stark and magnificent against the glower-ing dusk. Then we round a bend into fantasy: a great campfire burning on a grassy apron, with flickering lanterns at the water's edge, where a long table is set up, draped with a checked cloth and set for dinner. This is our camp for the night. Bedrolls have been laid out for us under a mosquito net, and an advance crew from the lodge has even set up a camp shower in a nicely sheltered stand of palms. A giraffe skull is the soap dish. Water is heating on the fire. My wife, with towel in hand, is setting out for her scrub-down when a wide-eyed watchman hurries toward her, just as a great crashing noise emanates from pretty much exactly the loca-tion of the shower. *"Tembo,"* he says—elephant! In fact, there are four elephants—a family, busily uprooting a sizable swath of palm trees for their supper. Their destructive power, and the presence in their party of a particularly tender young calf, make it clear that they should be allowed a very wide berth to finish their meal and get on their way before we bathe.

Meanwhile, the evening scene at the water's edge is in full swing: black-winged stilts wading delicately in the shallows;

Egyptian geese clamoring as they establish their roosts for the night; an African skimmer darting so low over the lake's surface that its wing tips sketch hyphenated wakes on either side of it; hippos yawning, their vast heads splitting open at the jawline; and six impala bucks—"a bachelor party," Santa says—trotting in for a drink. Fish are jumping, and pelicans, kingfishers, egrets, and eagles are there to catch them—until, all at once, the darkness thickens and closes in and quiet descends. We sit by the fire with whiskey sodas and hot roasted cashews until we're called to the lantern-lit table for chicken liver pâté, shish kebab, roast potatoes, and a dessert of honey crêpes—a feast about as far from my pre-conceptions of roughing it as you can get. My embarrassment about this level of comfort, however, is something I think I can learn to live with. I certainly fall asleep easily under the mosquito net at nine o'clock sharp, beneath a splendor of stars in a perfectly clear sky, and I sleep wonderfully until midnight, when I jerk awake drenched in sweat.

The air is heavy and still, the stars are gone, and every sound of the night seems ominously amplifed in the close, clinging dark-ness. Every drip, every little splash in the lake, every rattle of palm fronds, every soft strangled cry of a night bird, every snap of a twig, everything makes me sweat harder—my own heart sounds too loud—and then the air shakes gently with the unmistakable vocal rumblings of a not-too-distant lion. The power in that throat is magnificent, and listening to it, thrilled, I cannot forgive myself for failing to ask Santa just why it is that we will not be eaten while sleeping on the ground in the bush. Why isn't this arrange-ment insane? Are we not—laid out alongside one another—a per-fect buffet for lions? I can't grasp how I've come to be served up like this, with nothing but some gauze between me and the jaws of death. And I cannot fathom how my wife can sleep so happily through such peril. To be sure, just before dawn, when for three minutes exactly it rains, she sits abruptly upright to wipe her sprinkled face in alarm, but even before the rain stops—and long before the lion's roaring dies down—she is asleep again.

There is no greater relief than the dawn that follows such a night. Gradually the darkness softens, and as forms begin to define themselves in the mist, the cacophony of the lake at dusk seems to reverse itself, emerging now from the deep stillness into full blaring sound and blazing light. Santa jogs slowly by, following the edge of the lake. A cook puts a coffee pot on the fire. Then Santa returns at a much brisker clip—dashing toward us, really. "Lion," he says. "Come on." And, grabbing his gun, he hustles us, still in our pajamas, into the Land Rover. "They're in here, I'm sure of it," he says after we've driven a few hundred yards, pointing at a clump of bush and easing his foot on the clutch so that we drag forward no faster than a caterpillar, circling the spot where he swears he saw a few young males. There is nothing the first time around, and nothing the second. Then suddenly he hits the brakes and nods sharply as the bush we'd all been staring at on the previous passes begins to move. Ten feet from us, not more, an old lioness rises to her feet and pads quietly away without so much as a glance in our direction. She is a worn old cat, her scarred face such a distinctive record of past fights that, Santa tells us, she is known in the Selous as Alice Pacino. As we watch her stroll languorously down the dirt track, a burst of movement follows her: Her two cubs, husky one-year-old males, come bounding out of the bushes, cuffing each other and tumbling forward.

Sheer rays of morning sun slicing through palms light this exuberant frolic, and the dust the cats stir up sparkles around them. The joy of the scene makes me feel foolish for my nighttime fears. Then one of the cubs descends to the water's edge to drink, and seeing him crouch there—the rippling power of his muscle-bound haunches, his bared teeth, his hooked claws—I think again, Why don't they eat us? "Because they don't recognize you as a prey species," Santa explains when we're back in camp. "You're not on their smell menu. To them, you register as another predator, not a meal." I'm prepared to take comfort in this until Santa adds: "Except, of course, if there's a man-eater. If a lion gets a taste of us and discovers what an easy, delicious kill we are, you're doomed. He's got to be shot because he'll keep coming back for more." A moment later, Santa informs us that the lake on whose shores we just spent the night unprotected is home to an estimated eleven thousand crocodiles.

Food, sex, death—these are the forces that give drama to the spectacle of wildlife which we go out in the bush to behold and draw near. Our last day of walking and driving brings this home relentlessly. Everywhere we turn, we see mating, killing, or devouring: an impala buck circling a doe in a galloping frenzy, his nostrils flared and snorting, mane bristling and flashing, spittle flying; a tiny malachite kingfisher, its flamboyant plumage crying for a mate and in its candy-red bill a silvery minnow dying, and then swallowed. At lunchtime, at a place called Kipalala, on the shore of Lake Makubi, we watch elephants lumbering slowly across the water, a troop of cantering zebras, a rare intact family of giraffes— and after tea and biscuits and a nap, we swim in a hot spring and emerge to see a gathering of kudus and bushbucks. And at a lake called Sigezi, we come upon swarming crocodiles. They're big saurian monsters, these crocs—eight or nine feet long, with midriffs no slimmer than my own and jaws that open like vise grips, glistening with nearly a yard of teeth on either side. Out in the middle of the lake they're fighting, lashing their tails and snapping their great jaws and tussling over huge hunks of something dark, greasy gray, and deeply dead. The air is heavy with the fish-belly smell of putrefaction, and as we watch the tangled thrashing of the great lizards, it becomes apparent that they have killed a hippo—a small one, no doubt, perhaps even a sickly one. Now they are fighting over the tatters of what was once a hippo, and as they do so, a sizable posse of hippos moves in to surround the crocs. It is impossible to tell precisely what's going on, but the broad melodrama is unmistakable: The hippos are restoring order among the crocs that took one of them—and if there is something absurd in ascribing such anthropomorphic behavior to these animals, there is something equally absurd in denying that the hippos appear to be in mourning.

The day before, standing atop a ridge we'd just climbed, Santa looked around and spoke in a tone of what can only be called spiritual ecstasy about "the immense emptiness" that surrounded us. I knew what he meant, of course, but what really strikes me is how immensely full and vibrantly alive this landscape is.

We camp in the deep, soft billows of a sand riverbed, and this time when I awake to roaring in the night, it's terribly close—so close that I can hear the slow panting breath of the lion between the deep chesty rumblings. Across the sandy basin, I see the camp watchman's flashlight blaze, and the beam sweeps over our tents. But it is Santa's gun I'm thinking about, waiting for—the soft click of metal on metal that tells me our crack shot guide is awake and vigilant. Instead, from Santa's netting, I hear only a deep, satisfied snoring. I keep telling myself that only man-eaters need be feared and that if there was man-eater around, we would know. But then I get stuck on the thought that for every man-eater there has to be a first man.

At dawn, with the sun huge and red on the horizon and the softly stirring air loud with the primal breakfast-hour jabber of wild things in the bush, I awake to find myself uneaten. It is a marvelous way to start the day—triumphantly whole.

The Land Rover is waiting to carry us back to base camp. The track runs through narrow lanes of sand between thick walls of tangled, thorny vegetation teeming with a herd of restless buffalo. I feel that I could happily remain out here forever—until we reach the lodge and I see again the capacious bed. The breeze off the Rufiji River is billowing through the mosquito netting as I drop down among the pillows and make my peace with the journey's end.

2005

A Safari Packing List

What to bring (and not to bring)

 Isak Dinesen went on safari with little more than a rifle, a sun hat, and a bottle of Bordeaux. That's one way to go. But for those of us who aren't as at home in the African wild, consider the advice of seasoned bush guides: pack light but with great care.

The first thing that warrants consideration is the bag itself. Wheeled suitcases are all well and good in airport terminals and in the streets of Cape Town, but they're of little use in the bush. Most safari operators will only allow **soft-sided duffels,** which fit far more easily in the cargo hold of bush planes. Keep in mind, too, that baggage weight requirements on small planes don't generally exceed forty-four pounds per person in South Africa and Botswana, thirty-five pounds in Tanzania and Kenya, and just twenty-six pounds in Namibia and Zambia—and that includes all camera equipment. Luckily, most camps and lodges do laundry daily.

As for the bag's contents, **think casual, utilitarian, and inconspicuous.** Even the swankiest lodges don't require dressing for dinner, and though a wardrobe of all **tans** and **khakis** is hopelessly cliché, there are no better colors for hiding dirt, deflecting the sun, and blending into the surroundings. (Hues not ordinarily found on a savannah—neon green, hot pink—could easily startle the wildlife.) What other essentials should you bring? For walking safaris, you'll need **broken-in walking shoes,** a **hat with an ample brim,** and **lightweight trousers** for protection against the sun and acacia thorns. When game-viewing by jeep, boat, or canoe, you're better off with **sturdy, water-resistant sandals** and a hat or **headscarf** that'll stay firmly in place no matter how bumpy the drive or speedy the boat ride. For all safaris, you'll need a **good pair of binoculars** (don't skimp here—what are the odds you'll have another chance to see a lioness feeding her cubs?), and since nights and early mornings are often chilly (some parts of southern Africa dip below freezing in winter), you'd be wise to pack a **long-sleeved shirt** and a **warm jacket.** Your toiletry kit should include **sunscreen, lip balm, eyedrops, two kinds of bug repellent** (one for skin and the other for clothing and bed linens), an **antibacterial ointment** for nicks and scratches, and **malaria prophylaxis.** Since the bush planes tend to wobble in the heat, you may also consider taking along a few **motion-sickness tablets.** Photo and video junkies will need **extra batteries,** memory cards or film, and a charger and a **converter/adapter for 220/240AC voltage.** If you don't bring a **telephoto zoom lens,** you'll spend most of the safari wishing you had.

What to leave behind? Julian Harrison of Premium Tours in Philadelphia advises against bringing **blue jeans,** which take too long to dry when laundered in the bush and happen to be the same shade as the dye used for tsetse fly traps ("It's possible that in some locations, your jeans could make you a tsetse fly target," says Harrison in his book, *African Safari*). **Perfume** and **heavily scented lotions** also attract unwanted attention.

Finally, a word about safari etiquette: When viewing wildlife—or merely attempting to—common sense prevails. Keep voices lowered. Don't smoke. Resist the temptation to try to get an animal's attention or to insist your guide lead you closer to a photo op. Pay careful attention to where you are and what's around you: The fastest way to trouble is getting between a hunter and its prey, or worse, a mother and its child. A good and preferably local guide is essential. No one knows the temperament—and hiding places—of animals better than a native. If you're pleased with your guide, tip well. Mark Nolting, president of the Florida-based Africa Adventure Company, generally recommends ten dollars to twenty dollars per person per day you are on safari for your guide and camp staff combined. The happier you are with the guide, the higher the tip.

About the Authors

Russell Banks (b. 1940) is the author of fifteen books, including *Continental Drift* (1985) and *Cloudsplitter* (1988), both of which were finalists for the Pulitzer Prize, and *Affliction* (1989) and *The Sweet Hereafter* (1991), which were made into acclaimed feature films. The recipient of numerous awards, including a Guggenheim Fellowship, Banks, who is a fellow of the American Academy of Arts and Sciences, lives in upstate New York.

British rock journalist and historian **Nik Cohn** (b. 1946) always felt "an instinctive attraction" to Savannah, years before he visited the city in 1995 for *Condé Nast Traveler*. "Savannah has elaborate good manners, but a risky heart—a combination I've always found alluring," he says. The author of thirteen books, including *Yes We Have No: Adventures in the Other England* (1999) and, most recently, *Triksta: Life and Death and New Orleans Rap* (2005), Cohn lives in Shelter Island, New York.

Born in Scotland, travel writer and historian **William Dalrymple** (b. 1965) now divides his time between London and New

Delhi, where he lived for six years while researching his critically acclaimed 1993 book *City of Djinns: A Year in Delhi*. He is the author of six other titles, including 2002's *White Mughals* and, recently, 2006's *The Last Mughal: The Fall of a Dynasty, Delhi, 1857*.

Journalist **Philip Gourevitch** (b. 1961) spent years as a foreign correspondent in Africa. His 1998 book about the horrors of the Rwandan genocide (and the United Nations' failure to stop it), *We Wish to Inform You That Tomorrow We Will Be Killed with Our Families: Stories from Rwanda*, was awarded numerous honors, including the *Los Angeles Times* Book Prize and the National Book Critics Circle Award. In visiting the Selous Game Reserve in Tanzania for *Condé Nast Traveler*, Gourevitch was able to see the continent anew, as "an untouristed wilderness where the animals [were] as surprised to see me as I was them." Gourevitch lives in New York City, where he is editor in chief of *The Paris Review* and a contributor to *The New Yorker*. He is also the author of 2001's *A Cold Case*, a chronicle of an unsolved murder.

Novelist **Shirley Hazzard** (b. 1931) is the author of ten books, including 1980's *The Transit of Venus* (which received the National Book Critics Circle Award); 2003's *The Great Fire* (which received the National Book Award); and 2000's *Greene on Capri*, a memoir of her complicated friendship with the novelist Graham Greene. Hazzard, who was raised in Australia, is a fellow of the Royal Society of Literature and a member of the American Academy of Arts and Letters. She divides her time between New York and southern Italy.

Renowned cultural critic **Robert Hughes** (b. 1938) has been an art critic for *Time* magazine for more than thirty years and has authored ten books of nonfiction, including the highly influential *The Shock of the New* (1981); *The Fatal Shore* (1987), a history of his native Australia; *Heaven and Hell in Western Art* (1968); *Goya* (2003), a biography of the artist; and *Things I Didn't Know* (2006), a memoir. Hughes, who now lives in New York City, has been awarded countless literary prizes and distinctions, most recently an Academy Award in Literature from the American Academy of Arts and Letters.

In his nineteen years as a *Condé Nast Traveler* contributing editor, **Pico Iyer** (b. 1957) has reported on destinations from Argentina and Vietnam to Cambodia and Bolivia. Ethiopia, which he visited and profiled in 1994, was, he says, "among the most memorable places I've seen, with a spirit of intensity and devotion, a lit-up ardor, that I still haven't seen anywhere else." Iyer, who was born in Oxford, England, and now divides his time between Japan and California, is the author of six travel books (including 1988's *Video Night in Kathmandu: And Other Reports from the Not-So-Far East* and 1991's *The Lady and the Monk: Four Seasons in Kyoto*) and two novels, including *Cuba and the Night* (1995). A contributor to *Time* since 1982, he also contributes to *The New York Review of Books, Harper's,* and the *Financial Times,* among other publications.

Nicole Krauss (b. 1974) felt some hesitation about going to Japan for fear that the "strange and beautiful" pictures of her imagination would be erased. "But the Japan I found was far more spectacular than the Japan I'd invented," she says. Krauss, a poet and novelist, is the author of two works of fiction, *Man Walks Into a Room* (2002) and the best-selling *The History of Love* (2005). Her writing has appeared in *The New Yorker, Best American Short Stories,* and *Esquire.* She lives in Brooklyn.

Even after his travels through the Himalayas, **Suketu Mehta** (b. 1963) managed to retain a measured optimism about the region's future. "I think that pockets of this environment can be preserved," says Mehta, who was born in Calcutta, "but the local people really need to be trusted and listened to." Mehta, who lives in Brooklyn, New York, is the author of 2004's *Maximum City: Bombay Lost and Found,* which was a finalist for the Pulitzer Prize. His work has also been awarded a Kiriyama Prize, a Whiting Writers Award, and an O. Henry Award, among others. He is currently at work on a screenplay.

Jan Morris (b. 1926) is the author of thirty-six books, including the highly acclaimed *Pax Britannica* trilogy (1968–78), a history of the British Empire; *Last Letters from Hav* (1985); and portraits of cities such as Manhattan, Hong Kong, Venice, and Oxford, among others. She is also the author of a memoir, *Conundrum* (1974). Morris's most recent book is *Trieste and the Meaning of Nowhere* (2001), a meditation on the ancient Adriatic city. Recently awarded a Golden PEN Award for lifetime achievement, Morris lives in Wales.

After serving in the British Foreign Service, **John Julius Norwich** (b. 1929) began a literary career with his first book, *The Normans in the South* (1967), which was later republished, along with *The Kingdom in the Sun* (1970), in a volume entitled *The Normans in Sicily* (1992). An expert on the Byzantium age, he is also the author of *Byzantium: The Early Centuries* (1988); *Byzantium: The Apogee* (1992); and *Byzantium: The Decline and Fall* (1995), among numerous other titles. He currently lives in England and is co-chairman of the World Monuments Fund in Britain, for which he has lectured on the preservation of the city of Venice.

The author of twenty-four books, **Edna O'Brien** (b. 1930) made her literary debut with *The Country Girls Trilogy* (1960–64), which was widely acclaimed despite being banned in her native Ireland. Her novel *Lantern Slides* was awarded the *Los Angeles Times Book Prize* in 1990. O'Brien, who has also written numerous plays, children's books, and essays, lives in Ireland, where she is an adjunct professor of creative writing at University College in Dublin.

The author of nineteen books of fiction, criticism, and biography, including *Hunters and Gatherers* (1995), *The Peaceable Kingdom: Stories* (1993), and the National Book Award–nominated *The Blue Angel* (2000), **Francine Prose** (b. 1947) lives in New York City, and contributes essays and criticism to a number of publications, including *The New Yorker, The New York Times,* and *The Paris Review*. She is the recipient of two National Endowment for the Arts grants, as well as a Guggenheim Fellowship.

Gregor von Rezzori (d. 1998), the late novelist, essayist, and memoirist, often wrote about the changing political geographic landscapes of his native Eastern European homeland. Born in 1914 in Bukovina (at the time, part of the Austrian-Hungarian empire), he later became a Romanian citizen. He is the author of more than twenty books, the best known of which is *Memoirs of an Anti-Semite: A Novel in Five Stories* (1969), inspired by his coming-of-age in prewar Europe.

Poet and essayist **Patricia Storace** (b. 1956) spent a year living in Athens before recounting her time abroad for the magazine. "I lived in a neighborhood full of domineering old ladies," she says. "Athenians spend as much time as possible outdoors, acting out a kind of novel on the streets." A longtime contributor to *Condé Nast Traveler,* Storace has also written numerous pieces for *The New York Review of Books,* among other publications. She is the author of *Heredity* (1987), a collection of poetry, *Dinner with Persephone: Travels in Greece* (1996), and a children's book, *Sugar Cane: A Caribbean Rapunzel* (2007).

James Truman (b. 1958), the former editorial director of Condé Nast Publications, has long been drawn to the texture of Iran—its music, the poetry of Rumi and Hafiz, the landscapes, and the mosques. His 2002 journey for the magazine traced the last 2,500 years of Persian history. "Even on a preplanned itinerary, Iran is a source of constant surprise," says Truman. "Hospitality is considered a great social virtue, and you'll find yourself being invited into people's homes, where—unlike in public—they'll openly talk about their lives and feelings toward the Islamic regime." Truman, who was also the editor in chief of *Details* magazine, most recently served as C.E.O. of LTB Media, where he launched the magazine *Culture & Travel*. He lives in New York City.

Edmund White (b. 1940), a member of the American Academy of Arts and Letters and the American Academy of Arts and Sciences, lives in New York City and is the author of twenty-one books, including the memoirs *A Boy's Own Story* (1982) and *The Beautiful Room Is Empty* (1988); the biography *Genet* (1993), for which he received the National Book Critics Circle Award; and the short story collection *Skinned Alive* (1995). In 1993, White was made a Chevalier de L'Ordre des Arts et des Lettres by the French government. His most recent autobiography, *My Lives,* was published in 2005.

Author, journalist, and broadcaster **Simon Winchester** (b. 1944) has been a contributing editor to *Condé Nast Traveler* since its launch in 1987. A best-selling author, he has written twenty books of travel writing, history, and biography, including 1998's *The Professor and the Madman,* 2001's *The Map That Changed the World,* and, most recently, 2005's *A Crack in the Edge of the World: America and the Great California Earthquake of 1906.* A frequent broadcast and, radio presence (most notably on BBC's "From Our Own Correspondent" program, to which he is a regular contributor),

Winchester is also a sought-after lecturer; recent appearances have included those before London's Royal Geographical Society, of which he is a fellow. In 2006, he was made an Officer of the Order of the British Empire (OBE) by Her Majesty the Queen. He lives in New York City and the Berkshires.

About *Condé Nast Traveler*

Since its launch in 1987, *Condé Nast Traveler* has remained committed to its philosophy of "truth in travel." We are independent of the travel industry; this means we do not accept free or discounted trips or accommodations and, as far as possible, our correspondents travel anonymously. By doing so, they experience the world the way you do—good and bad—and their reports and recommendations are fair, impartial, and authoritative.

For more information on *Condé Nast Traveler*, visit cntraveler.com.

Acknowledgments

I would like to thank all of the writers who have contributed to *Condé Nast Traveler* over the past twenty years. Your travels—and the brilliant ways you committed them to paper—have given this magazine its heart and soul. My one regret is that more stories, by more of you, could not be included in this collection.

My gratitude goes to my predecessors as editor in chief of *Condé Nast Traveler*: Sir Harold Evans, the founding editor, and Thomas J. Wallace, under whose inspired stewardship most of these stories were originally commissioned, as well as to senior consulting editor Clive Irving, an invaluable sounding board for this and so many other projects. On behalf of all of us, I would like to thank S.I. Newhouse, Jr., chairman of Condé Nast Publications, for so staunchly supporting *Condé Nast Traveler* and recognizing the value and imperative of its "Truth in Travel" philosophy.

I am immensely appreciative of the energy, commitment, and unflagging attention to detail of features editor Hanya Yanagihara, the driving force behind this anthology. My gratitude as well to the magazine's publisher, Lisa Hughes; managing editor Dee L. Aldrich; and features editor Gully Wells, for their invaluable assistance in making this book a reality.

I would also like to thank the following for writing the service addenda included in this volume: Kelsey Blodget, Ondine Cohane, William Dalrymple, Deborah Dunn, John Grimwade, Manuela Holterhoff, Nandita Khanna, Nicole Krauss, Alexander Lobrano, Beata Loyfman, Azadeh Moaveni, Mimi Murphy, John Oseid, Jennifer Senator, Helena Smith, Dinah Spritzer, Gully Wells, and Simon Winchester. And thanks too to Kelsey Blodget, Paul Buckley, G. Y. Dryansky, Sylvia Espinoza, Sharon Gonzalez, Susan Hack, Rebecca Hunt, Nandita Khanna, Stephen Morrison, Hanna Robinson, Elke Sigal, and Ezekiel Turner for the myriad forms of their help.

—*K.G.*